THE UNITED STATES
AND NORTHEAST ASIA

Asia in World Politics
Series Editor: Samuel S. Kim

THE UNITED STATES AND NORTHEAST ASIA

Debates, Issues, and New Order

Edited by
G. John Ikenberry
and
Chung-in Moon

ROWMAN & LITTLEFIELD PUBLISHERS, INC.
Lanham • Boulder • New York • Toronto • Plymouth, UK

ROWMAN & LITTLEFIELD PUBLISHERS, INC.

Published in the United States of America
by Rowman & Littlefield Publishers, Inc.
A wholly owned subsidary of The Rowman & Littlefield Publishing Group, Inc.
4501 Forbes Boulevard, Suite 200, Lanham, Maryland 20706
www.rowmanlittlefield.com

Estover Road, Plymouth PL6 7PY, United Kingdom

British Library Cataloguing in Publication Information Available

Library of Congress Cataloging-in-Publication Data

The United States and Northeast Asia : debates, issues, and new order / edited by G. John
Ikenberry and Chung-in Moon.
    p. cm. — (Asia in world politics)
  Includes bibliographical references and index.
  ISBN-13: 978-0-7425-5638-6 (cloth : alk. paper)
  ISBN-10: 0-7425-5638-7 (cloth : alk. paper)
  ISBN-13: 978-0-7425-5639-3 (pbk. : alk. paper)
  ISBN-10: 0-7425-5639-5 (pbk. : alk. paper)
  1. East Asia—Relations—United States. 2. United States—Relations—East Asia.
I. Ikenberry, G. John. II. Moon, Chung-in.
  DS518.8.U588 2008
  327.7305—dc22
                        2007028436

Printed in the United States of America

∞™ The paper used in this publication meets the minimum requirements of American
National Standard for Information Sciences—Permanence of Paper for Printed Library
Materials, ANSI/NISO Z39.48-1992.

Contents

Illustrations

Preface

NORTHEAST ASIA IS TODAY a great geographical epicenter of world politics. The elemental forces of history are very much alive in this region. The rapid growth of China and the spread of its influence is one of the great dramas of the twenty-first century. So too is Japan's search for a mature sense of national identity and statehood. The flourishing of democracy in South Korea has given its leaders a new and independent voice with which to speak on issues of alliance relations and regional threats. The growth and integration of the East Asian economies have also altered old political relationships and created demands for greater regional cooperation. Meanwhile, the rise of India and the return of Russia have expanded the geopolitical "space" of Asia and brought a wider array of Eurasian great power politics into it. Finally, America's own changing global security priorities and alliance thinking—driven by the "war on terror"—have created new uncertainties and controversies in the region about Washington's long-term security ties and commitments to the region.

This volume brings together leading specialists who probe various aspects of this rapidly shifting Northeast Asian landscape. Together they provide a portrait of a region that is a mix of old and new. The old order in Northeast Asia—anchored in America's bilateral alliances and liberal hegemonic leadership—is giving way to something new, although the specific contours of that new order remain uncertain. The chapters in this volume provide maps and ideas with which to survey and assess this shifting regional landscape.

The idea for this volume began some years ago in discussions between the editors. The volume was originally initiated as a project of the Center for Global Studies, Yonsei University, which was headed then by Chung-in Moon. The Mortara Center of International Studies at Georgetown University under G. John Ikenberry's directorship became an institutional counterpart in launching the project. The discussion of chapter drafts occurred at two conferences held at Yonsei University and Georgetown University. Many individuals have provided assistance along the way. We want to thank individuals who attended the conferences and whose participation strengthened the chapters that followed. In particular, we are grateful for the participation of Muthiah Alagappa, Kurt Campbell, Victor Cha, Chung-min Lee, Jung-hoon Lee, Seok-soo Lee, and Daojiong Zha. We would also like to express our cordial thanks to Samuel S. Kim and Susan McEachern for encouraging us to submit the manuscript to Rowman & Littlefield. Support from Young-sun Lee and Sang-young Rhyu of Yonsei University as well as the editorial assistance of Jong-hyun Jung, John Kim, Iris J. Moon, and Ki H. Moon are also greatly appreciated. Finally, we thank Dae-yeob Yoon for his invaluable editorial and administrative contribution to bringing a successful end to the project.

Acknowledgments

THIS BOOK HAS BEEN SHAPED over the years with generous support from numerous sources. We would like to acknowledge and thank the Center for Global Studies at Yonsei University and the Mortara Center of International Studies at Georgetown University for their assistance. We are also deeply grateful for funding support from the following institutions: the SK Telecom and the East Asia Foundation in the Republic of Korea (ROK) and the Pacific Century Institute in the United States. Special appreciation goes to Gil-seung Son, chairman of SK Telecom and former chairman of the SK Group; Woo-shik Kim, deputy prime minister of ROK and former president of Yonsei University; and Spencer H. Kim, the founder of the Pacific Century Institute, for their keen interest in the future role of the United States in Northeast Asia and generous support of this project.

Introduction:
The Dynamics of Transition in Northeast Asia
Analytical Debates, Emerging Issues, and New Order

G. John Ikenberry and Chung-in Moon

DESPITE THE GEOGRAPHICAL SEPARATION of the United States from East Asia,[1] the United States has played a crucial role in shaping the region's geopolitical and geoeconomic destiny since World War II. The American hegemonic order replaced both the Sinocentric tributary system and the Japanese imperial order known as the Greater East Asian Co-Prosperity Sphere. During the Cold War era, the United States served as a hegemonic stabilizer that served as a military counterbalance to the Soviet Union, offering a security umbrella for its allies, and proving instrumental in the introduction of a liberal international economic order in the region. Indeed, the hegemonic order imposed by the United States brought about peace, stability, and prosperity for its regional allies. This functional interconnectedness with the region has made the United States in effect a salient member of East Asia.

However, the end of the Cold War, September 11, and major strategic alignments by the United States have unveiled new indications of a major transition in East Asia, where contending visions have come into view. The United States' maintenance of a status quo order buttressed by hegemonic leadership appears the most plausible from a unipolar power configuration. But as recent literature on China's rise illustrates, the tragedy of great power politics associated with power transitions might also become a new reality. A growing body of literature that evinces a pessimistic outlook on the East Asian security terrain is based on the scenario of a coming and inevitable clash between a hegemonic power (the United States) and a challenger (China).[2] Liberals are skeptical of the worst possibilities that might be associated with East Asian transitional dynamics. Power matters, but it does not unilaterally dictate geopolitical and geoeconomic destiny. Interests, norms, and a shared identity could foster cooperation among regional actors, transcending security dilemmas, prestige contests, and territorial disputes. Deepening economic interdependence, expanding social and cultural exchanges, and more importantly, informal networks formed through production, investment, and education would prevent conflict escalation in the region.[3] Beneath this liberal optimism lies the issue of national identity and nationalism. The collective memory of a history of domination and subjugation, the call to nationalist appeals, and the misuse of parochial nationalism in domestic politics would cause perpetual insecurity in the region. Unending cognitive dissonance, a structure of finite deterrence, and the logic of economic mercantilism could trap East Asia in a vortex of mutual suspicion, distrust, and potential and actual conflict.

What factors could affect the transitional dynamics of the East Asian regional order? America's stabilizing role seems crucial, but whether the United States can stabilize a regional order depends on the combination of changing power configurations and strategic positioning among regional actors, conjunctional dynamics of various events and issues, and the ability to chart out a new regional order. This volume aims at addressing these issues while giving a greater emphasis to the strategic role to be played by the United States.[4]

The United States and Northeast Asia: Debates on Power, Reality, and Realignments

A relatively long peace in East Asia can be attributed in part to a regional order shaped by American hegemonic presence. But since the end of the Cold War, signs of structural changes have begun to surface, not only because of shifting distribution of capabilities among regional actors, but also because of their new strategic positioning. Such trends have in turn provoked profound analytical and empirical debates on the changing nature of regional order in East Asia: Will the United States continue its hegemonic presence in East Asia so as to sustain the status quo? Is the "China threat" real or contrived? Can it challenge the United States as a new regional hegemon? What kind of "normal state" (*futsu no kuni*) is Japan striving to achieve? Is such a realignment of status feasible? Can Russia still be regarded as an Asian power even after the breakup of the Soviet empire? If so, what kind of Asian power would it constitute? What strategic choices would South Korea face in an altered security environment? Could it become a new middle power? Finally, what is the present status of North Korea? Is it truly a perpetual rogue state? The chapters in part I explore these issues.

The United States has become an inseparable part of East Asian geopolitical and geoeconomic destiny since the end of World War II. Its strategic posture is the single most important determinant of regional dynamics in East Asia. Have there been any changes in the political foundations of American relations with East Asia? Is the United States willing to sustain its security commitment to the region?

In chapter 1, G. John Ikenberry argues that there have not been any significant changes in American policy toward East Asia. He further contends that changes in security parameters, such as the end of the Cold War, shifting power realities in East Asia, the September 11 terrorist attacks, and the war in Iraq, have not altered American grand strategic relations with the region. Whereas a realist grand strategy based on bilateral alliance with regional actors has contributed to peace and stability, a liberal grand strategy framed around multilateralism has enhanced economic cooperation and prosperity in the region. Although concerns have been raised about the purpose of American power and its behavior in a unipolar world, the hegemonic order shaped by the United States will continue for the time being, and it is likely to be a stable one. This is so not only because alternative institutions such as ASEAN Regional Forum (ARF) are not likely to rival the American-led bilateral security structure, but also because no discernible political forces or coalitions capable of challenging the American position or transforming regional order are in purview.

China has recently been raised as a possible contender to the American position. What are the implications of China's rise for regional order? In chapter 2, Avery Goldstein explores these issues through the examination of two contrasting views. The power-transition theory sees China's rise as disruptive and dangerous because it is expected to pose a threat to others in the region as well as to the United States. On the other hand, the institutionalist theory envisions China's rise as presenting an opportunity for building international cooperation within East Asia. Goldstein observes that China has shown divergent behavior, depending on events. Events in the South China Sea and Korea lend credence to the expectations of institutionalist theory. Defying the expectations of a power-transition perspective, China has largely taken an institutionalist trajectory, seeking multilateral, cooperative ties with ASEAN countries. As was evidenced through its proactive, mediating role in the six-party talks on the North Korean nuclear issue, Beijing has championed multilateral negotiations and incremental steps toward arrangements beneficial to all, while rejecting confrontational solutions.

In contrast, the case of Taiwan lends credence to the expectations of a power-transition theory, as events in the Taiwan Strait over the past decade have deviated from institutionalist expectations. Recent events suggest that China's rise is causing concern to Taiwan's leaders over the country's future, despite the increasingly robust and mutually beneficial economic relationships that have developed among China, Taiwan, and the United States. For Goldstein, neither a power-transition theory, which interprets the absence of a challenge now as simply China biding its time, nor an institutionalist theory, which treats Taiwan as an important exception, can provide a full explanation. China's rise can be characterized as being both confrontational and cooperative, depending on events and issue areas, and he suggests that the United States pursue a hybrid strategy of containment and engagement to cope with China.[5]

Since Ozawa Ichiro popularized the concept of a normal or ordinary state in the early 1990s, the realignment of Japan's military status commensurate with its economic and global power has remained a major issue. What then would be the likely future of Japan as an ordinary power? And what implications can be drawn for regional order? In chapter 3, Takashi Inoguchi and Paul Bacon postulate that Japan has been making substantial adjustments to its foreign policy every fifteen years. These periods can be characterized as follows: an internal battle between pro-alliance and anti-alliance sections of Japanese society (1945–1960); adherence to the Yoshida doctrine (1960–1975); systemic support for the United States (1975–1990); an attempt to pursue the role of a global civilian power (1990–2005); and gradual consolidation of Japan's emerging role as a global ordinary power (2005–2020). Inoguchi and Bacon suggest three pathways to Japan becoming an ordinary country based on European precedents. First is the British pathway, in which Japan would model itself off of the United Kingdom, conceiving of itself as a country having special bilateral relations with the United States. The second is the German model, in which Japan emphasizes East Asian regional embeddedness more than a bilateral relationship with the United States, in turn aligning its national interests to broader regional and international interests. Finally, Japan could seek a French path to ordinary power, where autonomy is valued, rather than an American connection or regional embeddedness.

In adjusting to its new status as a normal state, Japan would be constrained by two kinds of deficits. One is a legitimacy deficit emanating from the Japanese Constitution, which forbids Japan from using force to settle international disputes and enforces the permanent renunciation of war. The other is a capability deficit stemming from the strictly defensive purposes of its Self-Defense Forces. According to Inoguchi and Bacon, political parties in Japan, both ruling and opposition, are likely to support the idea of constitutional revision for a normal statehood, as the pacifist stance no longer appeals strongly to the electorate. They predict that Japan will pursue the British path to a normal state, which is predicated on Japan's greater regional and international role within the framework of its bilateral alliance with the United States.

The decline of Russian power is one of the most dramatic and consequential geopolitical shifts in the twentieth century. The Soviet Union entered a period of relative economic decline beginning in 1975, which accelerated in the 1980s and in the 1990s reached near-catastrophic proportions. Transformation of the Soviet Union from a superpower into a strong power bears profound implications for East Asia. With the relinquishment of its global hegemonic ambition, can Russia still be considered an Asian power? How has Russia adjusted to its decline in East Asia? Why wasn't its relatively sudden decline associated with aggressive behavior?

William C. Wohlforth addresses these issues in chapter 4. Wohlforth starts with probing theoretical queries on the correlates of relative decline of national power and external behavior. Three postulates that suggest that Russia as a declining state was likely to show hostile or conflictual external behavior were made. First, Russia may be expected to use military force to "forestall or minimize expected future losses vis-à-vis rivals" in anticipation of its relative decline. Second, domestic political coalitions supporting the ideologies constructed for expansion could provoke external bellicosity. And finally, confronting decline, political leaders may be willing to take measures to maintain Russia's status at any cost, regardless of material aims. However, the above postulates did not dovetail with Russian reality. Although the country underwent a somewhat similar situation after 1989, it was able to handle its weakened status smoothly without external confrontation. Wohlforth attributes such behavior to an "anchoring" bias, or "the general human reluctance to update assessments in response to new information." Systematic exaggeration of its real power and prospects allowed Russia to avoid a more forceful reaction to decline. While there is a gap between the stated expectations of Russian policymakers regarding their regional role and any realistic outcome, the gap is not large. Russia understands that it is presently too economically and politically weak to take part in an Asian rivalry game, and thus, it is likely to pursue more pragmatic diplomatic lines, governed in the near-to-medium term by issues of general concern to the region, such as security, economic improvement, and modernization plans.

Being a small peninsular state, Korea was continually the victim of clashes between continental and maritime powers, caught in the midst of geopolitics and big-power politics. Ensuring its survival and prosperity through the prudent navigation of tough currents of regional power politics has remained the top priority of policymakers in South Korea. In chapter 5, Woosang Kim examines South Korea's strategic positioning and suggests the most desirable strategic choice available to South Korea. Kim argues that the country may be able to play a more constructive role in maintaining peace and prosperity in Northeast Asia, not as a great power but a middle power, with the potential to act in a pivotal role in local systemic affairs. Below the great powers in the international pyramid, there are the middle powers, which are most likely to be satisfied with the status quo. However, dissatisfied middle powers may want to side with the challenging great power and try to change the status quo.

The current picture in East Asia shows a uni-multipolar stability led by the United States. However, China is not satisfied with the Taiwan situation and the existing regional order largely established by the United States. The United States' strengthening of its ties with Japan also helps contribute to China's dissatisfaction. The alliance has been a major tool for blocking China's rise as a regional hegemon and also for checking Japan's revival as a regional destabilizer. When China perceives that it has successfully caught up with the United States, a power-transition crisis may come about. The United States may want to strengthen its existing military ties with both Japan and Korea and try to overcome China's challenge. Woosang Kim's prescription for South Korea is to remain a loyal ally in the U.S. camp. This will be the best option for Korea as a buffer state. Neutrality is often made untenable, and bandwagoning has the danger of losing the buffer state's independence. The best choice for Korea is to preserve peace and prosperity in the region by maintaining strong alliance ties with the United States.

How about North Korea? North Korea has long sought a self-reliant policy line. But self-imposed isolation through the banner of self-reliance (*Juche*) has fundamentally narrowed the scope of its external maneuverability, often leading to brinkmanship diplomacy. Such diplomatic behavior has in turn made the North earn the dishonorable label of a rogue state. What is the nature of its rogue behavior? Will North Korea remain a perpetual rogue state? Is there any chance of North Korea becoming a constructive member of the international community? In light of its current nuclear polemic, these questions have become all the more relevant. In chapter 6, Yongho Kim attempts to tackle these issues through an in-depth analysis of domestic determinants of North Korea's external behavior.

Yongho Kim contends that the dynamic interplay of North Korea's official ruling ideology, *Juche* (self-reliance), and domestic politics revolving around leadership succession are the key motivations behind North Korea's perception of its own situation and its decision to play the rogue. The key to a more manageable relationship with North Korea lies in understanding the rational roots of its identification as a "rogue state." According to Kim, most analysts "speculate" that North Korea's intentions are irrational, producing intolerable consequences, and thus label it a rogue regime. But such reasoning is misleading and even distorting. North Korea may in fact rationally choose to play rogue to make a credible deterrence against the United States and South Korea, to obtain more concessions from them, and to win external recognition of its national identity. North Korea's decision to play rogue can be ascribed to *Juche*, the North Korean ruling ideology. It was designed as an ideological instrument to liberate suppressed people by making themselves the masters of their own lives. Guerilla methods such as ambush tactics and surprise attacks constitute an integral part of the *Juche* ideology. Domestic politics provides another explanation for its roguish behavior. To outsiders, for example, brinkmanship diplomacy is a roguish behavior. But to North Koreans, it is an expression of the political leadership's toughness. Such tough behavior naturally invites reciprocally tough responses from outside, precipitating a crisis situation, which would in turn enhance its internal cohesion and ultimately Kim Jong-il's legitimacy. This is particularly true because the country's highest priority is placed on maintaining the Kim Jong-il regime. Kim concludes that North Korea is a rogue but rational state that consistently and flexibly responds to changes in the international environment, while utilizing them for domestic politics. If outside actors understand the logic of North Korea's playing rogue, they might be able to handle the North in a more effective manner.

Judged on new power realities and underlying realignments, the strategic outlook in East Asia does not seem bright. As Ikenberry aptly foresees, no country, even including China or a coalition of countries in the region, can readily challenge the American hegemonic position in the near future. Nevertheless, the unipolar moment under American hegemony cannot be permanent, nor can it assure peace and stability in the region. The American strategic position is crucial here. If the United States attempts to ensure its hegemonic position by encircling or containing China while strengthening its alliance with Japan and South Korea, a new Cold War divide could resurface between the Northern and Southern axes. Such an assertive move could turn China's rise into a real threat. After all, China is bound to grow in its national power, and could be destined to challenge the United States, resulting in the tragedy of great power politics. Japan's transformation into a normal state, without a corresponding resolution of its historical burdens, could heighten suspicion and distrust from neighboring countries, complicating the regional strategic outlook. Russia might be the only country that would not affect real politics in the region, since pragmatism will drive its East Asian policy. However, strategic moves by South and North Korea could significantly influence regional security dynamics. Contrary to Woosang Kim's prescription, South Korea's pursuit of a middle-power status or bandwagoning with China could also radically alter the regional strategic equation, though South Korea is too dependent on China to resort to an exclusive bilateral alliance with the United States. North Korea's potential new status as a nuclear state could serve as a new critical variable in reshaping regional security dynamics. All in all, new power realities and realignment patterns point to an uncertain outlook in which continuity and discontinuity, stability and instability, are precariously intertwined.

Emerging Issues: Understanding Challenges to the United States

Distribution of power and the resulting structure of a regional security system is an important, but static, predictor of change and continuity in East Asia. Interactions among regional actors and the resulting outcomes are by and large determined by actual events and issues. What issues and events are likely to influence the future strategic outlook of East Asia? We have identified three emerging events and issues: anti-Americanism and local resistance to American military presence, the rise of nationalism and its impacts on regional cooperation, and the North Korea nuclear problem.

The lasting legacies of the United States–led powerplay system are manifested through the continuing presence of American military bases in East Asia. The United States still maintains its military bases in Japan, South Korea, and the Philippines. Since the 1990s, however, the proliferation of democracy and anti-Americanism has seriously challenged American military hegemony which is based on forward troop presence in these countries. In chapter 7, Katharine H. S. Moon explores how the process of democratic deepening— namely, decentralization and heightened civil society activism—has shaped contemporary anti-Americanism in all three countries, adversely affecting the continuing presence of American military bases.

In South Korea, the democratic transition highlighted the importance of universally accepted values, such as human rights, environmental protection, and social welfare, in policy considerations. In the Philippines, the installation of "people power" through the political rise of Corazon Aquino ushered in a decade of heated and at times bitter jousting between the Philippines and the United States. The decentralization of government, the legalization and application of new rights for local residents, and people's increased access to public information and institutional accountability took place in all three countries throughout the 1990s. In Japan, former governor Masahide Ota of Okinawa was defiant against Tokyo's control over private lands to be used by the U.S. Forces in Japan, leading to the 1996 Okinawan referendum, in which 90 percent of the voters called for the consolidation and reduction of the U.S. military presence. In Korea, the responsiveness of some local governments to residents' complaints about the U.S. military presence and their cooperation with progressive civil groups are among the most novel and remarkable developments in the country's democratization process. In the Philippines, the logic of decentralization has yielded a very different outcome: eager support for U.S.

troop presence as a way to address Abu Sayyaf activities in the southern island of Mindanao. In tandem with decentralization in the three countries has been the exponential growth of and public interest in civil society organizations (CSO). In the 1990s, East Asian CSOs broadened and diversified their issue areas to peace, defense spending, national security, and troop deployment to Iraq. U.S. attempts to push for internal democratization have spawned a liberalization process and foreign policy repercussions that the United States did not bargain for. Katharine Moon eloquently illustrates how newly emerging democratic virtues in American allies in East Asia such as vibrant civil society activism and local empowerment have entailed unexpected structural constraints to the continuation of American military hegemony in the region.

An equally critical, but often neglected, issue in the region is the specter of nationalism widespread throughout Northeast Asia. Despite the end of the Cold War, growing economic interdependence, and social and cultural exchanges and cooperation, strong nationalist sentiments, emanating from the collective memory of the historical past, have been undermining efforts toward a regionalism in Northeast Asia. In chapter 8, Chung-in Moon and Seung-Won Suh attempt to unveil the impacts of nationalism on foreign policy behavior in China, Japan, and South Korea. They argue that the lack of subregionalism among Northeast Asian countries is closely associated with domestic political misuse and abuse of nationalism. An unintended coalition among nationalist adversaries in the three countries has been responsible for negatively amplifying chain reactions of suspicion and mutual distrust among them

Japan, South Korea, and China have all shown the revival of parochial nationalism. The burden of history and the social and political ambiance molded under the 1955 system prevented Japan from deliberating on the revival of nationalism. Since the mid-1990s, however, neonationalist movements have emerged, calling for revision of history textbooks as well as amendment of the Peace Constitution. Whereas some have even suggested the revival of the old imperial system, others have expressed xenophobic populism. South Korea is also witnessing a resurgent fever of nationalism that defies the forces of globalization and regionalization. Primordial nationalism, based on common ancestry, history, language, and culture; and instrumental nationalism, seeking to resist foreign domination and consolidate national sovereignty and unification, have thrived despite postmodern critiques. A socialist ideological template notwithstanding, China is also tilting toward nationalism. The Chinese government's attempts to tame and control nationalism through instruments of official patriotism have been subject to the law of diminishing returns. As shown by sweeping anti-Japanese demonstrations in May 2005, spontaneous popular nationalism has emerged as a new mode of nationalism. Resurgent nationalism in Japan, South Korea, and China threatens to seriously undermine the potential for a viable and harmonious regional order in Northeast Asia. Several opinion surveys indicate the deplorable state of mutual perception among the three countries. Moon and Suh contend that abuse and misuse of nationalist rhetoric for domestic political purposes in China, Japan, and South Korea has become one of most devastating hurdles to intraregional cooperation and integration. As long as collective memory of the historical past is politicized, they see no easy solution to the dilemma of nationalism in the region.

Along with nationalism, the North Korean nuclear problem has become another major security issue in Northeast Asia. Chapter 9 by Chung-in Moon examines motives, impacts, and management strategies associated with the North Korean nuclear quagmire. Moon ascribes North Korea's nuclear ambition to the combination of several factors: the logic of nuclear deterrence, regime survival, a move to balance inferiority in conventional forces, and bargaining leverage for economic gains and a tool for export earnings. What then is its nuclear capability? North Korea can be regarded as a nuclear state if and when it satisfies four conditions: possession of nuclear warheads, demonstration of delivery capability, actual nuclear testing, and production of miniaturized nuclear warheads that can be fitted on missiles. Moon believes that the North has acquired quite a sufficient amount of plutonium to manufacture between four and six nuclear warheads by reprocessing eight thousand spent fuel rods that were stored in a water tank as part of the Geneva Agreed Framework. However, the North is short of being able to manufacture highly enriched uranium bombs. As to delivery capability, Moon asserts that North Korea has acquired short-range and medium-range missile capability targeting South Korea and Japan, if not long-range ballistic missiles aiming at the United States. Although North Korea undertook an underground nuclear test on October 9, 2006, it proved to be a failure or at best partially successful. Finally, it is estimated that North Korea has not acquired the miniaturization technology required to fit nuclear warheads onto short- to medium-range missiles. Judged on this, while North Korea cannot be declared a "full-fledged nuclear weapons state," it is nonetheless a dangerous country with enormous nuclear weapons capability.

What is wrong with a nuclear North Korea? Moon gives three major security concerns associated with a nuclear North Korea: demise of peaceful coexistence on the Korean peninsula and resumption of a fierce inter-Korean arms race, nuclear domino effects in Northeast Asia, and global security implications resulting from the transfer of nuclear materials. He recommends a negotiated settlement through diplomacy as the best strategy to manage the North Korean problem. Reactivating and expediting the stalled six-party-talks process is essential in this regard. Neither military options nor a hostile neglect strategy would work. For whereas military actions could entail enormously high collateral damage without assuring a decisive political and military victory for the United States, a hostile neglect strategy to isolate and contain North Korea and to transform the Kim Jong-il regime will help the North achieve a de facto nuclear weapons state even before the strategy's intended objective of collapsing the North is achieved.

Examination of these newly emerging issues reveals that challenges to the United States are quite formidable, clouding the future of a stable and peaceful East Asia. It is more so because China's power has been on the rise, fostering the fear of the "China threat," and chances for greater multilateralism are getting slim. Meanwhile the United States has been strengthening its alliance with Japan in a move to prepare for confrontation with China. Such a move is likely to destabilize the overall security situation in the region. And as Katharine Moon perceptively points out, it will be increasingly difficult for the United States to maintain its military bases in East Asia because of opposition from civil society. If American military hegemony is measured by its overseas bases, it is certainly waning. The clash of nationalisms seems more troublesome. No matter how influential the United States could be, it will be extremely difficult to mitigate intraregional conflicts arising from contests over national identity and prestige. Failure to manage the North Korean nuclear problem could also result in one of the worst-case scenarios: a nuclear North Korea and regional nuclear domino effect or catastrophic conflict escalation in the process of controlling the situation.

Designing New Order

In light of the above, East Asia is at the vortex of uncertainty. Although elements of continuity framed around American hegemony still continue, overall configuration of power realities and strategic choice by regional actors portend a new strategic outlook in the future. What complicates the situation all the more is the proliferation of new events and issues. Changes in American alliance policy in the region can produce considerable strategic realignments. The Janus-like face of China's rise can also become a new source of anxiety in the region, while the proliferation of unruly, parochial nationalism in China, Japan, and South Korea could create a new security dilemma. Finally, the North Korean nuclear quagmire could become a lightning rod. How to manage all this? Chapters in part III attempt to suggest a new architecture of regional order.[6]

In chapter 10, Michael Mastanduno argues that the end of the Cold War has brought about a profound transformation in world politics from a bipolar to a unipolar system. It was in this context that the United States has pursued a hegemonic strategy for the maintenance of order in East Asia. As in the Cold War period, American hegemonic presence has played an important stabilizing role by not only providing collective goods, but also mitigating the insecurity that could have resulted from strategic uncertainty. Yet there are some dissenting voices toward the United States, and American hegemony may not be the ideal basis for regional order. Nevertheless, Mastanduno contends that at present, there are no other alternatives and that most countries in the region would agree that American engagement, rather than disengagement, is more beneficial to the stability of the region.

The events of September 11 have had a lasting impact on U.S. foreign policy, making U.S. foreign policy "more moralistic, more risk acceptant, and less wedded to particular institutional arrangements." This new policy stance, coupled with other developments, may foster the transformation of the existing East Asian security architecture. Shifting priorities of American foreign policy are bound to yield corresponding diplomatic consequences, and U.S. focus on the global war on terror will significantly affect the allocation of U.S. military assets, diverting American attention away from East Asia and giving a greater emphasis to the Middle East. Changing economic configurations could become another critical factor affecting American policy toward East Asia. East Asian countries enjoyed the fruits of economic prosperity during the Cold War under the American hegemonic leadership in East Asia, in which a liberal economic order and economic interdependence were integral to U.S. hegemony. But the East Asian geoeconomic landscape is changing. China's rapid rise, continuing economic stagnation in the United States, and subsequent economic conflicts between the two could further undercut American efforts to maintain the existing East Asian security order. Despite these constraints, Mastanduno asserts, the United States is likely to maintain its hegemony in the region, which will be beneficial to all regional actors.

Whereas Mastanduno sees a hegemonic order as an alternative, Vinod K. Aggarwal and Min Gyo Koo in chapter 11 call for a liberal institutional alternative focusing mainly on community building in Northeast Asia. Since the beginning of the Cold War, Northeast Asian countries have followed an interesting institutional path, in which bilateral alliance constituted the core of security relations, while trade relations were by and large governed by multilateral arrangements. This conventional bilateral-multilateral institutional mix has become increasingly untenable, as manifested by the burgeoning interest in preferential trade agreements (PTAs) and regional security dialogues. China, Japan, and South Korea held a tripartite summit on the sidelines of the formal summit of ASEAN Plus Three in Manila in November 1999. It was the first time that leaders of the three countries had met after decades of distrust. They agreed to conduct joint research to seek ways of institutionalizing economic cooperation among themselves. The Asian financial crisis of 1997–1998 and the debacle of the 1999 WTO ministerial meeting in Seattle revealed a number of institutional weaknesses that Northeast Asian economies shared. The growing ineffectiveness of multilateral trade and financial institutions in dealing with new challenges such as the rise of regional trading blocs and the proliferation of credit bubbles and currency speculators has encouraged them to seek regional and subregional institutional responses.

Aggarwal and Koo present an outlook of regional order that is quite different from that of Mastanduno. According to them, Northeast Asia may not be able to sustain the traditional pattern of the balance-of-power system. The protracted global war on terrorism could result in a significant departure from the region's emphasis on bilateral security ties. Changes are also taking place in the economic domain. Principal actors are now pursuing greater institutionalization at the regional level. The latest enthusiasm for PTAs in Northeast Asia seems to revolve around a bilateral free-trade agreement (FTA) as a popular mode of participation, while there are also strong indications of minilateral participation, such as the ASEAN Plus Three and the China-ASEAN Framework FTA. Likewise, Northeast Asian countries have been exploring a host of multiple institutional alternatives for regional trade and security cooperation by going beyond the combination of a bilateral-multilateral framework. As Aggarwal and Koo argue, the liberal institutional path is most desirable, but the path to deeper and wider economic and security integration in Northeast Asia is likely to be complex and time consuming.

Finally, in chapter 12, Ki-Jung Kim and Myongsob Kim give an overall picture of the United States and the East Asian regional order. They identify four ideal types of regional order: confrontational, reactionary, imperial, and multilateral. The configuration of the regional order is contingent upon the dynamic interplay of external powers' actions and regional actors' reactions. Whereas the confrontational order could result from regional actors' tough responses to coercive engagement by the external power, the reactionary one can emerge when a leading regional power, equipped with a strong resistant stance, strives for regional hegemony and meets little resistance from external power(s). Imperial order is predicated on the combination of a coercive engagement by the leading external power and compliant stance of the leading internal power. In contrast, the coincidence of cooperative engagement of the leading external powers with the compliance of the leading internal power will likely give rise to a multilateral order.

The East Asian regional order has experienced drastic changes since the mid-nineteenth century when the Western powers expanded to enter into the

Sinocentric sphere. With the mechanism of "unequal treaties," this Sinocentric order became entangled in the web of the world capitalist system. It evolved from a confrontational order to a reactionary one in which Japan actively pursued the "Greater East Asia Co-Prosperity Sphere" campaign by pitting the "Asian spirit" against "Western imperialists." Since the end of World War II, the regional order has demonstrated an "imperial" character under American hegemonic leadership. How about the future? Kim and Kim diagnose that three factors will eventually shape the future course of regional order. First is China's constructive engagement with East Asia as a partner and contributor to regional order without nostalgia for the Sinocentric order in premodern East Asia. The second factor is closely related to how Japan redefines its role in promoting a new order. Finally, the East Asian regional order will depend on how the United States maintains its properly engaged role, readjusting its place in this more complex and perhaps more flexible framework. They argue that "the current East Asian order resembles something between the confrontational order and from imperial order, where the United States holds the driver's seat in terms of managing regional affairs, with China perceived as a potential challenger." Kim and Kim conclude that it will not be easy to forge a multilateral regional order, which is the most desirable.

Together, this volume provides a panoramic view of the dynamics of change in East Asia. The old international order was anchored in America's postwar hegemonic presence in the region, tied to bilateral security partnerships with Japan and South Korea. For half a century that hegemonic order provided a stable structure of open markets and security as Japan, South Korea, and other Asian countries developed, democratized, and joined the wider modernized world. Today that order is in transition—to what, no one is sure, but change in indeed the hallmark of the region today.

As our survey of the chapters suggests, this book seeks to illuminate the character of East Asian regional order and the logic of change now underway. Partly by accident and partly by design, a relatively peaceful and stable regional system did emerge in East Asia over the last half-century. It is an order organized around "hard" bilateralism and "soft" multilateralism. At the core of this system has been the United States' bilateral alliances with Japan and South Korea. Over the decades a growing array of multilateral dialogues and gatherings have emerged—Asia-Pacific Economic Cooperation (APEC), ARF, and most recently the Asian Summit. From the outset, this bilateral security order has been intertwined with the evolution of regional economic and political relations. Free trade helped cement the alliances, and in turn the security partnerships helped soften economic disputes.

The chapters also highlight the factors that are propelling change in the region. The most potent drivers of change in East Asia are the rise of China and the "normalization" of Japan. China's growing political and economic influence across the region is one of the great themes in the unfolding drama of twenty-first century East Asia, as is Japan's search for a normal status on statehood, in terms both of the restoration of traditional rights of sovereignty and self-defense and of the development of a new national identity. Each of these grand developments alone would jeopardize stable relations in the region—but together they feed on each other and threaten to create vicious circles of antagonism and insecurity.

Other developments in the region are also undermining the old American-led order. The flourishing of democracy and populist politics in South Korea has made it easier for its leaders to question that country's client status and alliance dependence on the United States. The growth and integration of the East Asian regional economy has also reduced the centrality of American markets and investment and refocused commercial relations on China. Meanwhile, the rise of India and the return of Russia have expanded the geopolitical "space" of Asia and brought the wider array of Eurasian great power politics into it. Finally, America's own changing global security priorities and alliance thinking—driven by its war on terrorism—have created new uncertainties and controversies in the region about Washington's long-term security ties and commitments to the region.

The chapters that follow provide a vivid collective portrait on the region at this dynamic moment of transition. The distinctive confluence of shifting power relations, divergent developmental passages, and intensifying interdependence that is shaping the regional transition in East Asia ensures that the regional order that emerges in the years ahead will be unlike anything the world has seen before. But the concepts and debates in this volume will certainly help illuminate its complex contours.

Notes

1. East Asia is composed of Northeast Asia and Southeast Asia. In this volume, however, East Asia is interchangeably used with Northeast Asia, comprising China, Japan, Russia, North and South Korea, and the United States.

2. See John J. Mearsheimer, *The Tragedy of Great Power Politics* (New York: Norton 2001); Aaron Friedberg, "Ripe for Rivalry: Prospects for Peace in a Multipolar Asia," *International Security* 18, no. 3 (Winter 1993–1994); Denny Roy, "Hegemony on the Horizon: China's Threat to East Asian Security," *International Security* 19, no. 1 (Summer 1994).

3. See Mel Gurtov, *Pacific Asia* (Lanham, Md.: Rowman and Littlefield, 2002); Peter J. Katzenstein and Takashi Shiraishi, eds., *Network Power* (Ithaca, N.Y.: Cornell University Press, 1997).

4. This volume can be regarded as a sequel to a series of excellent books on East Asian security. See Samuel Kim, ed., *The International Relations of Northeast Asia* (Lanham, Md.: Rowman and Littlefield, 2004); J. J. Suh, Peter Kaztenstein, and A. Carlson, eds., *Rethinking Security in East Asia* (Ithaca, N.Y.: Cornell University Press, 2004); G. John Ikenberry and Michael Mastanduno, eds., *International Relations Theory and the Asia Pacific* (New York: Columbia University Press, 2003).

5. See Avery Goldstein, *Rising to the Challenge: China's Grand Strategy and International Security* (Stanford, Calif.: Stanford University Press, 2005), 218.

6. For a more detailed discussion on this issue, see Muthiah Alagappa, ed., *Asian Security Order* (Stanford, Calif.: Stanford University Press, 2003); Samuel S. Kim, "Northeast Asia in the Local-Regional-Global Nexus: Multiple Challenges and Contending Explanations," in *International Relations of Northeast Asia*, Samuel S. Kim, ed. 3–64.

Part I

THE UNITED STATES AND NORTHEAST ASIA
Debates on Power, Reality, and Realignments

1

The Political Foundations of American Relations with East Asia

G. John Ikenberry

A MERICAN FOREIGN POLICY TOWARD EAST ASIA—and the geopolitical organization of the region itself—have remained remarkably steady over the postwar decades. Despite the end of the Cold War, shifting power realities in East Asia, the rise of American unipolarity, the September 11 terrorist attacks, and the war in Iraq, American grand strategic relations with the region have remained largely unchanged. The United States has reaffirmed its alliance commitments and made clear its geopolitical and economic interests in the region. U.S. relations with China remain remarkably restrained and stable despite the steady growth of Chinese power and the Bush administration's hard-line foreign policy and war on terrorism. The U.S.-Japan alliance remains the organizational center of the region even as the evolving relationship between America and China grows in importance. America remains an East Asian great power and its hegemonic relations with states in the region continue to shape and influence its politics and economics.[1]

What explains the continuity of American policy toward East Asia? To answer this question it is necessary to see the larger logic and dynamics of the United States as a world power. The United States is a global hegemon that has constructed a political-security order in East Asia—as it has around the world—and in practical terms there is no viable alternative order that states in the region can conjure up that is more stable or mutually beneficial. Perhaps a new order will someday emerge, but not yet. American policy toward East Asia and the regional order that has evolved over the decades reflects this hegemonic reality: key countries in the region are dependent on American military protection and the American market. American extended deterrence and regional trade linkages are at the heart of this American–East Asian order. Moreover, this order—along with American foreign policy toward the region—is also supported by America's ideas and intellectual traditions about how to build regional and global order. These are realist ideas about power and containment but also liberal ideas about how best to build an international order and how to engage the region in the economic, political, and security spheres.

The Bush administration's policy toward the region—as well as its wider global vision—exhibits both these realist and liberal logics. The Bush administration is less committed to America's postwar orientation toward exercising global leadership through alliances and multilateral institutions. It has famously rejected a variety of arms control and environmental treaties and agreements. Yet five years after September 11, officials in the Bush administration seem to have rediscovered some usefulness in coalitions, alliances, and multilateral cooperation. In the long run, the American campaign to fight terrorism should reinforce cooperative relations with both of its allies in East Asia and create incentives for accommodating relations with China. These developments contribute to the continuity of America's presence in the region and the existing regional structures.

U.S. relations with East Asia have been less disrupted by the post–September 11 hard-line turn in American foreign policy and the crisis over the American invasion of Iraq than American relations with Europe. American foreign policy is preoccupied by the turmoil in the Middle East. The difficulties that the United States has encountered in the aftermath of the Iraq War have also served to moderate American global ambitions. The Bush administration has also articulated a constructive set of ideas to guide the evolution of U.S.-Chinese relations. There is some reason to think that the current administration—and certainly its successor—will return to a more mainstream foreign policy. This, in turn, will reinforce continuity of American policy in East Asia.

In this paper I do three things. First, I sketch American policy toward East Asia—built as it is around hegemony, bilateral security ties, and soft multilateralism—and trace how American policy has been evolving since the early 1990s. Second, I step back and look at the broader realist and liberal grand strategies that the United States wields in the region. Finally, I will look at the more recent U.S. efforts to maintain a hegemonic leadership position in the region by reinvigorating the bilateral U.S.-Japan alliance, pursuing multilateral cooperative arrangements in security and economic areas, and searching for a lasting rationale for the American presence in the region.

Postwar Foundations of America–East Asia Relations

American policy toward East Asia is built around hard bilateral security ties and soft multilateral economic relations. Embedded in these policies are a set of political bargains between the United States and other countries within the region. The U.S.-Japan alliance is the cornerstone of the regional security order, and the complex array of intraregional and trans-Pacific trade and investment agreements is the cornerstone of the economic order. The hub-and-spoke defense system has its roots in the early Cold War and the failure of more multilateral security arrangements that were intended to mirror the Atlantic security pact.[2] The U.S.-Japan alliance was established to deter the expansion of Soviet power and of communism more generally in the Asia Pacific. This Cold War anticommunist goal led the United States to use its occupation of Japan and military victory in the Pacific to actively shape the region—doing so more successfully in Northeast Asia than in Southeast Asia. The United States offered Japan—and the region more generally—a postwar political bargain. The United States would provide Japan and other countries security protection and access to American markets, technology, and supplies within an open world economy. In return, Japan and other countries in the region would become stable partners who would provide diplomatic, economic, and logistical support for the United States as it led the wider American-centered, anticommunist postwar order.

From the beginning, this bilateral security order has been intertwined with the evolution of regional economic relations. The United States facilitated Japanese economic reconstruction after the war and actively sought to create markets for Japanese exports, particularly after the closing of China in 1949. The United States actively promoted the import of Japanese goods into the United States during the 1950s to encourage Japanese postwar economic growth and political stability. The United States took the lead in helping Japan find new commercial relations and raw material sources in Southeast Asia to substitute for the loss of Chinese and Korean markets.[3] Japan and Germany were now twin junior partners of the United States—stripped of their military capacities and reorganized as engines of world economic growth. Containment in Asia would be based on the growth and integration of Japan in the wider noncommunist Asian regional economy—what Secretary of State Dean Acheson called the "great crescent" in referring to the countries arrayed from Japan through Southeast Asia to India. Bruce Cummins captures the logic: "In East Asia, American planners envisioned a regional economy driven by revived Japanese industry, with assured continental access to markets and raw materials for its exports."[4] This strategy would link together threatened noncommunist states along the crescent, create strong economic links between the United States and Japan, and lessen the importance of European colonial holdings in the area. The United States would actively aid Japan in reestablishing a regional economic sphere in Asia, allowing it to prosper and play a regional leadership role within the larger American postwar order. Japanese economic growth, the expansion of regional and world markets, and the fighting of the Cold War went together.

The solidification of a strategic partnership between Tokyo and Washington drove American policy after the fall of China. Japanese officials arrived in San Francisco in September 1951 to sign a peace treaty with forty-eight countries, and during the same visit Japan signed a bilateral security pact with the United States—anchoring the American security order in East Asia. It was only after the security partnership took shape that the economic integration of Japan into the world economy began. Throughout the last years of the Truman administration and into the Eisenhower years, American officials identified Japanese economic success with America's regional strategic interests. Unusual steps would be taken to boost Japan's economy and foreign trade. "The entry of Japanese goods into the United States should be facilitated," argued a National Security Council document in 1952. The United States was urged to "utilize Japan . . . as a source of supply on a commercial basis for equipment and supplies procured by U.S. armed forces or under United States aid programs for other countries."[5] Similar policies continued into the 1950s. The United States was willing to forego fully reciprocal trade relations if it meant that Japan's economy would be bolstered, leading to the growth and stabilization of noncommunist Asia.

The American military guarantee to partners in East Asia (and Western Europe) provided a national security rationale for Japan and the Western democracies to open their markets. Free trade helped cement the alliance, and in turn the alliance helped settle economic disputes. In Asia, the export-oriented development strategies of Japan and the smaller Asian tigers depended on America's willingness to accept their imports and live with huge trade deficits; alliances with Japan, South Korea, and other Southeast Asian countries made this politically tolerable.

The alliance system—and the U.S.-Japan security pact in particular—has also played a wider stabilizing role in the region. The American alliance with Japan has solved Japan's security problems, allowing it to forgo building up its military capability, and thereby making it less threatening to its neighbors. This has served to solve or reduce the security dilemmas that would otherwise surface within the region if Japan were to rearm and become a more autonomous and unrestrained military power. At the same time, the alliance makes American power more predictable and connected to the region. Even China has seen the virtues of the U.S.-Japan alliance. During the Cold War, China at least partially welcomed this alliance as a tool to balance Soviet power—an objective that China shared with the United States.

In the background, the American-led alliance system—in Europe and East Asia—has been a remarkably robust and critical support structure for the postwar global order. It is useful to see these alliances as the structural foundation—the beams and girders—that supports a larger, sprawling building. The U.S.-Japan alliance and the other bilateral security ties in the region provide institutional stability for the wider region. The alliances bind the United States to the other democratic states, providing both sides with reassurances about their future relations. The alliances serve to both extend American power and make it more predictable and "user friendly." The alliances give the weaker states in the alliance "voice opportunities"—that is, they provide channels for regular access to the United States—which makes these states more likely to work with the United States than to resist or work against it. The United States gains an institutionalized political presence in Europe and East Asia—paving the way for deeper economic integration and political cooperation.[6]

The end of the Cold War and the shifting economic and political environment in East Asia have altered the region and presented challenges to this postwar regional hegemonic order. The geopolitical landscape has changed. The Soviet Union has collapsed and now Russia is a weakened great power—too weak to play a dominant role in the region. The peace negotiations between the Koreas also are likely to lead to the reassessment of relationships and bargains. The end of the Cold War makes it more difficult for some Americans to understand why the United States continues to provide security protection to Japan and the wider region.

But in other ways, these relations and bargains remain critical to regional order—and they remain largely intact. The United States is even more powerful today than it was in the past, particularly with the ongoing economic malaise in Japan and the growth of America's new economy during the 1990s. The United States is still the world's leading military power. The United States also remains the leading destination for East Asian exports. (In the late 1990s, the United States passed Japan as ASEAN's largest trade partner.) There is a wide array of regional vested interests—on both sides of the Pacific—in favor of open trade and investment. This creates powerful and ongoing incentives for the countries of the region to engage the United States and encourage it to establish credible restraints and commitments on its power. The U.S. government clearly is convinced that its security and political presence in the region are as important as in the past, despite the end of the Cold War.

With the rise of China, the viability of this postwar logic of American-led regional order will presumably come under additional pressure. A more powerful China will be able to step forward and offer its own leadership and hegemonic services to the region. Already, the expanding importance of China's booming market is redirecting regional trade and investment toward China. China is also actively establishing a diplomatic presence in the region, playing a critical role in the six-party talks over North Korea's nuclear programs and cosponsoring the Asian Summit and other regional dialogues. As this China-centered regionalism grows, America's role will inevitably evolve to accommodate China and these shifting power realities. At the same time, the American-alliance system will also presumably continue to have an appeal to at least some of the countries in East Asia as a means to balance or hedge against future Chinese domination.

America's Realist and Liberal Grand Strategies

Behind American thinking toward East Asia stand at least two intellectual traditions. One is realist, of course, and it is exhibited in the balance-of-power and containment policies that the United States has pursued. America's hegemonic bargain with East Asia reflects this logic: the United States provides security protection and access to its technology and markets in exchange for diplomatic, logistical, and economic support from its partners as it leads the wider postwar order. America's wars in Asia and its forward military presence are all manifestations of this realist geopolitical orientation.

There is also a liberal orientation that has informed policies that have sought to create various sorts of integrative, reciprocal, and highly institutionalized relations. This tradition has stressed the importance of multilateral organization of economic relationships and it has placed a premium on the encouragement of democratic reform in defeated or transitional states. The liberal orientation toward order is also concerned with the management of power, but it brings a richer set of ideas about how economic interdependence, democratic community, political socialization, and binding institutions can contribute to stable and mutually agreeable order. America's "liberal grand strategy" is built around at least three elements of policy engagement, which seek to "open up," "tie down," and "bind together" countries in order to generate stable order.[7]

Opening up means directing the forces of trade and investment, cultural exchange, and transnational society into the closed politics of strong state rule. "These linkages bring with them powerful forces for change. Computers and the Internet, fax machines and photocopiers, modems and satellites all increase the exposure to people, ideas, and the world beyond China's border," as former president Bill Clinton explained in October 1998. Call this idea "strategic interdependence." The idea is to create realms of wealth and autonomy within the economy and society, which encourage political pluralism and erode the ironfisted control of the Communist Party. Expanding trade and investment also creates new and more vocal "vested interests" in closed societies who want to maintain continuous and stable relations with the outside world. Strategic interdependence is meant to accomplish at least two objectives: to help activate and reward internal groups and factions within the economy and society and to strengthen their domestic position, thereby giving a boost to political forces that favor democracy and a pluralistic political system.

Tying down means inviting other governments to get involved in international organizations such as the World Trade Organization (WTO) and the Asian-Pacific Economic Cooperation (APEC). Here the idea is to create expectations and obligations on governments through membership in regional and global institutions. Political conditionality for gaining membership in these organizations can itself create leverage, but the expectation is also that once inside the institution, government officials will slowly be socialized into embracing its principles and norms. The variety of multilateral security fora in East Asia—most importantly the ASEAN Regional Forum—are seen as playing a small role in socializing regional governments, providing mechanisms for conflict resolution, and fostering some small sense of common identity.

Binding together means establishing formal institutional links between countries that are potential adversaries, thereby reducing the incentives for each state to balance itself against the other. This is the security component of a liberal grand strategy. Rather than respond to a potential strategic rival by organizing a counterbalancing alliance against it, the threatening state is invited to participate within a joint security association or alliance. By binding to each other, states reduce the risk of surprises, and expectations of stable future relations dampen the security dilemmas that trigger worst-case preparations, arms races, and dangerous strategic rivalries. Also, by creating institutional connections between potential rivals, these associations establish channels of communication that provide opportunities to actively influence each other's evolving security policy. Even today, the United States and its European and Japanese partners ward off rivalry and balancing among themselves by maintaining their security alliances. It is the binding logic—more so than the response to external threats—that makes these institutions attractive today.

Behind these liberal and realist grand strategies, are political bargains that the United States has made with East Asian and European countries. One is the realist bargain, and grows out of its Cold War grand strategy of fighting

Soviet communism. The United States provides its East Asian and European partners with security protection and access to American markets, technology, and supplies within an open world economy. In return, these countries agree to be reliable partners that provide diplomatic, economic, and logistical support for the United States as it leads the wider international order. This is where America's alliance system matters in the most obvious way.

The other is a liberal bargain that addresses the uncertainties of American power. East Asian and European states agree to accept American leadership and operate within an agreed upon political-economic system. In return, the United States opens itself up and binds itself to its partners. In effect, the United States builds an institutionalized coalition of partners and reinforces the stability of these long-term mutually beneficial relations by making itself more accessible to other states—that is, by playing by the rules and creating ongoing political processes with these other countries that facilitate consultation and joint decision making. The United States makes its power safe for the world and in return the world agrees to live within this American-led system.

These strategies and bargains—realist and liberal—are long-standing, dating to the 1940s. They help explain the durability and legitimacy of the postwar American role in East Asia and the wider global system. But again, new realities—the end of the Cold War, September 11, and the rise of American unipolarity—have rendered these strategies and bargains more uncertain. It is in this new context that the Bush administration has stepped forward with a new grand strategic orientation.

Bush's Post-9/11 Grand Strategy

Since September 11, a third set of ideas have emerged in Washington—the so-called neoconservative grand strategy. The neoconservative vision of world order is built on unrivaled American military might and a belief in American exceptionalism. Beyond this, the pundits and policymakers who make up this radical school of thought tend to share four convictions. First, the United States should increasingly stand aloof from the rest of the world and use its unipolar power—most importantly, its military power—to arbitrate right and wrong and enforce the peace. In a Hobbesian world of anarchy, the United States must step forward as the order-creating Leviathan. The United States will refuse to play by the same rules as other states, but this is the price that the world must pay for the American unipolar provision of security. America's older, postwar approach to order—organized around alliance partnership, multilateral cooperation, binding ties, and strategic bargains with other key states—falls away.

This new global aloofness is reflected in Secretary of Defense Donald Rumsfeld's aphorism that "the mission determines the alliance" rather than the other way around. The United States will determine what is a threat and how to respond—and relevant and willing partners will be invited to join in. Gone is the notion that the alliance determines the mission. "New fundamentalists" are not against security partnerships—but coalitions of the willing will be formed only if other countries sign on to America's unilaterally defined goals. This global aloofness is also reflected in the October 2002 National Security Strategy report's new doctrine of preemption where the United States claims a new right to use force "to act against emerging threats before they are fully formed." Gone are the old justifications of war based on self-defense and imminent threat enshrined in Article 51 of the United Nations charter. "When it comes to our security," President Bush affirmed, "we really don't need anybody's permission."[8]

Second, the new strategic orientation argues that military power—and the willingness to use it robustly in pursuit of the national interest—must be put back into the center of American foreign policy. Early neoconservative thinking in the 1970s made this a central tenet—American foreign policy in the post-Vietnam era had become too liberal, too soft, and too unwilling to confront Soviet expansionism. Power must be put back in the service of American principles and the national interest. During the Clinton years, the new fundamentalists argue, the United States was not taken seriously as a global military power—commander in chief Clinton sent a few cruise missiles to Baghdad on several occasions but never threatened real force—and when enemies stop fearing the United States, they are emboldened to strike.

Third, the new Bush grand strategy evinces frustration with the entangling rules and institutions of liberal internationalism—so its supporters advocate pulling back from treaties and international agreements that jeopardize American sovereignty and constrain the exercise of power. The neoconservative pundit Charles Krauthammer calls it the "new unilateralism"—"After eight years during which foreign policy success was largely measured by the number of treaties the president could sign and the number of summits he could attend, we now have an administration willing to assert American freedom of action and the primacy of American national interests. Rather than contain power within a vast web of constraining international agreements, the new unilateralism seeks to strengthen American power and unashamedly deploy it on behalf of self-defined global ends."[9]

Some advocates of this view simply appeal to the new realities of terrorism: in an new era where small groups of determined individuals can unleash massive violence against the civilized world without warning, the old system of rules and multilateral cooperation must give way to action—whatever it takes to get them before they get us. Other new fundamentalists offer more political-philosophical attacks on multilateralism and rule-based order. In one of the most far-fetched versions, Undersecretary of State John Bolton, prior to joining the administration, argued that a great struggle was unfolding between what he calls Americanists and Globalists.[10] Globalists are depicted as elite activist groups that seek to strengthen "global governance" through a widening net of agreements on environment, human rights, labor, health, and political-military affairs and whose not-so-hidden agenda is to enmesh the United States in international laws and institutions that rob the country of its sovereignty. Americanists, according to Bolton, have finally awaked and are now seizing back the country's control over its own destiny. This is a cartoon view that not just evinces a healthy skepticism of multilateralism; it sees American resistance to the encroachment of those rules and agreements as a patriotic duty.

Fourth, the new strategic approach also incorporates Wilsonian ideas urging the spread of democracy. This is not just idealism—it is good national security policy. If democracy and the rule of law are established in troubled countries around the world, they cease being threats. This argument was given a conservative imprimatur in Ronald Reagan's celebrated 1982 speech to the British parliament in which he called for the promotion of democracy as a fundamental global security imperative. In the hands of new fundamentalists, this aspiration has become, in Pierre Hassner's apt phrase, "Wilsonian [diplomacy] in boots."[11] The promotion of democracy is not left to the indirect, long-term forces of economic development and political engagement—but, when necessary, it is purveyed through military force.

In recent years these transformational strategic ideas have begun to bump up against stubborn international realities. As the failing of America's war with Iraq painfully reveals, the United States is not able to impose its will on other countries or intimidate countries into cooperation. The neoconservative strategy is not sustainable. It is too costly and it generates more problems than it solves. America will inevitably move back to a more mainstream foreign policy—returning to liberal and realist grand strategies. This gradual shift back to a more traditional and pragmatic foreign policy only reinforces the continuity of American foreign policy in East Asia. It remains a policy built around American leadership manifest through alliances and markets.

America's East Asian Policies in the Post–Cold War Era

During the 1990s, the United States pursued a variety of realist and liberal-oriented policies in East Asia—and together they have reinforced continuity in the country's overall commitment to regional leadership and engagement. The Clinton administration may not have had a fully formed grand strategy in place, but its policies were informed by both traditional realist security objectives and liberal aspirations. Clinton officials described their policy toward China at one point as "constructive engagement," but it did so without loosening its commitment to the security of Taiwan. The warming of relations with China did not prevent the Clinton administration from sending two carriers to patrol the waters off Taiwan, and it was willing to debate how to press China on human rights and trade problems. Obviously, distinctions between "containment" and "engagement" are too simple to capture the mix of policies available to the United States.[12] We can look at American foreign policy toward East Asia during the Clinton administration and the current Bush administration in this light.

The Bush administration came into office with the goal of reestablishing Japan as America's core strategic partner in the region and ending the idea of a "strategic partnership" with China. Indeed, the Bush ambition appears to be to make Japan a heavier and more involved military partner in the region—sharing intelligence with Japan and expanding Japanese functional duties in the region. The initial steps by the Bush team have also been to signal a harder-line position toward North Korea. The post–9/11 language of the Bush administration portraying North Korea as part of a global "axis of evil" is a continuation of this hard-line approach to what it sees as rogue states.[13] But the major thrusts of the administration also involve liberal grand strategic ideas: the bilateral alliances will remain the core of America's commitment to the region; the United States will support soft multilateral dialogues in the region; trans-Pacific regional economic relations will be championed; and trade and investment flows will be encouraged in American relations with China.

In the economic area, the United States has had a very consistent policy of fostering expanded economic ties with China; encouraging cross-cutting trade and investment patterns within the region among the various economic centers; and raising the level of multilateral political management of intraregional economic relations. In many ways, the evolution of the East Asian region is already being driven by the forces of trade and investment. Japanese foreign investment exploded in the mid-1980s within Asia, reversing the earlier Western orientation of Japanese economic relations. At the same time, the overseas Chinese in Southeast Asia have also created a complex production and trade network in the region. The result is a growing intraregional economy, not dominated by either the United States or Japan. The very complexity and cross-cutting character of these relations are driving greater political and security engagement in the region.[14] The American policy appears to be aimed at deepening trade and investment interdependence and encouraging institutional groupings, such as APEC, to reinforce the open and "soft" character of Asia-Pacific economic regionalism. The United States has also consistently sought to make sure that Asia-Pacific regionalism encompasses the Western Hemisphere and not just Asia.

In the political arena, the United States has supported the expansion of wider and deeper institutional relations between China, Japan, Korea, the United States, and the ASEAN countries—at least as these contacts are manifest as dialogues or policy consultations. The United States has reaffirmed its commitment to bilateral security ties but it has offered support for multilateral and minilateral dialogues that are consistent with these underlying bilateral security commitments. Support for Chinese membership in the WTO and for various regional dialogues are meant to provide ways to foster agreement on regional norms and standards of conduct. One argument made by American officials during the Clinton administration was that institutions should be arrayed so as to enmesh the regional powers in a series of regional and global institutions that serve to establish explicit standards and expectations for government behavior in regard to human rights, political accountability, property rights, and business law. Yardsticks are erected that, often in subtle and indirect ways, allow governments and private groups to both support and criticize government policy and politics in neighboring countries. This in turn helps foster political community. Another argument is that a denser set of regional institutions provides forums and arenas for governmental and political elites to interact—thereby providing opportunities for the "socialization" of these elites into common regional norms and expectations.[15] Finally, dialogues can also provide functional problem-solving mechanisms that bring together leaders and specialists across the region to find common solutions to problems.

In terms of track two dialogues, the United States government has backed the Northeast Asia Cooperation Dialogue (NEACD), which is a consultation grouping aimed at enhancing mutual understanding and cooperation through unofficial dialogue among China, Japan, Russia, the United States, and the two Koreas. Although North Korea has not participated, this forum has brought together officials and policy experts from the five countries to talk about political, security, and economic issues. The Clinton administration was closely involved in the launching of this dialogue and secured government funding of it. Together, these various multilateral mechanisms serve various purposes. These multilateral venues are also a useful way to diffuse Chinese and Russian suspicion of the bilateral alliances.

The final area is regional security relations. The U.S.-Japan alliance and the U.S.-Republic of Korea (ROK) alliance—together with other bilateral pacts in the region—provide a vehicle for the United States to play an active role in the region. In this sense, they serve the same function as NATO does for American involvement in Europe. These alliances also stabilize relations between the United States and its Asian partners. The deepening of the U.S.-Japan alliance does appear to be driven by these multiple logics of tying down and binding together. The United States and Japan agreed to enhance security cooperation in the U.S.-Japan Joint Declaration on Security in 1996, and Japan enacted the U.S.-Japan Defense Guidelines in order to make the security treaty effective in 1998. The Taiwan Straits crisis in 1996 and North Korea's missile launching in 1998 both served to intensify American and Japanese efforts to reaffirm and update the alliance.

An important development in American thinking about its post–Cold War security involvement in East Asia came with the 1995 Nye Report, which made an argument that America's military umbrella in the region had real and important consequences for the stability and functioning of regional political and economic relations and for the success of America's economic, political, and security goals, including issues such as nonproliferation. Its famous phase that "security is like oxygen" sums up the rationale that was advanced.[16] The report made the case that the U.S.-Japan alliance and the engagement of China remain in the long-run interest of the United States—America's security presence had direct and indirect impacts on the stability of the region and on the ability of the United States to achieve its interests. Serious intellectual and policy challenges to this view have been raised from time to time but have not lasted, at least within the American defense and foreign policy community. At the end of the decade, the thinking remained the same. The 1998 Defense Department strategic report on East Asia argued that "maintaining an overseas military presence is a cornerstone of U.S. National Security Strategy and a key element of U.S. military policy to 'shape, respond, and prepare.'" It again makes the direct link between the bilateral alliances and their "critical practical and symbolic contributions to regional security."[17] Despite the end of the Cold War, it is the widely held view of the American foreign policy community that the United States needs to be permanently engaged with a forward deployed military presence in East Asia.

The American view toward multilateral military cooperation has fluctuated over the decade but it has generally been supportive of such initiatives—as long as they do not undermine the core bilateral security order. The 1995 Pentagon report on East Asia spent more time than the 1998 report discussing the positive contribution of these multilateral cooperative initiatives. But overall, the United States has warmed up to soft security multilateralism. President Clinton gave voice to the multilateral vision in a speech before the Korean National Assembly in July 1993, when he called for the creation of a "new Pacific community, built on shared strength, shared prosperity, and a shared commitment to democratic values." He identified four aspects to this vision of community: continued U.S. military presence and commitment, stronger efforts to combat the proliferation of weapons of mass destruction, support for democracy and open societies, and the promotion of new multilateral regional dialogues on the full range of common security challenges.[18]

In the following years, the United States has signaled its interest in organizing "coalitions of the willing" to address various regional security problems and to cautiously foster closer ties between its partners. It has given support to the ASEAN Regional Forum as a mechanism for dialogue. But the United States has also backed minilateral initiatives among its allies, including the U.S.-Japan-ROK Trilateral Coordination and Oversight Group (TCOG); the U.S.-Japan-ROK Trilateral Defense Talks; the Pacific Command's (PACOM) dialogue with Australia, Japan, ROK, and Singapore on establishing greater interoperability for future collective humanitarian operations; and PACOM's Asia Pacific Security Center, where Asian militaries study the conceptual and operational aspects of confidence-building measures and cooperative security. These cooperative security undertakings reflect the general American government view that the bilateral alliances should be strengthened and coordinated as much as possible. "Foremost," argues the 1998 Pentagon strategic statement of East Asia, "the U.S. will continue to strengthen its strategic partnerships with allies, which serve as important pillars from which to address regional political and military challenges. All of our alliance relationships promise to expand both in scope and degree in coming years to encompass more comprehensive concepts of security cooperation."[19]

Going beyond these minilateral groupings, the Bush administration is focusing on even greater cooperation among America's security partners in the region. This is an idea championed by now-retired admiral Dennis Blair, former commander in chief of the U.S. Pacific Command—and he calls it a proposal to build a "security community" in the region.[20] The idea is to "enrich bilateralism" with greater cooperation and shared strategic purpose among the East Asian security partners. These cooperative ties would build on the examples of ASEAN, the ASEAN Regional Forum, the Five-Power Defense Arrangements, and on America's bilateral ties with Australia, the Philippines, Singapore, and Thailand to provide a foundation for expanding shared expectations of peaceful relations among East Asian countries. This proposal for building security community ties in the region, of course, excludes China. The danger is that in the name of the liberal idea of security communities, the United States actually will end up building a containment ring around China.

Looking into the future, the United States is destined to continue to pursue realist and liberal strategies of order building in the region. It will seek to protect its bilateral alliances in the face of rising Chinese power. The Bush administration will also continue to seek to find ways to leverage defense cooperation with Japan and Korea in ways that will be relevant to wider regional and global security threats. At the same time, East Asian countries will certainly have incentives to continue to embrace these security pacts in elaborate strategies of hedging against Chinese military power. At the same time, the United States will continue to see engagement with China as a necessary part of its long-term strategy in the region. Conservatives and liberals alike in the United States believe that trade and investment with China are critical parts of the long-term solution to the problem of a rising China. Embedding China in the wider regional and global system helps ensure that China will be cooperative and integrative rather than belligerent and revisionist.[21]

Conclusion

American foreign policy toward East Asia is based on America's position as a hegemonic and status quo power in the region. It wants continuity more than change, and its security and economic strategies toward the region reflect this reality. The American presence in the region exhibits both realist and liberal logics. American security protection and market access are part of a practical convergence of interests between the United States and its partners in the region. But there is also a more diffuse liberal orientation manifest in American policy: it seeks to open up and tie together countries in the region so as to realize a more stable and integrative order. These realist and liberal impulses have coexisted and together reinforced continuity in America's role within the region.

There are at least five underlying challenges to this policy continuity. The first is the problem of a weak Japan. The United States wants Japan to play a more active role in the region. But will the weakness of Japan's economic and political situation allow it to do so? The weakness of Japan might seem to favor a continuation of the bilateral alliance structure of the region because there is no prospect in sight of a transformed regional security order organized around Japan or a Japanese-Chinese accord. But Japanese weakness makes it difficult for Japan to step up and expand its security role. A weak Japanese government might also be less able to explain and defend the American troop presence when some future incident creates a crisis and domestic outrage over the bases grows. If Japan does move in the direction envisaged by the Bush administration, the question is whether an expanded Japanese military role in the region will antagonize China and other countries and destabilize the very order that the United States seeks to preserve. American officials should also worry about how prolonged economic stagnation might transform Japanese political identity—which in the postwar decades was transformed from military great power to economic achiever. If Japan can no longer see itself as a great economic power, what sort of national identity will replace it? The problem of a too-strong Japan has long been appreciated in the region, but the problem of a too-weak Japan is just beginning to be understood.

The second challenge is redefining the patron-client character of the alliance. More so than within NATO, the American role in the U.S.-Japan alliance is that of the asymmetrical senior partner. Can this relationship be put on a more equal and reciprocal footing without unraveling the political bargain around which the partnership is based? When Japan and the United States talk about alliance reform, Japan thinks more about greater political equality and the United States thinks more about greater burden sharing. Can Japan have more of a voice in the alliance without the United States deciding that the political gains from being in the alliance are not worth the costs in tying itself to Japan and restricting its policy autonomy? The other challenge is that a more equal alliance will necessarily make Japan a more salient and active security player in the region, and again the question is whether this can be accomplished without unleashing new security dilemmas and arms races in the region, particularly with China.

A third—related—challenge is fostering greater cooperation among America's bilateral security partners without turning the security community impulses of multilateral security cooperation into a threatening new containment belt around China. Enhancing multilateral cooperation among the United States, Japan, South Korea, Singapore, Australia, and other allies could look very provocative from Beijing's perspective—even if it is cooperation dressed up in the liberal rhetoric of security community. After all, what is that enhanced cooperation aimed at? The form and content of great regional cooperation—at least cooperation that does not include China—will matter a great deal in determining if it is stabilizing or destabilizing. It would be a nice irony if hub-and-spoke security bilateralism were actually more congenial with regional stability than alliance multilateralism.

A fourth challenge to the existing order in East Asia is the stickiness of the American military commitment in the wake of future political reconciliation in Korea and the settlement of Cold War territorial disputes elsewhere in the region. Even if the United States is able to maintain a steady security commitment to East Asia, the question is how and where that military commitment will be forward deployed.

A final challenge is American power itself. The rise of a unipolar American order after the Cold War has not triggered a global backlash, but it has unsettled relationships worldwide. Asians and Europeans worry about the steadiness of American leadership. Some governments and peoples around the world resent the extent and intrusiveness of American power, markets, and culture. Some intellectuals in the West even suggest that an arrogant and overbearing America brought the terrorism of September 11 on itself.[22] Aside from diffuse hatreds and resentments, the practical reality for many states around the world is that they need the United States more than it needs them—or so it would seem. In the early months of the Bush administration the political consequences of a unipolar superpower seemed all too obvious. It could walk away from treaties and agreements with other countries—on global warming, arms control, trade, business regulation, and so forth—and suffer fewer consequences than its partners. But successfully to conduct a campaign against terrorism the United States now needs the rest of the world. This is a potential boon to cooperation across the board. To pursue its objects—fighting terrorism but also managing the world economy and maintaining stable security relations—the United States will need to rediscover and renew the political bargains upon which its hegemonic leadership is based. East Asia will be a critical location for this process.

But in the final analysis, the hegemonic order is probably a stable one. Alternative institutions are not likely to emerge to rival the American-led bilateral security structure. The ASEAN regional forum is not a template for a wider security system. The multilateral dialogues that are proliferating in the region seem to be actually serving to diffuse antagonism to the alliance pacts rather than to replace them. Just as there is no political coalition—within the United States or the wider region—that could support and sustain an American hard-line, containment-oriented approach to China, there is also no political coalition that could support or sustain a transformed regional order.

Notes

1. This paper draws upon my previous essays on American policy toward East Asia, including "The Future of Liberal Hegemony in East Asia," *Australian Journal of International Affairs* 58 (September 2004): 353–67 and "America in East Asia: Power, Markets, and Grand Strategy," in *Beyond Bilateralism: The Emerging East Asian Regionalism*, ed. T. J. Pempel and Ellis Kraus (Stanford, Calif.: Stanford University Press, 2003).

2. On the idea floated by the United States of a multilateral security institution in Asia in the early 1940s and during 1950–1951 that was to be a counterpart to NATO, see Donald Crone, "Does Hegemony Matter? The Reorganization of the Pacific Political Economy," *World Politics* 45 (July 1993).

3. Michael Schaller, "Securing the Great Crescent: Occupied Japan and the Origins of Containment in Southeast Asia," *Journal of American History* 69 (September 1982): 392–414.

4. Bruce Cummins, "Japan's Position in the World System," in *Postwar Japan as History*, ed. Andrew Gordon (Berkeley and Los Angeles, Calif.: University of California Press, 1993), 38.

5. Quoted in Stuart Auerbach, "The Ironies That Built Japan Inc.," *Washington Post*, July 18, 1993, A1.

6. See G. John Ikenberry, "America's Alliances in the Age of Unipolarity," unpublished paper.

7. This "liberal grand strategy" is discussed in G. John Ikenberry, "America's Liberal Grand Strategy: Democracy and National Security in the Post-War Era," in *American Democracy Promotion: Impulses, Strategies, and Impacts,* ed. Michael Cox, G. John Ikenberry, and Takashi Inoguchi (New York: Oxford University Press, 2000), 103–26.

8. Quoted in Dan Baltz, "President Puts Onus Back on Iraqi Leader," *Washington Post*, March 7, 2003, A1.

9. Charles Krauthammer, "The New Unilateralism," *Washington Post*, June 8, 2001, A29.

10. John Bolton, "Should We Take Global Governance Seriously?" *Chicago Journal of International Law* 1, no. 2 (2000): 205–22.

11. Pierre Hassner, "The United States: The Empire of Force or the Force of Empire?" *Chaillot Papers*, no. 54 (September 2002), 43.

12. An American strategy toward Asia was spelled out in a February 1995 Defense Department report, and it emphasized four overriding goals: maintain a forward presence of 100,000 in the region; put America's alliances with Japan and Korea on a firm basis; develop multilateral institutions such as the ASEAN Regional Forum to foster great security dialogue; and encourage China, for a position of strength, to define its interests in ways that are compatible with its neighbors and the United States. See *United States Strategy for the East-Asia Pacific Region* (Washington, D.C.: Department of Defense, 1995). This view is echoed in the last Defense Department strategic report on East Asia of the 1990s, *The United States Security Strategy for the East Asia-Pacific Region* (Washington, D.C.: Department of Defense, 1998).

13. See Peter Slevin, "Powell Offers Reassurance to South Korea," *Washington Post,* February 2, 2002, A19.

14. Yoichi Funabashi, *Asia Pacific Fusion: Japan's Role in APEC* (Washington, D.C.: Institute for International Economics, 1995); T. J. Pempel, "Gulliver in Lilliput: Japan and Asian Economic Regionalism," *World Policy Journal* 13, no. 4 (Winter 1996–1997): 13–26.

15. Iain Johnston, "Socialization in International Institutions: The ASEAN Regional Forum and I.R. Theory," in G. John Ikenberry and Micahel Mastanduno, eds., *The Emerging International Relations of the Asia-Pacific Region* (New York: Columbia University Press, 2003).

16. See Joseph S. Nye, "East Asia: The Case for Deep Engagement," *Foreign Affairs* (July–August 1995). For later reflections, see Nye, "The 'Nye Report': Six Years Later," *International Relations of the Asia-Pacific* 1, no. 1 (2001): 95–103. For background, see Yoichi Funabashi, *Alliance Adrift* (New York: Council on Foreign Relations, 1999).

17. U.S. Department of Defense, "1998 East Asia Strategy Report," Washington, D.C., November 1998, 9.

18. President Bill Clinton, speech to Korean National Assembly, July 10, 1993.

19. U.S. Department of Defense, "1998 East Asia Strategy Report," Washington, D.C., November 1998, 61.

20. Dennis C. Blair and John T. Hanley, Jr., "From Wheels to Webs: Reconstructing Asia-Pacific Security Arrangements," *Washington Quarterly* 24 (Winter 2001): 7–17.

21. See the Bush administration's major statement on U.S.-Chinese relations: Robert Zoellick, "Whither China: From Responsibility to Partnership," Remarks to the National Committee on U.S.-China Relations, New York City, September 21, 2005.

22. See for example, Steven Erlanger, "In Europe, Some Say the Attacks Stemmed from American Failings," *New York Times*, September 22, 2001; and Elaine Sciolino, "Who Hates the U.S.? Who Loves It?" *New York Times*, September 23, 2001. For imperial views of American power, see Chalmers Johnson, *Blowback: The Costs and Consequences of American Empire* (New York: Henry Holt and Co., 2000); and Michael Hardt and Antonio Negri, *Empire* (Cambridge, Mass.: Harvard University Press, 2000).

2

Power Transitions, Institutions, and China's Rise in East Asia
Theoretical Expectations and Evidence
Avery Goldstein

PERHAPS IT SHOULD NOT BE SURPRISING that the debate about the implications of a rising China is so heated. It is, after all, not just a high-stakes debate about the possible consequences of an emerging great power for international peace and security. It is also a debate that reflects strongly held, but sharply differing, political perspectives within the policy community that inform admiration, fear, or loathing of the Chinese regime. Moreover, it is a debate that reflects strongly held views within the academic community about the essential nature of international politics. Cross-fertilization between these communities on a topic of self-evident importance combines the intensity of ideological preference with that of intellectual turf battles in ways that probably overdetermine the outcome—rancorous exchanges that generate more "heat than light."[1] With a sense of conviction matched by urgency, writing on the subject often seeks to demonstrate the wisdom of a particular line of reasoning and then to offer conclusions about the challenges currently faced, predictions about the trajectory we will witness in the future, and policy recommendations that logically follow from the preferred interpretation of China's rise.

Adjudicating among the sternly defended positions in this ongoing debate may be an impossible task, since it goes well beyond factual questions to questions of political values and epistemological beliefs. Adjudication is, in any event, beyond the scope of this article, whose purpose is intentionally more restricted. What I offer below is a preliminary assessment of competing theoretical arguments about the implications of a rising China that considers some of the admittedly incomplete evidence available from the mere decade or so since observers began focusing on this topic. Moreover, rather than explore the full range of theoretical expectations, I look at just two perspectives. The two that I choose, power-transition theory and institutionalist theory, are selected because they arguably provide the intellectual foundation for two contrasting views about the implications of China's growing capabilities as well as for the alternative policy preferences these views justify.

A generally pessimistic view rooted in power-transition theory sees China's rise as disruptive and most likely dangerous because it is expected to pose a threat to others in the region that have long enjoyed the benefits of an international order underpinned by American power. This theory predicts that a more powerful China, dissatisfied with its hitherto marginal international influence, will try to use its increasing clout to reshape that order to its liking.[2] The upshot is a growing probability of conflict between a more demanding China and those, most importantly the United States, who will resist the changes China demands. This scenario also provides a rationale for those nervous about China's rise to embrace some form of containment strategy that combines coalition building with military preparations; these steps are expected to discourage even a dissatisfied China from using its growing clout to aggressively advance its international ambitions.[3]

A generally more optimistic view rooted in institutionalist theory sees China's rise as an opportunity for building international cooperation within East Asia that could forestall a replay of the sort of tragic great-power rivalry that often characterized world politics in previous centuries and that currently informs the power-transition perspective. Institutionalist arguments suggest reasons that a modernizing China will see its interests best served by cultivating organizations that facilitate cooperation and the peaceful resolution of conflicts with other states that will also recognize that their own interests are thereby advanced.

The chapter is divided into two parts. Part one provides a threefold categorization of international theories that might be employed to study the phenomenon of a rising power and then further explicates the two theoretical perspectives for interpreting China's rise that I consider here in greater detail. Part two sets forth the expectations from these theories about three putative flashpoints in East Asia—the South China Sea, Korea, and the Taiwan Strait— arenas where China's rise since the end of the Cold War has been seen as cause for concern. It also compares these competing expectations with the still-skimpy empirical record of the post–Cold War era. Events in the South China Sea and Korea lend some credence to the expectations of institutionalist theory, though this evidence is inevitably inconclusive and I suggest why it may also be interpreted as consistent with power-transition theory. In the Taiwan Strait, however, the picture is less ambiguous—most of the evidence lends credence to the expectations of power-transition theory.

International Relations Theory and Rising Powers:
The Theoretical Landscape

Inasmuch as I am setting aside many strands of international relations theory that might be tapped to explain the consequences of a rising power, it is worth at least indicating where the two theories I employ are situated on this broader intellectual landscape. To oversimplify greatly, theories that could be tapped to forecast the implications of China's rise can be grouped into three categories.[4] The first category includes theories asserting that states seek to maximize power to enhance their security or to acquire other benefits available to the internationally dominant. In such theories, power is in a sense only a means to other ends, but because it is viewed as *the* indispensable means in the dangerous and unpredictably anarchic realm of international politics, the pursuit of power is at least an essential interim goal for all states.[5] As indicated below in the discussion of power-transition theory, the expected result is recurrent disputes as each state seeks to enhance its standing relative to others, with rising powers making demands that currently dominant states are bound to resist.

A second category of theories includes those emphasizing the attributes of states, rather than their relative capabilities, and arguing that the implications of shifting power relations will vary depending on the type of state in question. Without denying the realist premise that all states coexist under the constraints of anarchy or the importance of their capabilities, such theories view states' goals as a key variable that determines how they will use the power at their disposal.[6] Their significantly different approaches notwithstanding, all the theories in this category logically direct attention to the attributes of particular rising powers, rather than the fact that they are rising, as the key to forecasting their effects on international politics.

A third category of theories includes those emphasizing the anarchic international context within which states, whatever their nature and capabilities, must interact. Neorealist balance-of-power theory, for example, assumes only that all states share a concern for survival (without denying that most have additional, internally generated, interests that shape foreign policy choices).[7] Such theory offers only limited insight into the phenomenon of a rising power like China, explaining why a weaker state will want to offset its vulnerability to exploitation by the strong, but not exactly how it will respond to these incentives or how others will react to these efforts.[8] Institutionalist theory, described below, also fits within this third category, accepting the importance of anarchy as a constraint on behavior. However, it argues that international organizations can mitigate the consequences of anarchy, enabling even rational egoists to focus on the absolute gains they can achieve through cooperation, rather than worrying about potential dangers that encourage a focus on relative gains. Institutions (both formal organizations and less explicit arrangements sometimes labeled "regimes") clarify the benefits available to all as long as cooperation endures and make it easier to monitor behavior in ways that reduce the fear, inevitable under anarchy, that those benefiting most will use their temporary advantage from short-term gains to exploit others. If a rising power can be integrated within international institutions, it should be possible to avoid the conflicts that anarchy's premium on hedging against vulnerability might otherwise induce.[9]

Theories within each of these three broad categories identify some subset of the many variables that shape international outcomes. The theories on which I focus below are singled out because they inform fundamentally different views about the consequences of China's growing capabilities and because they are closely tied to the most prominent policy alternatives—containment and engagement—in the debate about how to deal with a rising China.

Power-Transition Theory

Two closely related, though distinct, theoretical arguments focus explicitly on the consequences for international politics of a shift in power between a dominant state and a rising power. In *War and Change in World Politics,* Robert Gilpin suggested that peace prevails when a dominant state's capabilities enable it to "govern" an international order that it has shaped. Over time, however, as economic and technological diffusion proceed during eras of peace and development, other states are empowered. Moreover, the burdens of international governance drain and distract the reigning hegemon, and challengers eventually emerge that seek to rewrite the rules of governance. As the power advantage of the erstwhile hegemon ebbs, it may become desperate enough to resort to the *ultima ratio* of international politics, force, to forestall the increasingly urgent demands of a rising challenger. Or as the power of the challenger rises, it may be tempted to press its case with threats to use force. It is the rise and fall of the great powers that creates the circumstances under which major wars, what Gilpin labels "hegemonic wars," break out.[10]

Gilpin's argument logically encourages pessimism about the implications of a rising China. It leads to the expectation that international trade, investment, and technology transfer will result in a steady diffusion of American economic power, benefiting the rapidly developing states of the world, including China. As the United States simultaneously scurries to put out the many brushfires that threaten its far-flung global interests (the classic problem of overextension), it will be unable to devote sufficient resources to maintain its advantage over emerging competitors like China. While the erosion of the once-clear American advantage plays itself out, the United

States will find it ever more difficult to preserve the order in Asia that it created during its era of preponderance. The expectation is an increase in the likelihood for the use of force—either by a Chinese challenger able to field a stronger military in support of its demands for greater influence over international arrangements in Asia, or by a besieged American hegemon desperate to head off further decline. Among the trends that alarm those who look at Asia through the lens of Gilpin's theory are China's expanding share of world trade and wealth (much of it resulting from the gains made possible by the international economic order a dominant United States established), its acquisition of technology in key sectors that have both civilian and military applications (e.g., information, communications, and electronics linked with the revolution in military affairs), and an expanding military burden for the United States (as it copes with the challenges of its global war on terrorism and especially its struggle in Iraq) that limits the resources it can devote to preserving its interests in East Asia.[11]

Although similar to Gilpin's work insofar as it emphasizes the importance of shifts in the capabilities of a dominant state and a rising challenger, the power-transition theory A. F. K. Organski and Jacek Kugler present in *The War Ledger* focuses more closely on the allegedly dangerous phenomenon of "crossover"—the point at which a dissatisfied challenger is about to overtake the established leading state.[12] In such cases, when the power gap narrows, the dominant state becomes increasingly desperate to forestall this shift in power, and the challenger becomes increasingly determined to realize the transition to a new international order whose contours it will define.

Though suggesting why a rising China may ultimately present grave dangers for international peace when its capabilities make it a peer competitor of the United States, Organski and Kugler's power-transition theory is less clear about the dangers while a potential challenger still lags far behind and faces a difficult struggle to catch up. This clarification is important in thinking about the theory's relevance to interpreting China's rise because a broad consensus prevails among analysts that China's military capabilities are at a minimum two decades from putting it in a league with the United States in Asia.[13] Their theory, then, points with alarm to trends in China's growing wealth and power relative to the United States, but especially looks ahead to what it sees as the period of maximum danger—that time when a dissatisfied China could be in a position to overtake the United States on dimensions believed crucial for assessing power. Reports beginning in the mid-1990s that offered extrapolations suggesting China's growth would give it the world's largest gross domestic product (aggregate, not per capita) sometime in the first few decades of the twenty-first century fed these sorts of concerns about a potentially dangerous challenge to American leadership in Asia.[14] The huge gap between Chinese and American military capabilities (especially in terms of technological so-phistication) has so far discouraged prediction of comparably disquieting trends on this dimension, but inklings of similar concerns may be reflected in occasionally alarmist reports about purchases of advanced Russian air and naval equipment, as well as concern that Chinese espionage may have undermined the American advantage in nuclear and missile technology, and speculation about the potential military purposes of China's manned space program.[15] Because a dominant state may react to the prospect of a crossover and believe that it is wiser to embrace the logic of preventive war and act early to delay a transition while the task is more manageable, Organski and Kugler's power-transition theory provides grounds for concern about the period prior to the possible crossover.[16]

Institutionalist Theory

Institutionalist theory, especially as outlined in the work of Robert Keohane, offers grounds for qualified optimism that the rise of China is not necessarily destined to produce an intensification of international conflict among states seeking to maximize their power relative to rivals.[17] Even under the conditions of anarchy, international institutions provide information and shape expectations, clarifying for self-interested states that the price paid for seizing an immediate advantage may be that it forfeits the benefits available through sustained cooperation. Institutions highlight common interests and, perhaps more importantly, provide transparency about state behavior. Enhanced transparency enables states to recognize that continued cooperation is conditional, establishes the expectation that defection in pursuit of relative advantage will be punished and reciprocated, and thus reduces the temptation for any state to treat those with whom it has been cooperating as suckers.[18]

Analysts who rely on this theoretical perspective envision the possibility that a rising China will remain eager to be integrated with, rather than challenge, the institutions established in the U.S.-led international order. Cooperation need not be rooted in China's embrace of others' values or political beliefs, but simply in the recognition that integration with these institutions is essential to its own pursuit of wealth and power. And unlike the nervous anticipation of decline and challenge that power-transition theory posits, institutionalist theory highlights reasons why the United States would be likely to encourage the assimilation of a rising China within the existing international order—Washington, too, is expected to recognize its own self-interest in the economic and security benefits available through expanding cooperation with a wealthier and more powerful China.

Institutionalist theory, then, directs attention to China's efforts since 1980 to open up and join the international economic order that was established under American leadership beginning in the mid-twentieth century. The clearest manifestation of this trend was Beijing's accession to the World Trade Organization (WTO) in 2001. But more generally, over the past twenty-five years China's leaders have recognized the economic benefits their country derives from integration with existing international institutions. Indeed, they now view their policies fostering trade and foreign direct investment as keys to sustaining the growth necessary for China to emerge as a true great power.[19] Institutionalist theory suggests that this self-interest is a powerful incentive for Beijing to mute conflicts with valued economic partners and to manage, if not resolve, security rivalries that could disrupt mutually beneficial cooperation.[20] As such, institutionalist theory offers a perspective that sharply contrasts with the typically gloomy forecast offered by power-transition theory—intensifying conflict as a rising China assertively challenges the international order shaped by the long-dominant United States.

East Asia's "Flashpoints": Two Theories' Expectations and Evidence

South China Sea

Power Transition

Power-transition theory provides a foundation for pessimism about the numerous territorial disputes in the South China Sea.[21] Through its lens, China's rise in this theater is linked with Beijing's drive to establish a blue water navy, to secure vital sea lanes far from its homeland, and to control potentially valuable natural resources. Beijing's expanded influence in the South China Sea that would result from a shift in relative power challenges U.S. interests because the region is important not only to the American Navy's Pacific Command but also to nearby states that have been closely aligned with the United States—including the Philippines, Taiwan, Japan, and Indonesia. The logic of power-transition theory suggests that Beijing's ability to realize its objectives in the South China Sea disputes (recognition of its sovereignty claims and rules for economic and military activity it finds acceptable) may constitute an early indication of China's progress along the path to becoming a peer competitor of the United States. Indeed, China's ability to mount a challenge in the South China Sea would be more revealing of an emerging power transition than its growing influence in contiguous areas on the Asian mainland (Korea) or not far offshore (Taiwan). If and when Beijing can shape international events "out of area" this will herald a step up in class for China as a great power. Both China as a rising challenger and the United States as the unspoken target of the challenge will recognize that much more than the control of minor islands, reefs, shoals, and the waters surrounding them is at stake. Both, therefore, are expected to run grave risks if necessary to support their interests, increasing the likelihood of a confrontation between an emboldened, assertive China and a nervous, defensive United States.

Institutionalist

Institutionalist theory offers a sharply different perspective and forecast. It suggests that a desire to reap the benefits of the currently liberal trade and investment climate motivates China to seek solutions that facilitate cooperation, even if these do not enable China to advance its territorial claims against rivals. A rising China's interest in economic growth establishes incentives for it to avoid undermining future cooperation with the ASEAN (Association of South East Asian Nations) claimants to the disputed territory. And China's broader interest in maintaining its good standing in key regional and global economic institutions encourages restraint in the South China Sea to avoid alarming the United States and other major Asian countries.

Evidence?

In the mid-1990s, as observers were first taking note of China's rise, events in the South China Sea certainly seemed to lend credence to the expectations of power-transition theory. China's determination to expand its military power-projection capabilities in defense of increasingly strident sovereignty claims to maritime territories in the area inspired some of the first scholarly warnings about the dangerous implications of China's rise. Denny Roy wrote about the "hegemon on the horizon"; Desmond Ball predicted intensifying arms races among regional rivals sustained by their growing affluence. And Aaron Friedberg noted the historical absence of regional organizations that might mute conflicting interests, invoking the metaphor of a "thin gruel" to contrast the weak institutionalism of Asia with the "rich alphabet soup" that had come to characterize a deeply institutionalized Europe. From this perspective, China's rising power seemed to portend a dangerous challenge to a regional order that rested not on institutions, but on the power of a dominant United States.[22]

In 1992, apparently unfazed by an oft-repeated American policy supporting freedom of navigation in international waters and despite the potential for antagonizing rival ASEAN claimants, China declared its Law on the Territorial Sea and the Contiguous Zone, which asserted an expansive and unequivocal claim that the "PRC's [People's Republic of China] territorial land includes the mainland and its offshore islands, Taiwan and the various affiliated islands including Diaoyu Island, Penghu Islands, Dongsha Islands, Xisha Islands, Nansha (Spratly) Islands and other islands that belong to the People's Republic of China."[23] Worries about China's claims to the disputed territories and its apparent willingness to use military force in support of them quickly fostered anxiety among ASEAN states as well as the United States. Despite Beijing's occasionally reassuring rhetoric about a willingness to discuss opportunities for economic cooperation in the South China Sea, its behavior was defiant and uncompromising. Especially unsettling was Beijing's fortification of Mischief Reef in 1995 soon after it had ostensibly agreed to avoid military solutions to the outstanding disputes in the region.[24] Together with the broader perception that began to take root in the mid-1990s that China's economic and military capabilities were rapidly increasing, China's actions in support of these territorial claims raised red flags in the region about a looming challenge to the status quo.[25] Several Southeast Asian states increased their bilateral security ties to the United States; Indonesia and Australia inked a new security agreement.[26] The United States, for its part, reiterated its concern about freedom of navigation through potential chokepoints in the region, freedom that some of Beijing's assertions about territorial waters seemed to call into question.[27] Simply put, just five years after the Cold War, precisely the sort of dangerous dynamics power-transition theory expects to accompany the rise of a new challenger seemed to be developing.

But since the mid-1990s, a different story has emerged, one hardly consistent with the prediction that a rising China would use its growing power to push hard for changes in the status quo. Instead, as China's capabilities increased, Beijing altered its approach in the South China Sea. China backed away from its previously assertive posture and began to express surprisingly strong support for accelerating regional efforts at institutionalized multilateralism. Within less than a decade, Southeast Asia's political kitchen was unexpectedly serving up its own enriched alphabet soup of regional organizations and informal regimes whose influence varies, but whose significance has moved well beyond the early post–Cold War situation in which the few such institutions that did exist were little more than feckless regional talking shops.[28] After the mid-1990s China became an enthusiastic participant in many of these institutions, abandoning its previous position that regional organizations were venues in which the United States could encourage its friends and allies to gang up against China's growing influence. Beijing had apparently concluded that working through multilateral institutions would more effectively serve China's own interests than the approach it had adopted in the first half of the 1990s, seeking maximum leverage by dealing with smaller neighbors bilaterally.[29]

China's overall relations with the ASEAN states since 1996 have not followed the pattern of an increasingly powerful state pressing to expand its advantage as power-transition theory would anticipate. Instead, consistent with the logic of institutionalist theory, Beijing has attempted to craft cooperative solutions that promise absolute benefits for all. In tackling the problem of competitive currency devaluation during the Asian financial crisis in 1997–1998, in devising arrangements for resource exploitation and acceding to a common code of conduct in the South China Sea, and in agreeing to sign a protocol prohibiting the introduction of nuclear weapons in Southeast Asia, Beijing has chosen dialogue over confrontation, multilateralism over bilateralism, and joint absolute gains over exclusive relative gains. Indeed, on the code of conduct and the nuclear weapons–free zone, China basically accepted the preferred positions of its smaller neighbors. China's warmer embrace of regional multilateralism since 1996 culminated with a flurry of agreements in 2002–2003 that aimed not only to enhance cooperation in regulating relations in the South China Sea, but also to institutionalize a broad "strategic partnership" with ASEAN and to build upon the announced China-ASEAN Free Trade Area by expanding it to include the key economies of Northeast Asia.[30]

This recently accumulating evidence would seem to suggest that in the South China Sea since the end of the Cold War, institutionalist theory is proving to be more useful than power-transition theory for understanding the implications of a rising China. Beijing apparently decided that the country's interests are best served by forging cooperative solutions to outstanding disputes and managing potentially conflicting preferences with its Southeast Asian neighbors, solutions that permit all to continue benefiting from the regional prosperity that requires a peaceful environment. Such behavior lends credence to the claims of institutionalist theory. The evidence, however, may not be as decisive as it seems. China's rise has just begun; it is a story whose later chapters are not yet written. It is certainly possible that China's current shift to cooperative, multilateral approaches for handling disagreements with its Southeast Asian neighbors will prove to be a temporary phenomenon, perhaps retrospectively seen as a tactical adjustment that obscured a larger strategy.

In such an interpretation, consistent with the logic of power-transition theory, Beijing has simply adjusted to the counterproductive reaction its prematurely assertive posture in the early 1990s elicited. Alarmed ASEAN states had begun to unite in their opposition to China as they worried about its future intentions and began hedging their bets against future dangers by seeking the reassurance and support of the United States, whose power continued to overshadow China's. Beijing's subsequent mellowing, in short, may be only a temporary shift to buy time, reflecting China's still-limited capability to press its claims as well as its need to focus on other external concerns currently assigned higher priority. Indeed, the timing of Beijing's adjustment is arguably revealing. In 1996 China's leaders began to focus on two foreign policy priorities: (1) the need to address an old, but increasingly worrisome, prospect—that Taiwan might finally forsake any political ties to the mainland; and (2) the need to head off a new danger—that the PRC's greater power and regional assertiveness were enabling the United States to invoke an emerging "China threat" to cobble together a hostile, encircling coalition built on the trellis of American bilateral security treaties in Asia that dated to the Cold War.[31] China's more cooperative behavior in the South China Sea might, then, simply reflect the military requirement to focus on the more pressing contingency of Taiwan and to minimize the risk of provoking a confrontation with the United States and its allies before China is adequately prepared. Rather than a fundamental change in policy consistent with the expectations of institutionalist theory, it could be part of a strategy to create the breathing space China needs to build the capabilities that ultimately will enable it to press for the changes in the status quo that it actually prefers. If so, power-transition theory suggests that a stronger China will calculate differently in the future, especially if the Taiwan issue has been resolved. China's institutionalist turn, in short, may reflect a temporary accommodation to necessity rather than a durable commitment.[32]

Power-transition theory, then, suggests caution when interpreting the evidence of China's cooperative behavior in the South China Sea since the mid-1990s. It suggests that a more powerful China would abandon the pretense of cooperation unless international institutions can be shaped to serve China's national interests.[33] And because a fully risen China will have far-flung maritime interests, power-transition theory leads to the expectation that Beijing will want to tap its greater strength to ensure it enjoys a dominant position in the nearby South China Sea with its vital international shipping lanes and potentially valuable natural resources. Since China has not wavered in its assertion of sovereignty over most of the contested areas even as it embraces multilateralism, it might well forsake cooperation once the costs of doing so are no longer seen as prohibitive.

Nevertheless, in the absence of evidence from the South China Sea that confirms the dire warnings of power-transition theory, its predictions are best viewed as claims about a plausible future that has so far failed to materialize. Furthermore, institutionalist theory suggests that the accumulating benefits Beijing derives from sustained cooperation in the South China Sea may gradually erode the temptation to abandon multilateral cooperation; unilateral assertiveness could become more feasible for a rising China, but that does not necessarily mean it will become more desirable.

Korea

Power Transition

If only because of the Korean Peninsula's strategic location, situated between the Chinese heartland and Japan (the principal American ally in Asia), neither the United States nor China can remain indifferent to events there. Power-transition theory anticipates that a rising China will seek to expand its influence in this key arena, and that it will meet with determined resistance from Washington. The current U.S. military position in Korea is not merely a guarantee to the wealthy and powerful South against the unlikely prospect that an impoverished and militarily disadvantaged North Korea would use force to unify the peninsula. In the post–Cold War world, the U.S. deployment in Korea is also a key component of the American commitment to a forward military posture in East Asia. Power-transition theory indicates that the United States will oppose any change in the status quo in Korea that suggests a decline in American international influence relative to a rising China. As Chinese capabilities increase, however, power-transition theory predicts that Beijing will push harder to realize its preferences on the Korean Peninsula, even if that means reshaping a security order that was crafted and has been sustained by a dominant United States since the 1950s. An inkling of such changes could well be reflected in China's advocacy of a less militarized Northeast Asia that embraces a new security concept. In this vision, the major role long played by American armed forces and bilateral alliances (such as those with South Korea and Japan) would no longer be essential. At the same time, China's cultivation of robust economic ties with South Korea and Japan and its reduced support for the frightening North Korean regime may aim to encourage others to view a rising China as an indispensable economic partner rather than a worrisome emerging military rival.[34]

Through the lens of power-transition theory, the Korean Peninsula is but one of the venues where China is seeking to increase, and the United States is seeking to maintain, regional influence. The result there, as elsewhere, will be a competition that fuels the risk of dangerous confrontation. On the one hand, a rising China will gain confidence that it has the clout to push harder to shape events on the peninsula to suit its interests. On the other hand, a still-dominant United States will have strong incentives to respond to this challenge to its preponderance—especially since Washington will worry about preserving a reputation for resolve that may be needed if it faces challenges from China elsewhere in Asia.

Institutionalist

Institutionalist theory, by contrast, leads to quite different expectations about the role a rising China plays in Korea. China's booming economic ties with the Republic of Korea (ROK) are interpreted not as a grab for influence relative to an American competitor, but instead as part of Beijing's broader strategy of integration with the open international economic order. China's recent disdain for its troublesome ally, the Democratic People's Republic of Korea (DPRK), and its support for multilateral solutions to nuclear tensions on the peninsula are seen not as an attempt to reduce incentives for others to cleave to an American-led security order. Instead they are seen as reflecting Beijing's interest in working cooperatively toward a nonnuclear, stable, and prosperous Korea because this outcome sustains the peaceful environment essential for China's ongoing modernization built upon good relations with key economic partners like Japan, the United States, and South Korea. In short, from the perspective of institutionalist theory, China's Korea policy is not part of an effort to expand China's influence at America's expense.

Evidence?

In the first half-decade of the post–Cold War era, China's policy toward the Korean Peninsula, as in the South China Sea, reflected considerations that power-transition theory highlights. Even as Beijing followed Moscow's example and established formal diplomatic relations with Seoul despite Pyongyang's objections, the dual core of China's official Korea policy remained support for the North's unification agenda and opposition to the U.S. military presence in the South.[35] But after the end of the Cold War, Beijing also worried that its Korean ally's behavior jeopardized Chinese security by facilitating an American attempt to check China's growing power. The dangers that North Korea posed to its neighbors (especially its ballistic missile and nuclear weapons program) provided the United States with a convenient pretext to revise and update its Cold War security alliances with Japan and the ROK and to promote the deployment of missile defenses. Beijing saw both of these American moves as mainly aimed at dealing with the stronger China that would emerge in the future rather than with the weak and seemingly moribund DPRK rattling nerves today. In short, consistent with the logic of power-transition theory, Korea was not just about Korea; it was about the emerging rivalry between China, determined to use its growing clout to shape the international order in its neighborhood, and the United States, determined to preserve its position of regional preponderance.

Yet, as in the case of the South China Sea, China's approach to tensions on the Korean Peninsula evolved during the 1990s in ways hard to reconcile with a story about intensifying rivalry between a rising challenger and a dominant power. By the end of the decade, not only had South Korea become one of China's key economic partners, but PRC-ROK political relations had warmed substantially as well.[36] More broadly, Beijing began emphasizing the importance of containing tensions with, rather than countering the military power of, the United States and its Asian allies, including South Korea. A rising China was focusing less on the adverse consequences for traditional military balances and alliances in Asia that might follow from North Korea's nuclear mischief and focusing more on the prospect that it might undermine the peaceful international environment essential for China's continued economic modernization.[37]

At the end of the twentieth century, Korea's significance for China was being transformed, though not as power-transition theory would have it. Rather than an arena where the interests of a preponderant United States and a rising China clashed, Korea was becoming a venue where shared interests presented one of the greatest opportunities for Sino-American cooperation. The result has been Beijing's promotion of a Korea policy since the late 1990s that facilitates cooperative solutions consistent with the logic of institutionalist theory—multilateral discussions aimed at incremental steps toward arrangements that benefit all, with provisions for increased transparency and standards of verification to reduce the fear that any participant will exploit agreements to achieve a dangerous advantage over others. China's shifting posture on Korea was first signaled by the more constructive role it began to play at the four-party talks in 1999.[38] But the change is most clearly brought into focus by contrasting Beijing's position during the North Korean nuclear crisis in 1993–1994 with its position after renewed tensions developed in 2002–2003, culminating in Pyongyang's announcement that it had tested a nuclear weapon on October 9, 2006. In the earlier period, Beijing played a passive and peripheral role as the United States and DPRK forged the basic terms of the Agreed Framework. By contrast, in the latter period, Beijing has adopted an increasingly active and central role. It has employed highly visible diplomacy as well as discreet backchannel communications in repeated attempts to edge the United States and DPRK away from the precipice and into multilateral talks. These talks have pointed toward a bargain rooted in the logic of institutionalist theory, a new agreement expected to (1) meet the basic security needs of the parties (removing the intense relative-gains concerns that preclude cooperation); (2) provide for verification that is good enough to reduce fears of strategically significant cheating (increase transparency); (3) establish benchmarks for compliance with good-faith steps that incrementally implement the terms of agreement (transform a finite prisoner's dilemma into an iterated game); and (4) hold out the prospects of mutually beneficial regional economic development as cooperation unfolds (the shadow of a future that focuses on the absolute gains available to all, rather than the relative gains each might pursue through unilateral and risky immediate actions).

To be sure, it is far from certain that the six-party talks begun in 2003 focusing on North Korea's nuclear weapons program will produce an agreement satisfactory to all. The unraveling of what was initially portrayed as a breakthrough agreement in September 2005, followed by provocative North Korean missile tests in July 2006 and then a nuclear warhead test in October, cast serious doubt on Pyongyang's willingness to strike and comply with an acceptable deal. The fate of the most recent consensus achieved in February 2007 remains unclear. But the uncertain prospects for success notwithstanding, China's active role in nurturing the multilateral negotiations and the basic contours of the type of accord it has endorsed reflect behavior consistent with the expectations of institutionalist theory. Indeed, Beijing's decision to support the October 14, 2006, UN Security Council resolution imposing sanctions on North Korea in response to its nuclear test, as well as the personal-diplomatic and perhaps economic pressure it applied to Pyongyang to convince North Korea to return to the six-party talks, underscore the extent to which China is now invested in relying on multilateral cooperation and international institutions to deal with this pressing problem.[39]

Contrary to the expectation of power-transition theory that the peninsula should be a focal point for zero-sum competition between the regionally dominant United States and a rising Chinese challenger, it has instead become mainly a venue for positive-sum cooperation between the two.[40] Ever since the late 1990s, U.S. leaders have regularly cited common Chinese and American interests in Korea as a central reason it is important to maintain a sound working relationship with China.[41]

Nevertheless, the logic of power-transition theory does suggest an alternate interpretation of recent events in Korea. As in the case of the South China Sea, Beijing's cooperative behavior may simply reflect reluctant accommodation to its current weakness. More aggressively advancing its interests or otherwise seeking an advantage in Korea today would risk provoking resistance, alarming others, and perhaps motivating them to counter a rising China before it becomes strong enough to get its way. After all, Beijing's cooperative turn on Korea was distinctly limited until two American policy initiatives made clear the dangers China faced. First, in the late 1990s the United States accelerated its missile defense program and justified its initial East Asian orientation by pointing to the North Korean threat after its Daepodong missile test in late summer 1998. Unless this Pyongyang pretext for American missile defenses was addressed, China would face growing regional support for thickening U.S. missile defenses. In the near term, missile defenses seemed likely to cover areas of great importance to China, especially the Taiwan Strait. In the long term, they might offer protection for the American homeland, potentially compromising China's most impressive counter to U.S. military superiority—its relatively small, but still frightening, nuclear deterrent. Festering tensions in Korea, therefore, would only help the United States sustain and perhaps even increase its already daunting military advantage over China.

Second, in January 2002 President Bush articulated an American security policy that justified preventive strikes against rogue states seeking weapons of mass destruction and emphasized the strategic importance of regime change in such states, beginning with the troika (Iraq, Iran, and North Korea) he labeled an "axis of evil." This U.S. reaction to the terrorist attack of September 11, 2001, significantly increased Beijing's concern that the Bush administration might seek a unilateral, military solution to what Washington termed the unacceptable prospect of a nuclear-armed North Korea. In the period after the U.S.'s toppling of the Taliban regime in Afghanistan and before difficulties in Iraq altered perceptions of the war's significance, many saw a series of quick American military successes through April 2003 as increasing the plausibility of preventive strikes against East Asia's member of the Axis of Evil. For Beijing, such strikes could be disastrous. In addition to the risk that an unpredictable military conflict would disrupt the economic dynamo that is Asia and with which China's fate is enmeshed, Beijing would face an immediate increase in the already substantial burden of DPRK refugees flooding its depressed northeastern provinces. Just as important, preventive American strikes would constitute an unavoidable challenge to China's international and domestic political reputation, since Beijing has repeatedly indicated its opposition to such unilateral military action against North Korea. Direct Chinese support for the DPRK as occurred in the 1950s might be implausible. But with military attacks that it had publicly labeled unacceptable taking place on its doorstep, Beijing would likely feel constrained to go beyond the merely rhetorical opposition it has raised against other unilateral U.S. military action in the distant Balkans and Persian Gulf. The costs of doing more, however, especially while China remains relatively weak, could be devastatingly high.

Thus, through the lens of power-transition theory, China's shift to a more proactive role in fostering a multilateral, cooperative solution to tensions in Korea (especially to head off the most dangerous possible reactions to the nuclear warhead tests of October 2006) is readily interpreted as an effort to forestall the possibility of action that could benefit the United States at China's expense.[42] Beijing's current policy may then tell us more about its willingness to accommodate necessity today than it does about the preferences that may motivate a stronger China tomorrow. As in the case of the South China Sea, however, although this is a plausible interpretation of the limited evidence currently available, its validity is based on projections of future behavior. For now, events in Korea provide more empirical support for the expectations of institutionalist theory than for those of power-transition theory.

Taiwan

Power Transition

Beginning in the 1970s, the United States abandoned the fiction that the Republic of China (ROC) government on Taiwan represented China and began a slow process of upgrading relations with Beijing that culminated in formal recognition of the PRC in 1979. Despite this shift, however, ongoing U.S. support for Taiwan, especially since the passage of the Taiwan Relations Act in 1979, has aimed to ensure that its political reunification with the mainland would only take place peacefully and with the consent of the people on Taiwan. American economic, military, and diplomatic preponderance in Asia during the last decades of the twentieth century provided strong incentives for Beijing to respect, even if it did not accept, these limits on its effort to reincorporate Taiwan into the Chinese polity. At the start of the twenty-first century, however, a rising China is rapidly modernizing its economy; upgrading its military capabilities, with top priority assigned to improving weaponry relevant to potential conflict in the Taiwan Strait; and engaging in more active regional diplomacy that firms up support for the "one-China principle" (i.e., that Taiwan is a part of China) among most states in the region, including many American allies. From the perspective of power-transition theory, these are just the sorts of changes that will loosen the constraints on Beijing's Taiwan policy. As a rising China becomes more capable of challenging the de facto rules of the game established by the United States that have defined the delicate situation in the Taiwan Strait, power-transition theory predicts an increased risk of conflict. China may face daunting odds for the immediate future, but the theory anticipates that as the military balance in the strait gradually tips in favor of the mainland, it will be increasingly difficult for the United States to dissuade a dissatisfied China from pushing for a resolution of the Taiwan question that reflects its preferences.

Moreover, as the logic of Gilpin's work suggests, the American burden of attending to its vast array of interests beyond the Taiwan theater, such as coping with international terrorism and rogue states pursuing weapons of mass destruction, will require Washington to allocate substantial, perhaps increasing, resources elsewhere. If the United States must address more immediate or higher-priority concerns, these needs may accelerate the decline in the American ability (and perhaps willingness) to stand behind the rules governing cross-strait relations it had previously enforced. Well before any broader crossover in the relative standing of a rising China and a preponderant United States, dangerous conflict may result if China overestimates its ability to rewrite the rules governing the status quo in the Taiwan Strait without triggering an American response, or if the United States underestimates the task it faces in dissuading a more capable and less tightly constrained China from insisting that the rules be rewritten.[43]

Perhaps more importantly, although the origins of the Sino-American disagreement about Taiwan are rooted in the distant history of the mid-twentieth century, power-transition theory suggests that changes both in China and in the international landscape have transformed its basic meaning and significance. Through the lens power-transition theory offers, the situation in the Taiwan Strait today appears as yet another part of the broader challenge that China's rise poses to a regional security order long defined by a dominant United States. As with events in Korea, the Taiwan issue is now less about Taiwan than it is about this larger question of America's ability to preserve its leadership in Asia while China grows more powerful.[44] In this respect, Washington's enduring commitment to Taiwan may serve U.S. strategic interests by inducing China to focus its attention narrowly and concentrate its resources on the short-term demand that Taiwan contingencies may require.[45] These preparations, absolutely essential from Beijing's perspective, may be diverting resources from the investment in long-term, comprehensive military modernization that will be necessary for China to close the gap with American capabilities in the region and beyond. As such, the status quo in the strait underwritten by Washington's support for Taipei is a sponge absorbing China's resources and postponing the day when this rising challenger might become a true peer competitor. Beijing, then, has doubly strong incentives to do what it can to alter the status quo the United States prefers to maintain—dissatisfaction with the current uncertainty about Taiwan's political future and with the special military burden it imposes.

Institutionalist

Institutionalist theory provides grounds for a more optimistic assessment. It interprets China's continued restraint and tacit acceptance of the status quo in the Taiwan Strait as reflecting more than a straightforward power calculus that acknowledges current U.S. military preponderance. The institutionalist perspective emphasizes the increasingly strong incentives for leaders in Beijing to refrain from the use of force since that would jeopardize China's integration with an international economy from which it derives growing benefits. Although Beijing stands on principle in reiterating its right to use force within what it considers its sovereign territory, it clearly recognizes that choosing to defect from the search for a peaceful solution to disagreements about Taiwan's future status would entail sharp conflict with the United States and worry others in the region, imperiling China's ability to benefit from its good standing within institutions such as the WTO, APEC (Asia-Pacific Economic Cooperation), and especially the many venues affiliated with ASEAN that have become essential to the country's modernization strategy. In short, to the extent China sees participation in the regimes of the existing liberal economic order as an essential complement to domestic reforms, it is constrained by an unavoidable, if at times unwelcome, link between its stake in the broader international status quo and the status quo in the Taiwan Strait.

Institutionalist theory also provides grounds for optimism about the prospects for continued peace in the Taiwan Strait for two indirectly related reasons. First, integration with international institutions, from which China benefits, strengthens domestic political interests on the mainland (especially among the crucial party elite) likely to reject coercive options for dealing with Taiwan. Such advocates of restraint can more easily lay out the price China will pay if the use of force in the strait jeopardizes the country's reputation as a safe and responsible regional actor.[46] Second, these mainland advocates of patience can argue that forbearance rather than coercion also fosters trends on Taiwan likely to reduce the attractiveness of independence. As the substantial benefits Taiwan derives from economic exchange with the mainland grow, so do the costs of provoking Beijing by defying its warnings about the dangers of independence.

Evidence?

Unlike the cases of the South China Sea and Korea, events in the Taiwan theater over the past decade are more clearly consistent with the expectations of power-transition theory than with those of institutionalist theory. It is true that in the opening years of the post–Cold War era, talks between representatives from Beijing and Taipei raised some hope that a mutually acceptable solution to their sovereignty dispute could be discovered. The two sides not only engaged in regular discussions through nongovernmental (though tacitly state-supported) organizations but also expanded indirect trade and investment, and relaxed restrictions on social intercourse. In the early 1990s, these efforts suggested that Beijing and Taipei might be able to institutionalize cooperation and reduce the fear that either would jeopardize the prosperity they could jointly create and instead exploit a temporary advantage to get its way on the sovereignty question. And indeed, both sides of the strait have clearly grasped the substantial benefits they derive from their recently flourishing economic ties as well as the opportunity costs of disrupting them.

But even as the web of cross-strait economic interdependence has thickened, the reaction in Beijing and Taipei to its political implications has revealed the enduring prominence of their concerns about relative, rather than absolute, gains. Leaders in the two capitals oscillate between optimistic claims that time is on their side and nervous warnings that the other side is trying to exploit short-term benefits to impose its preferred solution to the sovereignty dispute. Neither stance reflects an expectation that cooperation will remain mutually beneficial. Both instead suggest that sooner or later one side will win at the other's expense. Put in the terms typically invoked by institutionalist theory, in this case the shadow of the future is not benign and does not inspire the necessary confidence that the parties are playing a game of indefinite duration. Absent these conditions, even institutionalist theory offers little room for optimism that cooperation will be sustained by self-interested actors. Instead, it suggests grounds for pessimism. Cooperation, if it is achieved at all, is expected to be fragile and prone to collapse.

Beijing's focus on relative gains has led it to waver between two basic positions on managing tensions in the Taiwan Strait, each informed by its larger concern about relations between a rising China and the United States. One position reflects the fear that Taipei and its ally in Washington may believe that the high costs of disruptive military action will keep the PRC from responding to events that test its determination to prevent Taiwan's independence. A desire to counter any such beliefs has motivated China's sharp reaction to the following: (1) statements from leaders on Taiwan that suggest new definitions of the island's status (Lee Teng-hui's 1999 "two states theory"; Chen Shui-bian's 2003 assertion that there was "one country on each side of the Strait"; the decision to add the word "Taiwan" to "Republic of China" passports); (2) a democratic political process on Taiwan that empowers supporters of independence (presidential elections in 1996 and 2000 that favored candidates Beijing saw as separatist; efforts to hold a referendum on a new constitution in 2006); and (3) moves to strengthen Taiwan's unofficial relationship with Washington (the U.S. show of force in response to Chinese coercion during the 1995–1996 crisis in the strait; the Bush administration's approval of an expanded package of arms sales to Taiwan in 2001 and its subsequently increased contacts with Taiwan's military; the American government acceding to requests from independence-minded Taiwanese presidents to make brief visits to the United States in May 1995 and November 2003 designed to elevate Taiwan's international visibility and boost their own electoral prospects). In response, Beijing has periodically reiterated its right to use force to prevent Taiwan's independence, even while insisting it prefers a peaceful solution to cross-strait tensions. This message has been conveyed not just through strident public statements from the Taiwan Affairs Office but also through alarming military exercises and missile tests in 1995–1996, publication of a Taiwan White Paper in February 2000 that added more ominous warnings about the consequences of indefinite stalemate in the search for a negotiated resolution of cross-strait differences, heavy investment in China's military modernization with a dedicated focus on the Taiwan contingency, and the enactment of an antisecession law in March 2005 specifically aimed at Taiwan.[47]

Beijing's sensitivity to what might seem to be minor, arguably semantic, provocations, and its felt need to underscore its resolve, reflect a belief that Taipei would never be so foolish as to forfeit its support from the powerful United States by crossing the one clear red line sure to trigger China's use of force—an open declaration of independence. Instead, China expects Taiwan to craftily adopt "salami tactics" that gradually expand its "international space," an effort initiated under President Lee Teng-hui in the late 1990s and continued by his successor, Chen Shui-bian. Beijing believes that the real risk it faces is a fait accompli as de facto autonomy seamlessly shades into de jure independence.[48] To combat this perceived danger, an increasingly powerful China's leaders periodically announce that they are prepared to jeopardize the undeniable economic benefits of the current framework for cooperative relations across the strait if they believe there is an urgent need to respond to developments on Taiwan that could preclude reunification.

Beijing's other basic position also focuses on relative gains in relations with Taiwan, but it is rooted in hope rather than fear. China has displayed greater patience at moments when it seems that Taiwan's subtle attempts to consolidate independence are failing, American support is ebbing, and longer-term economic and military trends are creating conditions that will make a settlement on China's terms more likely. Consistent with the logic of power-transition theory, this posture reflects Beijing's confidence that the shifting balance of economic and military power, not just in the Taiwan Strait, but also between China and the United States, will eventually make it possible to realize changes in the status quo that are too difficult and costly to make at present. In 2006, deepening U.S.-China cooperation on the Korean nuclear issue, American irritation over Taiwan's failure to follow through with the purchase of proffered U.S. military equipment, and the troubled political fortunes of President Chen Shui-bian and his Democratic Progressive Party (DPP) strengthened optimism in Beijing about trends that favor China and encourage it to adhere to its present cross-strait policy of patience and restraint.

The fears and hopes of Taiwan's leaders often mirror those of leaders on the mainland. When cross-strait trends seem to accentuate the shadow of a future in which Beijing, having grown stronger relative to the United States, is able to impose its preferred solution to the sovereignty dispute, Taipei resists even small steps to increase cross-strait ties that seemingly promise benefits for both sides. Taiwan worries that the result will not simply be institutionalized cooperation, but rather the initiation of a process that increases the risk Taipei will one day have to accept unification on Beijing's terms. Thus, Taiwan periodically eschews what might objectively seem to be the clear advantages of institutionalizing economic cooperation with a booming Chinese economy. Rather than warmly embracing the absolute gains available from reducing barriers to trade and investment, leaders in Taipei often insist on maintaining restrictions or only warily negotiate limited liberalization because they worry that relative gains favoring Beijing might enhance the mainland's political leverage over Taiwan's government and people.[49] Institutionalized cooperation is constrained, not only by Taipei's long-range concerns about the shadow of a potentially dangerous future in which the material benefits of cross-strait exchange eventually give China a stronger hand, but also by immediate concerns about significant symbolic concessions that Beijing seeks in agreements to regulate current China-Taiwan relations. Taipei, usually with American support, refuses to agree to talks with Beijing that explicitly or implicitly entail an acceptance of the "one country, two systems" vision or the "one-China principle," which Beijing typically insists must be the basis for managing cross-strait relations.[50]

A rising China poses an ever more difficult challenge for Taiwan's leaders, even if they only hope to prevent China from altering the status quo of de facto independence. Concern about Beijing's growing capabilities induces Taiwan to nurture its unusual nonstate military relationship with the United States that provides a deterrent discouraging wishful thinking in Beijing about the costs of any cross-strait military operations.[51] The island's leaders reckon that America's long-standing and highly visible support for their regime makes Washington's commitment quite credible despite the dubious basis in international law for this security relationship, and despite the limited economic and military value Taiwan represents for the United States. Abandoning Taiwan during a confrontation with China would, it is argued, harm America's interest in preserving its own credibility, even if the United States saw little intrinsic value in Taiwan itself. This connection between the Taiwan issue and a broader American concern that it not be perceived as reluctant to stand up to a rising China's challenge to the international status quo in Asia is surely what power-transition theory would lead one to expect.

The logic of power-transition theory also suggests another potentially dangerous consequence of the U.S. security connection to Taiwan. Advocates of Taiwan's independence could conclude that American backing provides not just a deterrent against a Chinese threat but also a shield behind which they, though not Beijing, can act to challenge the status quo. If so, they might calculate that China, whose continued rise depends on the benefits of integration with the international economy, would be reluctant to pay the stiff price sure to follow from a conflict in the strait in which Beijing would almost certainly confront Washington. In this view, the window of opportunity for Taiwan to exploit this Chinese fear and try for independence may only be open for a few more years while Beijing's prosperity still rests so much on good relations with the United States. But can independence supporters be sure that China's fear about the likely U.S. reaction means that the window is open even now? After all, in recent years, leading American officials, including the president, have publicly stated that the United States does not support Taiwan independence and many have privately signaled Taipei that it should not bank on U.S. intervention if Taiwan provokes China by ignoring the U.S. policy opposing unilateral challenges to the status quo in the strait. Essentially, the United States has offered assurances to Taiwan that it won't be abandoned in the face of Chinese coercion, but also warned Taiwan that the United States will not be entrapped in a conflict that results from Taiwanese recklessness. Yet political leaders in Taiwan may believe that regardless of whose actions trigger a crisis, once it unfolds, especially once military hostilities with China commence, they need not really fear American abandonment, because of Washington's self-interest in preserving its international reputation. Such beliefs may be bolstered by confidence that members of the U.S. Congress who are Taiwan's supporters or who (as power-transition theory would predict) have fretted about the emerging threat from a rising China since the mid-1990s would almost certainly emphasize larger concerns about America's international credibility in their public statements.[52]

In short, the Taiwan Strait is a setting where the conditions for the relevance of institutionalist theory are lacking. Leaders in China and Taiwan steeply discount the future and do not narrowly focus on the absolute gains available through institutionalized cooperation. Instead, giving priority to their ongoing political dispute about sovereignty in which Taiwan's position is inextricably intertwined with the regional security order underwritten by American preponderance, both sides keep a close eye on the prospects for relative gains and the advantages they would confer on China or Taiwan. Under such circumstances, power-transition theory identifies impediments to cooperation and illuminates why the Taiwan Strait remains a potential flashpoint for Sino-American conflict.

Conclusion

The Taiwan case offers the strongest evidence confirming the pessimistic predictions of power-transition theory. Yet the other cases described above suggest that power-transition theory may also have relevance beyond the Taiwan Strait. Despite China's currently cooperative behavior in Southeast Asia and Korea, power-transition theory predicts trouble ahead once a rising China gains the ability to press its demands against regional rivals and the currently dominant U.S. power behind them that it must now accommodate. The absence of a challenge while it is easily rebuffed is interpreted as simply the rational choice of a cost-sensitive actor, biding its time until it can act on its preferences with the expectation that it can prevail at an acceptable price. In considering the longer-term prospect of a rising China, power-transition theory directs attention to the vision that outgoing leader Jiang Zemin articulated in 2002—that at least the first two decades of the twenty-first century will be a "period of strategic opportunity" during which a less dangerous international environment provides China with a chance to emphasize the modernization program that will enable the country to achieve the status of a true great power.[53]

Power-transition theory, then, suggests that China's present policies in the South China Sea and toward tension on the Korean peninsula mean only that Beijing is stuck making the best of its disadvantageous position during the early stages of its ascent. The theory's expectation is that the current approach embracing multilateral institutions to manage sometimes conflicting interests in these two cases will not last. When China eventually has the power to shape outcomes in ways that serve its national interests, either the existing institutions will become vehicles for Beijing to exercise greater influence, or China will cease to rely on them. This perspective, in other words, envisions a Chinese great power treating international institutions in the American fashion—working through them when they can facilitate the exercise of Washington's power, but resorting to unilateral or U.S.-led ad hoc coalitions when it concludes that this approach better serves American interests.

Institutionalist theory and its expectations about the role an increasingly powerful, but also increasingly wealthy and economically integrated, China will play in coming decades have not, however, been decisively discredited by events thus far. Unless and until there is a noticeable change in China's currently cooperative, multilateral approach to managing relations in the South China Sea and on the Korean Peninsula, it is plausible to view the Taiwan case as an important exception to the broader usefulness of institutionalist theory, not as a preview of what China will do elsewhere when its growing power makes this feasible, as power-transition theory suggests. The assertion that Taiwan is an exception can be defended by arguing that few international issues rise to the level of existential zero-sumness that characterizes this dispute, certainly not any of the foreseeable disagreements in Asia that China may have with its neighbors or the United States in a world where the Manichaean Cold War–style struggle between rival ideological systems has disappeared.

Unlike typical territorial, boundary, or economic disputes, the Taiwan question is about the survival of the polity that has been created on the island since 1949, and to a lesser extent about the ability of the CCP (Chinese

Communist Party) regime on the mainland to ensure its leadership over the far-flung and ethnically diverse territories it inherited from its predecessors. For many on the island of Taiwan, however great the benefits of institutionalizing ties with the mainland, these material gains cannot offset the loss of political identity entailed in finally accepting that they are to be part of the Chinese nation-state. For many on the mainland, however small the cost that would follow from writing off political control of Taiwan (especially since the island's relative economic and military significance diminishes as China's capabilities grow, and since economic relations can continue without political integration), this material loss pales in comparison to the domestic and international implications for the regime's reputation. History (and, just as importantly, the interpretation of history fostered by the CCP over the past half century) make it difficult for Beijing's leaders to accept losing Taiwan without a struggle. Doing so would almost certainly be read as a betrayal of what they routinely describe as their obligation to finally fulfill the modern nationalist movement's central task of unifying a China whose territories were split apart during the era when Beijing was unable to stand up to foreign meddling. Unlike the other flashpoints examined here, the Taiwan dispute is one in which a rising China will almost certainly insist on satisfying demands long frustrated by American preponderance.

In sum, the available evidence about the merits of power-transition theory and institutionalist theory for anticipating the consequences of China's rise remains mixed and incomplete. Will additional evidence make it possible to decide which is more useful? For at least two reasons, definitive judgments will probably remain elusive.

First, it is possible that the usefulness of each theory will change over time, but not because power-transition theory is correct when it suggests that China's current behavior is merely a tactical ruse masking China's true preferences. Beijing's current foreign policy may in fact reflect current preferences and not just an accommodation to necessity. Yet those preferences may change as China's capabilities grow, either because power sparks greater ambition or because others react in ways that provoke China to reconsider its national interests.

Second, it is possible that the currently mixed picture will endure, and that the relevance of each theory will vary by issue area.[54] Institutionalist theory may continue to better illuminate some matters, perhaps questions of regional economic integration and disputes over territory on the periphery, matters where actors see little risk that a rising China would be interested and able to tap the absolute gains from cooperation to exploit others. At the same time, power-transition theory may better explain other matters, perhaps questions relevant to vital economic and territorial interests or military concerns manifested in regional arms races and arms control. In these cases, relative-gains concerns more tightly constrain the search for cooperative solutions, and a more powerful Chinese regime may be unwilling to forgo the option of seeking ways to improve upon the performance of its historically weaker predecessors.

The possibility, perhaps even probability, of such a theoretical mixed bag suggests the wisdom of peaceful coexistence among competing schools of international relations theory. But the stakes of the debate and its implications for policymakers are much higher and require that choices be made. For them, it may be less significant that the present balance sheet includes both the hopeful signs about a rising China's role in Southeast Asia and Korea and the dangerous signs about risks in the Taiwan Strait. The likelihood that the Taiwan problem, sooner rather than later, will demand attention suggests that events in this one among the many arenas in which an increasingly active China is engaged may well be decisive in shaping the implications of its rise for international security.

Notes

For their constructive criticisms, the author thanks Matt Tubin and Keren Yarhi-Milo. Material included in this chapter appeared in the author's article published in the *Journal of Strategic Studies*, Volume 30, Issue 4 (August 2007).

1. For an example of the strongly held views that cross the academic and policy communities, see Arthur Waldron, "Watching China: Arthur Waldron and Critics," *Commentary* 116, no. 3 (October 2003): 10–23.

2. Power-transition theory predicts conflict in cases where a "crossover" in relative power is imminent *and* the rising power is dissatisfied with the contours of the international system the currently dominant power has fostered. Thus, as often noted, at best power-transition theory establishes necessary but not sufficient conditions for great-power conflict. Those who have invoked the logic of power-transition theory to analyze the case of China, however, typically assume that Beijing is more or less dissatisfied with an international order that reflects Washington's handiwork, a legacy of the preponderant economic and military power of the U.S. during the twentieth century. But it is unclear whether China is in fact a dissatisfied power today, or will be one as it approaches the crucial crossover point in a power transition. Part of the problem is that the criteria for assessing a state's satisfaction are unclear. Does a strong disagreement about influence over outcomes constitute dissatisfaction, or must the disagreement focus on more fundamental principles or "rules of the game"? For a useful review of evidence questioning the assumption that China today is a revisionist power determined to rewrite the rules of international politics, see Alastair Iain Johnston, "Is China a Status Quo Power?" *International Security* 27, no. 4 (Spring 2003): 5–56.

3. Containment is not the only available response to the rise of a dissatisfied challenger. Preventive war is another historically important option. Germany's decision

for war in 1914 may well have been driven by the belief that it needed to confront a rising Russia before it became too powerful. See William C. Wohlforth, "The Perception of Power: Russia in the Pre-1914 Balance," *World Politics* 39, no. 3 (April 1987): 353–81. In the nuclear era, however, preventive war is a prohibitively dangerous option. For a wide-ranging consideration of the various possible policies for managing the dangers of power transitions see Ronald L. Tammen, Jacek Kugler, Douglas Lemke, Allan C. Stam III, Mark Abdollahian, Carole Alsharabati, Brian Efird, and A. F. K. Organski, *Power Transitions: Strategies for the 21st Century* (New York: Chatham House, 2000). For an exploration of possible American incentives to strike a nuclear China preventively or preemptively, see Keir A. Lieber and Daryl G. Press, "The End of MAD? The Nuclear Dimension of U.S. Primacy," *International Security* 30, no. 4 (Spring 2006): 7–44.

4. These groupings roughly parallel the three images Kenneth Waltz presented in *Man, the State, and War: A Theoretical Analysis* (New York: Columbia University Press, 1959).

5. See Hans Morgenthau, *Politics among Nations*, 5th ed. (New York: Knopf, 1973); John J. Mearsheimer, "The False Promise of International Institutions," *International Security* 19, no. 3 (Winter 1994–1995): 5–49; John J. Mearsheimer, *The Tragedy of Great Power Politics* (New York: Norton, 2001); A. F. K. Organski and Jacek Kugler. *The War Ledger* (Chicago: University of Chicago Press, 1980); Robert Gilpin, *War and Change in World Politics* (New York: Cambridge University Press, 1981).

6. See Michael W. Doyle, "Kant, Liberal Legacies, and Foreign Affairs," *Philosophy and Public Affairs* 12 (Fall 1983): 323–53; Edward D. Mansfield and Jack Snyder, "Democratization and the Danger of War," *International Security* 20, no. 1 (Summer 1995): 5–38; Edward D. Mansfield and Jack Snyder, "Democratic Transitions, Institutional Strength, and War," *International Organization* 56, no. 2 (Spring 2002): 297–337; Andrew Moravcsik, "Taking Preferences Seriously: A Liberal Theory of International Politics," *International Organization* 51, no. 4 (Autumn 1997): 513–52; G. John Ikenberry, *After Victory: Institutions, Strategic Restraint, and the Rebuilding of Order after Major Wars* (Princeton, N.J.: Princeton University Press, 2001); Alexander Wendt, *Social Theory of International Politics* (New York: Cambridge University Press, 1999); Randall L. Schweller, "Bandwagoning for Profit: Bringing the Revisionist State Back In," *International Security* 19, no. 1 (Summer 1994): 72–107; Randall L. Schweller, *Deadly Imbalances: Tripolarity and Hitler's Strategy of World Conquest* (New York: Columbia University Press, 1998).

7. Kenneth N. Waltz, *Theory of International Politics* (Menlo Park, Calif.: Addison-Wesley Publishing Co., 1979); Kenneth N. Waltz, "International Politics Is Not Foreign Policy," *Security Studies* 6, no. 1 (Autumn 1996): 54–57.

8. To the extent others perceive the accumulation of power as exceeding reasonable security requirements, neorealist theory predicts a counterbalancing reaction from others worried about the way such increased capabilities might be used. Because such perceptions are uncertain, neorealist theory must be supplemented with auxiliary arguments to explain why increases in power are sometimes viewed as excessive. See Stephen M. Walt, *The Origins of Alliances* (Ithaca, N.Y.: Cornell University Press, 1988). See also Robert Jervis, "Hypotheses on Misperception," *World Politics* 20, no. 3 (April

1968): 454–79; Robert Jervis, "Cooperation under the Security Dilemma," *World Politics* 30, no. 2 (January 1978): 167–214; Thomas J. Christensen and Jack Snyder, "Chain Gangs and Passed Bucks: Predicting Alliance Patterns in Multipolarity," *International Organization* 44, no. 2 (Spring 1990): 137–68; Thomas J. Christensen, "Perceptions and Alliances in Europe, 1865–1940," *International Organization* 51, no. 1 (Winter 1997): 65–98.

9. See Robert M. Axelrod, *The Evolution of Cooperation* (New York: Basic Books, 1984); Robert M. Axelrod and Robert O. Keohane, "Achieving Cooperation under Anarchy: Strategies and Institutions," *World Politics* 38, no. 1 (October 1985): 225–26; Robert O. Keohane, *After Hegemony: Cooperation and Discord in the World Political Economy* (Princeton, N.J.: Princeton University Press, 1984).

10. See Gilpin, *War and Change in World Politics*; See also Paul Kennedy, *The Rise and Fall of the Great Powers* (New York: Vintage, 1987).

11. On concerns about the security implications of economic engagement, see the annual reports of the U.S.-China Economic and Security Review Commission at www .uscc.gov.

12. See Organski and Kugler, *The War Ledger*; Tammen et al., *Power Transitions*. For a view that disputes the incentives for a challenger to initiate war, see Dale Copeland, *The Origins of Major War* (Ithaca, N.Y.: Cornell University Press, 2000).

13. See "Chinese Military Power, Report of an Independent Task Force," Council on Foreign Relations (June 12, 2003), http://www.cfr.org/pdf/China_TF.pdf. See also Keith Crane, Roger Cliff, Evan S. Medeiros, James C. Mulvenon, and William H. Overholt, *Modernizing China's Military: Opportunities and Constraints* (Santa Monica, Calif.: RAND Corporation, 2005); Office of the Secretary of Defense, *The Military Power of the People's Republic of China, 2005* (Washington, D.C.: Office of the Secretary of Defense, 2005).

14. Steven Greenhouse, "New Tally of World's Economies Catapults China into Third Place," *New York Times*, May 20, 1993, A1; William H. Overholt, *The Rise of China* (New York: W. W. Norton, 1993). For competing estimates of the Chinese GDP and an attempt to evaluate their merits during the mid-1990s, see Nicholas R. Lardy, *China in the World Economy* (Washington, D.C.: Institute for International Economics, 1994): 14–18. For an attempt to specify alternative trajectories and the factors shaping them, see Crane et al., *Modernizing China's Military*.

15. Select Committee on U.S. National Security and Military/Commercial Concerns with the People's Republic of China, Submitted by Mr. Cox of California, Chairman. *House Report*, 105–851 (June 14, 1999), http://www.gpo.gov/congress/house/ hr105851-html/index.html. See also the criticisms of the report in Walter Pincus, "Hill Report on Chinese Spying Faulted, Five Experts Cite Errors, 'Unwarranted' Conclusions by Cox Panel," *Washington Post*, December 15, 1999, A16; Alastair Iain Johnston, W. K. H. Panofsky, Marco DiCapua, and Lewis R. Franklin, *The Cox Committee Report: An Assessment Center for International Security and Cooperation* (Stanford, Calif.: Stanford University Press, December 1999), www.ceip.org/files /projects/npp/pdf/coxfinal3.pdf. Since the late 1990s, Congress has mandated various reports to assess the potential dangers a rising China might pose. For two of the most important annual efforts, see Department of Defense, *Annual Report on the*

Military Power of the People's Republic of China (www.defenselink.mil/news/Jul2005 /d20050719china.pdf) and the annual reports to the U.S. Congress filed by the U.S.-China Economic and Security Review Commission, available at www.uscc .gov. For discussion of the military significance of China's manned space program, see Arun Sahgal, "China in Space: Military Implications," *Asia Times*, November 5, 2003, http://www.taiwansecurity.org/News/2003/AT-051103.htm.

16. Indeed, among the historical referents usually invoked to illustrate the dangers that power-transition theory explains, Germany's decisions on the eve of World War I may have reflected precisely this sort of projection about future dangers that an allegedly rising Russia could pose rather than fear of an imminent crossover. See Wohlforth, "The Perception of Power."

17. Keohane, *After Hegemony*; Axelrod and Keohane, "Achieving Cooperation under Anarchy"; Robert O. Keohane and Lisa L. Martin, "The Promise of Institutionalist Theory," *International Security* 20, no. 1 (Summer 1995): 39–51. Also see John J. Mearsheimer, "The False Promise of International Institutions," *International Security* 19, no. 3 (Winter 1994–1995): 5–49.

18. In a summary contrasting institutionalist theory with realism, Keohane and Martin argue that "Realists interpret the relative-gains logic as showing that states will not cooperate with one another if each suspects that its potential partners are gaining more from cooperation than it is. However, just as institutions can mitigate fears of cheating and so allow cooperation to emerge, so can they alleviate fears of unequal gains from cooperation" (Keohane and Martin, "Promise of Institutionalist Theory," 45). Historical referents for the optimism about building conditional cooperation through institutionalized solutions include relations in the post–World War II period among Western European states and between the United States and Japan.

19. See Lardy, *China in the World Economy*; Nicholas R. Lardy, *Integrating China into the Global Economy* (Washington, D.C.: Brookings Institution Press, 2002).

20. In late 2003, Chinese analysts began to explicitly address the concerns expressed in power-transition arguments by arguing that China's economic and developmental requirements made integration with, rather than a challenge to, the current international system imperative. This claim was initially articulated in Zheng Bijian's speech at the Boao Forum in November 2003 outlining the thesis of China's "peaceful rise" (often relabeled "peaceful development") that has become a central plank of China's foreign policy. See Bijian Zheng, "New Path for China's Peaceful Rise and the Future of Asia," *Boao Forum for Asia*, November 3, 2003, http://history.boaoforum.org/english /E2003nh/dhwj/t20031103_184101.btk; Bijian Zheng, "China's 'Peaceful Rise' to Great Power Status," *Foreign Affairs* 84, no. 5 (September–October 2005): 18–24; Evan S. Medeiros, "China Debates Its 'Peaceful Rise Strategy,'" *Yale Global Online*, June 22, 2004, http://yaleglobal.yale.edu/display.article?id=4118; Avery Goldstein, *Rising to the Challenge: China's Grand Strategy and International Security* (Stanford, Calif.: Stanford University Press, 2005).

21. If one includes not just the Spratlys, but also the Paracels and disputed maritime zones, the competing claimants include China, Taiwan, Vietnam, the Philippines, Malaysia, Indonesia, and Brunei.

22. See Denny Roy, "Hegemon on the Horizon? China's Threat to East Asian Security," *International Security,* 19, no. 1 (Summer 1994): 149–68; Desmond Ball, "Arms and Affluence: Military Acquisitions in the Asia-Pacific Region," *International Security,* 18, no. 3 (Winter 1993): 78–112; Aaron Friedberg, "Ripe for Rivalry: Prospects for Peace in a Multipolar Asia," *International Security,* 18, no. 3 (Winter 1993/1994): 5–33.

23. See *Law on the Territorial Sea and the Contiguous Zone of 25 February 1992,* http://www.un.org/Depts/los/LEGISLATIONANDTREATIES/PDFFILES/CHN_1992_Law.pdf.

24. See Allen S. Whiting, "ASEAN Eyes China: The Security Dimension," *Asian Survey* 37, no. 4 (April 1997): 299–322; Masashi Nishihara, "Aiming at New Order for Regional Security-Current State of ARF," *Gaiko Forum* (November 1997): 35–40, FBIS-EAS-97-321; Michael Leifer, *The ASEAN Regional Forum.* Adelphi Paper 302 (London: International Institute for Strategic Studies, July 1996): 37, 43–44; and Mark J. Valencia, *China and the South China Sea Disputes.* Adelphi Paper 298 (London: International Institute for Strategic Studies, October 1995).

25. Avery Goldstein, "Great Expectations: Interpreting China's Arrival," *International Security* 22, no. 3 (Winter 1997–1998): 36–73; Goldstein, *Rising to the Challenge.*

26. See Fang Hua, "Yatai anquan jiagou de xianzhuang, qushi ji Zhongguo de zuoyong" [The current Asia-Pacific security framework, trends and China's Role] *Shijie Jingji yu Zhengzhi* 2 (2000): 12; Jianren Lu, "Yatai daguo zai dongnan yazhou diqu de liyi" [Asia-Pacific great powers' interests in Southeast Asia], *Shijie Jingji yu Zhengzhi* 2 (2000): 41, 45; Robert S. Ross, "The 1995–96 Taiwan Strait Confrontation: Coercion, Credibility, and the Use of Force," *International Security* 25, no. 2 (Fall 2000): 87–123.

27. Felix Soh, "U.S. Warns against Restrictions in South China Sea, Block Press Tour to Spratlys," *Straits Times* (Singapore), May 12, 1995, 1; Greg Torode, "Philippines Offered U.S. Jets: Manila Warns over Continued Chinese Construction Work on Mischief Reef," *South China Morning Post,* August 2, 1995, 12. See also Michael Richardson, "China's Push for Sea Control Angers ASEAN," *Australian,* July 23, 1996, 6(N).

28. On this burgeoning institutionalization, and China's embrace of it, see Association of South East Asian Nations, *Joint Declaration of the Heads of State/Government of the Association of Southeast Asian Nations and the People's Republic of China on Strategic Partnership for Peace and Prosperity,* October 8, 2003, www.aseansec.org/15265.htm.

29. Alastair Iain Johnston and Paul Evans, "China's Engagement with Multilateral Security Institutions," in *Engaging China,* ed. Alastair Iain Johnston and Robert S. Ross (London and New York: Routledge, 1999); Goldstein, *Rising to the Challenge,* chap. 6.

30. China was the first non-ASEAN state to accede to the Treaty of Amity and Cooperation. See Association of South East Asian Nations, *Instrument of Accession to the Treaty of Amity and Cooperation in Southeast Asia* (October 8, 2003), www.aseansec.org/15271.htm. For an example of the detailed, step-by-step measures for building economic transparency and cooperation, see *Protocol to Amend the Framework Agreement on Comprehensive Economic Cooperation between the Association of South East Asian Nations and the People's Republic of China* (October 6, 2003), www.aseansec.org/15157.htm. On the code of conduct, see *Declaration on the Conduct*

of Parties in the South China Sea, Phnom Penh (November 4, 2002), www.aseansec
.org/13163.htm. See also Philip P. Pan, "China's Improving Image Challenges U.S. in
Asia," *Washington Post*, November 15, 2003, A1.

31. See Avery Goldstein, "An Emerging China's Emerging Grand Strategy: A Neo-
Bismarckian Turn?" in *International Relations Theory and the Asia-Pacific*, ed. G. John
Ikenberry and Michael Mastanduno (New York: Columbia University Press, 2003):
57–106; also see Goldstein, *Rising to the Challenge*.

32. This interpretation, consistent with the logic of power-transition theory, reso-
nates with a common view of Deng Xiaoping's frequently cited admonition for the
Chinese to "bide our time and conceal our capabilities" (*tao guang yang hui*) and its
echo in the similar advice that Deng's successor, Jiang Zemin, offered—that China
should avoid trouble while it is at a material disadvantage and instead "enhance confidence, decrease troubles, promote cooperation, and avoid confrontation." Michael
Pillsbury, *China Debates the Future Security Environment* (Washington, D.C.: National
Defense University Press, 2000), xxxvix, xxiv. In China's contemporary thinking about
how to cope with the dominant United States, Pillsbury detects the influence of traditional Chinese strategic notions dating to the Warring States period that explain
"how to survive destruction at the hands of a predator hegemon" (Pillsbury, *China
Debates*, xxxv). See also Michael D. Swaine and Ashley J. Tellis, *Interpreting China's
Grand Strategy: Past, Present, and Future* (Santa Monica, Calif.: RAND, 2000), especially chap. 3.

33. For a summary of such concerns, see Michael Vatikiotis and Murray Hiebert,
"How China Is Building an Empire," *Far Eastern Economic Review* (November 20,
2003), www.taiwansecurity.org/News/2003/FEER-201103.htm.

34. On the new security concept and its growing relevance in the post–Cold War
world, see Benwang Sa, "Woguo anquan de bianhua ji xin de pubian anquanguan de
zhuyao tezheng" [The change in our country's security and the main features of the
new concept of universal security], *Shijie Jingji yu Zhengzhi Luntan* 1 (2000): 51. On
China's efforts to dilute American leverage by engaging in "all sorts of security cooperation" and participating in "various kinds of regional organizations for security
cooperation," see Xuetong Yan, "Dui Zhongguo anquan huanjing de fenxi yu sikao"
[Analysis and Reflections on China's Security Environment], *Shijie Jingji yu Zhengzhi*
2 (2000): 10.

35. To be sure, since the early 1970s this formal stance had partly obscured Beijing's
tepid support for its socialist ally, the DPRK. After the United States began disengag-
ing from Vietnam and as Beijing's top priority became opposition to Soviet influence
in Asia, it was an open secret that China was in no hurry to see U.S. forces leave the
region. Thus, the shared security concern that had long served as the chief reason for
close ties between these communist allies, opposition to the U.S. military presence on
the Korean Peninsula, was undermined. And as China embraced its post-Mao reform
program after 1978, the other basis for their close relations, a shared commitment to
revolutionary socialist ideology, also began to crumble.

36. By the end of the 1990s, their increasingly close ties led China and the Republic
of Korea (ROK) to establish a "Sino-Korean cooperative partnership oriented towards
the 21st century." See "Zhu Rongji Zongli tong Hanguo Zongtong Jin Dazhong juxing

huitan" [Premier Zhu Rongji and ROK President Kim Daejung Hold Talks], *Xinhua*, October 18, 2000. See also Zhengxue Liu and Linchang Wang, "Zhu Rongji tong Jin Dazhong huitan, shuangfang jiu shuangbian guanxi he diqu wenti jiaohuanle yijian" [Zhu Rongji and Kim Daejung Hold Talks, the Two Sides Exchange Opinions on Bilateral Relations and Regional Issues], *Renmin Ribao*, October 19, 2000; Weixing Hu, "Beijing's Defense Strategy and the Korean Peninsula," *Journal of Northeast Asian Studies* 14, no. 3 (Fall 1995): 50–67; Kay Moeller, "China and Korea: The Godfather Part Three," *Journal of Northeast Asian Studies* 15, no. 4 (Winter 1996): 35–48.

37. This position was part of China's larger post–Cold War grand strategy that rounded into shape after 1996. See Goldstein, *Rising to the Challenge*.

38. See Wenzhao Tao, "China's Position Towards the Korean Peninsula" (paper presented at the ASEM 2000 People's Forum, Seoul, Korea, October 17–20, 2000); Shichuan Ding and Qiang Li, "Chaoxian bandao heping jizhi ji qi qianjing" [A Peace Mechanism for the Korean Peninsula and Its Prospects], *Xiandai Guoji Guanxi* 4 (1999): 42–44; Guocheng Zhang, "Quadripartite Talks Enter Substantive Stage," *Renmin Ribao*, January 29, 1999, FBIS-CHI-99-030, Article ID: drchi01301999000119, 6. On China's initial reservations about the four-party talks see "PRC Spokesman: Beijing Hopes for Negotiations on Korea," *Agence France Presse*, April 18, 1996, FBIS-CHI-96-076, Article ID: drchi076_a_96005; Moeller, "China and Korea: The Godfather Part Three," 38.

39. See Warren Hoge, "Security Council Supports Sanctions on North Korea," *New York Times*, October 15, 2006, 1; Joseph Kahn, "China May Be Using Oil to Press North Korea," *New York Times*, October 31, 2006, 12; Joseph Kahn and Helene Cooper, "North Korea Will Resume Nuclear Talks," *New York Times*, November 1, 2006, 1.

40. See especially Thom Shanker and Joseph Kahn, "U.S. and China Call for North Korea to Rejoin 6-Nation Talks on Nuclear Program," *New York Times*, October 21, 2006, 8; Glenn Kessler, "Rice Sees Bright Spot in China's New Role since N. Korean Test," *Washington Post*, October 22, 2006, A21.

41. See Goldstein, *Rising to the Challenge*, 184–86.

42. The initial reactions to the nuclear test suggested that the risk of U.S. military strikes was only one danger. Other worrisome possibilities for China included a significant strengthening of the U.S.-Japan security alliance, growing support within Japan for increasing the country's own military capabilities, and perhaps even a reconsideration of Tokyo's commitment to eschew nuclear weapons. See, for example, Thom Shanker and Norimitsu Onishi, "Japan Assures Rice That It Has No Nuclear Intentions," *New York Times*, October 19, 2006, 14.

43. See Chas. Freeman, "China's Changing Nuclear Posture," *Proliferation Brief* 2, no. 10 (Carnegie Endowment for International Peace, May 11, 1999); Thomas J. Christensen, "Posing Problems without Catching Up: China's Rise and Challenges for U.S. Security Policy," *International Security* 25, no. 4 (2001): 5–40.

44. In a sense, this continues a tradition for the United States in which the American view of Taiwan has never really been based on the intrinsic value of Taiwan per se. From the moment President Truman ordered the Seventh Fleet into the Taiwan Strait following the onset of the Korean War until the Nixon-Kissinger opening to Beijing, Washington viewed the government of the ROC as a political-ideological asset in its

Cold War rivalry with a monolithic Soviet bloc. Following the Sino-American rapprochement in 1972 until the collapse of the Soviet Union, Washington viewed Taiwan as an inconvenient anomaly that could not be permitted to complicate the U.S. strategic entente with Beijing designed to counter Moscow's influence in Asia.

45. This is reflected in some of the arguments among American conservatives who see strategic value in U.S. support for Taiwan. See Ross H. Munro, "Taiwan: What China Really Wants," *National Review*, October 11, 1999; Aaron L. Friedberg, "The Struggle for Mastery in Asia," *Commentary* 110, no. 4 (November 2000): 17–26. Mirroring this American perspective, some Chinese analysts complain that the U.S. views Taiwan as an asset useful for checking or containing China. See Shikun Ma and Yong Zhang, "U.S. Arms Encourage the Arrogance of 'Taiwan Independence,'" *Renmin Ribao*, August 28, 1999, 3, FBIS-CHI-1999-0830, WNC Document Number: 0FHC8Y902206DY, World News Connection; "Promote Peaceful Reunification of the Two Sides of the Taiwan Strait with Greatest Sincerity and Effort," *Ta Kung Pao*, October 26, 2002, FBIS-CHI-2002-1026, WNC Document Number: 0H4P3K000GEIQQ, World News Connection.

46. Such advocates can argue that muting conflict and sustaining cooperation with a U.S.-dominated international order is a rational means to the end of increasing China's strength that will ultimately put the country in a position to produce a resolution of the Taiwan problem that Beijing finds acceptable. While this argument would be politically prudent behind closed doors in Beijing, its logic is not consistent with the expectations of institutionalist theory, since it envisions defection and exploiting relative gains at some date uncertain.

47. For a regularly updated collection of relevant Chinese, Taiwanese, and American documents, official statements, and academic analysis covering these topics and all major events affecting cross-strait relations, see taiwansecurity.org/TSR-Strait.htm.

48. Indeed, Taiwan's leaders stoke such smoldering fears in Beijing when they insist that there is no need for any formal declaration of independence because their country is already a sovereign state.

49. Since spring 2005, China's cultivation of relations with the main opposition party leaders from Taiwan (the KMT [Kuomintang] and PFP [People First Party]) suggests a more sophisticated proactive effort by Beijing to shape public opinion in Taiwan about the feasibility and desirability of negotiating a deal that both sides of the strait will find acceptable. The magnitude of the economic benefits available from ties with the mainland is reflected in the difficulty that Taiwan's leaders have faced in sustaining cross-strait restrictions as industrious islanders discover ways to circumvent many of the formal rules.

50. See, for example, Taiwan's rejection of "a Closer Economic Partnership Arrangement (CEPA) with China such as China signed with Hong Kong and Macau . . . because it is a product of China's 'one country, two systems' formula" (Melody Chen, "Taiwan Will Not Sign Pact with China, Mac States," *Taipei Times*, November 14, 2003), http://taiwansecurity.org/TT/2003/TT-141103.htm.

51. See, for example, "U.S.-Made Air-to-Air Missiles Delivered to Taiwan: Report," *Agence France Presse*, November 15, 2003, http://taiwansecurity.org/AFP/2003/AFP-151103.htm. Washington's military ties to Taiwan allegedly bolster the status quo by

(1) increasing Beijing's estimate of the likelihood the United States will intervene if a rising China tries to coerce Taiwan, (2) making it more difficult for China to destroy Taiwan's own defenses, and (3) introducing a grave but unspecified risk of American retaliation against China.

52. American actions have sent inconsistent signals. Washington's decision permitting Taiwan's president Chen to stop over in the United States and participate in highly visible political activities, along with Chen's commitment to holding a referendum on a new constitution for Taiwan during his second term, elicited strong warnings from Beijing that, intentionally or not, the United States was encouraging proindependence forces on Taiwan, and that a move to independence would mean war. See especially "Independence Stance May Trigger War," *China Daily*, 18 November 2003, www1 .chinadaily.com.cn/en/doc/2003-11/18/content_282630.htm; "Guo taiban fuzhuren Wang zaixi Zhichu: 'Taidu' shi yitiao dixian" [Taiwan Affairs Office Vice Chairman Wang Zaixi Indicates: "Taiwan independence" Is the "Red" Line], November 18, 2003, www.chinanews.com.cn/n/2003-11-18/26/370406.html. But during Chinese Premier Wen Jiabao's visit to the White House in November 2003, President Bush issued an unusually candid warning to Taiwan not to provoke a crisis by taking any steps that unilaterally challenged the status quo in the strait.

53. "Strategic Opportunities: This Is the Fourth Opportunity in Modern History." *Wen Wei Po*, March 13, 2003, FBIS-CHI-2003-0313, WNC: 0hbwldy0201wth.

54. See Charles Lipson, "International Cooperation in Economic and Security Affairs," *World Politics* 37, no. 1 (October 1984): 1–23; Michael Mastanduno, "Do Relative Gains Matter? America's Response to Japanese Industrial Policy," *International Security* 16, no. 1 (Summer 1991): 73–113; Robert Powell, *In the Shadow of Power: States and Strategies in International Politics* (Princeton, N.J.: Princeton University Press, 1999).

References

Agence France Presse. "PRC Spokesman: Beijing Hopes for Negotiations on Korea." April 18, 1996. FBIS-CHI-96–076, Article ID: drchi076_a_96005.

———. "U.S.-Made Air-to-Air Missiles Delivered to Taiwan: Report." November 15, 2003. taiwansecurity.org/AFP/2003/AFP-151103.htm.

Association of South East Asian Nations. *Declaration on the Conduct of Parties in the South China Sea, Phnom Penh*, November 4, 2002. www.aseansec.org/13163.htm.

———. *Declaration on the South China Sea.* Manila, Philippines, July 22, 1992. www .aseansec.org/1196.htm

———. *Instrument of Accession to the Treaty of Amity and Cooperation in Southeast Asia*, October 8, 2003. www.aseansec.org/15271.htm.

———. *Joint Declaration of the Heads of State/Government of the Association of Southeast Asian Nations and the People's Republic of China on Strategic Partnership for Peace and Prosperity*, October 8, 2003. www.aseansec.org/15265.htm.

———. *Protocol to Amend the Framework Agreement on Comprehensive Economic Cooperation between the Association of South East Asian Nations and the People's Republic of China*, October 6, 2003. www.aseansec.org/15157.htm.

Axelrod, Robert M. *The Evolution of Cooperation.* New York: Basic Books, 1984.

Axelrod, Robert M., and Robert O. Keohane. "Achieving Cooperation under Anarchy: Strategies and Institutions." *World Politics* 38, no. 1 (October 1985): 226–54.

Chang, Gordon G. *The Coming Collapse of China.* New York: Random House, 2001.

Chen, Melody. "Taiwan Will Not Sign Pact with China, Mac States." *Taipei Times,* November 14, 2003. taiwansecurity.org/TT/2003/TT-141103.htm.

China Daily. "Independence Stance May Trigger War," November 18, 2003. www1 .chinadaily.com.cn/en/doc/2003–11/18/content_282630.htm.

China News. "Guo taiban fuzhuren Wang Zaixi zhichu: 'Taidu' shi yitiao dixian" ["Former Deputy Director of the Taiwan Affairs Office, Wang Zaixi, Points Out: 'Taiwan Independence Is the Bottom Line.'"], November 18, 2003. www.chinanews.com .cn/n/2003–11–18/26/370406.html.

Christensen, Thomas J. "Perceptions and Alliances in Europe, 1865–1940." *International Organization* 51, no. 1 (Winter 1997): 65–98.

———. "Posing Problems without Catching Up: China's Rise and Challenges for U.S. Security Policy." *International Security* 25, no. 4 (2001): 5–40.

Christensen, Thomas J., and Jack Snyder. "Chain Gangs and Passed Bucks: Predicting Alliance Patterns in Multipolarity." *International Organization* 44, no. 2 (Spring 1990): 137–68.

Cody, Edward. "In Face of Rural Unrest China Rolls Out Reforms." *Washington Post,* January 28, 2006.

Copeland, Dale. *The Origins of Major War.* Ithaca, N.Y.: Cornell University Press, 2000.

Council on Foreign Relations. "Chinese Military Power, Report of an Independent Task Force." June 12, 2003. www.cfr.org/pdf/China_TF.pdf.

Crane, Keith, Roger Cliff, Evan S. Medeiros, James C. Mulvenon, and William H. Overholt. *Modernizing China's Military: Opportunities and Constraints.* Santa Monica, Calif.: RAND Corporation, 2005.

Ding, Shichuan, and Li Qiang. "Chaoxian bandao heping jizhi ji qi qianjing" [A Peace Mechanism for the Korean Peninsula and Its Prospects]. *Xiandai Guoji Guanxi* 4 (1999): 42–44.

Doyle, Michael W. "Kant, Liberal Legacies, and Foreign Affairs." *Philosophy and Public Affairs* 12 (Fall 1983): 323–53.

Freeman, Chas. "China's Changing Nuclear Posture." *Proliferation Brief* 2, no. 10 (Carnegie Endowment for International Peace, May 11, 1999).

Friedberg, Aaron L. "The Struggle for Mastery in Asia." *Commentary* 110, no. 4 (November 2000): 17–26.

Gilpin, Robert. *War and Change in World Politics.* New York: Cambridge University Press, 1981.

Goldstein, Avery. "An Emerging China's Emerging Grand Strategy: A Neo-Bismarckian Turn?" in *International Relations Theory and the Asia-Pacific,* edited by G. John Ikenberry and Michael Mastanduno. New York: Columbia University Press, 2003.

Goldstein, Avery. "Great Expectations: Interpreting China's Arrival." *International Security* 22, no. 3 (Winter 1997–1998): 36–73.

————. *Rising to the Challenge: China's Grand Strategy and International Security.* Stanford, Calif.: Stanford University Press, 2005.

Greenhouse, Steven. "New Tally of World's Economies Catapults China into Third Place." *New York Times,* May 20, 1993.

Hoge, Warren. "Security Council Supports Sanctions on North Korea." *New York Times,* October 15, 2006.

Hu, Weixing. "Beijing's Defense Strategy and the Korean Peninsula." *Journal of Northeast Asian Studies* 14, no. 3 (Fall 1995): 50–67.

Hua, Fang. "Yatai anquan jiagou de xianzhuang, qushi ji zhongguo de zuoyong" [The Current Asia-Pacific Security Framework, Trends and China's Role]. *Shijie Jingji yu Zhengzhi* 2 (2000): 12.

Ikenberry, G. John. *After Victory: Institutions, Strategic Restraint, and the Rebuilding of Order after Major Wars.* Princeton, N.J.: Princeton University Press, 2001.

International Monetary Fund. *World Economic Outlook.* "Revised Weights for the World Economic Outlook: Annex IV." Washington, D.C.: International Monetary Fund, 1993.

Jervis, Robert. "Cooperation under the Security Dilemma." *World Politics* 30, no. 2 (January 1978): 167–214.

————. "Hypotheses on Misperception." *World Politics* 20, no. 3 (April 1968): 454–79.

Johnston, Alastair Iain. "Is China a Status Quo Power?" *International Security* 27, no. 4 (Spring 2003): 5–56.

Johnston, Alastair Iain, and Paul Evans. "China's Engagement with Multilateral Security Institutions," in *Engaging China,* edited by Alastair Iain Johnston and Robert S. Ross. London and New York: Routledge, 1999.

Johnston, Alastair Iain, W. K. H. Panofsky, Marco DiCapua, and Lewis R. Franklin. *The Cox Committee Report: An Assessment Center for International Security and Cooperation.* Stanford, Calif.: Stanford University Press, December 1999. www.ceip .org/files/projects/npp/pdf/coxfina13.pdf.

Kahn, Joseph. "China May Be Using Oil to Press North Korea." *New York Times,* October 31, 2006.

Kahn, Joseph, and Helene Cooper. "North Korea Will Resume Nuclear Talks." *New York Times,* November 1, 2006.

Kennedy, Paul. *The Rise and Fall of the Great Powers.* New York: Vintage, 1987.

Keohane, Robert O. *After Hegemony: Cooperation and Discord in the World Political Economy.* Princeton, N.J.: Princeton University Press, 1984.

Keohane, Robert O., and Lisa L. Martin. "The Promise of Institutionalist Theory." *International Security* 20, no. 1 (Summer 1995): 39–51.

Kessler, Glenn. "Rice Sees Bright Spot in China's New Role since N. Korean Test." *Washington Post,* October 22, 2006.

Lardy, Nicholas R. *China in the World Economy.* Washington, D.C.: Institute for International Economics, 1994.

————. *Integrating China into the Global Economy.* Washington, D.C.: Brookings Institution Press, 2002.

Lau, Lawrence J. "China in the Global Economy." Presentation given at the UT-Starcom China Telecom Executive Management Program, Stanford Graduate

School of Business, September 22, 2003. www.stanford.edu/%7Eljlau/Presentations/Presentations/030922.pdf.

———. "Chinese Economic Outlook and Key Issues." Focus Ventures, Asian Forum, Shanghai, October 14, 2003. www.stanford.edu/%7Eljlau/Presentations/Presentations/031014.pdf.

Leifer, Michael. *The ASEAN Regional Forum.* Adelphi Paper 302. London: International Institute for Strategic Studies, July 1996.

Lieber, Keir A., and Daryl G. Press. "The End of MAD? The Nuclear Dimension of U.S. Primacy." *International Security* 30, no. 4 (Spring 2006): 7–44.

Lipson, Charles. "International Cooperation in Economic and Security Affairs." *World Politics* 37, no. 1 (October 1984): 1–23.

Liu, Zhengxue, and Wang Linchang. "Zhu Rongji tong Jin Dazhong huitan, shuangfang jiu shuangbian guanxi he diqu wenti jiaohuanle yijian" [Zhu Rongji and Kim Daejung Hold Talks, the Two Sides Exchange Opinions on Bilateral Relations and Regional Issues]. *Renmin Ribao,* October 19, 2000.

Lu, Jianren. "Yatai daguo zai dongnan yazhou diqu de liyi" [Asia-Pacific Great Powers' Interests in Southeast Asia]. *Shijie Jingji yu Zhengzhi* 2 (2000): 41, 45.

Ma, Shikun, and Zhang Yong. "U.S. Arms Encourage the Arrogance of 'Taiwan Independence.'" *Renmin Ribao,* August 28, 1999. FBIS-CHI-1999–0830, WNC Document Number: 0FHC8Y902206DY, World News Connection.

Mansfield, Edward D., and Jack Snyder. "Democratic Transitions, Institutional Strength, and War." *International Organization* 56, no. 2 (Spring 2002): 297–337.

———. "Democratization and the Danger of War." *International Security* 20, no. 1 (Summer 1995): 5–38.

Mastanduno, Michael. "Do Relative Gains Matter? America's Response to Japanese Industrial Policy." *International Security* 16, no. 1 (Summer 1991): 73–113.

Mearsheimer, John J. "The False Promise of International Institutions." *International Security* 19, no. 3 (Winter 1994–1995): 5–49.

———. *The Tragedy of Great Power Politics.* New York: W. W. Norton, 2001.

Medeiros, Evan S. "China Debates Its 'Peaceful Rise Strategy,'" *Yale Global Online,* June 22 2004. http://yaleglobal.yale.edu/display.article?id=4118.

Moeller, Kay. "China and Korea: The Godfather Part Three," *Journal of Northeast Asian Studies* 15, no. 4 (Winter 1996): 35–48.

Moravcsik, Andrew. "Taking Preferences Seriously: A Liberal Theory of International Politics." *International Organization* 51, no. 4 (Autumn 1997): 513–52.

Morgenthau, Hans. *Politics among Nations,* 5th ed. New York: Knopf, 1973.

Munro, Ross H. "Taiwan: What China Really Wants." *National Review,* October 11, 1999.

Nathan, Andrew J. "Present at the Stagnation," *Foreign Affairs* 85, no. 4 (July–August 2006): 177–82.

Nishihara, Masashi. "Aiming at New Order for Regional Security-Current State of ARF." *Gaiko Forum,* November 1997, 35–40, FBIS-EAS-97–321.

Office of the Secretary of Defense. *The Military Power of the People's Republic of China, 2005.* Washington, D.C.: Office of the Secretary of Defense, 2005.

Organski, A. F. K., and Jacek Kugler. *The War Ledger*. Chicago: University of Chicago Press, 1980.

Overholt, William H. *The Rise of China*. New York: W. W. Norton, 1993.

Pan, Philip P. "China's Improving Image Challenges U.S. in Asia." *Washington Post*, November 15, 2003.

Pei, Minxin. *China's Trapped Transition: The Limits of Developmental Autocracy*. Cambridge, Mass.: Harvard University Press, 2006.

———. "Will China Become Another Indonesia?" *Foreign Policy* 116 (Fall 1999): 94–109.

Pillsbury, Michael. *China Debates the Future Security Environment*. Washington, D.C.: National Defense University Press, 2000.

Pincus, Walter. "Hill Report on Chinese Spying Faulted, Five Experts Cite Errors, 'Unwarranted' Conclusions by Cox Panel." *Washington Post*, December 15, 1999.

Powell, Robert. *In the Shadow of Power: States and Strategies in International Politics*. Princeton, N.J.: Princeton University Press, 1999.

Richardson, Michael. "China's Push for Sea Control Angers ASEAN." *Australian*, July 23, 1996.

Rohwer, Jim. "Rapid Growth Could Make China World's Largest Economy by 2012." *South China Morning Post*, November 28, 1992.

Ross, Robert S. "The 1995–1996 Taiwan Strait Confrontation: Coercion, Credibility, and the Use of Force," *International Security* 25, no. 2 (Fall 2000): 87–123.

Sa, Benwang. "Woguo anquan de bianhua ji xin de pubian anquanguan de zhuyao tezheng" [The Change in Our Country's Security and the Main Features of the New Concept of Universal Security]. *Shijie Jingji yu Zhengzhi Luntan* 1 (2000): 51.

Sahgal, Arun. "China in Space: Military Implications." *Asia Times*, November 5, 2003. www.taiwansecurity.org/News/2003/AT-051103.htm.

Schweller, Randall L. "Bandwagoning for Profit: Bringing the Revisionist State Back In." *International Security* 19, no. 1 (Summer 1994): 72–107.

Schweller, Randall L. *Deadly Imbalances: Tripolarity and Hitler's Strategy of World Conquest*. New York: Columbia University Press, 1998.

Select Committee on U.S. National Security and Military/Commercial Concerns with the People's Republic of China. *House Report*. Submitted by Mr. Cox of California, Chairman, June 14, 1999. www.gpo.gov/congress/house/hr105851-html/index .html.

Shanker, Thom, and Joseph Kahn. "U.S. and China Call for North Korea to Rejoin 6-Nation Talks on Nuclear Program." *New York Times*, October 21, 2006.

Shanker, Thom, and Norimitsu Onishi. "Japan Assures Rice That It Has No Nuclear Intentions." *New York Times*, October 19, 2006.

Soh, Felix, "U.S. Warns against Restrictions in South China Sea, Block Press Tour to Spratlys." *Straits Times* (Singapore), May 12, 1995.

Swaine, Michael D., and Ashley J. Tellis, *Interpreting China's Grand Strategy: Past, Present, and Future*. Santa Monica, Calif.: RAND, 2000.

Ta Kung Pao, "Promote Peaceful Reunification of the Two Sides of the Taiwan Strait with Greatest Sincerity and Effort." October 26, 2002. FBIS-CHI-2002–1026, WNC Document Number: 0H4P3K000GEIQQ, World News Connection.

Tammen, Ronald L., Jacek Kugler, Douglas Lemke, Allan C. Stam III, Mark Abdollahian, Carole Alsharabati, Brian Efird, and A. F. K. Organski, *Power Transitions: Strategies for the 21st Century.* New York: Chatham House, 2000.

Tao, Wenzhao, "China's Position towards the Korean Peninsula." Paper presented at the ASEM 2000 People's Forum, Seoul, Korea, October 17–20, 2000.

Torode, Greg. "Philippines Offered U.S. Jets: Manila Warns over Continued Chinese Construction Work on Mischief Reef." *South China Morning Post,* August 2, 1995.

U.S.-China Economic and Security Review Commission annual reports. www.uscc.gov.

U.S. Department of Defense. *Annual Report to Congress: The Military Power of the People's Republic of China 2006.* http://www.defenselink.mil/pubs/pdfs/China %20Report%202006.pdf?

United Nations Secretariat, the Division for Ocean Affairs and the Law of the Sea (DOALOS). *Law on the Territorial Sea and the Contiguous Zone of 25 February 1992.* www.un.org/Depts/los/LEGISLATIONANDTREATIES/PDFFILES/CHN_1992 _Law.pdf.

Valencia, Mark J. *China and the South China Sea Disputes.* Adelphi Paper 298. London: International Institute for Strategic Studies, October 1995.

Vatikiotis, Michael, and Murray Hiebert. "How China Is Building an Empire." *Far Eastern Economic Review,* November 20, 2003. www.taiwansecurity.org/News/2003 /FEER-201103.htm.

Waldron, Arthur. "After Deng the Deluge." *Foreign Affairs* 74, no. 5 (September–October 1995): 148–53.

———. "The Chinese Sickness," *Commentary* 116, no. 1 (July–August 2003): 36–42.

———. "Watching China: Arthur Waldron and Critics." *Commentary* 116, no. 3 (October 2003): 10–23.

Walt, Stephen M. *The Origins of Alliances.* Ithaca, N.Y.: Cornell University Press, 1988.

Waltz, Kenneth N. "International Politics Is Not Foreign Policy." *Security Studies* 6, no. 1 (Autumn 1996): 54–57.

———. *Man, the State, and War: A Theoretical Analysis.* New York: Columbia University Press, 1959.

———. *Theory of International Politics.* Menlo Park, Calif.: Addison-Wesley Publishing Co., 1979.

Wendt, Alexander. *Social Theory of International Politics.* New York: Cambridge University Press, 1999.

Whiting, Allen S. "ASEAN Eyes China: The Security Dimension." *Asian Survey* 37, no. 4 (April 1997): 299–322.

Wohlforth, William C. "The Perception of Power: Russia in the Pre-1914 Balance." *World Politics* 39, no. 3 (April 1987): 353–81.

Xinhua. "Zhu Rongji Zongli tong Hanguo Zongtong Jin Dazhong juxing huitan" [Premier Zhu Rongji and ROK President Kim Daejung Hold Talks], October 18, 2000.

Yan, Xuetong. "Dui Zhongguo anquan huanjing de fenxi yu sikao" [Analysis and Reflections on China's Security Environment]. *Shijie Jingji yu Zhengzhi* 2 (2000): 10.

Zhang, Guocheng. "Quadripartite Talks Enter Substantive Stage." *Renmin Ribao,* January 29, 1999.

Zheng, Bijian. "New Path for China's Peaceful Rise and the Future of Asia." *Boao Forum for Asia,* November 3, 2003. http://history.boaoforum.org/english/E2003nh /dhwj/t20031103_184101.btk.

———."China's 'Peaceful Rise' to Great Power Status." *Foreign Affairs* 84, no. 5 (September–October 2005): 18–24.

3

Rethinking Japan as an Ordinary Country

Takashi Inoguchi and Paul Bacon

I N THIS CHAPTER WE ARGUE THAT since 1945 Japanese foreign policy has evolved through five phases, which will culminate in Japan's reemergence as a global ordinary power. We then discuss three potential models of ordinary power that are ideal-typical in nature, but which share some qualities with the respective political circumstances of France, Germany, and Britain. We also consider the legitimacy and capacity deficits that Japan possesses. We argue that Japan is using the British model as a foundation for the acquisition of ordinary power status. In doing so it is increasingly binding itself to the United States.

The Contours of Japanese Foreign Policy: Adjusting Every Fifteen Years

Henry Kissinger has suggested that Japan is slow to respond to significant political developments. In the past, he argues, it has often taken some fifteen years for Japan to respond decisively to a major political transformation.[1] He cites three examples: Commodore Perry's visit to Japan in 1853; the comprehensive defeat of Japan by the Allied Powers in 1945; and the collapse of the bubble economy in 1991. It took fifteen years for the Japanese to put an end to internal debate and strife and start de novo in 1868. It took fifteen years for the Japanese to firmly commit themselves to the United States before they announced the income-doubling plan in 1960 and indicated that they would focus on wealth accumulation. It has taken roughly fifteen years after the collapse of the bubble economy for the Japanese to decide how many employees to lay off and how to deal with bad loans. The Japanese economy started to pick up at long last toward the end of 2003. The substance of Kissinger's basic observation seems to ring true.

Bearing Kissinger's argument in mind, we first study the basic contours of Japanese foreign policy since 1945. Kissinger's argument is interesting and valuable, because it is often argued that postwar Japanese foreign policy has been unchanging. In fact, Japan has indeed been making substantial adjustments to its foreign policy every fifteen years. These periods can be characterized as follows. The first entailed an internal battle between pro-alliance and anti-alliance sections of Japanese society (1945–1960). The second period was characterized by adherence to the Yoshida doctrine (1960–1975). The third period saw Japan tentatively emerge as a systemic supporter of the United States (1975–1990). The fourth period saw Japan attempt to pursue the role of global civilian power (1990–2005), and the fifth, we argue, will see a gradual consolidation of Japan's emerging role as a global ordinary power (2005–2020).

The Contest between Pro-Alliance and Anti-Alliance Sentiment: 1945–1960

During the first period, between 1945 and 1960, there was extensive discussion of whether Japan should work closely with the United States or not. The die was cast in 1960 when Prime Minister Nobusuke Kishi passed the revision of the Japan–United States Security Treaty, despite vigorous resistance, and submitted his resignation to the National Diet.[2] The Yoshida doctrine was effectively pursued from the day of his resignation. The term Yoshida doctrine refers to the policy of seeking protection under the U.S. military umbrella and focusing Japan's national energy and resources on economic regeneration and wealth creation and accumulation.[3] There was vigorous internal debate about whether to adopt the Yoshida doctrine during the period between 1945 and 1960. Many Japanese were unable to come to terms with the humiliation of delegating national security to a foreign country. They were also concerned at the potential contradiction between the provisions of the Japan-U.S. Security Treaty and the provisions of the Japanese Constitution. The Yoshida doctrine was only embraced after Prime Minister Hayato Ikeda announced the income-doubling plan of 1960–1970. In 1960 it became clear that no significant internal or external opponents of the Yoshida doctrine remained.

Yoshida Doctrine or Free Ride?: 1960–1975

During this second fifteen-year period Japanese income levels rose so steadily that Japan became the target first of envy and then of enmity abroad. Internally, cumulative economic, social, and demographic changes were undermining the political base of the governing party, the Liberal Democratic

Party. French president Charles de Gaulle unkindly observed that Japan was a nation of "transistor salesmen." This remark caricatured Japan's decision, in accordance with the Yoshida doctrine, to focus on economics rather than politics and military affairs. De Gaulle's observation attempted to strip away the valor and pride of the visionary politician Shigeru Yoshida and expose what he believed to be the unsatisfactorily self-serving nature of his doctrine. De Gaulle claimed that Japan was a free rider that had no sense of responsibility for the management of world politics, even though it possessed the world's second-largest economy. This perception of Japan as a free rider prevailed for more or less the duration of this second fifteen-year period.

Systemic Supporter of the United States: 1975–1990

Toward the end of the second period the oil crisis erupted, and war broke out in the Middle East. Japan wavered between pro-American and pro-OPEC positions, as the accusation that Japan was a free rider echoed back and forth from both sides. This criticism prompted Japan to shift its position slowly but steadily from that of a free rider to that of a systemic supporter of the United States. The term systemic supporter refers to an actor that helps to maintain the United States-led international system. It is important to note that Japan's support was mostly of an economic nature, as exemplified by Japan's positions on free trade and energy security. Toward the end of this period, however, Japan's support began to assume a more political and military complexion, as exemplified by support for the United States on issues such as SS-20 missiles. However, Japan also highlighted the concept of "comprehensive security" during this period. It did so firstly to emphasize its limited support for the U.S.-led system, and secondly to highlight the importance of other aspects of security, whereas the United States focused excessively on the military aspect of security. This third period can therefore be characterized as one during which Japan played the role of a systemic supporter. Japan prosecuted this role in the spirit of Machiavelli's dictum that we should provide support to our friends but project our neutrality to enemies. Despite all the difficulties associated with the constitutional ban on the use of force for the settlement of international disputes, there was no shortage of rhetorical freedom. Prime Minister Yasuhiro Nakasone went so far as to characterize Japan as "an unsinkable aircraft carrier" toward the end of this period.

Global Civilian Power: 1990–2005

The start of this fourth period is marked by a steady decline in the frequency of wars among major powers and by the end of the Cold War.[4] These developments set the stage for what have been called "global civilian powers" to play a more significant role.[5] Before and during World War II both Japan and Germany had been revisionist, militarist, and expansionist powers. However, since 1945 both have been exemplary pacifist countries, and both Japan and Germany were delighted to be ascribed the role of civilian power after the Cold War. Germany and Japan had both suffered as a result of their quest for expansion prior to 1945, but both have emphatically relinquished this quest in the many years since.[6] Both are populous, large, and wealthy; both are pacifist; and both are good allies of the United States. However the legacy of the past and the ban on the use of force remain a burden for both countries. Despite these constraints, it was still possible for both countries to play a significant role in post–Cold War international relations. Using the emerging concept of human security as a guide for their actions, both countries engaged in peacekeeping operations and economic reconstruction projects in many parts of the Third World. Japan in particular was very generous in offering official developmental assistance to the Third World, with a focus on health, education, agriculture, manufacturing, and industrial infrastructure.

During the early 1990s the United Nations, under the leadership of Secretary General Boutros Boutros-Ghali, played a proactive role in the promotion of these activities. However, substantial problems began to emerge in the post–Cold War Third World. Global market integration deepened the predicament of poverty-stricken and strife-riddled countries. The end of the U.S.-Soviet Cold War confrontation meant that both had a reduced stake in many Third World countries. This contributed to the creation of failed states and bankrupt economies. Addressing these tasks is beyond the self-proclaimed global civilian powers, the United Nations, other international organizations, and nongovernmental organizations. Under such conditions the events of September 11 took place, as if calling for the United States to make its power felt and act decisively. Such a development would end the fourth period in Japanese postwar foreign policy, during which it aspired to be a global civilian power. This would also pave the way for Japan's reemergence as a global ordinary power.

Global Ordinary Power: 2005–2020

Japan has chosen to define itself as an emerging global ordinary power. It is in the process of consolidating this role for itself. Firstly, there is greater support for the use of force, provided that this force is used for solely defensive purposes. To defend Japan effectively against terrorism requires a number of courses of action. In an incident that took place in 2002, the Maritime Safety Agency used force on the Sea of Japan against an unidentified vessel that fiercely resisted the Japanese coast guard's attempt to investigate its actions.

Public opinion broadly supported this use of force. Furthermore, the Self Defense Forces (SDF) already have permission to use force, more specifically rifles, once they are attacked or they suspect that an enemy is about to attack, in the context of United Nations peacekeeping operations. This legislation was passed in 1991. The 2003 legislation that permits troops to be sent to Iraq also contains permission for the SDF to use force, more specifically person-to-tank weapons. Secondly, the nonprovocative use of force needs to be developed. In other words, strictly defensive methods must be practiced. If it is necessary to use force to such an extent that this goes beyond strictly defensive purposes, then it will be necessary to revise the constitution.

Although there have been substantial continuities in Japanese foreign policy since 1945, a closer look enables one to discern clear fifteen-year phases, and concomitant adjustments and shifts of emphasis to address emerging threats and conditions in world politics. It is important to stress that Japan has started a major transition in the direction of ordinary power. And it is clearly necessary to elaborate further on what Japanese ordinary power might entail.

Three Models of Ordinary Power, Japanese Style

It is likely that the Pax Americana will endure for some time to come.[7] Thus, any discussion of the extent to which Japan can regain ordinary-power status must be located firmly in the context of its relationship with the United States.[8] Here, alliance has arguably been replaced by partnership. As Francis Fukuyama argues, fundamental differences in values and institutions have vanished since the end of the Cold War.[9] In post–Cold War global politics, trust has gained increasing salience. When trust is ascertained, then partnership can be created. When the U.S.–Japan relationship is referred to, the idea of a transition from alliance to partnership should be kept firmly in mind. The following three models are useful in surveying and illustrating the range of partnerships with the United States that Japan might consider. We will look in turn at the following models: (1) French, (2) German, and (3) British. Each of these models invokes a different ideal-typical approach.

The French Model

The key idea here is that of autonomy. Japan is a close ally and partner of the United States. But this alliance has its roots in an ultimatum, an all-out war, complete disarmament, occupation, and regime change. Given Japan's economic performance since the Second World War, it is only natural that it should seek more autonomy. France has also recently asserted itself against the United States. It has accomplished this through Jacques Chirac's deft and adroit maneuvering in the debates surrounding the passing of UN Security Council resolutions permitting the use of force against Iraq. This French self-assertion is something Japan is quietly envious of, but also very apprehensive about. French self-assertion divides Europe, divides the West, and renders the United Nations less effective and the United States more unilateralist.[10]

Japan and France share some significant commonalities:

(1) Both are close allies of the United States.
(2) Both have a strong interest in peaceful and prosperous regional relations. Japan is sandwiched by China and the United States, as is France, by the United States and the United Kingdom on the one hand, and by Germany and Russia on the other.
(3) Both seek to cultivate a diverse range of diplomatic partners from outside their immediate spheres of activity, using such concepts as comprehensive security and the Francophone group respectively.

Gaullism is attractive to Japan, as it essentially boils down to an assertion of autonomy. Through its tight alignment with the United States, Japan has placed all of its diplomatic eggs in one basket. This excessively close alignment has generated a significant body of dissenting argument suggesting that Japan should strive for greater autonomy. I will briefly note three examples of such dissent. Akio Morita and Shintaro Ishihara famously published a book titled *The Japan That Can Say "No".*[11] Prime Minister Ryutaro Hashimoto, in a speech in Washington, D.C., suggested that converting all the Japanese-owned U.S. government bonds back into Japanese yen might lead Americans to think again about taking Japan for granted. Eisuke Sakakibara, vice minister for international affairs at the Ministry of Finance, was openly defiant when his idea of setting up an Asian Monetary Fund in the wake of the Asian financial crisis was flatly rebuffed by his American counterpart, Lawrence Summers. Summers wryly noted that he thought wrongly that Sakakibara was a true friend. When the first author of this chapter interviewed Sakakibara in 1997, his office was dominated by a big picture of a militant Islamic Mujahedeen fighter brandishing a sword. The alleged beauty of the French model is that, in the words of Jacques Chirac, France is a true friend, in the sense that true friends will often give you advice that you do not want to hear, before ultimately offering you their support. He also noted that sycophants will not do this, alluding perhaps to Tony Blair's United Kingdom.

The problem with the French model is that the Japanese leadership style is poles apart from the French. Japanese elites have not produced a Jacques Delor, a Pascal Lamy, a Jacques Attali, or a Valery Giscard D'Estaing. These men all exercise a strong leadership role in an articulate, aggressive, and adroit fashion. The Japanese political system, as an essentially decentralized consensus-oriented system, tends either not to create, or perhaps more importantly not to reward, such a leadership style at the highest level. Potential Japanese Gaullists endure great frustration as a result. However, former prime minister Junichiro Koizumi's articulate message and decisive response in support of the war against terrorism, and his dramatic Pyongyang summit, are not inconsistent with the French model of leadership and the French preparedness to pursue initiatives that might upset the United States.

Viewed from the United States, France and Japan are different, and thus they should not be expected to attempt to achieve similar levels of autonomy from the United States. The key intermediary variable is the perceived value to the United States of the roles they both play in their respective regions. France is critical to the aggregation of unity and stability in Europe, with the United Kingdom psychologically semidetached from the Continent, and Germany hampered by the institutional and historical constraints placed on its foreign policy initiatives, especially in the absence of a countervailing Soviet threat. France is perceived to be sufficiently critical to unity and stability in Europe that the United States is prepared to grant it considerable autonomy in its diplomatic affairs. However, one might also argue that the Gaullist policy of seeking autonomy not only for France but also a greater Europe stretching to Estonia and Cyprus does undermine the interests of the United States. Such a policy also undermines the interests of the North Atlantic Treaty Organization (NATO) and, to a lesser extent, those of Germany in central Eastern Europe, the Baltic nations, the Balkans, and the East Mediterranean.

Japan's role in East Asia is very different. Other than Japan, there is no country that the United States can count on as a key stabilizing power. China does not share core values and norms with the United States and the other leading, largely Western, liberal democracies who manage the international system. Korea is too small for the United States to count on. ASEAN is not only too small but also too fragmented and vulnerable. Hence the degree of autonomy the United States can afford to give to Japan is measurably smaller.

The German Model

The key idea here is regional embeddedness. Germany has been concealing itself within regional and international institutions such as the European Union and NATO, adroitly aligning its national interests with broader regional and international interests. With its technocratic competence, rule-based steadiness, and economic surplus deployed in pursuit of higher purposes, Germany has been quite successful in rehabilitating itself within a context where it does not regenerate old security concerns. This notwithstanding, Germany is also able to take initiatives that suit its own purposes within the broader context of European governance. This can be seen in the European Union's eastern expansion and in the introduction of the single currency, the Euro.[12]

Japan and Germany share some significant commonalities:

(1) Their past experience as revisionist powers. In the words of Hans-Peter Schwartz, Japan and Germany have progressed from *Machtbesessenheit* (self-aggrandizement before 1945) to *Machtvergessenheit* (an abstention from power politics after 1945). This experience, combined with significant economic strength, rendered both Japan and Germany significant global civilian powers throughout the 1990s.[13]

(2) Their strong alliances with the United States, sustained by a substantial American military presence.

(3) Their strong economic ties with and economic embrace of their respective regional hinterlands.

Despite its firm economic embrace of Asia, at least until the Asian financial crisis of 1997, Japan has not been characterized as being strongly embedded within the region.[14] First, Japan's traditional approach has been to conceive of itself as somehow external to Asia. For "Britain and Europe" read "Japan and Asia."[15] Second, China, which does not necessarily share basic norms and values with maritime East and Southeast Asia, has been on the rise, in terms of both economic might and military power. If Japan is to embed itself within Asia, then it has to reconcile itself to much deeper linkages to and alignment with China. This is a possibility that Japan is not willing to consider seriously at present, given its predominant emphasis on freedom, democracy, human rights, free trade, market economics, and strong alliance with the United States. Until 1997 Asia could be characterized as "in Japan's embrace,"[16] but since 1997 it can more aptly be characterized as "lured by the China market,"[17] albeit arguably still in Japan's embrace. China's offensive to lure foreign direct investment and conclude a regionwide free trade agreement has intensified since its accession to the World Trade Organization. Third, Japan's way of handling its historical legacy has not always been to the liking of other countries in the region. Japan's adherence to the U.S.-certified interpretation of its modern history has been solid, but has in recent times been partially diluted, due to both the passing of time and the rise of nationalism. Japanese nationalism should not be exaggerated. Japanese are much less likely than other Asians to conceive of national identity as their primary source of identity. Eighty to eighty-five percent of South Koreans and Thais depict national identity as their primary source of identity, but only 60 percent of Japanese do the same.[18]

In the war against terrorism in Afghanistan, as other countries did, Japan and Germany did their best to support the United States. They disregarded precedents, bent interpretations, and sent military personnel to the Indian Ocean and Afghanistan respectively. As the prospect of an American war with Iraq increased, German prime minister Gerhard Schroeder announced that Germany would not participate. On September 17, 2002, Prime Minister Koizumi visited North Korea, one of the members of the "axis of evil," and concluded a communiqué with Kim Jong-il. In this communiqué Japan acknowledged historical issues and pledged to extend compensation once diplomatic normalization was complete, while North Korea undertook to demonstrate its peaceful intentions, declaring that it would not seek to develop and maintain missiles and weapons of mass destruction. (One month later, Kim Jong-il admitted to James Kelly, U.S. undersecretary of state for East Asia and the Pacific, that North Korea had been developing nuclear weapons until recently, which is quite contrary to what Kim had said to Koizumi.) Depending on your view, the actions of Schroeder and Koizumi could be interpreted in two ways. They could be interpreted as constructive attempts to reduce tension and facilitate peaceful accommodation with axis of evil countries, or as maverick self-interested acts that undermine the focus and integrity of America's policy of seeking disarmament, and ultimately regime change, in axis of evil countries.

One should also bear in mind the fact that the greater a state's regional embeddedness, the less straightforward its process of preference ordering. This is especially so when domestic antimilitarism norms are so strong, and especially in countries where the legacy of war has played such a pervasive role in the construction of contemporary national identity. The United States is mildly apprehensive that if Germany and Japan become more regionally embedded, this will push their foreign-policy preference ordering still further out of kilter with American concerns. Schroeder's flat refusal, during the 2002 election campaign, to participate in the war on Iraq, and Koizumi's blitz summit diplomacy in Pyongyang, were both in broad disharmony with the evolving American campaign against the axis of evil (Iraq, North Korea, and Iran). The United States ascribes differing degrees of significance to the North Atlantic Treaty Organization and the Japan–United States Security Treaty. After September 11 the United States found Europe decreasingly problematic in terms of strategic priority. Its policy toward Europe has become more benign, if only because of the lack of threat from Russia and from its strategic nuclear forces. Instead the United States finds the Middle East and East Asia much more problematic and volatile, with each region having the potential to destabilize the peace and stability of the entire world. For this reason Germany has more latitude to pursue policies of which the United States does not approve. East Asia has greater strategic importance to the United States than

Europe does. Accordingly, Japan has less latitude to adopt anti–United States policy than Germany, because of East Asia's greater contemporary significance for international peace and security.

The British Model

The key idea is that of a special relationship. Japan conceives of itself as having special bilateral relations with the United States. Slightly more than a decade ago, the U.S. ambassador to Japan, Mike Mansfield, characterized the United States' relationship with Japan as its "most important bilateral relationship—bar none."[19] This phrase was often deployed as the defining concept of Japan–United States relations during the 1990s. The United Kingdom also conceives of itself as having a special relationship with the United States. In policy recommendations proposed by Richard Armitage, the U.S.-UK model was recommended as the best model on which to build future partnership between Japan and the United States.[20]

Japan and the UK share some significant commonalities:

(1) They both conceive of themselves as distinctive and somewhat distant from their respective continental neighbors.
(2) Both have high levels of economic interdependence with the United States and are embedded in the American complex of economic relations.
(3) Both have significant alliance links with the United States.

Since September 11 the United States has drawn on the cooperation of a very wide-ranging number of partners from the antiterrorist coalition, rather than on a few close allies hitherto distinguished by their perceived special relationship with the United States. It is true that the United Kingdom and to a lesser extent Australia have been regarded as reliable allies by the United States on many occasions since September 11, 2001. The United Kingdom and Australia are indeed qualitatively distinct from Japan, in that they can take military action without being subject to the same constraints. It can sometimes seem as if the United Kingdom and Australia act like America's mercenaries. This has provoked Japanese diplomats to remark that Japan is not as small as the UK (whose population size is one-half of Japan's), and does not feel it to be quite as necessary to fall into line so unquestioningly. Such observations suggest that the U.S.-UK model might not be so appropriate to the governing of the U.S.-Japan partnership.

The prospect of American war with Iraq initially drew an ambivalent response from Japan. Japan was mostly silent about the prospect of war with Iraq until after France and Germany took a very different position from the United States with regard to the postponement of the United Nations inspections in Iraq. As a result of this, in a speech given at the United Nations, Japan made explicit the fact that its position was more tightly aligned with the United States.[21] There is of course an element of contradiction in Japan staying out of a war that is so clearly important to America, and yet still aspiring to be recognized as its most important bilateral partner. Sending SDF personnel into Iraq aroused opposition at home. But sending state-of-the-art Aegis destroyers into the Indian Ocean, if not into the much closer Persian Gulf, was also argued by some to be both a prudent and a gallant strategy for Japan to adopt. There is also a contradiction between the deftness and decisiveness of the initiatives taken on the Korean Peninsula and the indecisiveness and ambivalence demonstrated over the issue of potential war with Iraq. What is more, Japan acted on the North Korea issue after little consultation with the United States. Presumably, North Korea wanted to extract concessions from Japan bilaterally, while Japan wanted to create a diplomatic success domestically.

Overcoming Legitimacy and Capability Deficits in Pursuit of Ordinary Power

Embracing defeat in 1945 resulted in two kinds of deficit that Japan must overcome as it attempts to become and behave like an ordinary power. Japan has a legitimacy deficit with regard to the use of force, and a capability deficit in using force as an instrument of defense, deterrence, and diplomacy.

Japan's Legitimacy Deficit

This deficit manifests itself in a number of ways. First, Article Nine of the Japanese Constitution forbids Japan from using force to settle international disputes. The preamble of the constitution also declares that Japan renounces war forever. The constitution has played a strong role in shaping Japanese politics, and the public has been tenaciously and overwhelmingly pacifist for more than half a century. The Yoshida doctrine, which advocated military reliance on the United States and the prioritization of wealth accumulation at home, was accommodated at the elite level with little difficulty as early as the 1950s. But at the mass level the Yoshida doctrine was not accepted during the 1950s, and anti-Americanism was an undeniable feature of Japan's domestic politics. Communists and socialists opposed alliance with the United States, and the conservatives advocated alliance with the United States. Even in the 1960s when the debate had been won and lost, and the focus had by and large turned to wealth accumulation, the security arrangements intermittently triggered large-scale anti-Americanism. In other words, of the two components of the Yoshida doctrine, the military reliance provided for in the Security Treaty was not fully embraced by a majority of the public.

The principal source of concern with regard to the Security Treaty for the public during the 1950s and 1960s was the possibility that Japan might be press-ganged into war by the United States. Elite sentiment with regard to the Security Treaty was the opposite of that of the electorate. The elites were concerned that unless Japan could demonstrate its willingness to abide by the provisions of the Security Treaty, it might be abandoned by the United States. Prevailing public sentiment was also to be a great hindrance to elite attempts to reposition Japan as a systemic supporter of the United States in later years. Economic, political, and military burden sharing were all debated extensively during this period. But acceptance of the possibility that Japan could legitimately use force in observance of its commitments under the Security Treaty was slow to emerge.

Japan's rapid economic penetration of world markets led it to reappraise its responsibilities, interests, and role in the international political economy. Japan's manufactured products and financial assets were ubiquitous, and yet Japan's capacity to influence the political and military forces that affect world markets was comparatively limited. Japan decided to support the United States and voice its demands from within the U.S. camp. This would be more effective than going it alone, and would make it less likely that the United States would interpret Japanese criticism as irresponsible or hostile. However, for some the fact that Japan was making it clear that it was a systemic supporter of the United States increased the possibility that Japan would be dragged into wars neither of its making nor vital to its own national security.

The 1990s saw the end of the Cold War and the further deepening of globalization. UN peacekeeping operations were a feature of the first half of the 1990s. UN secretary general Boutros Boutros-Ghali vigorously promoted a proactive role for the United Nations in the post–Cold War world. Superficially at least this post–Cold War world seemed best suited to global civilian powers like Japan and Germany. As was explained above, there are restrictions on the right of Japanese troops to use force. As Japan assumed a greater peacekeeping role, this created a new set of problems associated with the use of force in the execution of peacekeeping operations. The newly legislated Peacekeeping and Other Operations Law that permitted Japanese troops to participate in UN peacekeeping operations mandated troops to carry only small-scale weapons such as rifles, to indicate that their involvement in peacekeeping was not aggressive in intent. This legislation also stipulated that weapons could only be used when troops were attacked, or were about to be attacked, in the judgment of a troop leader. Because Japan conceived of itself and promoted itself as a global civilian power, it was necessary to address such operational matters.

The Japanese have invested a vast amount of time and effort, both inside and outside of the National Diet, to ensure that the participation of SDF troops in United Nations peacekeeping operations has been constitutionally appropriate. When this legislation was passed it was hailed as a major step toward Japan's reassumption of ordinary power status, although retrospectively this was only a comparatively minor step forward. This legislation stipulated that the overseas dispatch of troops for peacekeeping purposes could only be mandated by an appropriate United Nations Security Council resolution. It remained necessary for the overseas dispatch of troops to be legitimated by the United Nations.[22]

There were further developments in the 2000s. Japan's participation in the Afghan war of 2002 was limited to the prosecution of two tasks in the Indian Ocean. Firstly, Japan's state-of-the-art Aegis-equipped destroyers patrolled the Indian Ocean and monitored maritime traffic. Secondly, Japan supplied gasoline to the combat aircraft of the United States and the United Kingdom. It was not necessary to legitimize these support activities with a UN Security Council resolution, because the Indian Ocean was designated as a noncombat area. The stipulation of the Peacekeeping and Other Operations Law that SDF troops can only be sent to noncombat areas was not relevant for the same reason. Japan was able to avoid incurring casualties and fatalities in undertaking these support operations, unlike the United Kingdom and Germany, which both sent troops to Afghanistan.

With regard to the Iraq War, Prime Minister Koizumi indicated to the United States that Japan supported the war shortly before the outbreak of hostilities in March 2003. The divisions between the members of the UN Security Council emerged as it became clear that the council would not agree to a resolution authorizing the use of force in Iraq. The United States and the United Kingdom wanted such a resolution, while France, Russia, China, and Germany were strongly opposed. Defying the preferences of the three other permanent members of the Security Council and Germany, the U.S.-UK coalition forces attacked Iraq in March 2003. This complex and sensitive situation required Japan to perform a careful diplomatic balancing act. Japan justified its support for the coalition forces by referring to the fact that Iraq was in breach of numerous existing Security Council resolutions that had been passed since 1991. However, Japan did not make reference to the issue of weapons of mass destruction (WMD) in justifying its support for the intervention. By not invoking the WMD issue, Japan was simultaneously able both to sustain its argument that military action requires a United Nations resolution and to remain a close and demonstrably reliable partner of the United States.

The legislation mandating the dispatch of SDF troops to Iraq was passed in October 2003, shortly before Koizumi announced that elections to the lower house of the Diet would take place that November. There were some problematic aspects to this legislation. Firstly, it stipulated that troops should be sent to noncombat areas. However, the United States had clearly neither pacified the country nor eradicated militant terrorism. Second, the SDF mission was to be prosecuted within the context of a United Nations resolution that was passed after the conclusion of the war, as a result of sensible compromise diplomacy on the part of the United States. The purpose of the mission was to conduct peacekeeping operations and facilitate economic reconstruction. Such objectives are appropriate for a global civilian power guided by the concept and spirit of human security. However, dissidents and terrorists continue to attack not only United States troops and troops from other coalition countries but also the personnel of international organizations such as the United Nations and the International Red Cross.

Japan's Capacity Deficit

It is clear that overcoming the legitimacy deficit is of major importance if Japan is to become an ordinary power. However, Japan's capacity deficit in the use of force is no less serious. This deficit stems from the fact that the SDF were established on the assumption that they would operate for strictly defensive purposes. The constitution has effectively constrained and dictated the SDF's force structure up until now. Only since the mid-1990s has there been a general recognition that the most important function of the SDF is the protection of national security. Legal, institutional, and public opinion have typically placed constraints on the kind of weapons and forces with which it has been felt appropriate for the SDF to be equipped. These constraints have contributed to the emergence of Japan's capacity deficit.

Within the context of perceived Cold War security needs and restrictions, the SDF built a world-class army based on fighter aircraft, tanks, and submarines. Even though the SDF has periodically upgraded its forces since the end of the Cold War within this context, new types of weapons and new modes of force structure have also become necessary. Acquisition of the following capabilities and weapons has been deemed necessary by sections of the mass media and the National Diet: long-range fighter, bomber, and transport aircraft; nuclear submarines; aircraft carrier(s); a missile defense system; an intelligence-gathering satellite; destroyer vessels; and a greater capacity to conduct peacekeeping operations.

This list enables one to understand the extent to which constitutional and other constraints have contributed to the Japanese capacity deficit. The National Diet has stipulated all manner of constraints, specifying the nature and number of weapons that can be deployed. The guiding principle has been that the function of the SDF is strictly and exclusively defensive. One problem for the Japanese government is that weapons technology is constantly evolving, and therefore even armed forces configured in an exclusively defensive manner are periodically forced to upgrade their weapons and revise their force structures to keep pace with new developments. Military configurations and threat perceptions have changed, and, as a result, so has Japan's alliance with the United States.

Japan's Emerging Role as a Global Ordinary Power

We have traced the evolution of Japan's foreign policy since 1945, and examined the two deficits that Japan must overcome if it is to become an ordinary power. The constitutional issue remains unresolved, but in the last three decades three other important elements of Japanese foreign policy have been addressed. There has been a gradual strengthening of the SDF, a consolidation of the alliance with the United States, and a more substantial engagement in peacekeeping operations and disarmament. Japan's military development has kept pace with that of other countries in the region that are seeking to enhance their military capability. Alliance consolidation has been adroit and smooth. Japan has vigorously supported peacekeeping and disarmament initiatives. It is necessary to consider ways in which recent developments in domestic politics could impact Japan's transition toward the exercise of ordinary power.

Japan has adjusted its foreign policy roughly every fifteen years. Each time, some unforeseen combination of domestic and international factors has led its foreign policy to metamorphose, albeit within the broader framework of alliance with the United States and the nonuse of force in the settlement of international disputes. The tensions inherent in military alliance with the United States and a constitutionally stipulated nonuse of force afford considerable space for metamorphosis. That is why it is very important to realize that Japan has been changing much more dramatically each and every fifteen years than it appears at first glance.

What will be the emerging nature of Japan's ordinary power from 2005 to 2020? The legacy of pro-alliance orientation will remain firm. Firstly, there is an emerging consensus on foreign security policy based on the three key components: alliance, pacifism, and a pro-UN orientation. The two large parties, the Liberal Democratic Party (LDP) and the Democratic Party of Japan (DPJ), agree on these matters, and these three issues will be the pillars of Japan's global ordinary power. Differences between the LDP and DPJ foreign policy stances are likely to be a question of emphasis with regard to each pillar, rather than disputes over fundamental issues. The LDP is likely to give greater weight to the pro-alliance orientation than the DPJ, and attach less significance to the pro-UN and pacifist orientations. These three components aside, the LDP contains a large group of legislators who talk tough on self-strengthening. The LDP is more likely to endorse the overseas deployment of troops than the DPJ, and less concerned than the DPJ about whether such a dispatch is authorized by a UN Security Council resolution or not. The LDP would countenance the dispatch of Japanese forces to join a coalition not authorized by the UN, whereas the DPJ would not. The DPJ has been trying to differentiate itself from the LDP by giving greater weight to the pro-UN and pacifist orientations.

Secondly, constitutional revisions are more likely to take place during the 2005–2020 period. If the LDP continues to hold power in one way or another, as it seems set to, constitutional revisions are likely to take the following form: endorsement of the ordinary use of force in the settlement of international disputes; greater empowerment of the prime minister in the direction of the "Presidential Prime Minister" model, and an associated reduction in bureaucratic power; greater restraints on the scope, nature, and expense of social policy; and a greater inculcation of nationalism and patriotism.

In this article we have argued that since 1945 Japanese foreign policy has evolved through five phases, which will culminate in Japan's resumption of ordinary power. We then discussed three potential models of ordinary power, Japanese style, which are ideal-typical in nature, but which share some qualities with the respective political situations of France, Germany, and Britain. We also considered the legitimacy and capacity deficits that Japan possesses.

The events of the last decade, and in particular events since September 11, have highlighted the need for a reappraisal of conventional national security strategy. Japan must decide precisely what role it intends to play in international relations, as it gradually comes to acquire the status of a global ordinary power. It has been argued elsewhere that the German model may be a more appropriate basis for U.S.-Japan relations,[23] but perhaps an opportunity to move emphatically in this direction was lost during the period of alliance drift during the 1990s, when Japan had the opportunity to present and develop itself as a civilian power. It seems reasonably clear that of the three models we have discussed, Japan is moving in the direction of the British model and, as was suggested in the Armitage Report, toward tighter alliance coordination with the United States and the further cultivation of a special relationship in the region.

Two further important points need to be made. The first is that "the bilateral alliance [between the United States and Japan] is the most critical element ensuring regional stability and order in East Asia. There are no obvious alternatives to the alliance system on the horizon that are sufficiently credible and operable."[24] The second is that "the alliance is more than simply a military pact aimed at protecting the two countries from an external threat. The alliance is also a political partnership that provides institutional mechanisms that support a stable relationship between the countries within the alliance."[25] In other words, it is mistaken to assert that bilateral relations are always "thin" and instrumental in opposition to "thicker," more constitutive commitments to regionalism and multilateralism. As we suggested earlier, it is more appropriate to consider the alliance as a partnership based on shared values.

What this also means is that fears of resurgent Japanese nationalism and adventurism, perhaps fuelled by the LDP commitment to constitutional reform, are misplaced. It is true that Japan is becoming an ordinary great power in East Asia, and increasingly an ordinary global power. But it is doing so firmly in the context of a deepening relationship with the United States that places increasing constraints on its autonomous action in the security sphere. This closer alliance partnership that is developing need not preclude regional dialogue and collective action, as is sometimes argued.[26] It is more accurate to suggest that only a secure and binding alliance can provide a credible basis for such political progress as is possible in the region. It is mistaken to assume that it is necessary to choose between bilateralism and multilateralism, and that there is a zero-sum relationship between the two types of approach. Perhaps the most appropriate way to characterize the current state of Japan's international relations is one of bilateralism-plus, or supplementalism, as a number of commentators have suggested.[27] To put the point in terms of the models we have suggested here, Japan is clearly using the British model as a foundation for the acquisition of ordinary power status. In doing so it is increasingly binding itself to the United States.

Notes

This is a revised and abridged version of our article titled "Japan's Emerging Role as a 'Global Ordinary Power,'" which appeared in *International Relations of the Asia-Pacific* 6, no. 1 (2006): 1–21.

1. Henry Kissinger, *Does America Need a Foreign Policy?* (New York: Simon and Schuster, 2001), 123.

2. George Packard, *Protest in Tokyo: The Security Treaty Crisis of 1960* (Princeton, N.J.: Princeton University Press, 1966).

3. Masataka Kosaka and Saisho Yoshida Shigeru, *Saisho Yoshida Shigeru* [Prime Minister Yoshida Shigeru] (Tokyo: Chuokoronsha, 1968).

4. Francis Fukuyama, *The End of History and the Last Man* (New York: Basic Books, 1991).

5. Hanns Maull, "Germany and Japan: a New Civilian Power?" *Foreign Affairs* 69, no. 5 (1990): 91–106.

6. Saori Katada, Hans Maull, and Takashi Inoguchi, *Global Governance: Germany and Japan in the International System* (London: Ashgate, 2004); Hans-Peter Schwartz, *Die Gezähmten Deutschen: Von der Machtbesessenheit zur Machtvergessenheit* (Stuttgart: DVA, 1985.)

7. Joseph Nye, *The Paradox of American Power: Why the World's Only Superpower Can't Go It Alone* (Oxford: Oxford University Press, 2002); Henry Nau, *At Home Abroad: Identity and Power in American Foreign Policy* (Ithaca, N.Y.: Cornell University Press, 2002).

8. Richard Armitage, William V. Roth, Jr., Kurt M. Campbell, Michael J. Green, Kent M. Harrington, Frank Jannuzi, James A. Kelly, Edward J. Lincoln, Robert A. Manning, Kevin G. Nealer, Joseph S. Nye, Jr., Torkel L. Patterson, James J. Przystup, Robin H. Sakoda, Barbara P. Wanner, and Paul D. Wolfowitz, *The United States and Japan: Advancing toward a Mature Partnership* (INSS Special Report, October 11, 2000); Steven Vogel, ed., *U.S.–Japan Relations in a Changing World* (Washington, D.C.: The Brookings Institution, 2002); G. John Ikenberry and Takashi Inoguchi, Introduction to *Reinventing the Alliance: U.S.-Japan Security Partnership in an Era of Change* (New York: Palgrave Macmillan, 2003).

9. Francis Fukuyama, *The End of History* (New York: Penguin Books, 1993).

10. John Keeler and Martin Schain, eds., *Chirac's Challenge: Liberalization, Europeanization, and Malaise in France* (New York: Palgrave, 1996).

11. Akio Morita and Shintaro Ishihara, *No toieru Nippon* [The Japan That Can Say "no"] (Tokyo: Bungeishunsho, 1989).

12. Wolf-Dieter Eberwein and Karl Kaiser, eds., *Germany's New Foreign Policy: Decision-Making in an Interdependent World* (New York: Palgrave, 2001).

13. Maull, "Germany and Japan."

14. T. J. Pempel, ed., *The Politics of the Asian Financial Crisis* (Ithaca, N.Y.: Cornell University Press, 1999); Gregory W. Noble and John Ravenhill, eds., *Asian Financial Crisis and the Architecture of Global Finance* (Cambridge: Cambridge University Press, 2000); Stephan Hagaard, *The Political Economy of the Asian Financial Crisis* (Washington, D.C.: Institute of International Economics, 1999).

15. Takashi Inoguchi, "'Distant Neighbors? Japan and Asia," *Current History* 94, no. 595 (1995): 392–96.

16. Walter Hatch and Kozo Yamamura, *Asia in Japan's Embrace: Building a Regional Production Alliance* (Cambridge: Cambridge University Press, 1996).

17. Takashi Inoguchi, ed., *Japan's Asia Policy: Its Revival and Response* (New York: Palgrave, 2002).

18. Takashi Inoguchi, "A Northeast Asian Perspective," *Australian Journal of International Affairs* 55, no. 2 (2002): 199–212.

19. Embassy of Japan, "Japan–U.S. Relations" (Washington, D.C.: Embassy of Japan, 2004). http://www.embjapan.org/english/html/japanus/japanusoverview.htm.

20. Armitage et al., *The United States and Japan.*

21. Takashi Inoguchi, "The Japanese Decision," *Open Democracy* (7 August 2003), www.openDemocracy.net.

22. Inoguchi, "Japan's United Nations Peacekeeping."

23. Ikenberry and Inoguchi, *Reinventing the Alliance.*

24. Ikenberry and Inoguchi, *Reinventing the Alliance,* 2.

25. Ikenberry and Inoguchi, *Reinventing the Alliance,* 2.

26. Christopher W. Hughes, *Japan's Re-emergence as a "Normal" Military Power.* Adelphi Paper 368–9. (London: Routledge for the International Institute for Strategic Studies, 2005).

27. Christopher W. Hughes and Akiko Fukushima, "Japan–U.S. Security Relations: 'Towards Bilateralism Plus'?" in *Beyond Bilateralism: U.S.–Japan Relations in the New Asia-Pacific,* ed. Ellis S. Krauss and T. J. Pempel (Stanford, Calif.: Stanford University Press, 2003)

References

Armitage, Richard, et al. *The United States and Japan: Advancing toward a Mature Partnership.* INSS Special Report, October 11, 2000.

Asahi Shimbun, "Foreign Affairs Take Back Seat in Election," September 6, 2005. www .asahi.com/english/Herald-asahi/TKY200509060161.html

Eberwein, Wolf-Dieter, and Karl Kaiser, eds. *Germany's New Foreign Policy: Decision-Making in an Interdependent World.* New York: Palgrave, 2001.

Fukuyama, Francis. *The End of History and the Last Man.* New York: Basic Books, 1991.

———. *Trust: Social Virtues and the Creation of Prosperity.* New York: Simon and Schuster, 1995.

Funabashi, Yoichi. "Japan and the New World Order." *Foreign Affairs* (1991): 58–74.

Hagaard, Stephan. *The Political Economy of the Asian Financial Crisis.* Washington, D.C.: Institute of International Economics, 1999.

Hatch, Walter, and Kozo Yamamura. *Asia in Japan's Embrace: Building a Regional Production Alliance.* Cambridge: Cambridge University Press, 1996.

Hughes, Christopher W. *Japan's Re-emergence as a "Normal" Military Power.* Adelphi Paper 368–9. London: Routledge for the International Institute for Strategic Studies, 2005.

Hughes, Christopher W., and Akiko Fukushima. "Japan-U.S. Security Relations: Towards Bilateralism Plus?" in *Beyond Bilateralism: U.S.-Japan Relations in the New Asia-Pacific,* edited by Ellis S. Krauss and T. J. Pempel. Stanford, Calif.: Stanford University Press, 2003.

Ikenberry, G. John, and Takashi Inoguchi. Introduction to *Reinventing the Alliance: U.S.-Japan Security Partnership in an Era of Change.* New York: Palgrave Macmillan, 2003.

Ikenberry, G. John, and Michael Mastanduno. "Conclusion: Images of Order in the Asia-Pacific and the Role of the United States." In *International Relations Theory and the Asia-Pacific,* edited by G. John Ikenberry and Michael Mastanduno. New York: Columbia University Press, 2003.

Inoguchi, Takashi. "Distant Neighbors? Japan and Asia." *Current History* 94, no. 595 (1995).

———, ed. *Japan's Asia Policy: Its Revival and Response.* New York: Palgrave, 2002.

———. "Japan's Images and Options: A Supporter, Not a Challenger." *Journal of Japanese Studies* 2, no. 1 (1986).

———. "Japan's United Nations Peacekeeping and Other Operations." *International Journal* 50, no. 2 (1995).

———. "The Japanese Decision." *Open Democracy,* August 2003. www.openDemocracy.net.

———. "A Northeast Asian Perspective." *Australian Journal of International Affairs* 55, no. 2 (2002): 199–212.

———. "An Ordinary Power, Japanese-style." *OpenDemocracy,* February 2004. www.openDemocracy.net.

Japan Times. "For Koizumi, Risks Far Outweigh Benefits," August 16, 2005. search.japantimes.co.jp/print/news/nn08–2005/nn20050816a6.htm.

Katada, Saori, Hans Maull, and Takashi Inoguchi. *Global Governance: Germany and Japan in the International System.* London: Ashgate, 2004.

Keeler, John, and Martin Schain, eds. *Chirac's Challenge: Liberalization, Europeanization, and Malaise in France.* New York: Palgrave, 1996.

Kissinger, Henry. *Does America Need a Foreign Policy?* New York: Simon and Schuster, 2001.

Kosaka, Masataka, and Saisho Yoshida Shigeru. *Prime Minister Yoshida Shigeru.* Tokyo: Chuokoronsha, 1968.

Maull, Hanns. "Germany and Japan: A New Civilian Power?" *Foreign Affairs* 69, no. 5 (1990): 91–106.

Morita, Akio, and Shintaro Ishihara. *No toieru Nippon* [The Japan That Can Say "No"]. Tokyo: Bungeishunsho, 1989.

Morris, Dick. *Power Plays: Win or Lose, How History's Great Political Leaders Play the Game.* New York: Regan Books, 2002.

Mueller, John E. *Retreat from Doomsday: The Obsolescence of Major War.* New York: Basic Books, 1989.

Nau, Henry. *At Home Abroad: Identity and Power in American Foreign Policy.* Ithaca, N.Y.: Cornell University Press, 2002.

Noble, Gregory W., and John Ravenhill, eds. *Asian Financial Crisis and the Architecture of Global Finance.* Cambridge: Cambridge University Press, 2000.

Nye, Joseph. *The Paradox of American Power: Why the World's Only Superpower Can't Go It Alone.* Oxford: Oxford University Press, 2002.

Packard, George. *Protest in Tokyo: The Security Treaty Crisis of 1960.* Princeton, N.J.: Princeton University Press, 1966.

Pempel, T. J., ed. *The Politics of the Asian Financial Crisis.* Ithaca, N.Y.: Cornell University Press, 1999.

Schwartz, Hans-Peter. *Die Gezähmten Deutschen: Von der Machtbesessenheit zur Machtvergessenheit.* Stuttgart: DVA, 1985.

Vogel, Steven, ed. *U.S.–Japan Relations in a Changing World.* Washington, D.C.: Brookings Institution, 2002.

4

Defying Expectations
Russia's Missing Asian Revisionism

William C. Wohlforth

R USSIA COUNTS AS ONE OF Asia's most dynamic powers in the post–Cold War era. By many measures, the scale and rapidity of its decline in the 1990s dwarfed other changes in the region's international politics. Measured against the collapse of Moscow's military and economic capabilities, the rise of China appears glacial. This precipitous fall from grace poses two puzzles for international relations scholarship. First is the puzzle of peaceful decline, presented most clearly in Moscow's response to the end of the Cold War and the collapse of the Soviet Union. Scholars have exerted considerable effort seeking to explain why Russia defied expectations by accepting great-power decline peacefully.

Less noticed is the fact that most scholars' answers to the first puzzle only deepen the second one: why Russia's loss of status in 1989–1992 did not generate a subsequent revisionist reaction. And the puzzle became even more salient when the new millennium brought something of a turnaround in Russia's fortunes. Between 2000 and 2006, Russia's economy grew at an annual rate of 5–6 percent, resulting in a 50 percent increase in gross domestic product (GDP) and dramatically improved government finances. While considerably slower than China's spectacular performance, this shift—against the backdrop of a more coherent, assertive, and authoritarian government—suggested that Russia might once again chafe against a status quo perceived as unjust.

My purpose in this chapter is to provide an explanation for Russia's surprisingly graceful adjustment to decline that helps answer the key questions about Russia's role in Asia. I begin by placing the Russian case in the larger context of scholarship on great-power decline. In the next section, I find the answer to the puzzle of Russia's response to decline in a complex interaction between material capabilities and actors' perceptions and intellectual understandings—precisely the nexus of variables that lies at the core of "neoclassicial realist" scholarship.[1] I then document how this response applied specifically to Russia's Asia policy. With this assessment of Russia's adjustment to its new global and regional role as a key backdrop, I then analyze Putin-era Asia policy. Does the new gas- and oil-fueled "turn" toward Asia reflect, at long last, the assertive revisionism predicted by scholarly theories? I find scant evidence for risky revisionism. Russian officials want to increase their trade and energy links with Asian partners, but show no inclination to rock the boat. In short, Russia's remarkable and unexpected adjustment to decline in Asia appears stable.

The Puzzles of Russian Decline

In July 1986, Mikhail Gorbachev gave a speech in Vladivostok calling for a revamped Asian security architecture and a larger role for the USSR in the region's economics and politics. Coming from the leader of a superpower that had made massive investments in its military position in Asia for the previous generation, the speech generated excited commentary in the region and globally. Few observers noticed that much of Gorbachev's time in Siberia was devoted to dealing with the region's housing shortage and other problems endemic to its moribund planned economy. As it turned out, the infrastructure problems the general secretary tried unsuccessfully to remedy were better predictors of the Soviet Union's fate in the region than the portentous words he uttered to foreign audiences. Five and a half years after giving that speech, Gorbachev presided over the dissolution of the Soviet Union. By the middle of the 1990s, Russia's military and economic capabilities were in free fall while its Asian regions suffered under corrupt politics, depressed economies, and rapid population decline owing to increased mortality and outmigration.

As dramatic as it was globally, Moscow's decline was especially precipitous in Asia because its grasp on great-power status in that region was more tenuous and vulnerable than was the case in Europe. Geography dictates that Russia be an Asian country, but not necessarily an Asian great power. Historically, Russian governments have only managed to act in Asia as a great power when they have been willing and able to devote the fantastic resources that a real strategic presence in Russia's Far East demands.[2] Long, expensive, and slow transportation lines; the North-South flow of rivers; poor soil quality; problematic coastal geography; and, most important, the inhospitable climate make it very expensive to deploy and maintain a significant strategic presence in Russia's Far Eastern and southeastern provinces. Moscow overcame these obstacles in the 1970s in a typically Soviet way: through massive, uneconomic, and ultimately unsustainable state-led resource commitments. Just as Moscow's international position in Asia was a concentrated reflection of its overall reliance on military power, its economic and even demographic position in its own Far East was a concentrated reflection of its reliance on state coercion, central planning, and subsidies. While the collapse of the Soviet state hurt all regions, in gross economic terms it hit the Far East the hardest of all.

According to formidable bodies of theoretical and historical scholarship, this decline was a recipe for war. Three distinct scholarly literatures posit links between decline and bellicose international behavior. First, writings on preventive war suggest that states that anticipate relative decline in terms of military power or aggregate resources may use force to forestall or minimize expected future losses vis-à-vis rivals.[3] A second body of theory relaxes the assumption that states are unitary and rational decision makers, and finds the origins of bellicosity in the domestic political coalitions undergirding expansionism. Military and other elites vested in empire not only stand to lose status and legitimacy under imperial retrenchment but may find the road to peaceful adaptation blocked by the very political coalitions and supporting ideologies they constructed for expansion in the first place.[4] Finally, theories and research findings from social psychology show that people tend to prefer higher status for the groups with which they identify.[5] Applied to international relations, this literature suggests that decision makers may place a value on the international status of their state that is independent of material goals such as security and welfare.[6] Confronting decline, decision makers may be willing to pay costs for the maintenance of their country's status that would not make sense for purely material aims.[7]

And if these theories were widely believed to be true in general, they were thought to be especially relevant to Russia, a country with a four-hundred-year history as a great power and an elite whose affection for international prestige was legendary. Paul Kennedy expressed a consensus view when he wrote in 1987 that "there is nothing in the character or the tradition of the Russian state to suggest that it could ever accept imperial decline gracefully."[8]

Scholars proffering explanations for change in Soviet foreign policy are therefore compelled to unpack the logic of forceful responses to decline. As a result, the vast literature on Soviet and Russian foreign policy during and after the end of the Cold War is in part a response to the puzzle of Moscow's peaceful adaptation to decline. Analysts generally find that the preventive war argument did not apply to late–Cold War Moscow, mainly because both the Soviet Union and its principal rivals were armed with secure second-strike nuclear capabilities. A necessary condition for preventive war is the belief that fighting a winnable war now will leave the state in a better position later—a notion unlikely to come to the minds of the leaders of nuclear-armed states.

The domestic and psychological theories, however, are far more applicable to the Soviet-Russian case and indeed reinforce each other. As an authoritarian state with deeply entrenched military and ideological elites whose political power and legitimacy were tightly bound up with empire, the Soviet Union appeared primed for the use of force to arrest decline. And psychological writings on group identity and status seeking seem tailor-made for the Russian case: both popular and elite evidence indicates strong attachment to great-power status. To the degree that both theories apply to the case of the Soviet Union and the end of the Cold War, leaders would be expected to treasure status, and powerful imperial institutions could count on mass affection for status as a reliable resource in any political struggle over policy responses to decline.

Why, in the final analysis, did Soviet Russia avoid the fate theory had set for it? Analysts forward two main answers. First is the leadership/domestic structure argument. The Soviet Union's totalitarian political institutions endowed the leader with the potential to defy the powerful pressures from entrenched elites, and Mikhail Gorbachev possessed precisely the mix of talents needed to realize this potential.[9] Second is the ideas argument. Soviet "new thinking" about international relations obscured the tough trade-offs of coping with decline by feeding the conviction that Moscow could maintain and even enhance its international status even while scaling back the costs of empire.[10] As Deborah Larson and Alexei Shevchenko put it, "Gorbachev and his like-minded colleagues chose the idealistic new thinking over competing foreign policy programs because it offered a new global mission that would enhance Soviet international status while preserving a distinctive national identity."[11]

Both explanations are plausible, and a great deal of evidence supports them. They are, however, partial answers at best, for they both apply only to the 1985–1991 period, and in many ways they only deepen the puzzle of what occurred after 1991. If Soviet new thinking was supposed to bring Moscow enhanced international status, then it must count as one of history's most consequential cases of collective self-delusion. Nearly everything that happened after 1989, from the settlement of the Cold War largely on Western terms to the collapse of the USSR itself, decisively undermined any notion that a foreign policy based on new thinking would preserve or enhance Russia's prestige. Predictably, the new thinking quickly fell from favor in post-Soviet Russia, replaced by a hard-nosed geopolitical realism. Similarly, the totalitarian political institutions that are widely credited with allowing Gorbachev to subvert his imperialistically minded elites gave way to precisely the kind of chaotic quasi democracy that provides the most fertile soil for nationalistic and cartelized politics.[12]

Russia's Solution

The intervening factors that smoothed Russia's adaptation to decline in 1989–1991 were thus transitory. Their passing from the political scene presented Moscow with a new need to adapt to decline in the middle and late 1990s, as the belated realization of the country's true international trajectory filtered into Russians' political consciousness. The result, in terms of the theoretical literature, was a perfect storm for a violent attempt to revise the status quo that emerged from the events of 1989–1991: peace-loving "new thinking" was decisively discredited, conditions were ripe for a "stab in the back" myth to mobilize masses on the platform of remedying national humiliation, and the weak political institutions of postcommunist Russia were particularly vulnerable to capture by domestic forces that would profit from new revisionism.

The question of how Russia adapted this time is complex, but the interaction between ideas and domestic politics remains an important part of the story. The starting point is the general human reluctance to update assessments in response to new information.[13] This bias of "anchoring" means that, given an initial high assessment, perceptions of power tend consistently to lag real decline. In the Russian case, the ideas politically in play served to increase this natural lag. As noted, this may have been one of the most important causal effects of Gorbachev's new thinking. Yet, even as new thinking faded from the scene, new ideas came to the fore that had a similar if shorter-lived effect. New thinking was replaced for a brief two-year period by a clearly articulated liberal worldview, personified by Foreign Minister Andrei Kozyrev, who sought "alliance-like" relations with the West.[14] Though little noticed at the time, the liberal ideas shared with new thinking a robust optimism about Russia's prospects as a major power once the intellectual shackles of the past were thrown off. For Kozyrev and his ilk, Moscow would gain immense leverage in world politics by unambiguously joining the United States as a partner in upholding world order.

Hence, despite the shift in official ideology from new thinking to liberalism, from roughly 1989 until 1993 Russian policymakers believed that their state had the power to sustain bipolarity. That is, even after the formal loss of the outer and inner empires, Russians still talked as though their country remained a superpower—inferior to the United States, to be sure, but well above all the rest. Moscow's swing to the West under Boris Yeltsin in 1991–1993 thus took place under the optimistic assumption of Russia's continued superpower standing.

Kozyrev-style Westernism never achieved the hegemonic position formerly occupied by the new thinking. Immediately it contended with powerful intellectual challenges from a peculiarly Russian geopolitical version of realpolitik. By 1993, the liberal paradigm had been officially abandoned by the Foreign

Ministry and the Kremlin, replaced by a mild form of Realpolitik.[15] Indeed, a consistent pattern emerged over the first years after the dissolution of the Soviet Union: the more that feedback about the decline of Russia's power and prestige mounted, the more that official Russian discourse became dominated by geopolitics. It was the dominance of this discourse that caused many analysts to argue that a consensus on foreign policy had emerged within the Russian elite by the mid-1990s. The impression was strengthened by the appointment of the widely respected and bureaucratically skilled Yevgeny Primakov to replace Andrei Kozyrev as foreign minister, and it was further consolidated during Primakov's tenure as prime minister. Of course, the convergence toward geopolitical language to describe foreign policy hid major differences of emphasis, especially regarding the relative salience of "old" versus "new" security threats. But the prevalence of geopolitical language in official Moscow, compared to most other major capitals, remained striking.

Though geopolitics appears to represent a major departure from liberal and new-thinking ideas, it retains one key feature in common with the paradigms that preceded it: a bias toward overestimating Russian power.[16] Notwithstanding the loss of the fourteen other Soviet republics, Russia remains the world's largest state. And its location in the heart of Eurasia does make it a political factor in most of the world's key regions, from East and South Asia to Central Asia, the Caucasus, the Middle East, and Europe. Space, location, nuclear weapons, and superpower pedigree are the only plausible sources of Russia's claim to great-power status. And only on the geopolitical dimension does Russia truly stand out. While there are many different strands of Russian geopolitical thinking, they all lead to the conclusion that owing mainly to its size and location, Russia will take a (if not the) leading role in the creation of a new world order. As Sergei Rogov, director of the Russian Academy of Sciences Institute of the United States and Canada, put it: "the Russian Federation, unlike the Soviet Union, cannot pretend to the role of a superpower. But due to the size of its territory and population, as well as its military and scientific potential, and as a great Eurasian power, it can become a leading participant in a multipolar world, playing an active role in resolving problems in which it has an interest."[17]

Russia's Solution Applied to Asia

This was the intellectual underpinning of Russia's "multipolar" diplomacy in Asia. At the global level Moscow presented itself as a—if not the—key organizer of multipolar policy coalitions to rein in U.S. power. Yevgeny Primakov's tenure at the helm of Russian foreign policy inaugurated a parade of ostensibly anti-U.S. diplomatic combinations: the "European troika" of France, Germany, and Russia; the "special relationship" between Germany and Russia; the "strategic triangle" of Russia, China, and India; and, most important, the "strategic partnership" between China and Russia.

Rhetorically, Russian diplomacy was characterized by the desire to team up with Asian centers of power in order to reduce America's regional sway. But the language Primakov, Foreign Minister Igor Ivanov, and other Russian officials used to describe their policy was misleading on two counts.[18] First and most important is the plain fact that Russia never counterbalanced U.S. power—either globally or in Asia. Balancing power involves taking specific actions alone or in concert with others that promise to provide some counterweight to America's overweening capabilities—actions, moreover, that would not have been taken if the United States had not been so powerful. The most reliable way to balance power is to build up one's own capabilities. Needless to say, Russia's multipolar strategy did not entail any such "internal balancing": the country's military power continued to decay throughout the 1990s. Neither did Russia engage in "external balancing"—that is, aggregating its power in alliance with other states in a meaningful way. Russia's treaty relationships with China and India simply were not such power-aggregating alliances. All three powers continued to cooperate closely with the United States on a very large range of security and economic matters. Indeed, throughout the 1990s each placed greater priority on relations with the United States than with each other—behavior bearing scant resemblance to any normal understanding of balancing.

Moreover, Moscow's multipolar rhetoric was misleading because the bulk of Russia's security relationships in East, Southeast, and South Asia had little to do with America's global hegemony and regional presence. Had U.S. power been magically cut in half, Russia would have still sought rapprochement with China and would still have faced a powerful incentive to work with rather than against Beijing in the effort to manage the security problems created by its own imperial retrenchment. The Soviet Union's effort to contain China in the 1970s and 1980s strapped its capabilities and contributed significantly to its imperial overstretch. By the mid-1990s, a much weaker and still weakening Russia had to preserve amicable security ties and had a strong interest in developing economic relations with a much stronger and growing China.

The substantive core of Russia's relationships with India and China was not the diplomatic partnerships but major arms sales and extensive military coproduction arrangements. Russia's interest in these exports, however, was not driven by the need to counterbalance U.S. power. Rather, they were and remain desperately needed to slow the inexorable decline of Russia's military-industrial complex. The crucial background here is that between 1992 and

1998 Russia experienced what was probably the steepest peacetime decline in military power by any major state in history.[19] Arms sales are a substrategy that aids Russia's more general interest in staving off further military decline. Given the collapse of domestic orders (in 2001, only 10 percent of Russian defense firms received state orders), Russia's defense sector possesses massive excess capacity.[20] Exports are a crucial lifeline for a military industry producing less than one-third of its 1992 output and rapidly losing technological competitiveness. Russia wants to sustain a core defense manufacturing capacity until economic growth affords it the opportunity to modernize its surviving military infrastructure and to transfer excess defense workers and production capacities into more productive sectors. Even more immediately, exports aid a defense sector that supplies income and welfare services to hundreds of thousands of workers and their families, provides the economic lifeblood of dozens of cities, and enriches numerous managers and public officials.

Aside from arms transfers, the partnership with China has three elements: regional, economic, and multipolar. The last item received the most attention; the first two elements are where most of the concrete actions have taken place. During the 1990s, the two sides demarcated most of their 2,600-mile border.[21] They sought to cooperate on cross-border trade and immigration issues. They endeavored to boost bilateral trade, although politicians in both capitals have only a limited ability to affect the underlying demand in each country for the other's goods. And they instituted confidence-building measures and negotiated numerical limits on troop deployments in the region.

The multipolar rhetoric surrounding the essentially pragmatic Russia-China partnership correlated with the two countries' disapproval of specific U.S. policies. For example, the Friendship Treaty contained a laundry list of U.S. policies the two sides opposed. Article 11 stipulated support for the principles and norms of international law, which means that the two sides opposed any repetition of the Kosovo scenario anywhere in the world and any revision of international treaties (e.g., the Anti-Ballistic Missile [ABM] Treaty). Articles 11 and 12 reinforce both parties' commitment to the treaty, while Article 12 enjoins both to maintain the "global strategic balance and stability." In short, the sole "multipolar" aspect of this treaty was an attempt to signal Washington that it could pay some unspecified price if it unilaterally abandoned the ABM Treaty.

In sum, geopolitical ideas served to inflate Russian rhetoric about the country's role in Asia and the world. While Russia's real behavior was generally pragmatically driven management of current security and economic challenges, the discourse was about Moscow leading the world to multipolarity. The ideas may have fed the anchoring bias, slowing Russians' updating of their power assessments in the face of new evidence. The geopolitical fixation on territory and location may thus have inculcated a real policy bias toward overplaying Russia's hand in Asian and global affairs. A second possibility, however, was that the ideas were used strategically by politicians to defuse domestic pressures for more bellicose foreign policies. Throughout the 1990s, Russia talked the talk of revisionism but never truly walked the walk. To the extent that Russia was able to follow a coherent policy at all in the 1990s, it was about managing decline. Globally, the multipolar talk served to divert attention from a reality of steady concessions to, powerlessness to oppose, or eager cooperation with the United States. In Asia the multipolar dimension served to mask an uncomfortable reality: that what the policy was really doing was managing the power transition in the region from Russia to China.

In reality, both processes likely worked in tandem to defuse the effects of the reactions to decline highlighted in the scholarly literature. Domestic groups did mobilize on themes of national humiliation and revanche, just as the theoretical literature expected. And the psychological anguish occasioned by a rapid fall from status was strongly present in postcommunist Russia, exactly as predicted by social identity theory. But in combination with the natural anchoring bias, ideas—sincerely believed and strategically manipulated—magnified Russia's remaining strengths and dampened the psychological and political shocks of decline.

If this analysis is valid, it still begs important questions. Is the story of Russia's adaptation to decline over, or might there be potential trouble ahead? If Russia's robust economic growth continues, might Moscow seek to use force to leverage a revision in its recently humbled international status? Certain answers to these questions are impossible, but the evidence concerning Russia's official thinking and behavior under Vladimir Putin does not suggest an affirmative answer.

Putin's rise to power in 1999 occurred as a growing cadre of officials and analysts had concluded that the multipolar line was not working, mainly for one reason: the world was unipolar, and it was likely to stay that way.[22] The multipolar approach, they argued, was beyond Russia's limited capabilities. Russia clearly lacked the power to affect the polarity of the international system, and underlying trends toward multipolarity would occur independent of Russian diplomacy. If local hegemony in the former Soviet space and global multipolarity were each daunting objectives, the combination was formidable indeed.

In addition, the old approach scattered Russia's limited foreign-policy energies around the globe, preventing a necessary concentration on priority issues. It constrained Russia's flexibility, trapping it into taking a lead position in most global anti-U.S. policy coalitions. Other powers, such as the European Union (EU) and China—often with greater interests at stake and far greater capabilities—were letting Russia do the dirty work of seeking to constrain the United States, all the while making lucrative deals with Washington on the side. Why should Russia, often the weakest player on the multipolar team, always lead the charge? Moreover, if relations between any of the other multipolar partners and Washington were to deteriorate seriously—for example, between Beijing and Washington over Taiwan—Russia would be drawn into a confrontation in which it has no stake and which it cannot afford.

Notwithstanding support from some analytical and commercial circles for reining in the multipolar line, it remained popular among many politicians and state officials. Putin made positive efforts to revise strategy along more modest lines. As prime minister and then president, he oversaw revisions in Russia's national security and defense doctrines that increased the emphasis on the modernization imperative and new transnational threats, especially from terrorism.[23] More notably, the entire discussion of Russia's strategic priorities shifted. The bottom line of the newer view was that Russia's chief priorities are and will remain modernization and economic rejuvenation, which create powerful incentives to maintain productive partnerships with the governments of the world's richest and most influential states. Putin appeared to be well aware that the fate of Russia's rejuvenation will be determined mainly by the success of domestic institution building. But he and his aides also understood that too much tension in relations with the other major powers may have negative spillover on a range of international economic matters where their support is crucial. A serious polarization in relations with the United States or any other major power could have catastrophic consequences for the state budget and the Russian economy. Moreover, Putin continued to insist that the major near- and medium-term security threats Russia faces do not emanate from other great powers but rather demand their cooperation. New security issues, such as terrorism, weapons proliferation, Islamic fundamentalism, organized crime, unregulated migration, and the like, assumed an increased salience in Russia's hierarchy of strategic interests as opposed to traditional great-power security concerns.

What emerged from this rethinking was less a coherent grand strategy than a new strategic emphasis on modernizing Russia so that it has a chance to recover as a real great power in the middle decades of this century. In the medium term, that means exploiting Russia's existing resources to finance the creation of the institutions and relationships it needs to succeed over the long term. And the chief resource Russia has at its disposal now is petroleum. Russia is becoming a petro-power in order to create the preconditions for its re-emergence as a full-fledged great power. In the meantime, it will use the influence it gains as a major oil and gas power—with the limits created by the need to maintain a reputation as a reliable supplier—mainly to leverage its way into better economic arrangements that further its modernization objective.

Russia's Asian Hedge

Russian officials have long played on the ambiguity of Russia's geopolitical location to stress their country's status as an Asian as well as European power. After he took office in 2000, Putin reduced this ambiguity, stressing that Russia is fundamentally a European country with a lot of territory in Asia. As he noted in an interview, "the European Union (EU) accounts for 37 percent of Russia's external trade turnover, and after the expansion of the EU this will increase to 52 percent. Russia is a European country in its geography, history, culture and mentality of the population."[24] Reducing this ambiguity did not mean eliminating it, however, for even in the heyday of the post–9/11 "honeymoon" with the West, Putin and his foreign policy team continued to believe that eliminating all ambiguity would eliminate Moscow's diplomatic flexibility and hence its bargaining power. Unless the costs become too high, Putin's default strategy is to hedge his bets by nurturing good relationships with all parties. At the same time, the evidence suggests that Putin and his aides believe that Russia cannot allow such diplomatic maneuvering to risk a genuine deterioration of relations with key economic and strategic partners, including the EU and the United States.

This trademark hedging strategy is the key background for assessing Russia's post–2003 turn toward Asia. Russia's renewed economic growth, increased authoritarianism, and tightened state control over major petrochemical firms, followed by EU and U.S. criticism and a predictable Russian response, fueled talk of a strategic reassessment in Moscow. Highlighted on the economic front by energy projects—which include oil and gas pipelines to China and possibly South Korea, as well as liquefied natural gas and oil projects off Russia's Pacific coast—and on the security front by arms sales and regional security cooperation, Russia's Asia policy clearly took on renewed vigor after 2003.

China

Putin began his presidency by reducing the multipolar emphasis in relations with China, and made immediate efforts to take a more realistic and bottom line–oriented approach to the strategic partnership. In the months leading up to September 2001, all the usual preconditions for an intense bout of multipolar diplomacy were in place. Resentment of U.S. hegemony had been stoked by the prominent unilateralist tendencies and rhetoric of the early

Bush administration, the galvanizing push of U.S. plans concerning missile defense, the new administration's cooler and more distant stance toward both Russia and China, and the U.S. spy plane incident. Yet even in this hothouse atmosphere for nurturing a serious anti-U.S. policy alignment, the parties were reluctant to commit publicly to real policy coordination. Indeed, it was during the summit with Jiang Zemin in July 2001 at which the Sino-Russian Friendship Treaty was signed that Putin publicly defected from the "multipolar" policy coalition against U.S. national missile defense.

After Putin's celebrated decision to align Russia with the U.S.-led war on terrorism, he accelerated the strategic shift toward selective accommodation and retrenchment that was already underway. The trend toward de-emphasizing multipolarity now encompassed both rhetoric and behavior. The centerpiece of the effort was a retreat on issues Putin knew Russia would eventually have to compromise on in any case: NATO and the ABM Treaty. Once Russia further softened its stance on these issues, the path was open to major improvements in relations with the United States, signified by Russia's signing a strategic arms reductions treaty during George W. Bush's May visit to Moscow and St. Petersburg and formally joining the new NATO-Russia Council later that month. Adding weight to these modest policy moves was a dramatic increase in the clarity with which Putin and other top officials described the rapprochement with the West.[25]

The shift altered the tone of the strategic partnership with China. In effect, Russia chose to defect from the multipolar policy coalition against U.S. abrogation of the ABM Treaty and NATO expansion. Putin's relaxed reaction to the announcement of formal U.S. withdrawal from the treaty in December 2001 put the nail in the coffin of that coalition, while his acceptance of a revamped Russian role in the NATO-Russia Council pulled the rug out from years of campaigning against that organization's role in international security. The immediate implication was clear. Russia's role in the antiterror campaign meant that it did not need China—or the threat of closer security ties to China—to enhance its importance to Washington. More fundamentally, it reflected the long-germinating assessment that Russia's forward-leaning stance on multipolarity only set it up to be suckered by China (and the Europeans) as they shrank from paying the up-front political costs of confronting Washington.

Putin has tried to ensure that the strategic partnership with China works to his own benefit. For now, that implies a focus on the key near-term security threats that both sides regard as most important—terrorism, North Korea's nuclearization or meltdown, drug trafficking, Islamic extremism, separatism, organized crime, migration, and weapons proliferation—and the avoidance of commitments that would subordinate Russia's larger policies to China's. At their December 2002 summit meeting in Beijing, Putin and Jiang Zemin reiterated their support for a multipolar world order to contain U.S. unilateralism, but the substance of the meeting concerned deepening energy and trade cooperation and the struggle against terrorism within the framework of the Shanghai Cooperation Organization.[26] The reason for the focus on the pragmatic core of their strategic partnership was self-evident: both countries had made major efforts to improve their relations with the United States. While Chinese commentators fretted about Russia's westward drift, Beijing's new leadership proved much more cautious about risking ties with the United States over Iraq than Russia was.

As Russia's political and economic relations with both the United States and the EU entered a rocky period in 2005, the strategic partnership with China took on steam. Hu Jintao's visit to Moscow in July 2005 was accompanied by a joint Sino-Russian statement on "world order," once again highlighting multipolarity. But the substance remained the same. Trade between Russia and China remained anemic ($29.1 billion, as opposed to China's $210 billion with the United States and $185 billion with Japan) and dominated by military hardware and petrochemicals. Notably, Russia's default hedging strategy was on display in a new "competing pipeline" drama: the East Siberia–Pacific Ocean pipeline, expected to carry some 600,000 barrels of oil a day to Asian customers. Japan lobbied insistently for a $5 billion, 2,300-mile project that would link oilfields near the Siberian city of Angarsk to the port city of Nakhodka on the Japan Sea. Beijing championed a smaller and cheaper route to the Chinese city of Daqing.

Characteristically, Moscow played both sides, partly for political reasons but almost certainly also in order to seek the best commercial terms.[27] Russia's Yukos Oil and China National Petroleum signed a preliminary agreement on the Angarsk-Daqing deal on the sidelines of the summit meeting between Putin and Hu Jintao in May 2003. But in subsequent interviews, Putin expressed a clear preference for the Nakhodka plan, stressing its potential to diversify Russia's energy exports in Asia. "The only question is whether it is well-grounded economically," he stressed.[28] Japan took the bait by offering generous subsidies, while Putin and other Russian officials tried to keep everybody happy with the idea of a branch line from Angarsk-Nakhodka to Daqing, provided there is enough oil. As of early 2007, it remained unclear whether the twin routes would be economically feasible and, if not, which one would find favor with Moscow.

Central Asia and the Shanghai Cooperation Organization (SCO)

A similar pattern characterized Sino-Russian cooperation in Central Asia under the umbrella of the SCO. At first, the U.S. and Russian response to

September 11 sapped the modest momentum that had been building behind the organization. The main impetus behind the strengthening of the SCO (including Uzbekistan's decision to join it in 2001) had been the terrorist threat emanating from Afghanistan. Now, the SCO's Central Asian members were hosting the U.S. military, which went on to accomplish the membership's cherished goal of destroying the Taliban. To restore a certain degree of normalcy in the post-Taliban era, SCO foreign ministers met in Beijing in early January to assess the new situation in the region. Russia's immediate response was, as in much of its diplomacy in recent years, to make a virtue of necessity. Russian defense minister Sergey Ivanov explicitly linked the SCO to the global antiterror coalition. With the formation of the NATO-Russia Council, whose mandate explicitly highlights counterterrorism, he stressed, Moscow has indeed become a crucial link in a Eurasian counterterrorist coalition encompassing two regional security organizations covering the North Atlantic and Central Asia.[29] The SCO officials agreed to set up a regional counterterrorism agency and an emergency response mechanism.

The cycle shifted in 2004–2005 with U.S. and European support for the "color revolutions" in Georgia, Ukraine, and Kyrgystan, as well as their criticism of Uzbekistan's violent suppression of antigovernment protests in Andijon. U.S.-Uzbek relations soured, and Russia and China saw an opportunity to rejuvenate the SCO. At their summit in Astana, Kazakhstan, in July 2005, SCO heads of state effectively called for an end to the U.S. military bases in Central Asia. Uzbekistan ordered the American forces out of their Kershi-Khanabad base, while Kyrgyzstan used the SCO resolution as a lever to increase rent on the U.S. airbase in Manas. Nevertheless, even after the organization's fifth-anniversary summit in Shanghai in June 2006, its structure, mode of operation, financing, rules for accession, participation of observers, and membership criteria all remain ill defined.

Japan

Predictably, Russia's Japan diplomacy tracked the overall course of relations with the United States. As Putin oversaw a sustained effort to improve relations with the United States early in his presidency, a weaker but measurable attempt to add impetus to ties with Japan was also in evidence. In March 2000, Putin restated an earlier offer to return two of the disputed Kurile Islands to Japan and created momentum toward a breakthrough in negotiations over normalization. Although the negotiations about the islands soon bogged down in familiar ruts, modest progress was evident in other areas.[30] Military contacts between the two countries increased after a visit by Russia's defense minister in December 2001 initiated regular exchanges of delegations between security institutions and expanded confidence-building measures. At their summit in January 2003, Putin and Prime Minister Junichiro Koizumi signed a "Japan-Russia Action Plan" that reiterated their commitment to overcome the Kuriles territorial dispute and broaden energy cooperation beyond the existing projects on Sakhalin. In precisely this period, Moscow backed out of the pipeline commitment to China while expressing support for Japan's favored route.

Despite increasing trade and progress in developing Sakhalin Island gas projects, the relationship stalled in 2004–2005. In part this loss of momentum stemmed from the two sides' inability even to appear to make progress on the islands dispute as well as structural and political limitations on trade and investment. Another cause was likely Japan's ever-closer security relationship with the United States, given new emphasis in the April 2006 U.S.-Japanese agreement on relocating U.S. military bases in Japan as well as bilateral military cooperation.

Korea

Perhaps the most spectacular initial Russian initiative in Asia was Putin's reengagement in Korean affairs. In July 2000 and August the following year, he and North Korea's Kim Jong-il exchanged visits after a decade-long freeze in the two countries' relationship. Russian officials argued that rebalancing Moscow's relations between North and South Korea would aid their expressed interest in reengaging the strategic dialogue on the peninsula after years of having been shunted aside by Beijing and Washington. In addition, the Russians hoped to prod the North Koreans to abandon their missile program in order to defuse one U.S. argument for missile defense. But much of the substance of the meetings concerned economic relations with both Koreas: connecting the Trans-Siberian Railway to the North Korean rail network and the inter-Korean railway; refurbishing power plants and other facilities constructed with Soviet aid in the 1950s and 1960s (with Moscow refusing barter transactions and attempting to induce South Korean banks and firms to finance the projects); and, of course, possible arms sales to both Koreas "within the limits of reasonable sufficiency."[31]

After Putin's March 2001 visit to Seoul, Russia and South Korea announced close cooperation to promote the Irkutsk (Kovykta) gas project, involving an $11 billion pipeline to bring gas down from Siberian fields through China and North Korea, and then to the industrial heartland of South Korea. They also consulted on South Korea's participation in projects to develop oil and gas fields on Sakhalin and in other Russian regions.[32] Other pipeline projects currently in discussion or planning phases include an oil pipeline from Sakhalin to Japan, South Korea, and Taiwan (or a shorter line to a Russian transshipment terminal); a Russia-China oil pipeline from Siberian fields running through either Mongolia or North Korea into China; natural gas pipelines to China and South Korea; and a trans-China gas pipeline.[33]

Russia's policy on North Korea fits the general pattern of Russian maneuvering for economic advantage and political influence, but within the limits dictated by relative weakness and a basic interest—in this case, in nuclear nonproliferation—that it shares with the other major powers.[34] Moreover, the main lesson of Russia's Korea policy has been to underline its limited leverage over the parties. Time has not been kind to the more grandiose plans for Russia's role in Korean affairs. Failure to make progress on the North Korean standoff stymied ambitious plans to build pipelines and railroads on the peninsula, and other means of bolstering economic links to Seoul remained in the talking phase.

Assessment and Prospects

Each of Russia's key Asian relationships has exhibited a similar pattern of great expectations followed by restraint and realism until another bout of optimism occurs. The cycles are governed in part by developments specific to each relationship, but there is a rough strategic logic of hedging bets and using one relationship as bargaining leverage in another. Thus, when relations with Washington sour, Russia looks to Brussels, Berlin, and Paris. When both the United States and the EU prove troublesome, there is talk of a shift to Asia. Within Asia, subtle shifts of emphasis among China, Japan, and India reflect similar dynamics. There is, in sum, scant evidence of a fundamental reorientation. Rather, the turn toward Asia was a subtle shift in emphasis made to seem more portentous than it really was by the very same Russian response to decline that has remained stable since the early 1990s. The shifts in Russia's emphasis on Asia are limited by four key conditions.

First, despite Russia's economic recovery, the country's policy in Asia still must be framed in response to relative decline. Though it is growing, the Russian economy remains tiny, with a GDP in 2004 that was estimated at $582 billion at market exchange rates—roughly the economic size of Illinois in that same year. Even if Russia averages steady 6 percent annual average economic growth, the gap with China will probably widen rapidly. The raw numbers obscure a deeper and more troubling reality: while China and now India have experienced growth based increasingly on knowledge-based industries and investments in physical and human infrastructure, Russia remains a marginal economy bolstered by natural resource exports. And Russia's decline transcends economic indices to encompass a demographic meltdown (the population is shrinking by 750,000 per year), a public health crisis, a catastrophic degradation of the environment, an educational system in crisis, and the systematic deterioration of social and physical infrastructure throughout the country.[35] In the years and decades ahead, Russia's population will continue to decline and age, and it will face the daunting economic costs of today's deep and well-documented social, institutional, and infrastructural crises.

The problem of relative decline in Asia encompasses even Russia's traditionally strong suit: military power. Even after the defense budget increases began in 1999, maintenance and training remain dismal; personnel problems are dire and getting worse; and, most important, little has been done to advance real military or defense industrial reform, in part owing to the entrenched recalcitrance of the top brass.[36] Meanwhile, the military capabilities of all of Russia's potential great power rivals in Asia—China, India, Japan, and the United States—are increasing rapidly. Hence, Russia faces the prospect of continued relative decline in conventional military power both globally and in Asia. In short, even in simplistic neorealist terms that ignore economic interests and the requisites of entry into the global economy, Russia faces every incentive to avoid alienating any other great power—east, west, or south.

The second reality that limits the significance of Russia's shift toward Asia is that economic incentives pull consistently westward. The geographical center of Russia's economy is in the West. Eighty percent of Russians live in the European portion of their country. Trade is heavily weighted to the EU and North America. Meanwhile, the northeastern and, in all likelihood, the southeastern sections of Russia are currently overpopulated as a result of uneconomic "strategic investment" by Soviet authorities.[37] If Russia continues to reform its economy on market principles, much of the current industrial activity in the Far East will relocate or become unviable and the federal government will face ongoing pressure to minimize subsidies. The major economic activity that will remain profitable will be resource extraction—a much smaller employer than manufacturing. And the payrolls of oil, gas, and mineral concerns will decline as new investment and technology increase the productivity of those activities. As one noted Russian expert summed it up, "Eastern Siberia and the Far East have become the weakest link in Russia's economic security."[38]

Third, Russia's trade portfolio in Asia is particularly distorted. Trade is a larger share of Russia's GDP (over 45 percent) than for all other major Asian powers, and over 55 percent of Russian exports are energy and metals.[39] Hence, Russian officials will remain preoccupied with developing markets for these products in Asia. Moreover, Asia remains the chief market for Russia's high-value-added and technology exports, with China and India by far the principal buyers. Military hardware and nuclear and space technology—both declining assets inherited from the Soviet Union—loom large in Russia's small share of such exports. Revenues from arms sales have varied between 1.2 and 4 percent of total exports since the mid-1990s, and from nuclear materials and technology about half that figure.[40] Despite their small share in Russia's trade portfolio, in both cases there is relatively weak domestic demand for either of these industries. With abundant hydrocarbon-fuelled electrical generation capacity and declining demand compared to Soviet times, the domestic market for the Ministry of Atomic Energy (Minatom) has dried up. Similarly, even with recently increased defense spending, the Russian military's procurement needs are minuscule compared to the capacity of the military industry Russia inherited from the Soviet Union. Foreign military sales, therefore, are essential to keeping these two domestic industries alive, and the major markets are in Asia—China and India together accounted for nearly 70 percent of Russia's record arms exports in 2005.[41]

Fourth, Russian policy in Asia is driven by a common core of security interests that Moscow shares with the other regional powers, including the United States. While Moscow, Beijing, and (much less frequently) New Delhi periodically played up the anti-U.S. aspect of their nebulous "strategic triangle," each continued to maintain deeper and wider relations with Washington than with others, and none sought to engage in any costly balancing of the United States. All the key powers have defined their near- to medium-term core interests in complementary ways. It follows that Russia's interests require amicable relations with all, including the United States and Japan. Indeed, Moscow's sense of weakness fosters wariness of China's growing economic and diplomatic clout, and a general preference for balancing Russian relationships in the region.

Conclusion

Russia has experienced the greatest peacetime decline of any major power in history. But the path from material shift to policy change is hardly direct or smooth. Ideas and domestic politics are crucial intervening variables. Indeed, strategic ideas played an important role in smoothing Russia's adjustment to decline. They help to explain how Russia came to terms with its own decline remarkably smoothly despite the fact that its national experience after 1989 fitted the parameters scholars associate with bellicosity and revisionism. Paradoxically, by systematically exaggerating Moscow's real power and prospects and thus enabling policymakers to delay and obfuscate the psychological and domestic political costs of retrenchment, a series of three distinct sets of ideas helped Russia avoid the potential costs and risks of a forceful reaction to decline. The theories linking decline and war are not shown to be outright wrong in this instance, for the causal effects they predict did occur. Rather, the literature can be accused of insufficient attention to the likelihood that strategic actors will behave in ways that thwart theoretical expectations. After all, both the domestic political and the psychological theories explicitly treat bellicose responses to decline as suboptimal from a rational perspective. It is little wonder that leaders seek ways of staying in power while avoiding such costly foreign policies.

A notable byproduct of Russia's solution to the anguish of decline is perennial rhetorical inflation concerning the country's geopolitical orientation and grand strategy. Substantively subtle shifts in focus between West and East are trumpeted as tectonic shifts of global significance. Closer analysis reveals a policy that is sensitive to the limits of Russian power and faces few incentives for risky revisionism. It follows that if Asia is "ripe for rivalry," Russia knows that it is presently too poor and weak to take part.[42] The implication is that Russia's diplomacy in Asia will continue along pragmatic lines, governed in the near to medium term mainly by the mix of "new security issues," economic incentives, and modernization imperatives that have come to the fore in the last half decade.

Notes

1. See Gideon Rose, "Neoclassical Realism and Theories of Foreign Policy," *World Politics* 51, no. 1 (1998): 144–72.

2. For an excellent, concise analysis, see Robert S. Ross, "The Geography of the Peace: East Asia in the Twenty-first Century," *International Security* 23, no. 4 (Spring 1999): 81–118.

3. See Jack S. Levy, "Declining Power and the Preventive Motivation for War," *World Politics* 40, no. 1 (1987): 82–107.

4. Exemplars of this literature are Jack L. Snyder, *Myths of Empire: Domestic Politics and International Ambition* (Ithaca, N.Y.: Cornell University Press, 1991); Charles A. Kupchan, *The Vulnerability of Empire* (Ithaca, N.Y.: Cornell University Press, 1994).

5. Henri Tajfel and John C. Turner, "An Integrative Theory of Intergroup Conflict," in *The Social Psychology of Intergroup Relations,* ed. William G. Austin and Stephen Worchel (Monterey, Calif.: Brooks/Cole, 1979).

6. Jonathan Mercer, "Anarchy and Identity," *International Organization* 49, no. 2 (1995): 229–52; Deborah Welch Larson and Alexei Shevchenko, "Shortcut to Greatness: The New Thinking and the Revolution in Soviet Foreign Policy," *International Organization* 57, no. 1 (2003): 77–109.

7. On the microfoundations of the phenomenon in general, see Barry O'Neill, *Honor, Symbols, and War* (Ann Arbor: University of Michigan Press, 1999); for the Russian case, William C. Wohlforth, "Honor as Interest in Russian Decisions for War, 1600–1995," in *Honor among Nations: Intangible Interests and Foreign Policy,* ed. Elliot Abram (Washington, D.C.: Ethics and Public Policy Center, 1998).

8. Paul Kennedy, *The Rise and Fall of the Great Powers* (New York: Random House, 1987), 514.

9. The two best-known examples are Matthew Evangelista, *Unarmed Forces: The Transnational Movement to End the Cold War* (Ithaca, N.Y.: Cornell University Press, 1999); and Archie Brown, *The Gorbachev Factor* (New York: Oxford University Press, 1996).

10. See William Curtis Wohlforth, *The Elusive Balance: Power and Perceptions during the Cold War* (Ithaca, N.Y.: Cornell University Press, 1993); Jacques Lévesque, *The Enigma of 1989: The USSR and the Liberation of Eastern Europe* (Berkeley: University of California Press, 1997); and, for the version grounded most explicitly in social psychology, Larson and Shevckenko, "Shortcut to Greatness."

11. Larson and Shevckenko, "Shortcut to Greatness," 78.

12. Jack L. Snyder, *From Voting to Violence: Democratization and Nationalist Conflict* (New York: Norton, 2000)

13. Amos Tversky and Daniel Kahneman, "Judgment under Uncertainty: Heuristics and Biases," *Science* 185 (1974): 1124–30; Robert Jervis, *Perception and Misperception in International Politics* (Princeton, N.J.: Princeton University Press, 1976).

14. For Kozyrev's views, see "Russia: A Chance for Survival," *Foreign Affairs* (Spring 1992): 1–16; interviews with *Nezavisimaia Gazeta,* April 1, 1992, A1 and A4 and *Izvestiia,* June 30, 1992, A3; Kozyrev, "Preobrazhenie ili kafkianskaia metamorfoza," *Nezavismiaia gazeta,* August 20, 1992: 1, 4. A good sampling of the distribution of views in the period is provided by the Foreign Ministry Conference on "A Transformed Russia in a New World," reported in *International Affairs* (Moscow), April–May 1992.

15. The Foreign Ministry of the Russian Federation published its revised foreign policy concept in December 1992, and submitted it to the Duma in March 1993. See "Foreign Policy Concept of the Russian Federation," Foreign Broadcast Information Service—Daily Report: USSR: 93–37, March 25, 1993, 1–20.

16. For more on this, see W. C. Wohlforth, "Heartland Dreams: Russian Geopolitics and Foreign Policy," in *Perspectives on the Russian State in Transition,* ed. Wolfgang F. Danspeckgruber (Princeton, N.J.: Liechtenstein Institute on Self-Determination, 2006).

17. S. Rogov, "Kontory Rossiiskoy geopolitikoi," *Nezavisimaia gazeta—stsenarii* 3 (1998), 5.

18. Indeed, even in their books, both Primakov and Ivanov are much more circumscribed than in many of their public presentations. Evgeny Primakov, *Gody v bolshoi politike* (Moscow: Kollektsiia Sovershenno sekretno, 1999); Igor S. Ivanov, *Novaia rossiiskaia diplomatiia: desiat let vneshnei politiki strany* (Moscow: Olma-Press, 2001).

19. Christopher Hill, "Russian Defense Spending," in United States Congress, Joint Economic Committee, *Russia's Uncertain Economic Future* (Washington, D.C.: Government Printing Office, 2002), 168.

20. Kevin P. O'Prey, "Arms Exports and Russia's Defense Industries: Issues for the U.S. Congress," in Joint Economic Committee, *Russia's Uncertain Economic Future.*

21. Local tensions over contested islands in the Ussuri River continued. See Oleg Zhunusov, "Spornye ostrova otob'yut u Kitaya s pomoshch'yu pontonov," *Izvestiya,* July 19, 2002, 2.

22. See, e.g., "Strategiia dlia Rossii IV," available on the website of the council on foreign and defense policy at www.svop.ru. A more detailed analysis of the strategic shift from which portions of this section are drawn is William C. Wohlforth, "Russia," in *Strategic Asia 2002–2003: Asian Aftershocks*, ed. Aaron L. Friedberg and Richard J. Ellings (Seattle, Wash.: National Bureau of Asian Research, 2003).

23. Drafts of the three key national security documents were made available at the website of the Security Council of the Russian Federation at www.scrf.gov.ru /Documents/Documents.htm.

24. Transcript of Putin's interview with the BBC at www.kremlin.ru, as reported on Johnson's Russia List, no. 7236, June 24, 2003.

25. See, for a good example, the interview with Igor Ivanov by Svetlana Babaeva reported in "'Igor' Ivanov: Glavnoa-stoby vneshnyaya politia ne privodila k raskolu vnutri strany," *Izvestiya*, July 10, 2002, 1.

26. For more on this, see W. C. Wohlforth and Kathleen Collins, "Central Asia: Defying 'Great Game' Expectations," in *Strategic Asia, 2003–2004: Fragility and Crisis*, ed. Richard Ellings and Aaron Friedberg, with Michael Wills (Seattle, Wash.: National Bureau of Asia Research, 2003).

27. As Peter Rutland notes, "Part of the problem is that the Chinese . . . reportedly were offering low-ball prices." "Russia's Economic Role in Asia: Toward Deeper Integration," in *Strategic Asia 2006–2007: Trade, Interdependence, and Security*, ed. Ashley J. Tellis and Michael Wills (Seattle, Wash.: NBR, 2006), 184.

28. Transcript of Putin's Kremlin press conference on June 20, 2003, at www .kremlin.ru.

29. Dmitry Safonov, "Sergey Ivanov Views Shanghai Cooperation Organization's Antiterror Mission," *Izvestiia*, May 15, 2002, FBIS-CHI-2002–516.

30. Alexei Zagorsky, "Three Years on the Path to Nowhere: The Hashimoto Initiative in Russian–Japanese Relations," *Pacific Affairs* 74, no. 1 (Spring 2001): 75–93.

31. Interfax/ITAR-TASS (Moscow), January 9, 2001; Roald Saveliev, "The New Russian Leadership's Foreign Policy and Russian-Korean Relations," *Far Eastern Affairs*, no. 2 (2001): 10–15.

32. Interfax, *Oil and Gas Report*, March 2–8, 2001.

33. EIA Report, "Russia: Oil and Natural Gas Pipelines," March 2002, www.eia.doe .gov.; and Mikhail Klasson, "Gazprom Breaks into Asia," *Moscow News*, July 17, 2002, 7.

34. Russia's official policy—which Putin reiterated emphatically at the G-8 summit in Evian—is that proliferation of weapons of mass destruction "is the main threat of the 21st century." Transcript of Putin's BBC interview on June 22, 2003, reprinted in Johnson's Russia List, no. 7236, June 24, 2003. See for an insightful discussion Gilbert Rozman, "The Geopolitics of the North Korean Nuclear Crisis," in *Strategic Asia, 2003–2004: Fragility and Crisis*, ed., Richard Ellings and Aaron Friedberg, with Michael Wills (Seattle, Wash.: National Bureau of Asia Research, 2003).

35. See Murray Feshbach, "The Demographic, Health and Environmental Situation in Russia," draft report presented at the Liechtenstein Institute on Self-Determination Conference "The Future of the Russia State," Triesenberg Liechtenstein, March 14–17, 2002; and Feshbach, "Russia's Demographic and Health Meltdown," testimony in United States Congress, Joint Economic Committee, *Russia's*

Uncertain Economic Future: Hearing before the Joint Economic Committee, Washington, D.C.: Government Printing Office, 2002.

36. See, especially, Dale R. Herspring, "Putin and Military Reform," in *Perspectives on the Russian State in Transition,* ed. Wolfgang F. Danspeckgruber (Princeton, N.J.: Liechtenstein Institute on Self-Determination, 2006); Walter Parchomenko, "The Russian Military in the Wake of the Kursk Tragedy," *Journal of Slavic Military Studies* 14, no. 4.

37. Fiona Hill and Clifford Gaddy, *The Siberian Curse: How Communist Planners Left Russia out in the Cold* (Washington, D.C.: Brookings Institution Press, 2003); Vladimir Kontorovich, "Economic Crisis in the Russian Far East: Overdevelopment of Colonial Exploitation?" *Post-Soviet Geography and Economics* 42, no. 6 (2001): 391–415; Allen C. Lynch, "The Roots of Russia's Economic Dilemmas: Liberal Economics and Illiberal Geography," *Europe-Asia Studies* 54, no. 1 (January 2002): 31–49.

38. Vilia Gel'bras, "Velikoderzhavnyi i voenno-promyshlennyi kompleksy," *Expert,* June 11, 2001, 29.

39. Data from the National Bureau of Asian Research's "Strategic Asia" database at http://strategicasia.nbr.org/Data/CView/.

40. Calculated from statistics presented in Celeste A. Wallander, "Russia's Interest in Trading with the 'Axis of Evil,'" testimony in House Committee on International Relations, *Russia's Policies toward the Axis of Evil: Money and Geopolitics in Iraq and Iran: Hearing before the House Committee on International Relations,* February 26, 2003.

41. Data from the Stockholm Peace Research Institute's "SPRI Arms Transfers" database at http://armstrade.sipri.org/.

42. Aaron L. Friedberg, "Ripe for Rivalry: Prospects for Peace in a Multipolar Asia," *International Security* 8, no. 3 (Winter 1993–1994): 5–33.

References

Brown, Archie. *The Gorbachev Factor.* New York: Oxford University Press, 1996.

Council on Foreign and Defense Policy. "Strategiia dlia Rossii IV." www.svop.ru.

Evangelista, Matthew. *Unarmed Forces: The Transnational Movement to End the Cold War.* Ithaca, N.Y.: Cornell University Press, 1999.

Feshbach, Murray. "The Demographic, Health and Environmental Situation in Russia." Draft report presented at the Liechtenstein Institute on Self-Determination Conference, "The Future of the Russia State," Triesenberg Liechtenstein, March 14–17, 2002.

Friedberg, Aaron L. "Ripe for Rivalry: Prospects for Peace in a Multipolar Asia." *International Security* 18, no. 3 (1993–1994): 5–33.

Gel'bras, Vilia. "Velikoderzhavnyi i voenno-promyshlennyi kompleksy." *Expert,* June 11, 2001.

Herspring, Dale R. "Putin and Military Reform." In *Perspectives on the Russian State in Transition,* edited by Wolfgang F. Danspeckgruber. Princeton, N.J.: Liechtenstein Institute on Self-Determination, 2006.

Hill, Christopher. "Russian Defense Spending." In *Russia's Uncertain Economic Future,* United States Congress, Joint Economic Committee. Washington, D.C.: Government Printing Office, 2002.

Hill, Fiona, and Clifford Gaddy. *The Siberian Curse: How Communist Planners Left Russia out in the Cold.* Washington, D.C.: Brookings Institution Press, 2003.

Ivanov, Igor. "'Igor Ivanov': Glavnoa-stoby vneshnyaya politia ne privodila k raskolu vnutri strany: Interview with Igor Ivanov." By Svetlana Babaeva. *Izvestiya,* July 10, 2002.

Ivanov, Igor S. *Novaia rossiiskaia diplomatiia: desiat let vneshnei politiki strany.* Moscow: Olma-Press, 2001.

Kennedy, Paul. *The Rise and Fall of the Great Powers.* New York: Random House, 1987.

Klasson, Mikhail. "Gazprom Breaks into Asia." *Moscow News,* July 17, 2002.

Kontorovich, Vladimir. "Economic Crisis in the Russian Far East: Overdevelopment of Colonial Exploitation?" *Post-Soviet Geography and Economics* 42, no. 6 (2001): 391–415.

Kupchan, Charles A. *The Vulnerability of Empire.* Ithaca, N.Y.: Cornell University Press, 1994.

Larson, Deborah Welch, and Alexei Shevchenko. "Shortcut to Greatness: The New Thinking and the Revolution in Soviet Foreign Policy." *International Organization* 57, no. 1 (2003): 77–109.

Lévesque, Jacques. *The Enigma of 1989: The USSR and the Liberation of Eastern Europe.* Berkeley: University of California Press, 1997.

Levy, Jack S. "Declining Power and the Preventive Motivation for War." *World Politics* 40, no. 1 (1987): 82–107.

Lynch, Allen C. "The Roots of Russia's Economic Dilemmas: Liberal Economics and Illiberal Geography." *Europe-Asia Studies* 54, no. 1 (January 2002): 31–49.

Mercer, Jonathan. "Anarchy and Identity." *International Organization* 49, no. 2 (1995): 229–52.

Nezavisimaia Gazeta. "Russia: A Chance for Survival: Interview with *Nezavisimaia Gazeta.*" By A. Kozyrev. *Foreign Affairs* (Spring 1992): 1–16.

O'Neill, Barry. *Honor, Symbols, and War.* Ann Arbor: University of Michigan Press, 1999.

O'Prey, Kevin P. "Arms Exports and Russia's Defense Industries: Issues for the U.S. Congress." In Joint Economic Committee, *Russia's Uncertain Economic Future.*

Parchomenko, Walter. "The Russian Military in the Wake of the Kursk Tragedy." *Journal of Slavic Military Studies* 14, no. 4.

Primakov, Evgeny. *Gody v bolshoi politike.* Moscow: Kollektsiia Sovershenno sekretno, 1999.

Putin, Vladimir. "Kremlin press conference," June 20, 2003. www.kremlin.ru.

———. "Proliferation of Weapons of Mass Destruction Is the Main Threat of the 21st Century: Interview with Vladimir Putin." *Johnson's Russia List,* no. 7236, June 24, 2003.

Rogov, S. "Kontory Rossiiskoy geopolitikoi." *Nezavisimaia gazeta—stsenarii* 3 (1998): 5.

Rose, Gideon. "Neoclassical Realism and Theories of Foreign Policy." *World Politics* 51, no. 1 (1998): 144–72.

Ross, Robert S. "The Geography of the Peace: East Asia in the Twenty-first Century." *International Security* 23, no. 4 (1999): 81–118.

Rozman, Gilbert. "The Geopolitics of the North Korean Nuclear Crisis." In *Strategic Asia: 2003–2004: Fragility and Crisis,* edited by Richard Ellings and Aaron Friedberg, with Michael Wills. Seattle, Wash.: National Bureau of Asia Research, 2003.

"Russia: Oil and Natural Gas Pipelines." EIA Report, March 2002. www.eia.doe.gov.

Russian Federation Foreign Ministry. "Foreign Policy Concept of the Russian Federation." Foreign Broadcast Information Service—Daily Report: USSR: 93--37, March 25, 1993.

Rutland, Peter. "Russia's Economic Role in Asia: Toward Deeper Integration." In *Strategic Asia 2006–2007: Trade, Interdependence, and Security,* edited by Ashley J. Tellis and Michael Wills, 184. Seattle, Wash.: NBR, 2006.

Safonov, Dmitry. "Sergey Ivanov Views Shanghai Cooperation Organization's Antiterror Mission." *Izvestiia,* May 15, 2002, FBIS-CHI-2002–516.

Saveliev, Roald. "The New Russian Leadership's Foreign Policy and Russian-Korean Relations." *Far Eastern Affairs,* no. 2 (2001): 10–15.

Security Council of the Russian Federation. www.scrf.gov.ru/Documents/Documents. html.

Snyder, Jack L. *From Voting to Violence: Democratization and Nationalist Conflict.* 1st ed. New York: Norton, 2000.

———. *Myths of Empire: Domestic Politics and International Ambition.* Ithaca, N.Y.: Cornell University Press, 1991.

Tajfel, Henri, and John C. Turner. "An Integrative Theory of Intergroup Conflict." In *The Social Psychology of Intergroup Relations,* edited by William G. Austin and Stephen Worchel. Monterey, Calif.: Brooks/Cole, 1979.

Tversky, Amos, and Daniel Kahneman. "Judgment under Uncertainty: Heuristics and Biases." *Science* 185 (1974): 1124–30.

United States Congress. Joint Economic Committee. *Russia's Demographic and Health Meltdown.* Washington, D.C.: Government Printing Office, 2002.

Wallander, Celeste A. "Russia's Interest in Trading with the 'Axis of Evil.'" *Russia's Policies toward the Axis of Evil: Money and Geopolitics in Iraq and Iran: Hearing before the House Committee on International Relations.* February 26, 2003.

Wohlforth, W. C., and Kathleen Collins. "Central Asia: Defying 'Great Game Expectations.'" In *Strategic Asia, 2003–2004: Fragility and Crisis,* edited by Richard Ellings and Aaron Friedberg, with Michael Wills. Seattle, Wash.: National Bureau of Asia Research, 2003.

Wohlforth, William C. "Heartland Dreams: Russian Geopolitics and Foreign Policy." In *Perspectives on the Russian State in Transition,* edited by Wolfgang F. Danspeckgruber. Princeton, N.J.: Liechtenstein Institute on Self-Determination, 2006.

———. "Honor as Interest in Russian Decisions for War, 1600–1995." In *Honor among Nations: Intangible Interests and Foreign Policy,* edited by Elliot Abram. Washington, D.C.: Ethics and Public Policy Center, 1998.

———. "Russia." In *Strategic Asia 2002–2003: Asian Aftershocks,* edited by Aaron L. Friedberg and Richard J. Ellings. Seattle, Wash.: National Bureau of Asian Research, 2003.

Wohlforth, William Curtis. *The Elusive Balance: Power and Perceptions during the Cold War.* Ithaca, N.Y.: Cornell University Press, 1993.

Zagorsky, Alexei. "Three Years on the Path to Nowhere: The Hashimoto Initiative in Russian–Japanese Relations." *Pacific Affairs* 74, no. 1 (Spring 2001): 75–93.

Zhunusov, Oleg. "Spornye ostrova otob'yut u Kitaya s pomoshch'yu pontonov." *Izvestiya,* July 19, 2002.

5

Korea as a Middle Power in the Northeast Asian Security Environment

Woosang Kim

FOR THE PAST THREE DECADES in Northeast Asia, we have witnessed dynamic changes in power distribution, mainly due to uneven growth rates among such regional actors as China, Taiwan, South Korea, North Korea, Russia, and Japan. Most of all, China's rapid economic growth and its increased political capacity have signaled the possible future of the Northeast Asian political system.

In recent decades South Korea has also been very successful economically and politically. With its rapid economic growth the Republic of Korea (ROK) has recently obtained the membership in the Organization for Economic Cooperation and Development (OECD). Although South Korea has suffered the so-called IMF (International Monetary Fund) financial crisis in the late 1990s, it has recovered from the foreign reserve crisis and its current gross domestic product (GDP) per capita is approximately $20,000. In the past two decades South Korea has upgraded its visibility and diplomatic status through a series of events. For example, Korea has successfully hosted two worldwide sports festivals—the Summer Olympics in 1988 and the World Cup Soccer tournament in 2002. The former foreign minister Ban Ki Moon has been elected as the next secretary general of the United Nations. As one of the leading middle powers, South Korea is also leading the discussions on the issues of comprehensive and human security with such other countries as Canada, Australia, and Japan.

However, the Korean Peninsula is probably the most potentially explosive area in Northeast Asia. Together with the Taiwan Strait, the Korean Peninsula is the very place where American and Chinese strategic interests collide with each other. The Korean Peninsula has been the historical demarcation between maritime power and continental power.[1] Again in the new millennium, the rivalry between the continental power China and the maritime power America seems to be the most important determinant in molding the future Northeast Asian regional system.

Historically, surrounded by major powers, Korea has almost always been a victim of the conflict of interests among Japan, China, Russia, and the United States. In the twenty-first century, however, Korea may be able to play a constructive role of maintaining peace and prosperity in Northeast Asia. In this chapter, I argue that Korea is not a great power but a middle power and has its pivotal partnership role as the middle power in the local systemic affairs.

In this study, I utilize the power transition theoretical framework mainly for two reasons. First, the power transition theory captures very well the dynamic changes of power distribution in the international system, identifies the behavior of the declining dominant power and the rapidly growing power, and explains the instability of the system caused by a power transition situation. Second, the power transition theory differentiates a middle power from a great power and a small power and discusses the role of the middle power. In this research, I also investigate the future scenarios of Northeast Asian regional security, suggest the security strategy that the middle power Korea should follow, and provide the raison d'etre of the Korea-U.S. alliance in the twenty-first century.

A Middle Power in the Power Transition Theoretical Framework

Power Transition Theory

A. F. K. Organski has challenged the balance of power theory's main assumption that the strength of each nation is relatively constant unless it wins a war or makes new alliances. According to him, internal changes are constantly occurring within modern nation-states, and many of these changes have great significance in terms of national capabilities. Industrialization and political and social modernization are particularly important in this respect. The great shifts in power through internal development of nation-states cause change in the distribution of power in the system, and that change, most of the time, introduces a new type of security environment in the system.[2]

In the power transition theoretical framework, the differential rates of growth among great powers in the system provide a chance for the rapidly challenging power to catch up with the declining dominant power. This more or less equally distributed power condition between the two sides, usually witnessed during the power transition period, influences the likelihood of conflict between the dominant power and the challenger.

Together with the equal distribution of power between the two contenders in the system, the challenging power's level of dissatisfaction is another crucial factor. According to Organski, the dominant power creates and maintains the international status quo. But there are always some members of the international system that are not satisfied with the existing international order. These states are dissatisfied states, and their dissatisfaction makes them desire to alter the status quo. So long as the dominant power remains preponderant it can preserve the international status quo. But when a dominant power declines relative to a dissatisfied great power so that the dissatisfied challenger roughly equates its power with that of the declining dominant power, the status quo may no longer be preserved. Power transition theory thus suggests that, during a power transition between the rising challenger and the declining dominant power, if the challenger is more or less satisfied with the existing systemic order, war is less likely. But, if the challenger is dissatisfied, then conflict between the rising challenger and the declining dominant power is highly likely.[3]

Woosang Kim has introduced the alliance factor in the original power transition framework. While Organski and Jacek Kugler emphasize solely internal development as the main source of increase in power, Kim suggests the importance of the alliance relationship in Organski's power transition thesis. In fact, alliances as well as internally derived capabilities provide power. These internally and externally derived capabilities complicate the question of judging power transitions. Because declining powers are likely to form alliances to bolster their capabilities, actual transitions may occur later than when the challenger passes the dominant state in internal capabilities. Which allies are chosen is critical in determining whether or not a war expands. To understand stability and conflict in the system, therefore, we need to understand not only the dynamics of relative power over time, but also alliances and the interests that drive nations into conflict.[4]

Douglas Lemke has made another important contribution to the power transition framework. With his multiple-hierarchy model, Lemke has applied the power transition framework to the regional systemic context. He suggests that there are many regional hierarchical international systems and that those systems operate much like the overall international system. In each regional hierarchical system, there are a regional dominant power and regional major powers and minor powers. Here, the regional dominant power may be the same as the dominant power in the international order. He notes that a local status quo concerns issues related to local interests that are omitted from the international status quo. Such interests include access to strategic territory or transit routes, important cultural or religious sites, or the ability to exploit natural resources.[5]

Many recent empirical studies on the causes of conflict have supported the power transition views of the relationship between the distribution of power, alliance, dissatisfaction, and the outbreak of war.[6] In particular, Kim's and Lemke's recent empirical works have shown that the power transition framework can be applied to the regional systemic context.[7]

South Korea as a Middle Power

In Organski's power transition framework, a dominant power is at the apex of the international hierarchical order. Just below the apex of the international pyramid are great powers. The difference between the dominant power and the great powers is to be found, not only in their different national capabilities, but also in the differential benefits they receive from the international order. Great powers receive substantial benefits from the international order, although they receive fewer benefits than the dominant power. Because great powers are so important, the dominant power requires the help of at least some of the great powers to easily maintain the status quo. So, some of the great powers are allied with the dominant power, sharing in the leadership of the dominant international order and in the benefits that flow from it. Of course, there may be dissatisfied great powers that do not feel that they are properly treated by the dominant power.

Below great powers in the international pyramid, there are middle powers. Many of them have accepted the existing international order and found a place in it that assures them certain benefits. Those middle powers are most likely to be satisfied with the status quo, for their support is also important in keeping the international status quo. However, there are other middle powers that have risen to that status recently and are dissatisfied with the existing order since the order had been set up a long time before they rose to the middle power status. Those dissatisfied middle powers may want to side with the challenging great power and try to change the status quo. That kind of challenge by the dissatisfied group of a great power and a middle power poses a threat against the dominant power that wants to maintain the status quo.[8]

Although many studies have differentiated a great power from a small power, very few have discussed the definition of a middle power. In general, a great power with enough power projection capabilities has geographically general interests that lead it to be an active political and military player in the international system. On the other hand, a small power has limited geographical interests with its relative inability to influence political and military activities in the international system. Based on these definitions of a great power and a small power, both a middle power and a minor power in the power transition framework can be considered a small power. Both a middle power and a minor power, with their relatively limited power projection capabilities, are forced to focus only on local matters. But, as power transition theorists imply, a middle power is different from a minor power since it has considerable capabilities that can be mobilized for local affairs or occupies a geostrategic location in the regional system. With its capabilities or geostrategic location, a middle power can help the dominant power in maintaining the local status quo, or it can even pose a threat against the dominant power's leadership in the regional system by allying with a dissatisfied major power.[9] When a small power's support is required by the dominant power or at least helps the dominant power to successfully deal with the key local issues, then that small power can be considered a middle power. Unlike a minor power, which has little or no influence in local systemic affairs, a middle power can exert significant influence on regional systemic affairs.[10]

When a dominant power in a regional system anticipates a challenge from one of the dissatisfied major powers, a satisfied middle power's supporting role in maintaining the status quo increases. When the location of the middle power lies between two rival major powers, that middle power is considered a buffer state. In that case, the middle power's strategic value to both neighboring major powers as well as the dominant power may drastically increase.[11] Korea is contiguous to three major powers: China, Japan, and Russia. Historically, the Korean Peninsula has been geostrategically very important to such major powers as China, Japan, Russia, and the United States. So, those powers from time to time have competed with each other over their spheres of influence in the peninsula. The importance of the future Korea's role as a successful buffer state in the Northeast Asian security environment will no doubt increase further.

William Riker's minimum winning coalition thesis seems to suggest that Korea can play the role of pivotal partner in the region. In any coalition formation, the greater the necessity to include a player in a coalition in order to make it a winning one, the greater the player's pivotal power. Despite the player's relatively small resource base, the player is as valuable a member of a coalition as any other great power member and can rationally demand a payoff as big as any other great-power member might demand.[12] The Korean Peninsula is geopolitically and strategically very important for all of the neighboring states, as well as the United States. None of them will be willing to let any other state take control over the peninsula. Each of the great powers would want to maintain its sphere of influence in the Korean Peninsula. Therefore, Korea can play the role of the pivotal partner in Northeast Asia. Although Korea has limited resources and national capabilities compared to those of the neighboring great powers, Korea may be able to exert a disproportionate influence on alliance politics in Northeast Asia.

In the Northeast Asian security order, South Korea is a middle power that helps promote peace and stability in the region. The United States has been the balancer in the region, and for about five decades the Americans have successfully managed the regional stability through both the U.S.-Japan and the ROK-U.S. alliance partnerships. Although South Korea's role may not be so crucial in maintaining the international systemic order in general, its supporting role of maintaining the Northeast Asian regional status quo with its American partner is critical. Indeed, the power transition theory suggests that the dominant power that anticipates a threat from a dissatisfied challenger should maintain its preponderance in power over the potential challenger through alignment with other satisfied powers in the region. When the two Koreas are united through peaceful measures twenty to thirty years from now, a united Korea as a middle power in the international hierarchy can play an important supporting role in keeping the status quo in the regional security order. The buffer state Korea can play the role of a pivotal partner successfully as long as it keeps the right combination of its relative capability and foreign policy orientations.

Future Security Scenarios and the Middle Power Korea's Role

As with the power transition theoretical framework, alliance formation, as well as internal developments of major powers and middle powers in the region, is an important variable in understanding the future changes of the regional security structure. In forecasting the future regional security environment, individual actors' national interests, goals, preferences, and willingness to pursue their own national interests and preferences should be taken into account as well.

The China Factor

The current picture shows a uni-multipolar stability led by the United States. However, the velocity and magnitude of Chinese economic and military growth may lead to different situations. China is obviously the country to watch in terms of the differential rates of growth—the highest among the great powers in the system. One important question about China is its potential growth in national capabilities. Can China manage to maintain rapid growth rates for two to three decades and eventually catch up with the United States? A number of studies suggest that China may likely become the world's economic superpower and overtake the United States' position.[13] However, this view of China as a potential regional hegemon is not universally held. Others suggest that China's power is in fact still quite weak and is likely to remain so for many years to come.[14] Since the death of Deng Xiaoping in

February 1997, they contend, leadership unity in China increasingly depends upon the effective management of socioeconomic problems, in addition to the ethnic minority and unification issues, including Taiwan, Tibet, and Xinjiang. The increasing gap between economic development in the hinterland and the coastal areas, in tandem with growing regional disparities, defies any early or conclusive solution.

When considering the China factor, however, we should always estimate one national power relative to that of other powers. To speculate about China's potential to catch up with the United States in terms of national power, China's rates of growth must be estimated in connection with those of the United States. We should also keep in mind that perception and misperception really matter. That is, how the United States and China perceive their relative national powers is probably more important than their actual relative national capabilities. For example, one country may overestimate its own power, while the other may underestimate its competitor's power. Others also suggest that although China cannot be a peer competitor to the United States globally, China can pose a threat to the United States' interests in the region.[15]

China's level of dissatisfaction with the international and regional security order is another important factor that will influence regional stability. China has long maintained that its foreign policy is based on two main principles—the one-China principle and the five principles of peaceful coexistence. Even if the principle of one China has been honored by most of the countries in the world, China is not satisfied with recent changes in the relationships between Taiwan and other major powers in the region. China appears to believe that the United States, Russia, Japan, and South Korea have improved their unofficial ties with Taiwan, allowing the latter to garner greater international support at the expense of China. Such views illustrate China's continuing dissatisfaction with the existing regional order mainly set up by the United States.[16]

The United States' strengthening of its ties with Japan also helps contribute to China's dissatisfaction. China envisions a future in which it might be squeezed out by the United States and the American ally. Together with the Taiwan issue, the United States' leadership, or its active engagement in the region, may eventually be considered one of the most important factors contributing to China's dissatisfaction with the future regional security environment.

The America Factor

Another important factor determining the future Northeast Asian security environment is U.S. foreign policy toward East Asia. Two types of U.S. foreign policy can be identified: a policy of internationalism or engagement, and a policy of isolationism. Historically, the United States has pursued one or the other. Since the United States became the leading power in the postwar international system, it has pursued a policy of internationalism. However, we do not know for sure how long the United States will maintain this policy of active engagement in Northeast Asia, forward deployment of forces, and military alliances with the regional powers.[17]

In considering the America factor, a discussion of the U.S.-Japan alliance is necessary, because the U.S.-Japan alliance has been the primary factor contributing to economic prosperity and political stability in the region. If current trends continue, Japan will become a normal state sooner or later, and its economic and political role will expand in the region. It is a prevailing view, however, that Japan's security role will be restrained within the current framework of the U.S.-Japan alliance structure. That is, Japan's future role in regional security issues will be dependent on United States security policy toward the region.[18] The New Guidelines for U.S.-Japan security cooperation assume the dual functions of increasing Japan's military role in the region on the one hand and further binding it into the bilateral treaty on the other. Thus, in the short term, no dramatic change in the bilateral alliance is likely to take place.

In the long term, however, if a significant change of this partnership in the future occurs, the region's security environment would be drastically shaken. To begin with, the change would imply withdrawal of the U.S. presence. Then, the resurgence of Japan would be expected, and that would have to be balanced or deterred by China. It means the end of stability in Northeast Asia.[19] The U.S.-Japan alliance has functioned as a balancer between China, Japan, and the United States. Some suggest that the alliance has been a major tool for blocking China's rise as a regional hegemon and also for checking Japan's revival as a regional destabilizer.[20] For them, an erosion of the alliance would be detrimental to the security of the region and also become the cause of changes in the distribution of regional power.

There are other factors that might influence the future Northeast Asian security environment. The Russia factor may be one of them. However, Russia's future influence depends on its growth and the stabilization of its politico-economic situation. No matter how successful its processes of economic modernization and political stabilization are, however, Russia's potential influence on East Asian regional security issues may not substantially increase anytime soon.[21] As Robert Ross has pointed out, for example, the "inhospitable geography separating the Russian Far East from western Russia" would block it from devoting the necessary resources to become as influential an actor as China or the United States in the Northeast Asian security order in the near future.[22]

Future Regional Security Environments and Korea's Options

If the United States maintains its current "internationalist" foreign policy of active engagement in Northeast Asia through forward deployment of forces and military alliance with regional powers, there are two possible long-term scenarios, depending on the prospects for dissatisfied socialist China. The first, which would result if China fails to catch up with the United States in national capabilities, is a strengthening of stability based on the United States' leadership in the region. This kind of situation can be called the U.S.-led uni-multipolar security scenario. The second, if socialist China succeeds in catching up with the United States, is power equality between the United States, the declining status quo power, and China, the rising revisionist power. This type can be called the power transition scenario.

As long as the United States maintains its hegemonic status in the system through preponderance in power over other potential challengers as well as its policy of internationalism, the Northeast Asian regional system will be stable based on the United States' leadership. When, on the other hand, China perceives that it is successfully catching up with the United States, the power transition crisis may come about. When the United States anticipates that China's challenge is imminent, it will try to protect its sphere of influence in the region and maintain the existing security order, notwithstanding its relative power decline. Here, China may not directly challenge the United States, but its intention to unify with Taiwan by force may indirectly challenge the U.S.'s leadership in the region.

If the United States anticipates dissatisfied China's challenge, it may take a set of preventive measures. First of all, the United States may want to strengthen its existing military ties with both Japan and Korea and try to overcome China's challenge. The United States may even attempt to build a virtual triangular alliance with Korea, and Japan.[23] The United States may strengthen its ties with Taiwan and improve its relationship with India and other Southeast Asian countries as well. The United States would also strengthen its ties with the North Atlantic Treaty Organization (NATO), since NATO will play a crucial role in tying Russia down so as not to form an alliance with China. In this kind of situation in which the United States pursues the policy of containing China, a major conflict between the declining status quo power and rising revisionist power is highly likely. This power transition scenario suggests increased military and political roles for Japan and Korea, and an improved relationship between the United States and Taiwan.

In this scenario, the middle power Korea has two options. Remaining as a loyal ally in the U.S. camp would be an option for Korea, but it would endanger its security by turning the peninsula once again into a collision point between continental and maritime powers. As long as the two Koreas have been united by this time, another option is to ally with China. When a middle power shares a border with the threatening regional hegemon, the threatened middle power is very likely to bandwagon to the threatening neighboring hegemon to avoid conflict in its territory.[24] Unless the United States chooses a policy of isolationism and lets China become a regional hegemon, however, Korea will be a crucial partner for the United States in countering the Chinese challenge in the region. This argument holds for the case of Japan as well. That is, unless Japan decides to appease China, Japan has to face the Chinese threat. In that case, Japan will seriously need the military and political support of the buffer state, Korea. United Korea, with an army of more than one million and a population of more than eighty million, would be a pivotal middle-power partner for both the United States and Japan in maintaining the regional status quo.

In fact, Korea-U.S. alliance is the best option for the buffer state, Korea. A buffer state usually has three primary options: neutrality, bandwagoning or leaning to one side, and the third-power strategy. Historically, neither neutrality nor leaning to one side was always a satisfactory strategy for the buffer state. Neutrality is often made untenable by constant pressures from neighboring great powers. Bandwagoning has the danger of losing the buffer state's independence or at least a part of its territory. The third-power strategy, however, is often utilized by the buffer state. Since the third power is physically remote from the region, it may be less interested in dominating the buffer state and more concerned with blocking any of the regional major powers from expanding to be the regional hegemon. Allying with the United States must be Korea's third-power option. The United States is far away from the region and strong enough to mobilize its troops very quickly to the region. As long as the United States has vital national interests in the region, it can be Korea's third-power option.[25]

What if China becomes more satisfied and cooperative with the existing regional security order? Here, a satisfied and cooperative China may mean a fully democratic China that will not have any serious problem in merging democratic Taiwan into China. Or it may mean a China that will be less challenging to the existing regional order and be less provocative and more flexible in handling foreign affairs, that is, in carrying out its one-China principle. China, with a lower level of risk acceptance; with less dependence on armed force; and at the same time, with continued interests in the pursuit of economic prosperity, would be less threatening even when it is put under socialist leadership.

If a satisfied and cooperative China fails to catch up with the United States in national capabilities, regional stability will be at its highest under the

United States' leadership. In case a more or less satisfied China succeeds in catching up with the United States, the two great powers will be less likely to resort to arms to resolve the conflict of interests in the region. Instead of challenging the existing U.S.-led regional security order, China is likely to accept the status quo, and therefore the United States will allow China to share its regional leadership position without a struggle. In this kind of security structure, the transition of power between the declining leader country and the rising regional challenger will be peaceful.

The above security structures are based on the long-term perspective. In the short-term security environment, however, it is very clear that China will not have enough time to catch up with the United States in national power and is less likely to become satisfied and cooperative with the existing regional security order. Dissatisfied China will pursue economic reform and its one-China policy, while maintaining its current form of socialist free-market system. The United States will maintain its policy of active engagement. In the next five to ten years, North Korea will still pose a considerable threat to Northeast Asian stability with its continued efforts to develop weapons of mass destruction. Russia will still face political and economic vulnerabilities and uncertain international status. Japan will be more likely to accomplish the status of normal state, but will still be dependent upon the United States in security matters. Therefore, we can rather confidently forecast that the status quo will be maintained, and thus the future system in the short-term perspective will still be the United States–led uni-multipolar system.

Korea: A Middle-Power Ally

We have witnessed the rapid growth of China for the past two decades and are expecting that the trend will continue in the years to come. Therefore, the likelihood that the power transition scenario will materialize twenty to thirty years from now is not low. Although there is a possibility that by that time China will become a satisfied and responsible democratic power through domestic political modernization and external engagements with other democratic countries, the future is still uncertain.[26]

Under this uncertain future security environment, Korea can be a very important middle-power ally to the United States. First of all, surrounded by China, Japan, and Russia, unified Korea will be a buffer state. As long as the United States maintains the alliance ties with Korea, it may be very successful in preventing any of the neighboring major powers from expanding to be the regional challenger. Second, Americans may think that keeping the existing alliance ties with Japan is the best strategy for them in the region. However, maintaining alliance ties with Japan may become burdensome for the United States since those ties may pose a considerable threat to China and thus encourage it to be more dissatisfied with the regional security order as China becomes stronger. Strategically speaking, the middle power Korea can be a better partner for the U.S.'s regional ally. Third, because the Korean Peninsula is geostrategically so important, no single neighboring country is likely to give up its potential sphere of influence in the peninsula. But, so long as the United States keeps its ties with Korea, the United States can monopolize its sphere of influence in the Korean Peninsula. The Korean Peninsula is at the heart of the Northeast Asian market, and for the United States to keep its sphere of influence here means that the United States can promote free trade in the region. Finally, in the short term, the alliance ties with South Korea will be helpful in preventing the proliferation of weapons of mass destruction in the region. So, if the United States wants to be the major western Pacific power in the coming decades, it will be crucial for the United States to keep its sphere of influence in the Korean Peninsula. If the United States is eager to maintain the current U.S.-led uni-multipolar international system in the coming decades, it will be critical for the United States to maintain its military alliance not just with Japan but with Korea, either unified or not.

The ROK-U.S. alliance has been a classic type of the asymmetric, autonomy-security trade-off alliance in which the stronger great power provides security protection to the weaker-power partner in return for influence over the domestic or foreign policies of its weaker partner.[27] Indeed, for the last fifty years, the U.S. provision of extended deterrence in the Korean Peninsula has been successful.

However, the fifty-year-long Korea-U.S. alliance seems to be on shaky ground. As the capability relationship between the great-power ally and the weaker-power ally becomes less and less asymmetric, the weaker partner is likely to request adjustment of the existing alliance relationship. If the request is not met, the alliance relationship can become very unstable. When the weaker party becomes stronger, it may think that it is in less need of the strong party's support and come to value the existing alliance less. In addition, when perceptions of common threat among alliance partners are different, the change of power in a weaker partner may have a significant influence on the existing asymmetric alliance.[28]

Domestic politicization of the existing alliance relationship is also likely to deteriorate the alliance. First of all, demographic and generational changes in the society of the weaker partner could undermine its traditional alliance commitment. Second, an existing alliance may be jeopardized if influential elites decide that they can improve their internal positions by attacking the alliance itself. Third, when regime change or leadership change occurs and consequently, the basic nature, identity, or ideology of the regime changes, then the alliance is likely to be dissolved.[29]

Indeed, there is a perception gap on North Korea. The common perception that North Korea represented a serious security threat was the glue that bound the alliance together. But there is a growing difference over the North Korean threat perception. Many South Koreans tend to think that the possibility of war between the two Koreas has disappeared. There is also a difference over how to deal with the North Korean nuclear weapons crisis between the alliance partners. These changing perceptions of threat and the ensuing policy gap may deteriorate the existing ROK-U.S. alliance relationship.

Recently Korean society has experienced changes in its demographic and generational composition, especially in the leadership groups. Together with the advent of the Roh Moo-Hyun administration, the new generations in their thirties and forties, especially the so-called 386 generation, have become the key players in domestic political and foreign policy decision-making processes as well as in the opinion formulation processes. They are ideologically more progressive and liberal, and their values and objectives in relation to the alliance issue are very much different from those of the old-generation leaders who have vested interests in the status quo. In fact, widespread anti-American sentiment among the younger generations right before the 2002 presidential election made a significant impact on the election result. The existing alliance may be jeopardized if influential elite groups decide that they can improve their domestic political positions by criticizing the existing alliance relationship.

The fifty-year-long ROK-U.S. alliance has survived many changes in domestic and security environments. It seems to be very natural for the existing alliance relationship to be in a shaky condition after lasting for fifty years. The hegemonic power has its own role to play in strengthening the shaky alliance relationship. Americans could show their willingness to pay special attention to South Korean concerns about ongoing issues related to sporadic anti-American sentiment. Protests or demonstrations by Koreans against the U.S. alliance policy or its unilateral foreign policy may be the weaker partner's prerogative. Through the channels of protest and demonstration, Koreans can let Americans know what the growing differences are between the two sides and give the two governments chances to adjust and resolve the problems before they get out of control.[30] By showing its willingness to remedy problems and misunderstandings at the right moment, the United States can promote pro-American sentiments in Korea. If Americans correctly catch the Koreans' psychology and cultural understandings, they could find effective and easy measures to improve their relationship with South Korean people.

Some Koreans criticize U.S. unilateralism and worry about a potential U.S. preemptive strike against the North Korean regime. They tend to think that the ongoing U.S. force restructuring on the peninsula has something to do with the U.S. strategic plan for a preemptive strike against North Korea. Others are beginning to blame the unpopular Roh regime for the domestic politicization of Korea's precious alliance ties with the United States. They are disappointed with what they perceive as the incapable progressive Roh regime and thus are eager to change the situation by electing a more capable and conservative candidate as the new president in the 2007 presidential election.

A majority of the Koreans still believe that the ROK-U.S. alliance is crucial for peace and prosperity in the Korean Peninsula. Although during the current Roh administration there may be no hope for revitalizing the deteriorating ROK-U.S. alliance relationship, they believe that the newly elected government after the 2007 election will start to seriously tackle the unnecessary misunderstandings between the two allies. As a matter of fact, issuing a joint declaration or a set of guidelines between the ROK and the United States will be an option. In the guidelines such issues as how to readjust and strengthen the existing alliance with the changing environments and how to deal with the potential crisis situations around the Korean Peninsula, including the North Korean nuclear weapons problem, can be included. Since institutionalization of an alliance is supposed to be helpful in strengthening it,[31] a joint declaration or a set of guidelines will be a good idea for reviewing the fifty-year-old mutual defense treaty and for increasing the level of the institutionalization of the alliance.

Conclusion

Korea, either unified or not, is a small power. But a small power Korea is not a minor power but a middle power. Korea, surrounded by three major powers, is a buffer state. A small power Korea alone cannot pose a real threat against any neighboring major power. However, in a situation in which those three major powers—China, Japan, and Russia—compete with each other as rivals, a major power that successfully holds an alliance relationship with a middle power Korea will be in an advantageous position. Indeed, when a major power forms an alliance with Korea, a small power Korea may be perceived as a threatening force against any remaining major power.

A middle power Korea can also play a significant role of maintaining the status quo in local systemic affairs as long as it remains a satisfied power within the existing regional order set up by the dominant power, the United States. Indeed, Korea can be a reliable partner for the United States in preventing any major power from becoming a regional hegemonic challenger in the twenty-first century. The future is always uncertain. In case the power transition scenario is realized, Korea will be an indispensable partner to the United States in Northeast Asia.

When the mutual defense treaty between South Korea and the United States was signed in 1953, South Korea was a minor power. South Korea then became a middle power. As the relative capabilities of South Korea and the United States become less asymmetric, the weaker partner is likely to request transformation of the alliance ties into a more equal mechanism. As the North Korean threat perception gap between them increases, the existing ties are in danger of dissolution. During this uneasy period, one thing that the elites and decision-making groups in South Korea should not do is domestically politicize the shaky alliance relationship. As the hegemonic power, the United States also has its share of the role of strengthening the shaky alliance relationship.

With the existence of a North Korean threat perception gap, the ROK-U.S. alliance inevitably has to try to adjust to the new circumstances. The raison d'etre of the alliance for the twenty-first century should be based not only on common threats but also on common values and interests. The alliance is likely to persist when the allies share common values of democracy and the free-market system. Moreover, the alliance ties will be strengthened when the relationship is highly institutionalized. For that matter, a more effective management mechanism for the ROK-U.S. alliance is needed. In addition, a joint declaration or a guideline to rewrite the fifty-year-old mutual defense treaty needs to be seriously considered. Before it is too late, South Korea and the United States must make efforts to readjust and strengthen the existing alliance ties between them.

Notes

1. For example, in the late sixteenth century between Japan during the shogunate and China's Ming dynasty, in the late nineteenth century between imperial Japan and the Qing dynasty, and in 1950 between the United States and the People's Republic of China.

2. A. F. K. Organski, *World Politics* (New York: Alfred A. Knopf, 1958).

3. Organski, *World Politics*; Woosang Kim, "Alliance Transitions and Great Power War," *American Journal of Political Science* 35, no. 4 (November 1991): 833–50; Woosang Kim, "Power Transitions and Great Power War from Westphalia to Waterloo," *World Politics* 45, no. 1 (October 1992): 153–72.

4. Kim, "Power Transitions"; Kim, "Alliance Transitions"; Woosang Kim and James D. Morrow, "When Do Shifts in Power Lead to War?" *American Journal of Political Science* 36, no. 4 (November 1992): 896–922; Jonathan M. DiCicco and Jack Levy, "Power Shifts and Problem Shifts," *Journal of Conflict Resolution* 43 (1999): 675–704.

5. Douglas Lemke, *Regions of War and Peace* (Cambridge: Cambridge University Press, 2002); DiCicco and Levy, "Power Shifts."

6. A. F. K. Organski and Jacek Kugler, *The War Ledger* (Chicago: University of Chicago Press, 1980), chap. 1; Henk Houweling and Jan Siccama, "Power Transitions as a Cause of War," *Journal of Conflict Resolution* 32, no. 1 (1988): 87–102; Kim, "Power Transitions"; Kim, "Alliance Transitions"; Woosang Kim, "Power, Alliance, and Major Wars, 1816–1975," *Journal of Conflict Resolution* 33, no. 2 (June 1989): 255–73; Daniel S. Geller, "Capability Concentration, Power Transition, and War," *International Interaction* 17, no. 3 (1992): 269–84; Daniel S. Geller, "Power Differentials and War in Rival Dyads," *International Studies Quarterly* 37, no. 2 (1993): 173–93; Douglas Lemke and Suzanne Werner, "Power Parity, Commitment to Change, and War," *International Studies Quarterly* 40, no. 2 (1996): 235–60.

7. Woosang Kim, "Power Parity, Alliances, Dissatisfaction, and Wars in East Asia, 1860–1993," *Journal of Conflict Resolution* 46, no. 5 (October 2002): 654–71; Lemke, *Regions of War and Peace.*

8. Organski, *World Politics,* 365–69.

9. However, a middle power alone cannot pose a real threat against a major power, since it is a small power.

10. Martin Wight, *Power Politics* (London: Riyal Institute of International Affairs, 1946); Maria Papadakis and Harvey Starr, "Opportunity, Willingness, and Small States," in *New Directions in the Study of Foreign Policy,* eds., Charles Hermann, Charles Kegley, and James Rosenau (London: Harper Collins Academic, 1987); Robert Rothstein, *Alliances and Small Powers* (New York: Columbia University Press, 1968); Louis J. Cantori and Steven L. Spiegel, *The International Politics of Regions: A Comparative Approach* (Englewood Cliffs, N.J.: Prentice Hall, 1970); Lemke, *Regions of War and Peace;* Samuel P. Huntington. "The Lonely Superpower," *Foreign Affairs* 78, no. 2 (March–April 1999): 35–49.

11. Michael Partem, "The Buffer System in International Relations," *Journal of Conflict Resolution* 27, no. 1 (March 1983): 3–26.

12. William Riker, *The Theory of Political Coalitions* (New Haven, Conn.: Yale University Press, 1962).

13. John Naisbitt, *Megatrends in Asia* (London: Nicholas Brealey, 1995); Joseph Nye, "China's Re-emergence and the Future of the Asia-Pacific," *Survival* 39, no. 4 (1997): 65–80.

14. Gerald Segal, "Northeast Asia and the Containment of China," *International Security* 20, no. 4 (Spring 1996): 107–35; William Wohlforth, "The Stability of a Unipolar World," *International Security* 24, no. 1 (Summer 1999): 5–41; Avery Goldstein, "Great Expectations: Interpreting China's Arrival," *International Security* 22, no. 3 (Winter 1997): 36–73.

15. See Thomas J. Christensen, "Posing Problems without Catching Up," *International Security* 25, no. 4 (Spring 2001): 5–40.

16. David Shambaugh, "Containment or Engagement of China? Calculating Beijing's Responses," *International Security* 21, no. 2 (Fall 1996): 180–209.

17. Segal, "Northeast Asia"; Shambaugh, "Containment or Engagement." In addition to the policies of engagement and of isolationism, Robert Art adds a policy of selective engagement. Robert J. Art, "Geopolitics Updated: The Strategy of Selective Engagement," *International Security* 23, no. 3 (Winter 1998–1999): 79–113.

18. For Japan's dependence on the United States on the economic and security area, for example see Robert Ross, "The Geography of the Peace: East Asia in the Twenty-first Century," *International Security* 23, no. 4 (2002): 81–119.

19. Yoichi Funabashi, "Bridging Asia's Economics-Security Gap," *Survival* 38, no. 4 (1996): 101–17.

20. For example, Thomas Christensen sees the U.S. presence in Japan either as a "bottle cap" or as an "egg shell." See Thomas Christensen, "China, the U.S.-Japan Alliance, and the Security Dilemma in Northeast Asia," *International Security* 23, no. 4 (Spring 1999): 49–80.

21. Recently, Russia has been paying serious attention to the Korean Peninsula issue. The main interests of Russia in the Korean Peninsula must have something to do with the economic benefits that Russia can collect in case the Trans-Siberian Railroad is successfully connected to the Trans-Korean Railroad and the gas pipeline is built from Siberia through the Korean Peninsula to Japan.

22. Ross, "Geography of the Peace."

23. Ralph A. Cossa, ed., *U.S.–Korea–Japan Relations: Building toward a "Virtual" Alliance* (Washington, D.C.: CSIS, 1999).

24. Stephen M. Walt, *The Origins of Alliances* (Ithaca, N.Y.: Cornell University Press, 1987).

25. Partem, "Buffer System"; Woosang Kim, "Korea and the Northeast Asian Security System in the Twenty-first Century," in *U.S.–Korea–Japan Relations: Building toward a "Virtual" Alliance,* ed. Ralph A. Cossa (Washington, D.C.: CSIS, 1999).

26. Constructivists may think that such possibility is very high. But again the problem is the uncertain future. No one constructivist can confidently predict that the future Northeast Asian regional system will be based on the Kantian culture in which all major actors are friends rather than foes and rivals. Alexander Wendt, *Social Theory of International Politics* (Cambridge: Cambridge University Press, 1999); Dale Copeland, "The Constructivist Challenge to Structural Realism," *International Security* 25, no. 2 (Fall 2000): 51–87.

27. James D. Morrow, "Alliances and Asymmetry: An Alternative to the Capability Aggregation Model of Alliances," *American Journal of Political Science* 35, no. 4 (1991): 904–33.

28. Stephen M. Walt, "Why Alliances Endure or Collapse," *Survival* 39, no. 1 (Spring 1997): 156–79.

29. Walt, *Origins of Alliances.*

30. As a matter of fact, in the 1970s and 1980s both Japanese and German societies experienced anti-American protests and demonstrations.

31. Walt, *Origins of Alliances.*

References

Art, Robert J. "Geopolitics Updated: The Strategy of Selective Engagement." *International Security* 23, no. 3 (Spring 1998–1999): 79–113.

Cantori, Louis J., and Steven L. Spiegel. *The International Politics of Regions: A Comparative Approach.* Englewood Cliffs, N.J.: Prentice Hall, 1970.

Christensen, Thomas. "China, the U.S.-Japan Alliance, and the Security Dilemma in Northeast Asia." *International Security* 23, no. 4 (Spring 1999): 49–80.

Christensen, Thomas J. "Posing Problems without Catching Up." *International Security* 25, no. 4 (Spring 2001): 5–40.

Copeland, Dale. "The Constructivist Challenge to Structural Realism." *International Security* 25, no. 2 (Fall 2000): 51–87.

Cossa, Ralph A., ed. *U.S.–Korea–Japan Relations: Building toward a "Virtual" Alliance.* Washington, D.C.: CSIS, 1999.

DiCicco, Jonathan M., and Jack Levy. "Power Shifts and Problem Shifts." *Journal of Conflict Resolution* 43 (1999): 675–704.

Funabashi, Yoichi. "Bridging Asia's Economics-Security Gap." *Survival* 38, no. 4 (1996): 101–17.

Geller, Daniel S. "Capability Concentration, Power Transition, and War." *International Interaction* 17, no. 3 (1992): 269–84.

———. "Power Differentials and War in Rival Dyads." *International Studies Quarterly* 37, no. 2 (1993): 173–93.

Goldstein, Avery. "Great Expectations: Interpreting China's Arrival." *International Security* 22, no. 3 (Winter 1997): 36–73.

Houweling, Henk, and Jan Siccama. "Power Transitions as a Cause of War." *Journal of Conflict Resolution* 32, no. 1 (1988): 87–102.

Huntington, Samuel P. "The Lonely Superpower." *Foreign Affairs* 78, no. 2 (March–April 1999): 35–49.

Kim, Woosang. "Alliance Transitions and Great Power War." *American Journal of Political Science* 35, no. 4 (November 1991): 833–50.

———. "Korea and the Northeast Asian Security System in the Twenty-first Century." In *U.S.–Korea–Japan Relations: Building toward a "Virtual" Alliance,* edited by Ralph A. Cossa. Washington, D.C.: CSIS, 1999.

———. "Power, Alliance, and Major Wars, 1816–1975." *Journal of Conflict Resolution* 33, no. 2 (June 1989): 255–73.

———. "Power Parity, Alliances, Dissatisfaction, and Wars in East Asia, 1860–1993." *Journal of Conflict Resolution* 46, no. 5 (October 2002): 654–71.

———. "Power Transitions and Great Power War from Westphalia to Waterloo." *World Politics* 45, no. 1 (October 1992): 153–72.

Kim, Woosang, and James D. Morrow. "When Do Shifts in Power Lead to War?" *American Journal of Political Science* 36, no. 4 (November 1992): 896–922.

Lemke, Douglas, and Suzanne Werner. "Power Parity, Commitment to Change, and War." *International Studies Quarterly* 40, no. 2 (1996): 235–60.

Lemke, Douglas. *Regions of War and Peace.* Cambridge: Cambridge University Press, 2002.

Morrow, James D. "Alliances and Asymmetry: An Alternative to the Capability Aggregation Model of Alliances." *American Journal of Political Science* 35, no. 4 (1991): 904–33.

Naisbitt, John. *Megatrends in Asia.* London: Nicholas Brealey, 1995.

Nye, Joseph. "China's Re-emergence and the Future of the Asia-Pacific." *Survival* 39, no. 4 (1997): 65–80.

Organski, A. F. K. *World Politics.* New York: Alfred A. Knopf, 1958.

Organski, A. F. K., and Jacek Kugler. *The War Ledger.* Chicago: University of Chicago Press, 1980.

Partem, Michael. "The Buffer System in International Relations." *Journal of Conflict Resolution* 27, no. 1 (March 1983): 3–26.

Papadakis, Maria, and Harvey Starr. "Opportunity, Willingness, and Small States." In *New Directions in the Study of Foreign Policy,* edited by Charles Hermann, Charles Kegley, and James Rosenau. London: Harper Collins Academic, 1987.

Riker, William. *The Theory of Political Coalitions.* New Haven, Conn.: Yale University Press, 1962.

Ross, Robert. "The Geography of the Peace: East Asia in the Twenty-first Century." *International Security* 23, no. 4 (2002): 81–119.

Rothstein, Robert. *Alliances and Small Powers.* New York: Columbia University Press, 1968.

Segal, Gerald. "Northeast Asia and the Containment of China." *International Security* 20, no. 4 (Spring 1996): 107–35.

Shambaugh, David. "Containment or Engagement of China? Calculating Beijing's Responses." *International Security* 21, no. 2 (Fall 1996): 180–209.

Walt, Stephen M. "Why Alliances Endure or Collapse." *Survival* 39, no. 1 (Spring 1997): 156–79.

———. *The Origins of Alliances.* Ithaca, N.Y.: Cornell University Press, 1987.

Wendt, Alexander. *Social Theory of International Politics.* Cambridge: Cambridge University Press, 1999.

Wight, Martin. *Power Politics.* London: Riyal Institute of International Affairs, 1946.

Wohlforth, William. "The Stability of a Unipolar World." *International Security* 24, no. 1 (Summer 1999): 5–41.

6

North Korea
A Perpetual Rogue State?

Yongho Kim

H OW TO RESOLVE NORTH KOREA's nuclear issue has been a hot potato
since the early 1990s. The Agreed Framework in 1994, the four-party
talks proposed in 1996, and the current six-party talks failed to generate an
undisputed conclusion of the debate. Right after the inauguration of George
W. Bush in 2001, his administration put the issue on the table as it repeatedly labeled North Korea a rogue state, one of the axis of evil, and an outlaw
regime. The acknowledgment of Pyongyang's first deputy foreign minister,
Kang Sok-joo, of the clandestine nuclear development project to a visiting
U.S. assistant secretary of state, James Kelly, in October 2002, ignited a new
series of debates on the eve of the Iraq War. The stalemate continues between
U.S. calls for complete, verifiable, irreversible dismantlement (CVID) and
North Korea's call for simultaneous economic benefits in return for suspension of nuclear development. In October 2006, North Korea opened another
page through its conduct of a nuclear test.

This chapter explores the question of whether North Korea will remain
a perpetual rogue state by examining its provocative and coercive foreign
policy through an eclectic approach. This chapter starts with a reorientation
of our perception for understanding the logic behind North Korea's rogue
behaviors. In this, the chapter scrutinizes the North Korean version of the
rationality of playing rogue by indicating that epistemological biases have
been involved in analyzing North Korea's provocative behavior. Subsequently,
the chapter outlines circumstantial variants on both international and
domestic levels, and traces why North Korea has chosen to play rogue under
certain circumstances.

On this, I argue that North Korea's official ruling ideology, *Juche* or self-reliance, and domestic politics revolving around leadership succession have affected Pyongyang's perception of its situation and its decision to play rogue. If one understands the unique logic and rationale behind its rogue behavior, and if one can successfully interpret it as a dependent variable, the chapter concludes, North Korea would be manageable by controlling independent variables.

Definition of a Rogue State: Is North Korea a Rogue State?

By definition, the word "rogue" contains negative connotations; it refers to "a dishonest, unprincipled person," "a rascal; scoundrel," and "one who is of a mischievous disposition." As a verb, it means "to cheat," "to destroy as biological rogues," or "to live or act like a rogue."[1] To define "a rogue state" requires a merging of these negative meanings with malicious intentions and, at the same time, possession of the technology to produce weapons of mass destruction and ballistic missiles, as U.S. president George W. Bush indicated.[2]

So far, the most "authoritative" definition of a rogue state can be found in the National Security Strategy of the United States, published by the National Security Council in September 2002.

> In the 1990s we witnessed the emergence of a small number of rogue states that, while different in important ways, share a number of attributes. These states:
>
> · brutalize their own people and squander their national resources for the personal gain of the rulers;
> · display no regard for international law, threaten their neighbors, and callously violate international treaties to which they are party;
> · are determined to acquire weapons of mass destruction, along with other advanced military technology, to be used as threats or offensively to achieve the aggressive designs of these regimes;
> · sponsor terrorism around the globe; and
> · reject basic human values and hate the United States and everything for which it stands.[3]

Then, is North Korea eligible for the label of a rogue state? The answer is, of course, yes! If we apply the above standards to North Korea, it surely deserves the "rogue" label. The North Korean people have suffered from starvation for many years since the 1990s, contrary to the steady increase in its defense budget. It also neglects to observe Nuclear Nonproliferation Treaty (NPT) regulations and declared withdrawal from the treaty twice in 1993 and again in 2003.

North Korea physically and verbally demonstrates its intention and capability to develop and deploy weapons of mass destruction in 2006. In addition, it is still on the list of terror-supporting countries due to its protection of Japanese ultraleftist terrorist groups of the Red Army who kidnapped the airliner Yodo in 1970. It still rejects and even condemns many calls for ameliorating its human rights situation and regards the United States as its principal enemy. The aim of this chapter is neither to argue that Pyongyang's label as a rogue state is inappropriate nor to defend North Korean positions. Rather, this chapter proposes to clarify the process by which external environments and domestic concerns trigger North Korea's rogue behaviors.

How to Analyze North Korean Foreign Policy?
Introducing an Alternative Approach

This section introduces an eclectic approach for analyzing North Korea's rogue behavior simultaneously from the inside and the outside.[4] Views from the inside and the outside are not incompatible; both are critical elements in analyzing North Korea's policies and behaviors.[5] However, an overemphasis either on international environment, domestic politics, or ideological elements would only produce misperception, misunderstanding, and misinterpretation.

When we label somebody as a "bad" person, our judgment is usually based on his or her overt behavior, and we assume that his or her intentions are equally bad. We categorize persons as being irrational when their behavior is hardly understandable. If, however, we were to judge only on the basis of the outcome of their specific behavior, evaluations might vary. Especially if their irrational behavior were to generate a beneficial outcome that serves their interest, how would we evaluate their behavior? Could we still justify their behavior by saying that they have irrational objectives?[6] People tend to think that the end (outcome) does not justify the means (behavior), because they think that favorable outcomes are not produced by irrational procedures or extralogical factors.[7]

The adjective "rational" usually describes an actor's behavior in accordance with his preferences, which he or she regards as being in his best interests.[8] Rationality requires two central conditions, connectedness and consistency. If an actor connects choices "by saying that choice A is more desirable to me than choice B" in a consistent way, then the actor's behavior may be labeled as rational.[9] If we label the behavior as irrational because the outcome is not welcome to us, or because we focus on his incomprehensible behavior, we would be unable to understand the logic that motivates his "irrational" behavior. Failure to understand the logic lying behind the behavior would cause misunderstandings and counterproductive measures. Decisions by Hitler to spark World War II, Kim Il-sung to ignite the Korean War in 1950, or Saddam Hussein to invade Kuwait in 1990 can all be regarded as rational choices because these leaders thought that doing so would best represent their interests.[10]

Likewise, understanding North Korea's behavior requires probing into its version of rationality, which can be found in its unique way of reasoning through its interests and policy alternatives. Many analyses have tended to regard North Korea's irrationality as the source of its instability. They have often labeled its behavior with adjectives such as impulsive, eccentric, renegade, erratic, and paranoid. "Epistemic imperialism" impels us to expect North Korea to behave in accordance with Western norms, not with the perceptions of the North Koreans themselves. However, there are some aspects of North Korean behavior that are hardly understandable from outside perspectives, especially from the Western standard.[11]

Understanding North Korean behavior becomes complicated if we consider only the effects. Most analyses start by evaluating the effects of certain North Korean behaviors, such as withdrawal from the NPT, test-firing of a missile, and disclosure of the clandestine nuclear program. Rather than scrutinizing what has caused such behavior, most studies either focus on the "carrots and sticks" method for getting the Pyongyang regime back on track, or the political implications and influences on regional and international order.

Discussion of the causes and effects, and more specifically, the intentions, behaviors, and their consequences is relevant. Mistaking effects as causes can result in erroneous assumptions and evaluations.[12] When we label somebody as irrational, our judgment is usually based on his or her behavior, not on his or her intentions or consequences, because only behavior is visible. Likewise, most indications of Pyongyang's irrationality concentrate on its actions. On the basis of the observation of its behavior, most analysts "speculate" that North Korea's intentions are also irrational, which produces intolerable consequences, and thus label it a rogue regime as in figure 6.1.

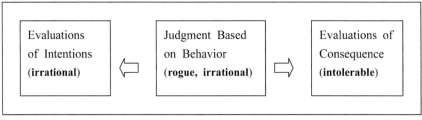

FIGURE 6.1
Conventional judgment of North Korean foreign policy behavior

If, however, North Korea's rogue behavior generates satisfactory conces-sions either from the United States or South Korea without prompting mili-tary sanctions, the consequence is productive in the eyes of Pyongyang, and thus North Korea's rogue behavior can be labeled as rational. We can infer that North Korea rationally chooses to play rogue to deter the U.S. or South Korean military threat or to make its will to provoke more credible under a continued threat.[13]

Then, as in figure 6.2, intentions generating rogue but rational behavior are also rational. North Korea's nuclear program produced two light-water reactors in addition to free heavy oil, while its negotiations over the missile program and the return of KIA (killed in action) bodies from the Korean War brought about economic benefits. In the 2000s, it succeeded in achieving the status of nuclear weapons state without prompting military sanctions. In figure 6-2, our judgment is based on the evaluations of consequences. In this sense, Pyongyang's decision to play rogue is a rational choice.

Then, one question arises; why did North Korea choose to play rogue while other states chose different options under similar situations? The answer lies in its unique logic inherited from the anti-Japanese struggle[14] and embedded in its threat perception, which resulted in an unconventional way of reasoning out alternatives.

A leader's choice is not explainable without some reference to his assump-tions, views, preexisting beliefs, and most important, his perceptions of inter-national relations.[15] Perceptions matter when decision makers are uncertain about the intentions and policy preferences of the adversary, or about the character of a given situation.[16] This is especially true when perceptions of the world are indoctrinated to evolve into an ideology. The ideology in this case would limit how a leader perceives specific policies and intentions of the ad-versary and would frame the situation in a way that emphasizes possible gains

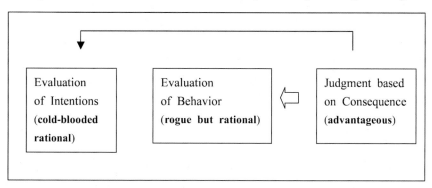

FIGURE 6.2
Alternative judgment of North Korean foreign policy behavior judged from consequences

or possible losses. This would ultimately lead him to take greater risks than he had intended.[17] In this regard, North Korea's rogue behavior is the result of Pyongyang's unique "mediating orientations" in which subjective processing involves reacting to stimuli from the international environment.[18]

Pyongyang's unique choice of playing rogue can be found in *Juche,* the North Korean ruling ideology implying self-reliance. Explaining Pyongyang's rogue behavior requires understanding the particular beliefs and perceptions that shape the behavior because "attempts to influence or manipulate what others believe require the actor to know what they already think."[19] The choice of an offensive strategy is determined by the interaction of a rational cost-benefit calculation. Motivational biases are embedded in the decision-making process and cognitive biases for doctrinal simplification; motivational biases assert the greatest influence when central values and key interests are severely threatened.[20] Another issue is that North Korea's Cold War perceptions still function as constraints.[21]

The lack of consideration of the perceptional variants behind Pyongyang's behavior has misled outside observers in the estimation of its policy objectives and its resolve to take risks. North Korea's rogue behavior has seldom been the object of analytical evaluations. Rather, most have taken Pyongyang's irrationality for granted. If one grasps North Korea's operational mindset of the Juche ideology, it may be possible to elicit rationality from the seemingly irrational behavior by finding a consistency and connectedness inherent in its rogue behavior. The common belief that terrorists are an unusual type of people who are "crazy, irrational fanatics with no sense of morality or decency"[22] has been applied to North Korea, influenced by normative biases and information paucity, as Han S. Park indicates.[23]

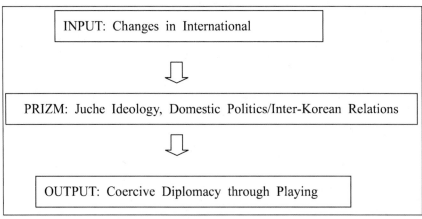

FIGURE 6.3
Alternative approach for interpreting North Korean foreign policy behavior

Figure 6.3 depicts the process by which North Korea perceives and responds to its international environment through the prism of, and under the guidelines of, the Juche ideology, its principle of conduct.

According to Kim Jong-il, Kim Il-sung opened the *Juche* era when the suppressed people emerged as the masters of their own lives. He was the main actor in the sociohistorical context, following Marx and Engels, who had opened the realm of the international communist movement, and Lenin, who had developed Leninism at an era when capitalism entered onto the stage of imperialism. Being a human-centered ideology arguing that men determine everything through their independent and creative struggles,[24] the *Juche* ideology incorporates such principles as militant nationalism, human beings as the locus, spiritual determinism, collectivism, and transcendentalism.[25] Wada Haruki sums up three themes of the *Juche* ideology.[26] The first is human determinism: nothing is impossible if man tries hard enough. This phraseology became the core of North Korea's society-wide principles of conduct. The second is that national independence is the highest ideological value. The third is *Suryong*, or the leader who embodies the omnipotent ability of men to preserve their national independence.

The ideology guides men, when faced with an unfavorable environment, to try hard to convert it into a favorable one. At issue here is the Juche ideology's human determinism intermingled with a mythology of the partisan spirit stemming from the experience of anti-Japanese struggles. Human determinism makes up the core of North Korea's view of the world. Kim Jong-il stated, "the Juche view of the world based on philosophical principles that men are the master of everything and determine everything, is the most right view in our time."[27] From the logic that humans can determine everything in the world, we can infer that humans can also alter the environment.

Then how can humans alter the environment? The answer lies in guerilla tactics such as *maebok-chon* (ambush tactics) and *kisup-chon* (surprise attacks). The Juche ideology may be a product of history, especially of experiences such as the anti-Japanese struggles in the 1930s and 1940s and the confrontation with the United States since the Korean War in the 1950s.[28] During Kim Il-sung's anti-Japanese struggles, his unpredictable and unconventional tactics, even with a small number of troops, let him become one of the most wanted partisan leaders by the Japanese army. A dramatization of his anti-Japanese guerilla warfare in Manchuria is still one of the most frequently aired TV programs in Pyongyang today. The doctrine is that conventional tactics and direct confrontations with the enemy would be counterproductive under the asymmetry of military capability.[29] Scott Snyder posits that two themes derived from Kim Il-sung's historical experience are embedded in the psychological aspects of North Korean negotiation behavior: "the will to persevere despite tremendous odds for the sake of redeeming the nation" and "defiance of fate and assertion as the actor" or as "the creator of history rather than as the passive object."[30]

International Environment, Domestic Politics, and Playing Rogue

How a state frames a situation or "encodes a decision" drastically affects its policy choices.[31] A different interpretation of the adversary's motivations leads to different policy prescriptions, even under similar situations. Defensive realism is relevant on this point. It underlines the diagnosis of the adversary's motivations embedded in its policies. As Robert Jervis puts it, interpreting North Korea's motivations behind its nuclear program determines U.S. policy on the program.[32] A state's policy is made "not just by power calculations, but by the varying points on the spectrum" of motivations "from pure harmony to zero-sum conflict."[33] Defensive realism implies the pursuit of a realist policy toward North Korea, whereby the interpretation of Pyongyang's intention—which is embedded in its nuclear and missile program—is a vital requirement. In addition, whether North Korea intends to launch a covert attack on America also requires thorough investigation.

In the case of North Korea, a calculation of options against external threats and the domestic need for cohesion led to aggressive behaviors. Judging from the brinkmanship of terrorism, violations of the armistice treaty, and its nuclear and missile programs, North Korea appeared provocative during international and domestic difficulties. The fact that the two nuclear crises share common circumstantial links with North Korea's terrorist activities before the 1990s supports the main argument of this chapter.

North Korea's coercive diplomacy has undergone significant changes. As shown in figure 6.4, until the mid-1980s, North Korea had used terrorism and military provocations against South Korea as its main tools. It reacted to aspects of an unfavorable international environment, such as the U.S. intervention in Vietnam in the late 1960s and South Korea's involvement in the war, and the strengthened security cooperation among the United States, Japan, and South Korea in the early 1980s. Faced with broad international criticism of terrorism and with structural changes after the end of the Cold War, North Korea gradually ceased its terrorist activities and increasingly relied on nuclear diplomacy instead.[34]

Another finding in examining North Korea's provocative behavior is that its hostile verbal statements do not accompany actual military behavior as shown in figures 6.5, 6.6, 6.7, and 6.8.[35] Crises originated from North Korea since the 1990s were prompted by its hostility and provocation, mostly in the form of

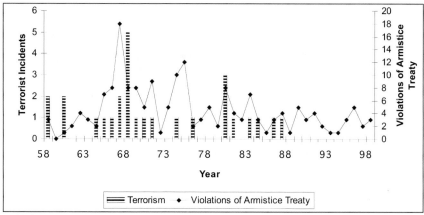

FIGURE 6.4
North Korea's terrorism and violations of armistice treaty, 1958–1999

verbal threats and, in some cases, minor military provocations against South Korea. While North Korea's verbal statements demonstrated extreme belligerence, its rhetoric was not accompanied by abrupt policy changes. Thus, it is notable that North Korea's verbal provocations do not usually develop into a real crisis. In the same vein, verbal warnings from Washington appeared to produce little coercive influence. North Korea's reaction to verbal warnings was very belligerent and usually disproportionate to the U.S. accusations. At times, North Korea reacted to the U.S. verbal warning with military provocation directed at South Korea, not at the United States.

North Korea stepped back when the United States demonstrated willingness to impose military sanctions. It was in June 1994 that the Clinton administration asked the UN to impose sanctions against North Korea.[36] The U.S. forces in South Korea disclosed a plan according to which a large number of U.S. citizens living in Seoul would participate in an evacuation exercise.[37] At a House hearing on June 9, 1994, Robert Gallucci, the chief U.S. negotiator with North Korea, confirmed that several measures to reinforce U.S. forces in South Korea had been undertaken.[38] A series of newspaper articles also indicated a U.S. buildup in South Korea.[39] It was also reported that the then defense secretary William Perry issued an order to the USS *Independence* to stay within a one-week distance of the Korean Peninsula.[40] Then, a resolution calling for sending more troops to South Korea was passed by 93 to 3 in the U.S. Senate on June 16.[41] As Bill Clinton later wrote,

> I was determined to stop North Korea from developing a nuclear arsenal, even at the risk of war. In order to make absolutely certain that the North Koreans knew we were serious, Perry continued the tough talk over the next three days, even saying that we would not rule out a preemptive military strike.[42]

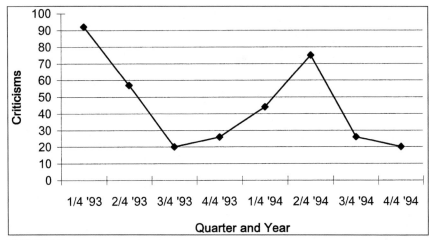

FIGURE 6.5
North Korea's verbal criticisms toward the United States, 1993–1994

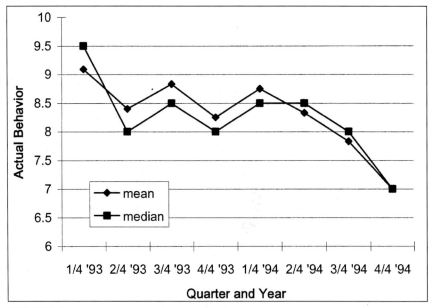

FIGURE 6.6
North Korea's actual behavior toward the United States, 1993–1994
Source: Yongho Kim and Yurim Yi, "Security Dilemmas and Signaling during the North Korean Nuclear Standoff," Asian Perspective, vol. 29, no. 3 (2005): 89–92.
Note: North Korea's actual behavior toward the United States was measured in accordance with Edward Azar's method introduced in his Conflict and Peace Data Bank (COPDAB), 1948–1978, 3rd ICPSR Release (Ann Arbor, Mich.: Inter-University Consortium for Political and Social Research, 1993).

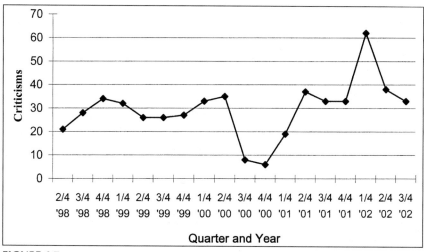

FIGURE 6.7
North Korea's verbal criticisms toward the United States, 1998–2002

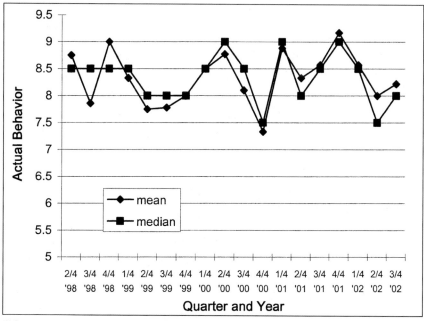

FIGURE 6.8
North Korea's actual behavior toward the United States, 1998–2002
Note: North Korea's actual behavior toward the United States was measured in accordance with Edward
Azar's method introduced in his Conflict and Peace Data Bank (COPDAB), 1948–1978, 3rd ICPSR Release
(Ann Arbor, Mich.: Inter-University Consortium for Political and Social Research, 1993).

It was on June 22, right after Jimmy Carter's visit to Pyongyang (June 15–18), that President Clinton announced that North Korea would return to the third round of nuclear negotiation with the United States.

In 2002, when North Korea publicized its clandestine nuclear program, it also faced unfavorable international circumstances: the hard-line policy of the Bush administration, especially after 9/11 and the war in Iraq. "It was like a declaration of war"[43] was Pyongyang's official response to George W. Bush's State of the Union address that labeled North Korea as a member of the "axis of evil" in 2002.[44] One day later, the U.S. president issued another warning that "all options are on the table" in protecting the United States and its allies from Iran, Iraq, and North Korea, during his meeting with the visiting King of Jordan. Again in 2003, President Bush named Pyongyang as an outlaw regime. Absolute U.S. victories in major international conflicts, including those in Iraq, Kosovo, and Afghanistan, demonstrated that a war against the United States would only devastate North Korea.

Bush's hard-line policy was surely a frustrating development for North Korea. In the early stages of the Bush administration, North Korea appeared to anticipate a continuation of Clinton's policy. North Korea maintained a balanced stance between China and the United States over the clash of an American EP-3 reconnaissance plane with a Chinese F-8 fighter over Hainan Island. Pyongyang's official party newspaper, *Rodong Sinmun,* reported official briefings by both the U.S. and Chinese foreign ministries and even carried President Bush's comments, together with those of Jiang Zemin.[45] North Korea also registered regrets over 9/11 by reaffirming Pyongyang's antiterrorism stance and expressed its opposition to all types of terrorism and relevant supporting activities.[46] While Clinton's bottom-line policy was to halt North Korea's nuclear development, Bush's policy aimed to achieve the total abandonment of North Korea's nuclear program even at the risk of an armed conflict on the Korean Peninsula. In doing so, the Bush administration put an end to the U.S.–North Korean rapprochement symbolized by exchange visits of Madeleine Albright and North Korean vice marshal Cho Myong Rok.

What is notable is that the two nuclear crises paint somewhat different pictures. In the first nuclear crisis, the security dilemma did not bring about a spiral effect; only North Korea experienced a security dilemma while the United States cared only to block nuclear proliferation. The crisis was negotiable because the positive sanction of providing heavy oil and two light-water reactors, in return for the halt of Pyongyang's nuclear program, brought improved bilateral relations between Washington and Pyongyang. This was vital in relieving the latter's security dilemma.

The second nuclear crisis in 2002–2003 was accompanied by a spiral effect. To begin, it was 9/11 that stimulated a security dilemma on the part of the

United States, which in turn drove the Bush administration's foreign policy objectives toward removing all weapons of mass destruction from the hands of rogue nations. North Korea was thus included on the list of axis of evil and outlaw regimes. This hard-line policy deepened North Korea's security dilemma and drove it into confirming its clandestine nuclear program, thereby creating another nuclear crisis. South Korea registered its grave concern over the possibility of a unilateral U.S. attack, and Japan took a similar posture, stating its preference for a peaceful solution of the second nuclear crisis. The six-party talks are in some sense a compromise between the peaceful solution that is preferred by neighboring countries and their concern with overburdening the United States, which is entangled in the disorder of postwar Iraq.

North Korea's domestic politics provides an explanation in a different context by offering a link between its roguish behavior and its domestic politics, especially in terms of the succession. Several North Korea watchers suggest the feasible expectation that an early stage of the second succession is underway. Their speculation, although in the absence of any reliable evidence, is not rootless. Following several years of preparation from the late 1960s, Kim Jong-il's rise in the main political scene started in 1972 when he was appointed as the director of the propaganda bureau of the ruling Korean Worker's Party.[47] The year 1972 also marked Kim Il-sung's sixtieth birthday. It was also one year after Mao Zedong's heir, Lin Biao, died in a plane crash. Kim Jong-il was born in 1942. As a man in his sixties who had been his father's designated successor for several decades and as the successful heir who has survived political struggles with his uncle and stepmother, he may be aware that it is about time to initiate a search for the next successor to the throne.

The correlation between North Korea's playing rogue and the initiation of the major stages in the succession agenda implies that North Korea utilized terrorism and coercive diplomacy as means of encouraging domestic cohesion. Kim Jong-il was well aware that the collapse of the Soviet Union was in part due to internal rivalry between Gorbachev, Ligachev, and Yeltsin. Right before Kim Il-sung launched his succession plans for his son in the late 1960s, he initiated several campaigns for purging cadres who were disloyal to him. At the Fifteenth Plenum of the Fourth Party Central Committee held May 4–8, 1967, high-ranking cadres were purged under the charge of spreading antirevolutionary ideologies. They included Park Kum-ch'ol, member of the standing committee of the Politburo and party secretariat; Ko Hyok, vice premier of the cabinet; Kim Do-man, party secretary; and Ho Sok-son, party chief in charge of science and education. However, Kremlinologists working on North Korea indicated that they were in fact charged for their attempt to dissolve Kim Il-sung's personal cult.[48] Another purge in 1969 was targeted at high-ranking military figures such as Kim Ch'ang-bong, then vice premier and defense minister, and Ho Pong-hak, who was in charge of counterintelligence for South Korean affairs. They were charged with mishandling cadre policy in the military.[49]

Domestic variables generated from political burdens are usually overlooked in an analysis of international disputes, even when calculations about domestic political costs outweigh apparently visible costs such as body counts, financial damage, and loss of military resources.[50] North Korea's highest priority is placed on maintaining the Kim Jong-il regime. Massive economic reform that would relieve economic destitution only attracts marginal attention due to "unhealthy" capitalist elements that would ultimately jeopardize the survival of the Kim regime. Domestic sources of foreign policy have long been one of the popular subjects among scholars in international relations studies. However, North Korea's domestic concerns and, in a more specific way, the succession issue have hardly been regarded as variables influencing North Korea's rogue behavior. Thus, including this issue in the general framework for making predictions about North Korea's policies would yield more reliable guidelines for understanding what assurances would satisfy North Korea. This would also determine whether North Korea will remain a perpetual rogue state.[51]

We may infer, thus, that North Korea has attempted to reshape its environment through unpredictable tactics and rogue behavior. The point here is not whether North Korea is feasibly capable of changing its environment at its will, but its belief that it is able to do so or that "doing something is better than doing nothing."[52] Fortunately for Pyongyang, in most cases this strategy has worked. The United States and South Korea have abandoned a tit-for-tat strategy against North Korea's provocations because the political burden was too heavy. As a result, North Korea, obviously in a weak position, has emerged victorious.[53] When North Korea shot down an EC-121 intelligence aircraft in 1969, Washington's response was far from being retaliatory: "The weak can be rash. The powerful must be more restrained."[54] The Clinton administration employed a similar logic with North Korea's nuclear and missile brinkmanship by preferring positive sanctions to other military options. North Korea's rogue behavior usually elicits weak responses from the United States, with the exception of certain cases.

North Korea's rogue behavior may be understood as signals that convey messages. A heightened frequency level of Pyongyang's rogue behavior under unfavorable international circumstances may be a rational choice because peaceful gestures may be decoded as an acknowledgment of desperation. Jervis posits that "signals designed to reassure or frighten others will backfire if they believe that strong messages are being used to cover up a weak position."[55] Inferences from signals are hardly drawn in a straightforward way, especially when the importance of the inferences increases.[56] This level of analysis reveals that a quasi homeostasis has operated surrounding North Korea's rogue behavior. Playing rogue is a way to demonstrate Pyongyang's displeasure and convey a message of threat to do more if the United States and South Korea refuse to "moderate" their behavior that is causing an unfavorable international environment for North Korea. The most commonly chosen countertactic is to ignore these signals, which in turn drives North Korea to escalate the level of its rogue behavior to ensure that the message gets through.[57]

North Korea appears to have established an acceptable level of risk and danger stemming from its conflict with the United States and South Korea. Until that acceptable level is reached, North Korea intentionally offends Washington, Seoul, and occasionally, Tokyo, as in 1998 when Pyongyang test-fired a missile, in 2002 when Pyongyang acknowledged its nuclear program, in 2005 when it declared possession of nuclear weapon, and in 2006 when it conducted nuclear missile tests. Even though North Korea does not want a war, it needs to convey the signals that a war remains possible. Thus, by employing rogue tactics, North Korea usually proceeds in the opposite direction than that which produces the desired results of defusing an unfavorable environment. When tensions escalate more than Pyongyang expects due to the U.S.'s or South Korea's resolute reactions accompanied by firm resolve, Pyongyang then tries to defuse the situation by diplomatic initiatives such as the unprecedented invitation to Jimmy Carter in 1994.[58]

Conclusion

Most analyses indicate North Korea's nuclear program as the source of regional instability, thus regarding it as a cause. To the contrary, the discussion in this chapter so far has led to an argument that North Korea's playing rogue is its own reaction to the changes in the international environment while utilizing them for domestic coherence. Regarding Pyongyang's behavior as effects rather than causes can generate a new set of discussions. Identifying one or more independent variables that have operated to produce North Korea's playing rogue provides a tool not only to understand but also to predict North Korea's future moves under certain circumstances.

Viewing North Korea in this way does not always lead to recommending dovish policies. North Korea's playing rogue has been implemented within a certain risk-acceptant boundary. North Korea has employed the strategy of playing rogue, not for a war, but to escalate from small-scale, deliberate, and limited violence to a heightened tension through which it can start bargaining.[59] This implies that its behavior is aimed at an objective that is short of an armed conflict. North Korea's rogue behaviors have ranged from one that incited a crisis situation to one that brought a near-war crisis. Indeed, in 1994, the Korean Peninsula fell into a near-war situation as the United States mobilized troops for handling ammunition in case of a war. North Korea accepted Jimmy Carter's mediation and finally signed the Agreed Framework. Likewise, in August 1976, North Korea stood still with arms crossed when it encountered the strong risk-taking will of the United States and South Korea. On August 18, two U.S. Army officers were killed by axe-wielding North Korean soldiers in Panmunjom during their escort mission for the South Korean workforce to trim a large poplar tree. President Ford approved Operation Paul Bunyan, in which American and South Korean troops cut down the poplar tree. The operation was backed by an armed platoon, twenty-seven helicopters, and B-52 bombers flying around the Korean Peninsula. North Korean solders held their fire. North Korea could keep on crossing the red line in the second nuclear crisis because the United States failed to generate convincing signals toward military sanctions due to its prolonged involvement in the postwar disorder in Iraq.

Notes

1. *The Compact Edition of the Oxford English Dictionary,* 1st ed., 22nd printing (Oxford: Oxford University Press, 1982), 2566; *Webster's New World Dictionary of the American Language,* 2nd ed. (Springfield, Mass.: Merriam-Webster, 1985), 1233.

2. George W. Bush, Graduation Speech at West Point, www.whitehouse.gov/news /releases/2002/06/20020601–3.html (accessed September 20, 2003).

3. National Security Council, *The National Security Strategy of the United States of America* (September 2002), www.whitehouse.gov/nsc/nss5.html (accessed September 20, 2003).

4. For details on the eclectic approach, see Peter J. Katzenstein and Nobuo Okawara, "Japan, Asian-Pacific Security, and the Case for Analytical Eclecticism," *International Security* 26, no. 3 (Winter 2001–2002): 167–82; and Joseph S. Nye, "Seven Tests: Between Concert and Unilateralism," *National Interest,* no. 66 (Winter 2001–2002): 9–13.

5. For various perspectives on how to analyze North Korea, see Samuel S. Kim, ed., *The North Korean System in the Post–Cold War Era* (New York: Palgrave, 2001); Bruce Cummings, "Corporatism in North Korea," *Journal of Korean Studies,* vol. 4; Haruki Wada, "Yugekitai Kokkano Seiritsuto tenkai," *Sekai,* October 1993; Han S. Park, *North Korea: The Politics of Unconventional Wisdom* (London: Lynne Rienner Publishers, 2002); Charles Armstrong, *The North Korean Revolution, 1945–1950* (Ithaca, N.Y.: Cornell University Press, 2003); Jong-seok Lee, *Hyundae Pukhanui ihae* [Understanding Modern North Korea] (Seoul: Yoksa Pip'yong-sa, 1995); Byung Chul Koh, ed., *North Korea and the World* (Seoul: Kyungnam University Press, 2004); Kong-

dan Oh and Ralph C. Hassig, *North Korea through the Looking Glass* (Washington, D.C.: Brookings Institution, 2000); Michael O'Hanlon and Mike Mochizuki, "Toward a Grand Bargain with North Korea," *Washington Quarterly* 26, no. 4 (2003); Michael Horowitz, "Who's Behind That Curtain? Unveiling Potential Leverage over Pyongyang," *Washington Quarterly* 28, no. 1 (2004); Roland Bleiker, "A Rogue Is a Rogue Is a Rogue: U.S. Foreign Policy and the Korean Nuclear Crisis," *International Affairs* 79, no. 4 (2003); James T. Laney and Jason T. Shaplen, "How to Deal with North Korea," *Foreign Affairs* 82, no. 2 (2003); Victor D. Cha and David C. Kang, *Nuclear North Korea: A Debate on Engagement Strategies* (New York: Columbia University Press, 2003); Joel S. Wit, "North Korea: The Leader of the Pack," *Washington Quarterly* 24, no. 1 (2001); Daniel A. Pinkston and Phillip C. Saunders, "Seeing North Korea Clearly," *Survival* 45, no. 3 (2003); Hazel Smith, "Bad, Mad, Sad or Rational Actor? Why the 'Securitization' Paradigm Makes for Poor Policy Analysis of North Korea," *International Affairs* 76, no. 3 (2000).

6. Bruce Bueno de Mesquita, *Principles of International Politics: People's Power, Preferences, and Perceptions,* 2nd ed. (Washington, D.C.: CQ Press, 2003), 292.

7. Robert Jervis, *System Effects: Complexity in Political and Social Life* (Princeton, N.J.: Princeton University Press, 1997), 231.

8. For various conceptualization on rationality, see Robert Jervis, "Commentaries on Part III: Images and the Gulf War," in Stanley A. Renshon, ed., *The Political Psychology of the Gulf War: Leaders, Publics, and the Process of Conflict* (Pittsburgh: University of Pittsburgh Press, 1993), 173–79; Thomas C. Schelling, *The Strategy of Conflict* (Cambridge, Mass.: Harvard University Press, 1960, reprinted in 1994), 15–18; Bueno de Mesquita, *Principles,* 292–93; Robert Jervis, *The Meaning of the Nuclear Revolution: Statecraft and the Prospect of Armageddon* (Ithaca, N.Y.: Cornell University Press, 1989), 40–41. On rationality and bias and misperception, see Robert Jervis, *Perception and Misperception in International Politics* (Princeton, N.J.: Princeton University Press, 1976); Jack Snyder, *The Ideology of the Offensive: Military Decision Making and the Disasters of 1914* (Ithaca, N.Y.: Cornell University Press, 1984), 15–34. On psychological and cognitive explanations of rationality, see Robert Jervis, "Models, Cases, and the Study of International Conflict" (paper presented at the Dean's symposium at the University of Chicago, May 4–5, 1989), 11.

9. David Austen-Smith and Jeffrey Banks, "Social Choice Theory, Game Theory, and Positive Political Theory," in *Annual Review of Political Science,* ed. Nelson Polsby (Palo Alto, Calif.: Annual Reviews, 1998); Bueno de Mesquita, *Principles,* 293.

10. Bueno de Mesquita, *Principles,* 293.

11. For details, see David Kang, "Getting Asia Wrong: The Need for New Analytical Frameworks," *International Security* 27, no. 4 (Spring 2003): 84; Victor D. Cha, "Hawk Engagement and Preventive Defense on the Korean Peninsula," *International Security* 27, no. 1 (Summer 2002): 46; David Kang, "International Relations Theory and the Second Korean War," *International Studies Quarterly* 47, no. 3 (September 2003): 304–10; Park, *North Korea,* 9.

12. Robert Jervis, "Theories of War in an Era of Leading-Power Peace: Presidential Address, American Political Science Association, 2001," *American Political Science Review* 96, no. 1 (March 2002): 4–6.

13. Schelling, *Strategy of Conflict*, 143.

14. North Korea asserts its legitimacy is rooted in the Alliance of Breaking Up Imperialism [T'adochekukjoui Tongmaeng], which Kim Il Sung is argued to have organized in 1927. It is often referred to as < ㅌ · ㄷ > in Korean initials.

15. Robert Jervis, *The Logic of Images in International Relations* (Princeton, N.J.: Princeton University Press, 1970), 4.

16. Bueno de Mesquita, *Principles*, 332.

17. Bueno de Mesquita, *Principles*, 16.

18. Harry Eckstein, "A Culturalist Theory of Political Change," *American Political Science Review* 82, no. 3 (1988): 790; Park, *North Korea*, 9. See also Jervis, *Perception and Misperception*, 35–48.

19. Jervis, "Commentaries on Part III," 174–76.

20. Snyder, *Ideology of the Offensive*, 30.

21. Bueno de Mesquita, *Principles*, 300–302.

22. Bueno de Mesquita, *Principles*, 371.

23. Park, *North Korea*, 7.

24. Kim Jong Il, "Juchesasange Taehayo" [On Juche Ideology], *Kim Jong-il Juyo Non-munjip* [Major Writings of Kim Jong-il] (Seoul: Ministry of Unification, 1993), 23.

25. Park, *North Korea*, 31–40.

26. Wada, "Yugekitai," 272–73.

27. Kim Jong Il, "Juchesasange," 23.

28. Park, *North Korea*, 13–14. For the process of Juche's evolution, see 17–30.

29. Scott Snyder, *Negotiating on the Edge: North Korean Negotiating Behavior* (Washington, D.C.: USIP Press, 2000), 24.

30. Snyder, *Negotiating on the Edge*, 22.

31. Cha, "Hawk Engagement," 54–55.

32. Robert Jervis, "Realism, Neoliberalism, and Cooperation: Understanding the Debate," *International Security* 24, no. 1 (Summer 1999): 52–53. On North Korea's nuclear program, see Leon V. Sigal, *Disarming Strangers: Nuclear Diplomacy with North Korea* (Princeton, N.J.: Princeton University Press, 1998).

33. Jeffrey W. Legro and Andrew Moravcsik, "Is Anybody Still a Realist?" *International Security* 24, no. 2 (Fall 1999): 22–23.

34. For circumstantial variants, see Yongho Kim, "North Korea's Use of Terror and Coercive Diplomacy: Looking for their Circumstantial Variants," *Korean Journal of Defense Analysis* 14, no. 1 (2002): 45–68.

35. Yongho Kim and Yurim Yi, "Security Dilemmas and Signaling during the North Korean Nuclear Standoff," *Asian Perspective* 29, no. 3 (2005): 73–97.

36. *New York Times*, June 3, 1994, A1.

37. *Seoul Sinmun*, June 2, 1994, 4.

38. *Segye Ilbo*, June 11, 1994, 2.

39. Bill Gertz, "Pentagon Plans for Buildup in the South," *Washington Times*, June 14, 1994, A1; Michael R. Gordon, "Clinton May Add G.I.'s in Korea While Remaining Open to Talks," *New York Times*, June 17, 1994, A1; Art Pine and Jim Mann, "Clinton Weighs List of Military Options for Korea Buildup," *International Herald Tribune*, June 20, 1994, 7.

40. *Chosun Ilbo,* June 12, 1994, 2.

41. See thomas.loc.gov/cgi-bin/bdquery/z?d103:SP01799.

42. Bill Clinton, *My Life* (New York: Alfred A. Knopf, 2004), 591.

43. *Rodong Simmun,* January 30, 2001, www.kcna.co.jp; *Kookmin Ilbo* [Kookmin Daily News] (Seoul, Korea), February 1, 2002, 3.

44. *New York Times,* January 31, 2002, A1.

45. *Rodong Sinmun,* April 5, 2001, 6.

46. *Korean Central News Agency,* September 12, 2001; *Chosun Central Broadcasting,* 14 September 2001; *Pyongyang Broadcasting,* September 14, 2001; *Pukhan Tonghyang* [Weekly report on North Korea], no. 556.

47. Jong-sok Lee, *Hyondae Pukhaneui Ihae* [Understanding Modern North Korea] (Seoul: Yoksa Pipyongsa, 1995), 291.

48. For details of the 1967 purge, see Lee, *Hyondae,* 427–32.

49. Kim Il Sung's speech at the fourth plenum of the People's Army Committee of the fourth KWP, 14 January 1969.

50. Bueno de Mesquita, *Principles,* 278.

51. Jervis, *Logic of Images,* 99.

52. Cha, "Hawk Engagement," 53–54.

53. Bueno de Mesquita, *Principles,* 279.

54. Quotation of statement by then secretary of state Rogers from Seymour Hersh, *The Price of Power: Kissinger in the Nixon White House* (New York: Summit Books, 1973), 72; Jervis, *System Effects,* 255–56.

55. Jervis, *System Effects,* 146.

56. Jervis, *System Effects,* 256.

57. Jervis, *System Effects,* 276.

58. Jervis, *System Effects,* 277–87.

59. Larry A. Niksch, "North Korea's Nuclear Weapons Program," Issue Brief for Congress (IB91141), 2; Cha, "Hawk Engagement," 53.

References

Armstrong, Charles. *The North Korean Revolution, 1945–1950.* Ithaca, N.Y.: Cornell University Press, 2003.

Austen-Smith, David, and Jeffrey Banks. "Social Choice Theory, Game Theory, and Positive Political Theory." In *Annual Review of Political Science,* edited by Nelson Polsby. Palo Alto, Calif.: Annual Reviews, 1998.

Bleiker, Roland. "A Rogue Is a Rogue Is a Rogue: U.S. Foreign Policy and the Korean Nuclear Crisis." *International Affairs* 79, no. 4 (2003).

Bueno de Mesquita, Bruce. *Principles of International Politics: People's Power, Preferences, and Perceptions,* 2nd ed. Washington, D.C.: CQ Press, 2003.

Bush, George W. Graduation Speech at West Point. www.whitehouse.gov/news/releases/2002/06/20020601–3.html (accessed September 20, 2003).

Cha, Victor D. "Hawk Engagement and Preventive Defense on the Korean Peninsula." *International Security* 27, no. 1 (Summer 2002).

Cha, Victor D., and David C. Kang. *Nuclear North Korea: A Debate on Engagement Strategies.* New York: Columbia University Press, 2003.

Clinton, Bill. *My Life.* New York: Alfred A. Knopf, 2004.

Cummings, Bruce. "Corporatism in North Korea." *Journal of Korean Studies* 4 (1983).

Eckstein, Harry. "A Culturalist Theory of Political Change." *American Political Science Review* 82, no. 3 (1988).

Gertz, Bill. "Pentagon Plans for Buildup in the South." *Washington Times,* June 14, 1999.

Gordon, Michael R. "Clinton May Add G.I.'s in Korea While Remaining Open to Talks." *New York Times,* June 17, 1994.

Hersh, Seymour. *The Price of Power: Kissinger in the Nixon White House.* New York: Summit Books, 1973.

Horowitz, Michael. "Who's Behind That Curtain? Unveiling Potential Leverage over Pyongyang." *Washington Quarterly* 28, no. 1 (2004).

Jervis, Robert. "Commentaries on Part III: Images and the Gulf War." In *The Political Psychology of the Gulf War: Leaders, Publics, and the Process of Conflict,* edited by Stanley A. Renshon. Pittsburgh: University of Pittsburgh Press, 1993.

———. *The Logic of Images in International Relations.* Princeton, N.J.: Princeton University Press, 1970.

———. *The Meaning of the Nuclear Revolution: Statecraft and the Prospect of Armageddon.* Ithaca, N.Y.: Cornell University Press, 1989.

———. "Models, Cases, and the Study of International Conflict." Paper presented at the Dean's Symposium at the University of Chicago, May 4–5, 1989.

———. *Perception and Misperception in International Politics.* Princeton, N.J.: Princeton University Press, 1976.

———. "Realism, Neoliberalism, and Cooperation: Understanding the Debate." *International Security* 24, no. 1 (Summer 1999).

———. *System Effects: Complexity in Political and Social Life.* Princeton, N.J.: Princeton University Press, 1997.

———. "Theories of War in an Era of Leading-Power Peace: Presidential Address, American Political Science Association, 2001." *American Political Science Review* 96, no. 1 (March 2002).

Kang, David. "Getting Asia Wrong: The Need for New Analytical Frameworks." *International Security* 27, no. 4 (Spring 2003): 84.

———. "International Relations Theory and the Second Korean War." *International Studies Quarterly* 47, no. 3 (September 2003): 304–10.

Katzenstein, Peter J., and Nobuo Okawara. "Japan, Asian-Pacific Security, and the Case for Analytical Eclecticism." *International Security* 26, no. 3 (Winter 2001–2002): 167–82.

Kim, Il-sung. Speech at the Fourth Plenum of the People's Army Committee of the Fourth KWP, January 14, 1969.

Kim, Jong-il. "Juchesasange Taehayo" [On Juche Ideology], *Kim Jong-il Juyo Nonmunjip* [Major Writings of Kim Jong-il]. Seoul: Ministry of Unification, 1993.

Kim, Samuel S., ed. *The North Korean System in the Post–Cold War Era.* New York: Palgrave, 2001.

Kim, Yongho. "North Korea's Use of Terror and Coercive Diplomacy: Looking for Their Circumstantial Variants." *Korean Journal of Defense Analysis* 14, no. 1 (2002): 45–68.

Kim, Yongho, and Yurim Yi, "Security Dilemmas and Signaling during the North Korean Nuclear Standoff." *Asian Perspective* 29, no. 3 (2005): 73–97.

Koh, Byung Chul, ed. *North Korea and the World.* Seoul: Kyungnam University Press, 2004.

Laney, James T., and Jason T. Shaplen. "How to Deal with North Korea." *Foreign Affairs* 82, no. 2 (2003).

Lee, Jong-seok. *Hyundae Pukhanui ihae* [Understanding Modern North Korea]. Seoul: Yoksa Pip'yong-sa, 1995.

Legro, Jeffrey W., and Andrew Moravcsik. "Is Anybody Still a Realist?" *International Security* 24, no. 2 (Fall 1999): 22–23.

National Security Council. *The National Security Strategy of the United States of America,* September 2002. www.whitehouse.gov/nsc/nss5.html (accessed September 20, 2003).

Niksch, Larry A. "North Korea's Nuclear Weapons Program." Issue Brief for Congress (IB91141).

Nye, Joseph S. "Seven Tests: Between Concert and Unilateralism." *National Interest,* no. 66 (Winter 2001–2002): 9–13.

O'Hanlon, Michael, and Mike Mochizuki. "Toward a Grand Bargain with North Korea." *Washington Quarterly* 26, no. 4 (2003).

Oh, Kongdan, and Ralph C. Hassig, *North Korea through the Looking Glass.* Washington, D.C.: Brookings Institution, 2000.

Park, Han S. *North Korea: The Politics of Unconventional Wisdom.* London: Lynne Rienner Publishers, 2002.

Pine, Art, and Jim Mann. "Clinton Weighs List of Military Options for Korea Buildup." *International Herald Tribune,* June 20, 1994.

Pinkston, Daniel A., and Phillip C. Saunders. "Seeing North Korea Clearly." *Survival* 45, no. 3 (2003).

Schelling, Thomas C. *The Strategy of Conflict.* Cambridge, Mass.: Harvard University Press, 1960. Reprinted in 1994.

Sigal, Leon V. *Disarming Strangers: Nuclear Diplomacy with North Korea.* Princeton, N.J.: Princeton University Press, 1998.

Smith, Hazel. "Bad, Mad, Sad or Rational Actor? Why the 'Securitization' Paradigm Makes for Poor Policy Analysis of North Korea." *International Affairs* 76, no. 3 (2000).

Snyder, Jack. *The Ideology of the Offensive: Military Decision Making and the Disasters of 1914.* Ithaca, N.Y.: Cornell University Press, 1984.

Snyder, Scott. *Negotiating on the Edge: North Korean Negotiating Behavior.* Washington, D.C.: USIP Press, 2000.

The Compact Edition of The Oxford English Dictionary, 1st ed., 22nd printing (Oxford: Oxford University Press, 1982), 2566.

Wada, Haruki. "Yugekitai kokkano seiritsuto tenkai." [The Founding of the Partisan State and Its aftermath] *Sekai,* October 1993.

Webster's New World Dictionary of the American Language, 2nd ed. (Springfield, Mass.: Merriam-Webster, 1985), 1233.

Wit, Joel S. "North Korea: The Leader of the Pack." *Washington Quarterly* 24, no. 1 (2001).

Part II

EMERGING ISSUES
Understanding Challenges to the United States

7

Challenging U.S. Military Hegemony

"Anti-Americanism" and Democracy in East Asia

Katharine H. S. Moon

"Anti-Americanism" has become the new buzzword to describe a panoply of discontents. For many Americans, it represents fear of a world that seems unfamiliar, out of control, and uncontrollable. For others, it is a reflection of guilt or embarrassment at having enjoyed so much power and plenty for half a century. But the meaning, intensity, and political enactment of anti-American sentiments and ideology have a wider range outside of the United States, from violent attacks against Americans and their political supporters to a malaise regarding U.S. military power even among historical allies and friends. Germany, France, South Korea, Australia, and the Philippines are just a few of the latter.[1] In the early 2000s, nationally elected leaders and government officials in the first three countries, together with their general public, voiced anti-American sentiments and positions. In others, like Australia and the Philippines, the heads of state eagerly expressed their nations' loyalty to the United States (and its war on terror), while segments of their populations demonstrated vigorously against the Bush administration and its policies abroad.

The nature, dynamic, and intensity of the anti-American malaise in East Asia are variable, sometimes sporadic, and often inconsistent. The 2002 Pew survey noted strong support for the United States among two allies—Japan (72 percent) and the Philippines (90 percent)—and much lower support in Korea (53 percent).[2] Anti-Americanism is certainly not as hateful or violence prone as the versions in the Middle East. On some occasions, anti-American protests take on carnival-like dimensions, with hip-hop, punk, and rap bands, folk dance, and drama troops entertaining the audience. And many Asians generally view Americans in a favorable light, even if the U.S. government or specific policies are harshly criticized.[3] Yet, anti-American sentiments can be emotionally intense and politically explosive, as the Korean demonstrations against the acquittal of the two U.S. soldiers whose sixty-ton vehicle had run over and killed two teenage girls in 2002 graphically showed. And organized anti-American sentiment, whether in civil society or among political elites, can overturn the established political order and the structure and content of alliances. For example, it is now a cliché to say that Korean president Roh Moo-hyun rose to power and planted his "new guard" of left-oriented actors by riding the wave of anti-Americanism in the winter of 2002. About a decade earlier, the Senate of the Philippines kicked out the U.S. naval and air facilities that had been a fixture in the U.S.-RP (Republic of the Philippines) relationship since the Military Bases Agreement (MBA) of 1947.

The task of recognizing and understanding the reasons for anti-Americanism among self-declared foes of the United States is challenging enough. But in some ways, the task is more confusing and difficult when the "perpetrators" are friends—especially those who have received large amounts of U.S. military assistance, development funds, skills training, market access, and tutelage on democracy. Americans cannot simply claim that the Korean families participating in candlelight protests were "thugs" or that Okinawan housewives' antibase activism is motivated by religious fundamentalism. To the contrary, anti-American sentiments and political acts among U.S. allies in East Asia tend to observe law and order and uphold democratic procedures and norms: registering with government authorities to hold protests; holding popular referendums; filing lawsuits for personal or community damages in court; voicing political opinions in print and assembly; lobbying local and national elected officials; mobilizing public support through civil society organizations (CSOs). Even if Asian anti-American sentiments share the opposition to or resentment of U.S. hegemony apparent in other parts of the world, their particular characteristics are unique. U.S. policymakers need to be cognizant of the specific historical, institutional, and cultural manifestations of anti-Americanism in order to assess and address them more accurately and constructively.

I argue that the redistribution of power *within* a nation significantly explains pro- and anti-American responses in East Asia. In all three Asian societies, the balance of power between state and society, especially with respect to the state's monopoly of power over national security, has been shifting since the 1990s. Tom Berger's observation that national security involves ongoing "renegotiation," persuasion, legitimation, and institutionalization of political-military culture by competing political actors applies aptly to the Asian cases.[4] In particular, analyzing the process of democratization and democratic deepening—namely, decentralization and heightened civil society activism—in Japan, Korea, and the Philippines is central to understanding the particular nature and enactment of contemporary anti-Americanism in all three countries.

Japan, Korea, and the Philippines serve the purpose of comparative inquiry for the following reasons: (1) each has a bilateral security treaty with the United States and has housed significant numbers of permanently stationed American troops for most of the last half-century; (2) they share similar histories of personal and community grievances toward U.S. troops, such as crimes against civilians, engaging in prostitution, abandoning their Amerasian offspring, and racist and humiliating treatment by Americans; (3) antibase activism has taken place periodically in all three countries, with anti-American undercurrents; (4) all three instituted government decentralization in the 1990s; and (5) despite these similarities, there are significant national differences in support for U.S. military presence in each country.

Building Democracy

Democratization itself unleashes social and political forces that challenge the state's ability to define nationalism and national security interests. In an early postwar study of Japanese nationalism, Delmer Brown highlights the growth of "people's nationalism" in Japan during the early years of the U.S. military occupation: "The removal of the thought-control structure and the weakening of the authoritarian system by democratic reforms made it possible for the newly organized peasant and labor groups to express their views and aspirations.... The great mass of the people were now beginning to express national sentiments in their own terms,"[5] sometimes in direct conflict with those of the Japanese ruling class.[6]

One could apply a similar observation to Korea from the democratic transition in the late 1980s to the present. In the 1990s, Koreans got an extra push from the administration of President Kim Young Sam (1994–1998), which early on encouraged the diversification and democratization of policymaking. The new government highlighted the importance of "universally accepted values such as democracy, human rights, environmental protection, and social welfare" in policy considerations.[7] Hyuk-rae Kim underscores the rapidity and intensity of public response to such political liberalization:

> Improving the quality of life, overshadowed over the years as a result of the country's growth-first strategy, was now to be an important part of the government's mission. Multiple dimensions of national security from economic and ecological security . . . to communal and societal security . . . were also emphasized as forming the new and more comprehensive foreign and security policy agenda for South Korea.[8]

In particular, the first half of the 1990s served as a crucible for the creation of organizations that have assumed leading roles in the organized criticism of U.S. policies and the terms and operation of the bilateral alliance. For example, the National Campaign for the Eradication of Crimes by U.S. Troops against Korean Civilians (National Campaign), the "clearinghouse" organization focused solely on collecting, investigating, publicly addressing, and monitoring such crimes, both alleged and proven, by U.S. military personnel, was established in 1993 in response to the brutal murder of Yun Geumi. Yun, a young woman who had worked and died in the entertainment/prostitution industry that caters to American personnel in Dongducheon (home of the Second Infantry Division) posthumously became a nationalist symbol of Korea's powerlessness and "victimization" by the United States and catalyst for organized activism on issues related to the U.S. troop presence.[9] In 1994, the *banhwan* (return-of-land) movement was launched in response to the proposed relocation of the U.S. Forces-Korea Yongsan headquarters (in Seoul) to Pyongtaek/Osan in the early 1990s. In the middle of the decade, both the Korean Confederation of Trade Unions (KCTU) and Green Korea United (GKU) were created, and Women Making Peace was launched in 1997. Moreover, People's Solidarity for Participatory Democracy, the nationwide umbrella organization for progressive issues and citizen participation and representation in domestic and international policy matters, was established in 1994. And from 1995 on, when negotiations on the revision of the Status of Forces Agreement (SOFA) were reintroduced onto the bilateral security agenda, activists and CSOs began to introduce their voices through the media and transnational networks.

Earlier in the Philippines, the ousting of Ferdinand Marcos and the installation of "people power" through the political rise of Corazon Aquino in the mid-late 1980s ushered in a decade of heated and at times bitter jousting between the Philippines and the United States over the presence and price tag of the U.S. Air Force base and naval facility stationed on the islands. Left-leaning or nationalist activists had acceded to elected office by the early 1990s, which enabled them to push for tough terms if the United States wanted to continue using the bases. For example, some of the most outspoken Senate opponents of a new base agreement, like Jovito Salonga, Orlando Mercado, and Aquilino Pimentel, had been imprisoned by Marcos under martial law. Others, like Sotero Laurel and Wigberto Tanada, descended from well-known nationalists who had been highly critical of American intervention in the Philippines; Tanada was the principal sponsor of the nonratification resolution in the Senate.[10] The long-standing, though marginalized, activist critics of U.S. bases, who had regarded them as explicit symbols of U.S. neoimperialism, were able to assert their voices and pressure political leaders without fearing punishment, since they no longer could be labeled as dissidents and punished at the will of the state. And like many political regimes that assume power after ousting their authoritarian predecessors, the Philippines under Aquino attempted to distance itself from the image that had stuck with Marcos, that of a U.S. lackey dependent on its patron for economic largesse and its claim to power.

The privileged position of the Armed Forces of the Philippines (AFP) also ended as constitutionally backed civilian rule became the norm throughout the 1990s. Democratization reduced the power of this central institution and, by extension, the role of the United States in the internal affairs of the Philippines. For the AFP, the loss of the U.S. bases meant a dramatic loss of funds and equipment. In order to retain U.S. military assistance, the AFP and the Department of National Defense entreated the Philippine Senate to pass the Treaty of Friendship, Cooperation and Security (PACT), which was intended to replace the fast-expiring MBA of 1947 for economic and security reasons. Lacking any political interest group to lobby on its behalf, the AFP undertook a media campaign for the extension of the U.S. bases, but to little effect. Wielding its new authority over the military, the Senate "belittled" and "chastised the AFP for publicly advocating the ratification of the PACT which a senator claimed was a policy matter, and that the military officials should not interfere unless authorized by civilian leadership."[11]

Throughout the 1990s, the AFP had the most antiquated military hardware in Southeast Asia, yet it had to struggle to get the Philippine Congress to enact and allocate funds for its modernization program. For example, Senate defense committee chairman Orlando Mercado had raised the bar even higher in mid-1993 with a new condition for upgrade funds: "the AFP acquisition program will be directed more at protecting the natural environment than for conventional warfare and external defense."[12] The military therefore had to accept such nonmilitary missions and identity or be left out in the cold. Former lieutenant general Arturo Enrile, who became the head of the AFP in 1994, "was realistic enough to know that to improve the AFP's equipment necessitates that he should 'follow a certain line,'" one that shows the "'civilian community that the AFP is part of the country, part of the community.'"[13] Enrile was reading the political mood of the legislature and civil society, and under his leadership, all three services of the military adapted their modernization goals to the new environmental and developmental mandate.

In a postauthoritarian environment, not only did the military have to improve its identity by identifying with civilian-defined "soft" projects like environmental protection and community development, but it also had to compete for public funds and support with other political institutions and actors. Facing public opinion that was against "militarization" and the rise of nongovernmental organizations (NGOs) that demanded government funds for socioeconomic development and welfare projects, the military was politically placed at the end of the line. Moreover, congressional funding for the military was "further complicated by the fact that many legislators were in one way or another ill-affected by the AFP's actions during the Martial Law years."[14] In short, democratization had changed the political and institutional landscape such that the military's organizational needs and national security outlook fell far from being a public priority. One report in November 2001 found that "of the 331.6 billion pesos earmarked to modernize the Armed Forces in 1995, only 11 percent was released by 2000."[15]

Decentralization and Local Empowerment

The decentralization of government, the legalization and application of new rights for local residents, and people's increased access to public information and institutional accountability took place in all three countries throughout the 1990s. Shin'ichi Yoshida's characterization of local empowerment in Japan—as a "series of epoch-making phenomena . . . that amounted to an open revolt by local communities against the central government's idea of what constituted the national and public interest"—applies to Korea and the Philippines as well.[16] In Japan, the process began with a recommendation by the Third Provisional Council for the Promotion of Administrative Reform (1990–1993), of which former prime minister Morihiro Hosokawa was a member. Having survived opposition from sections of the Liberal Democratic Party (LDP) and the central bureaucracies, the Law for Promoting Decentralization was enacted in May 1995, followed by the 1999 Omnibus Law of Decentralization, which strengthened and widened local government power and authority. Similarly, Korea adopted new laws to restore local self-rule after more than thirty years of centralized authoritarian control, permitting the establishment of local assemblies (1991) and the election of local government officials by popular vote (1995). Comparable changes took place in the Philippines with the establishment of the Local Government Code in 1991. Terrence George highlights the fact that "the Philippines enjoys the most supportive statutory environment for local political participation in all of Southeast Asia" and boasts the only law that explicitly requires NGO participation in local governance.[17]

In all three countries, "democratization, globalization, and public-sector reform have contributed most to decentralization."[18] These very forces have shifted the balance of power between central and local government and between the state and civil society in all three countries, so that national security and foreign policy no longer remain the sole purview of the central government. "Never before have mayors and governors been expected to accomplish so much for their constituents nor given so much power to do so. And never before have citizens been so legally equipped to participate in local government affairs."[19] Again, this reference to the Philippines could easily describe local politics in Korea and Japan. Local autonomy also means that local leaders require the votes and support of everyday residents and therefore must be accountable to them, even if some financial and other resources get distributed by the capital. In short, decentralization has created new push and pull factors, making power struggles between the center and localities an inevitable part of the political process of deepening democracy.[20]

Japan offers several examples of this tension as it relates to national security policy, the most prominent being the defiance of former governor Masahide Ota of Okinawa against Tokyo's control over private lands to be used by the U.S. Forces-Japan and the 1996 Okinawan referendum, in which 90 percent of the voters called for the consolidation and reduction of the U.S. military presence. In Tsuneo Akaha's view, the rape of the twelve-year-old Okinawan girl by three U.S. marines in September 1995, which triggered the defiant reactions, presented the "most serious challenge to the Japan-U.S. security treaty since the end of the Cold War."[21] It was domestic political changes, not primarily geopolitical changes or a strategic debate between the two governments, that generated the explosive antibase activism in Okinawa. With the weight of voters behind him, Governor Ota went head to head with Tokyo, pitting the "public interest" (i.e., local) against the "national interest." Specifically, armed with the new Local Autonomy Law of 1995, he brought his case to the Japanese supreme court. Although he lost the battle, "Ota sought not only to change Tokyo's policy on U.S. military bases in Okinawa but also to 'renegotiate the policymaking process itself by giving the prefectural government a greater role.'"[22]

Tokyo's monopoly over foreign policy and national security has been challenged by other localities. Although more than two thousand towns and cities had declared themselves nuclear-free by the 1980s, the antinuclear/disarmament movement in Japan for the most part had "failed to seriously challenge the [central] government's nuclear disarmament policy, which strictly avoids any initiative that might jeopardize U.S. nuclear deterrence capabilities."[23] But in 1998, Kochi Prefecture adopted the Kobe Formula of 1975, in which the city mandated visiting foreign ships to certify their nuclear-free status or be denied port privileges. But the legal premise could not have been more different: Kobe had relied on port law to claim local jurisdiction over the civilian port and had not raised the central government's ire for two decades. But after the passage of the Local Autonomy Law, Tokyo understood that localities would be able to exercise new legal muscle to challenge the central government's policies and adopted a hard line in the legal and political debate over jurisdictional authority to permit or prohibit port visits by foreign ships. Naoki Kamimura underscores Kajimoto Shushi's observation that "behind the vigorous opposition to Kochi's nuclear-free proposal by the national government and LDP lies the fear that the spread of the Kobe Formula would effectively ban U.S. warships from these ports at a time when the U.S. and Japanese governments are trying to give U.S. warships easier access to Japanese civilian ports and other facilities."[24]

Even if localities are not directly exerting their political muscle on Tokyo's foreign policy and national security prerogatives, those housing U.S. installations voice complaints related to the quality of life of the local residents. For example, Japanese living near the bases in Yokota (Tokyo), Atsugi (Kanagawa Prefecture), Misawa (Aomori Prefecture), in addition to Kadena and Futenma (Okinawa), "have been battling in Japanese courts to protest noise pollution, inadequate safety measures, and environmental concerns."[25] They are not necessarily anti-American or antibase protests, especially in the more politically conservative locales like Misawa; nevertheless, they reflect long-accumulated grievances that local inhabitants and officials had sought to address and redress for decades. Local autonomy has granted legitimacy and legal standing to what were once considered private, local, peripheral interests.

In Korea as well, local activism has increased its coordination, voice, and power to assert interests usually not considered by the central government. But unlike in Japan, antibase issues–cum–local interests in Korea have been more coherent as a national agenda item and potent as the common "glue" that brings together disparate groups of people. In particular, complaints against the bases have served to bridge regional, political, and social gaps between the activist elite in Seoul and the "periphery," where most residents of U.S. camptowns live. Antibase activism has facilitated the cross-fertilization of standpoints, issues, and approaches among hitherto disconnected communities. For example, villagers living near U.S. bases who have been complaining about damage to private property are learning about environmental issues and values, and environmentalists, who tend to be from the educated, [urban] middle class, are exposed to people, communities, and livelihoods that have existed on the fringes of Korean society.[26]

The economic, environmental, and social impact of military basing and closure has attracted much national and local attention in the United States and facilitated at times the cooperation of unlikely political partners.[27] But in Korea, the responsiveness of some local governments to residents' complaints about the U.S. presence, and their cooperation with progressive civil groups, are some of the most novel and remarkable developments in the country's democratization process. Until only a few years ago, local officials and citizen-activists who criticized U.S. bases or troops or advocated for the (alleged and real) victims of crimes and abuses by U.S. personnel had treated one another with distrust and hostility. And generally, local governments had kept a lid on local tensions and conflicts related to U.S. troops in order to avoid the ire of the authoritarian Park and Chun regimes, as well as negative reactions by the U.S. commands. For one, local leaders served at Seoul's whim and pleasure; for another, local camptown economies were dependent on the U.S. bases for employment and revenues from the 1950s until the 1980s.[28]

However, in recent years, local governments have become active players in the larger anti-American movement. Some joined forces with local residents, businesses, and a variety of CSOs to voice their views of the U.S. facilities as obstacles to economic progress and city planning and U.S. troops as threats to the environment and public safety (particularly of girls and women). Incheon City Council, which formed the "Citizens' Congress for the return of land used by the USFK in Bupyong" in May 2000 to reclaim land that the U.S. military was using as a junkyard, is a case in point. According to one Korean daily, "This is the first time for a city council to participate in a movement for the return of land used by U.S. forces together with a civic group."[29] Participation included demonstrations in front of the U.S. Camp Market for its relocation out of downtown Bupyong. Also in May, officials of the fourteen local governments that house U.S. bases within their jurisdictions established the first-ever "nationwide consultative body" of local governments to exchange information about their relationship with base commands and the impact of the bases on local and regional development. They also sought to forge a collective front to demand more financial and development assistance from the central government.[30] In October 2001, they submitted a legislative proposal to the National Assembly. They claimed that their localities suffer a disproportionate share of the economic, environmental, and social burden of maintaining U.S. troops for the security of the entire nation.[31]

This argument echoes that raised in Okinawa. Accounting for only 0.6 percent of Japanese territory, the prefecture houses 75 percent of the U.S. bases (in acreage) and about half of the troops stationed in Japan. The sense of disproportionate burden is intensified because the prefecture's per capita income is the lowest in Japan and the unemployment rate is twice the national average.[32] In the context of local autonomy and empowerment in Korea and Japan, it is obvious that the U.S. base issue and the anti-American movement have become means through which local governments can assert their interests vis-à-vis the central government.

In the Philippines, the logic of decentralization has yielded a very different outcome: eager support for U.S. troop presence through Balikatan (shoulder-to-shoulder) military training exercises in 2002. Initiated by the United States as a way to address Abu Sayyaf activities in the southern island of Mindanao, Balikatan turned the Philippines into the Asian front in the war against global terrorism. Although the arrival of 660 U.S. troops with the purported purpose of training 5,000–7,000 Philippine soldiers to hunt down Abu Sayyaf members in the southern region created a political crisis in Manila, the locals welcomed Americans in uniform. For example, when in January 2002 the U.S. troops arrived in Zamboanga City, Mindanao—the site of their training camp—they were greeted with friendly placards reading "Welcome back, GI Joe."[33] Later in March, Zamboanga residents "staged a large march . . . to thank the Americans for their presence."[34]

Although the Philippine public held a favorable view of the U.S. military presence in the southern islands, the people of Basilan, where the actual exercises were concentrated from winter through July 2002, were particularly eager to host the foreigners. According to the *Manila Standard* (July 30, 2002),

> Before the [U.S.] soldiers came, the Basilan folk lived in constant fear. It was, for them, a hellish existence as the Abu Sayyaf bandits sowed their seeds of terror on the island and neighboring areas. Some of the Basilan women were raped and killed; many of their men and children were forced into servility or slaughtered by the bandits during murderous orgies.

In Lamitan, a rural town on Basilan island, the local parish priest regularly carries a 9-mm submachine gun and a .45 caliber pistol for self-protection against Abu Sayyaf thugs who were prone to hide in the jungles and take along Filippino and American hostages. So, an official sigh of relief at the American presence seemed logical: "'To be honest, I'd be very glad. I trust the Americans,' said Wahab Akbar, a stocky former Muslim rebel who is now the island's governor. 'We're very thankful the U.S. government has not abandoned this corner of the world.'"[35]

Pro-Americanism stemming from the U.S. troop presence was the prevailing sentiment in the southern islands and the general public throughout 2002. By contrast, a small minority of left-oriented students, activists, and intellectuals staged public demonstrations against Balikatan and U.S. hegemonic policies, including daily protests in front of the U.S. Embassy in Manila during the winter of 2002. They carried "Yankee Go Home!" signs and by late February were burning American flags at what were deemed the largest rallies as of then (two thousand people). They campaigned aggressively against the reentry of U.S. forces into the Philippines on two grounds: (1) nationalism and Philippine sovereignty; (2) constitutional authority. For many Filipinos, the return of American soldiers was not only a reminder of a bygone colonial era, but also a source of fear that the United States was seeking to reclaim the former bases, which had been returned to the Philippines in the early 1990s. As one Manila resident put it, "I think that the American government would be happy to have us as a colony again." Such suspicions were spray-painted on Manila's street curbs: "U.S. troops out now."[36]

The relationship between the center and the localities significantly determines the nature and force of antibase and anti-American activism and their effect on policymaking. Despite the politicization and political activities (referendum on the U.S. bases, legal battles with Tokyo over base-related policies, widespread media coverage of citizen movements) in Okinawa in the mid-late 1990s that were targeted against the U.S. bases and the Japan-U.S. Status of Forces Agreement, mainland Japanese activists never adopted the cause as their own. The fact that the overwhelming majority of U.S. forces resides on an island whose cultural and historical identity is already marginal to the mainland's means that overlapping interests, personnel, and alliances are weak. On the other hand, the much smaller landmass of South Korea makes communication and travel between Seoul and the localities much more accessible. Plus, there is no historical or cultural divide per se between the periphery and the center. Additionally, democracy activists and radical students began targeting U.S. military camptowns in the mid-late 1980s as symbols of subjugation by the U.S. government and its authoritarian "lackeys," former presidents Chun Doo Hwan and Roh Tae Woo. After the murder of Yun Geumi, the former prostitute, by Private Kenneth Markle in 1992, military camptowns became central to CSO activism on foreign policy, national security, and reunification issues. The growth of such activism was part and parcel of the dynamic spread of civil society participation in politics in general.

Civil Society Organizations in the World of Policy

In tandem with decentralization in the three countries has been the exponential growth of and public interest in civil society organizations (CSOs, including nongovernmental organizations—NGOs; nonprofit organizations—NPOs; and transnational networks), local residents' associations, and volunteerism, such that Yoshinobu Yamamoto argues that "the development of civil society itself has become the issue of governance."[37] In the 1990s, East Asian CSOs broadened and diversified their issue areas, ranging from consumer rights, social welfare, political reform, the environment, and human rights to peace, defense spending, national security, and troop deployment to Iraq. Hyuk-rae Kim notes the "unprecedented growth of the [Korean] NGO sector," with a concentration in the following areas: between 1993 and 1996, 62 percent of organizations advocating citizens' rights, 51.4 percent for the environment, 48.9 percent for youth, and 44.8 percent for human rights were established. In sum, 74.2 percent of NGOs in Korea were established between 1987 and 1996.[38] In Japan, Shin'ichi Yoshida observes that the number of NGOs focusing on international cooperation has increased significantly.[39]

In the Philippines, NGO communities were highly supportive of the Local Government Code and the potential for "people power" that it promised, such that a prominent rural development NGO lauded it as "arguably the most significant legislation passed under the Aquino administration."[40] Specifically, "at least one-fourth of the seats on local development councils" and "at least one seat on four other boards, dubbed 'local special bodies' [e.g., school and health boards, peace and order council]" must be filled by NGOs, NPOs, and "in some cases private sector individuals.[41] The code empowers local governments by substantially increasing their access to financial resources, enhancing their regulatory powers, and broadening their authority over planning, development, and social service provision.[42] In order to facilitate capacity building and delivery of services, the central government transferred tens of thousands of workers from central bureaucracies to localities: "The Department of Health alone devolved forty-five thousand staff—two-thirds of its total personnel—to provincial and municipal government from 1992 and 1994."[43]

Although leftist students and intellectuals in the Philippines began targeting the U.S. bases and the local camptowns as incarnations of American neoimperialism and militarism as early as the 1960s and 1970s, they were never able to mobilize the larger population around such issues. Their successors are still active, for example, putting out statements against the U.S. war in Iraq and their government's support of the Bush administration or protesting in front of the U.S. embassy in Manila against Balikatan. But they are a very small minority, and there is a wide ideological and social gap between them, who are concentrated in Manila universities, and poor peasants of the southern islands. For residents of Basilan and Mindanao, U.S. military presence is more about immediate daily survival, as long as the Abu Sayyaf and other "bandits" can be eliminated. They are not enamored of the U.S. presence, especially the Muslim populations, but poverty and underdevelopment are what bind the various communities together to support the temporary presence of U.S. forces.

It is also important to recognize that the identity and interests of NGOs in the Philippines have become moderate and society oriented rather than state oriented since democratizaton. That is, they believe that societal changes must occur first before the state can act constructively, whereas before democratization, most civic organizations were either pro- or antistate (Marcos). The majority of NGOs are also development oriented, reflecting economic priorities in the Philippines. It is also not a coincidence that heavy funding by international sources, particularly USAID (United States Agency for International Development), tends toward moderation in issue orientation and political activities. In general, NGOs have paid less sustained attention to security issues than socioeconomic ones. This is in stark contrast to Korea, where economic development is no longer a policy concern, but national security and reconciliation and reunification are hot issues.

Regional and International Networks

The national anti-American movements need to be understood in the context of regional and international antibase activism. For starters, networks of activists in Korea, Okinawa, the Philippines, and Vieques (Puerto Rico) exchange information about organizational activities, agendas, political strategies, mobilization of resources, and methods of political expression. Second, transnational networks help broaden the audience for each national movement. Third, the transnational solidarity provides a kind of international legitimacy to each national movement. Fourth, international interaction provides new ideas and interpretive schemes.

Korean and Okinawan activists have been exchanging and in some cases coordinating information, agendas, and "personnel" since the late 1980s. The initial participants were women from Korea, Okinawa/Japan, and the Philippines who began to meet to discuss problems related to the U.S. troop presence and women and gender relations in each country or locale. After the 1995 gang rape of an Okinawan girl by U.S. marines in Okinawa, the antibase activism on the island broadened and intensified within and reached outward toward Korea. Korean activists also extended their solidarity and network to Okinawa. For example, in 1997, Okinawans visited Seoul to participate in the weekly Friday demonstration in front of Yongsan Garrison (organized by the National Campaign). In August 1996, Kim Yonghan (coleader of the National Campaign in the early-mid 1990s) went to Japan at the invitation of peace activists there. He participated in activities commemorating the fifty-first anniversary of the bombing of Hiroshima; learned about the particularities of the U.S. presence in Japan, namely "private" leasing of land and "rent" paid by the Japanese government; and was impressed by the diversity and dynamism of peace and antibase activism among Japanese. Arriving during the lead-up period to the referendum, he inquired about the procedures and details of the return-of-land movement there. He also enlisted Okinawans' help in the Korean *banhwan* movement and proposed an international, collective demonstration (with activists in Okinawa, Philippines, Australia, Germany, and other NATO countries) for the following spring.[44] In 1998, Okinawans formed the *Han-Oki minjung yondae* (people's solidarity) with the purpose of educating themselves about U.S. military–related problems affecting Koreans in particular, and of networking with peace activists in Taiwan, Philippines, and Puerto Rico.[45]

In addition to Okinawan support for Koreans through joint conferences, visits, and other gestures of solidarity,[46] activists from Vieques, Puerto Rico, have built bridges of cooperation and solidarity with Koreans, especially those protesting the American use of Gun-ni (Maehyang-ri) range for bombing practice. Ismael Guadalupe Ortiz, a leader of the antibase movement in Vieques, visited Maehyang-ri in July 1999 and expressed alarm at how much worse the situation is for the Korean villagers, given that they live much closer to the strafing area than their Vieques counterparts.[47] Such words of empathy were highlighted by the Korean media and NGO groups in their newsletters and periodicals. More recently, Guadalupe sent a message of "solidarity with the people of Korea" condemning and protesting the U.S. troops' role in the deaths of the two teenage girls in 2002: "This is one more abuse added to those crimes perpetrated by the U.S. military against the Korean people since the Korean War. These crimes committed by the U.S. are awaiting the repudiation of the world community."[48] This message was not only delivered to Koreans but also made available to netizens around the world by various websites.

Democratization, then, unleashes new political actors and interests in the domestic and international arena. It also creates new opportunities for dissent and solidarity that complicate national and multinational policymaking. Amitav Acharya offers evidence of this trend in Southeast Asia:

> Civil societies in Indonesia and elsewhere in the region have felt resentful towards ASEAN for its reluctance to support their cause or involve them in its decision making. This has led to a call from the NGO community in Indonesia, Thailand, the Philippines, Cambodia and Malaysia for ASEAN to become more open. Democratisation has thus undermined the legitimacy of ASEAN's elite-centred regionalism.[49]

Additionally, the diversification of issue areas across national boundaries mirrors those within boundaries. In Asia at large, CSO scrutiny of and activism around human rights, the environment, and inequalities abound and confront official policy priorities and interpretations. National security is no exception: "Southeast Asian [and Northeast Asian] NGOs have also called for alternative approaches to national security that emphasise the security of people over that of states and regimes."[50]

U.S. Interpretive Frames and Policy Responses

It is clear that the Cold War changed the meaning of old enmities and alliances, facilitating the active exploration among East Asian nations of new configurations of cooperation and neighborliness with one another. Numerous regional cooperation schemes have been nurtured to simultaneously advance national and regional interests and ensure against an overbearing U.S. regional hegemony. The large majority of Japan's trade is with its regional neighbors, and China is now Korea's top trading partner. Without doubt, the anticommunist "glue" that once held together the military and political commitments between the United States and its East Asian partners and propped up American cultural hegemony in the region has lost much of its adhesive power with the changes in the international system. Koreans, who had for decades imitated nearly everything American and set aside things Korean, now buy and view more homemade music and films and videos than American imports. Moreover, Korean pop culture is a commodity with a fast-growing audience in Japan, China, and Southeast Asia. And Japan plays the leading role in introducing concepts and techniques to "Asianize" Western culture and thereby forge an eclectic but distinct Asian system and aesthetic for media entertainment and pop culture.[51] In this dynamic context, the role of the United States in East Asia has become ambiguous and open to question by Asian publics, generating what John Ikenberry calls a "legitimacy deficit" that stems from the changing distribution of global and regional power.[52]

But without understanding of the changes in the internal political systems of Asian countries, explanations of external relations and outcomes remain limited. If authoritarian rule had remained the dominant trend in much of Asia, the crisscrossing transnational linkages between private actors, experimentation with entrepreneurial and cultural risk taking, the exchange of information and political opinions across cultures, the willingness to construct new political interests and identities, and the freedom to challenge the official framing and justification of policy priorities and implementation would not characterize today's East Asia. Without the freedom to scrutinize U.S. policies and their respective governments' relations with the United States, Asian societies could have kowtowed to elite perceptions and explanations of foreign policy and national security and harnessed more tightly U.S. power and protection in the face of rapid change and accompanying uncertainty in the region. But democratization (along with liberalization) since the mid-late 1980s has challenged the domestic political power structures and the established versions of the relationship with the United States that had been the modus operandi for much of the authoritarian period in Cold War Asia. Here, Samuel Kim's critique of realist approaches to Northeast Asian security is worth emphasizing: "Differences in internal constructions and resulting domestic politics have a greater impact on how states or their decision makers define threats and vulnerabilities [as well as opportunities], and therefore on the whole security problematic, than does the structure of the international system."[53]

America is good at invoking democracy in its foreign policy, but not good at responding to it during the tough times. Ironically, it is the very success of post–World War II American hegemony that has gotten the United States into the current predicament of having to ward off both enemies and friends who are hostile to its power and policies. The very fact that the United States believed it was able to fashion the world according to its own image abetted a type of liberal myopia regarding the process and progress of democracy. As revealed by the United States' rather painful attempts to "rally" its European and Asian allies behind its cause in Iraq, democratic nations simply don't fall into line. They don't easily play follow-the-leader, and their own leaders contend with the wrath of public opinion as much as, if not more than, the wrath of the United States. The soil that the United States helped make hospitable for the seeds of democracy in Western Europe and East Asia has yielded fruit that is both sweet and bitter. On the one hand, democracy promotion serves the U.S. national interest by advancing peace, stability, legality, and human dignity, but it also risks the creation of democratically elected regimes that are hostile to U.S. interests[54] or a democratization process that degenerates into civil strife and regional instability.[55]

Democratic realities in the three East Asian cases are not prone toward extremes in terms of civil strife or hostility to the United States, but U.S. attempts to push for internal democratization have spawned a liberalization process and foreign policy repercussions that the United States did not bargain for. The example of U.S.-RP relations in the mid-late 1980s is most obvious. Following the fraudulent presidential election victory of Ferdinand Marcos in early February 1986, the Reagan administration put a dent into decades of U.S. economic and military support for the corrupt authoritarian regime of Marcos. Then President Ronald Reagan warned the dictator "against suppressing the independent poll-watching group, NAMFREL; vigorously challenged the election's credibility; and finally told Marcos it was time to go."[56] The United States shared the credit for enabling people power to transform the Philippines nearly overnight into a political democracy, but within a few years that very democracy also enabled the Philippines government to kick the U.S. bases out. Even though Corazon Aquino tried to overturn the Senate's decision by appealing to people power through a national referendum, she backed down because of the political and legal battle she would have had to wage against "constitutionalists": Aquino's populist move was sure to "set off a series of time-consuming court challenges by lawmakers and others who [would] assert that the Constitution permits voters to overrule a vote by the Senate on a regular law, but not on a treaty."[57] Even if nationalism served as a motivation for the Senate decision against the U.S. military, it was constitutional authority that was served and advanced through the political struggle over the bases.

The United States was also quite blunt about the need to democratize the highly centralized Japanese political establishment as a way to liberalize the Japanese economy in the late 1980s and early 1990s. Fueled by frustration and nationalism, "Japan-bashing" became commonplace in the United States in response to America's economic woes. "Senator John Danforth publicly referred to Japanese as 'leeches' as U.S. politicians began to publicly blame the Japanese for the $59 billion bilateral trade deficit."[58] According to Takashi Inoguchi, the "United States government may not have been the only actor engineering the 1993 dismantling of the LDP's one-party dominance; nevertheless, it played an important part."[59] The year 1993 ushered in Morihiro Hosokawa as prime minister and the rise of the Japan New Party. Although observers have focused on his efforts to liberalize the electoral and party system as soon as he stepped into office, "If Hosokawa had a particular cause, it was not electoral reform but deregulation and decentralization. For years, he railed against what he viewed as excessive power of central-government bureaucrats," and immediately prior to assuming his newly elected office, he served on the council that proposed recommendations for decentralization.[60] The U.S. government found a Japanese politician who was willing to push a political and economic liberalization agenda, but one of those agenda items, decentralization, had the effect of redistributing power to local governments and CSOs in the localities that house U.S. bases, most prominently, Okinawa. For the United States, antibase activism and policy initiatives by residents are just some of the costs of local empowerment.

In the last two years, policymakers, academics, the media, and other "Korea observers" in the United States have been quick to offer generational change (i.e., from old to new) as the main reason for the sudden outpouring of anti-American sentiments. But youth does not necessarily translate into historical amnesia, blind nationalism, radicalism, or anti-Americanism. In Japan, it is the older generation that keeps its eyes, ears, and minds closed to the realities of Japan's war atrocities, while the younger generations are more eager to step up to the historical plate and acknowledge past wrongs, mend old wounds, and forge new friendships with their regional neighbors and the country that dropped the atomic bomb on them. They are the ones busily exchanging views on the Internet, working together with regional CSOs, and admiring the cultural products (film, videos, music) imported from their nation's ex-colonies.

In Korea, as critical and nationalistic as the younger generations might be about the bilateral relationship and U.S. foreign policy, they are also pragmatic and know how to differentiate between sentiment and interests, both personal and national. According to Youngshik Bong, Koreans in their twenties and thirties "think negatively of America, but many of them prefer to have U.S. citizenship. They denounced the U.S. war against Iraq as an unjust invasion, but support the government decision to dispatch troops for U.S.-Korean cooperation over the North Korean issue."[61] More importantly, Bong points out their one constancy: they acknowledge the importance of the alliance relationship and support it for the sake of national security and economic stability.

Moreover, it is the younger generations, folks in their twenties and thirties, who have been developing a new consciousness about peace, human rights, and multicultural orientation. They have been at the forefront of forging peace movements, something that had been an oxymoron in a Korean society steeped in Cold War thinking. And whatever the cause for their nationalism, it is not of the myopic variety. They criticize U.S. policies, but they also have taken the initiative to investigate and repent for Korea's own war atrocities and human rights violations of the past—specifically toward Vietnamese civilians. Even though they had to confront aggressive criticism from Korean veterans and other conservative (nationalist) "elders" who wanted them to keep a lid on these less-than-heroic images of Korean troops, the young activists have been engaging in people-to-people reconciliation projects with Vietnamese villagers since the 1990s as a way to apologize for human rights violations perpetrated by Korean soldiers who fought in the Vietnam War. They put pressure on their own government in the mid-1990s to offer a formal apology to the Vietnamese but failed to get such a result.

Regarding young Koreans as politically naïve or economically complacent because they grew up in times of relative stability and wealth does not make sense unless one also emphasizes the fact that they grew up in a social and political environment of relative freedom in the 1990s. They don't long for the right to speak out against the government or for independent opinions as their predecessors had in the 1960s and 1970s; they take it for granted. And no form of authority, including the U.S. government and its troops, is off limits to them. Korean sociologist Sook-Jong Lee makes this clear:

> One consequence of democratization and institutional reforms has been the economic decline of the older generation and the rise of the younger generation. . . . The older generation is also being pushed to the political and social sidelines. This generation is perceived as supporting the status quo and resistant to reform. . . . In addition, [the younger generation's] easy access to information [technologies] and ability to create and mobilize political networks gives them the ability to be an effective political force.[62]

In short, forging a democracy means not only constructing political and social institutions but also creating empowered citizens. In Korea, the labors of the past for a democratic society have produced progressive-minded, outspoken youth.

Conclusion

Despite the missionary-style zeal with which American leaders tout democracy and work to export it abroad, Americans do not live up to democratic realities very well. In some sense, the United States likes to take credit for giving birth to democracies, but it does not like the youthful nature of new democracies when they are unruly (disobedient), assertive (nationalistic, emotional), and quite willing to challenge the power of the United States (rebellious and ungrateful). This was the case in the Philippines in the late 1980s and early 1990s and more recently in Korea. And when Japan, the most established democracy in East Asia, began to define national interests in a way that threatened U.S. economic hegemony, it no longer was treated as the chosen son in Asia.

In the midst of current U.S. attempts to offer democracy and freedom as candy-coated medicine to cure the ills plaguing Afghan and Iraqi societies, the East Asian alliance partners of the United States serve as timely reminders of what democracy can bring: vibrant civil society activism and local empowerment in the historical context of overcentralization and social oppression. With them may come acute challenges to the ability of even pro-U.S. governments to toe the U.S. line. They also teach the United States to be careful and wary of how it uses its power in the country of occupation, for today's foibles, faux pas, and slights by the foreign government can accumulate in the country's collective memory and become potent sources of mistrust and hostility toward the United States in the future. Outright acts of humiliation and disrespect will bear even more bitter fruits. National interest can only serve the national interest when other societies' histories, pride, and perspectives are taken into account. The East Asian cases show that peoples' political identities and expressions may end up directing, rather than following, policies. If the United States does not keep abreast of and adapt to the serious changes within other societies, its superpower days may be numbered.

Notes

1. For coverage of opposition in the Asia-Pacific to U.S. war plans in Iraq, see National Network to End the War Against Iraq, "Anti-war protests begin in Asia-Pacific," October 15, 2002, www.endthewar.org/features/asiapacific/htm (accessed November 19, 2003).

2. Pew Global Attitudes Project, *What the World Thinks in 2002* (Washington, D.C.: Pew Research Center for the People and the Press, 2002), 55.

3. South Korea is a case in point. Although it was the venue of widespread and intense public protest against the United States in the winter of 2003 and 50 percent of the respondents in the Pew 2003 survey had a negative image of the United States, 74 percent held favorable views of Americans (up from 61 percent in 2002, prior to the explosive anti-American demonstrations). In contrast, the most vocally anti-

American nations in Europe, France, and Germany, had significantly less friendly feelings toward Americans: 67 percent in Germany; 58 percent in France. The comparison is particularly interesting, given that 45 percent of Germans and 43 percent of French respondents viewed the United States favorably (19, 21). See Global Attitudes Project, *Views of a Changing World* (Washington, D.C.: Pew Research Center for the People and the Press, 2003).

4. Thomas U. Berger, "Norms, Identity, and National Security in Germany and Japan," in *The Culture of National Security: Norms, and Identity in World Politics,* ed. Peter J. Katzenstein (New York: Columbia University, 1996), 326–27.

5. Delmer M. Brown, *Nationalism in Japan: An Introductory Historical Analysis* (Berkeley: University of California, 1955), 252.

6. Brown, *Nationalism in Japan,* 252–53.

7. Jung-Hoon Lee, "Globalization, Nationalism, and Security Options for South Korea," in *Democratization and Globalization in Korea: Assessments and Prospects,* ed. Chung-in Moon and Jongryn Mo (Seoul: Yonsei University, 1999), 240.

8. Hyuk-rae Kim, "The State and Civil Society in Transition: The Role of Non-Governmental Organizations in South Korea," *Pacific Review* 13, no. 4 (Winter 2000): 603.

9. See Katharine H. S. Moon, "Resurrecting Prostitutes and Overturning Treaties: Gender Politics in the 'Anti-American' Movement in South Korea," *Journal of Asian Studies* (February 2007).

10. Many thanks to Professor Patricio "Jojo" Abinales of the Center for Southeast Asian Studies, Kyoto University for information on the profiles of senators and their political histories.

11. On the relationship between democratization and changes in the AFP, see Renato De Castro, "The Military and Philippine Democratization: A Case Study of the Government's 1995 Decision to Modernize the Armed Forces of the Philippines," in *Democratization: Philippine Perspectives,* ed. Felipe B. Miranda (Quezon City: University of the Philippines Press, 1997), 241–79. The quote is from 252.

12. De Castro, "Military and Philippine Democratization," 259.

13. De Castro, "Military and Philippine Democratization," 262.

14. De Castro, "Military and Philippine Democratization," 255.

15. See www.worldpress.org/article_model.cfm?article_id=789&dont=yes (accessed November 19, 2003).

16. Shin'ichi Yoshida, "Rethinking the Public Interest in Japan: Civil Society in the Making," in *Deciding the Public Good: Governance and Civil Society in Japan,* ed. Tadashi Yamamoto (Tokyo: Japan Center for International Exchange, 1999), 33.

17. Terrence R. George, "Local Governance: People Power in the Provinces?" in *Noble Organizing for Democracy: NGOs, Civil Society, and the Philippine State,* ed. G. Sidney Silliman and Lela Garner Noble (Honolulu: University of Hawaii, 1998), 225, 227.

18. Shun'ichi Furukawa, "Decentralization in Japan," in *Japan's Road to Pluralism: Transforming Local Communities in the Global Era,* ed. Shun'ichi Furukawa and Toshihiro Menju (Tokyo: Japan Center for International Exchange, 2003), 23.

19. George, "Local Governance, " 228.

20. Ilpyong J. Kim and Eun Sung Chung refer to this dynamic as a "dialectic relationship between centralization and decentralization." See Ilpyong J. Kim and Eun Sung Chung, "Establishing Democratic Rule in South Korea: Local Autonomy and Democracy," *In Depth* 3, no. 1 (1993): 212. Also see Kyoung-Ryung Seong, "Delayed Decentralization and Incomplete Democratic Consolidation," in *Institutional Reform and Democratic Consolidation in Korea,* ed. Larry Diamond and Doh Chull Shin (Stanford, Calif.: Hoover Institution Press, 2000). For general discussions of this tension in the context of democratization and democracy, see Desmond King and Gerry Stoker, eds. *Rethinking Local Democracy* (London: Macmillan, 1996), chaps. 1 and 2; Dilys M. Hill, *Democratic Theory and Local Government* (London: Allen & Unwin, Ltd., 1974), particularly chap. 8; Diamond, *Developing Democracy,* chap. 4.

21. Tsuneo Akaha, "Three Faces of Japan: Nationalist, Regionalist and Globalist Futures," in *Globalism, Regionalism and Nationalism: Asia in Search of Its Role in the Twenty-first Century,* ed. Yoshinobu Yamamoto (Malden, Mass.: Blackwell, 1999), 191.

22. Cited in Naoki Kamimura, "Japanese Civil Society and U.S.-Japan Security Relations in the 1990s," *Medicine and Global Survival* 7, no. 1 (April 2001): 21. For a detailed discussion of Okinawa-Tokyo politics over U.S. bases in the context of local autonomy, see Sheila A. Smith, "Challenging National Authority: Okinawa Prefecture and the U.S. Military Bases," in *Local Voices, National Issues: The Impact of Local Initiative in Japanese Policy-Making,* ed. Sheila A. Smith (Ann Arbor: University of Michigan Press, 2000).

23. Kamimura, "Japanese Civil Society," 23.

24. Kamimura, "Japanese Civil Society."

25. Haruo Iguchi, "Complication: American Military Presence in Okinawa and Enhancing the U.S.-Japan Alliance," in *United States–Japan Strategic Dialogue: Beyond the Defense Guidelines* (Honolulu: Center for Strategic and International Studies, Pacific Forum, 2001), 83, www.csis.org/pacfor/us_japan_dialogue.pdf (accessed November 17, 2003).

26. K. Moon, "Nationalism, Anti-Americanism, and Democratic Consolidation," in *Korea's Democratization,* ed. Samuel S. Kim (New York: Cambridge University, 2003), 145.

27. Fred Rose, *Coalitions against the Class Divide: Lessons from the Labor, Peace, and Environmental Movements* (Ithaca, N.Y.: Cornell University Press, 2000).

28. For a detailed description of the evolution of and the politics and social interactions in U.S. military camptowns in Korea, see Katharine H. S. Moon, *Sex among Allies: Military Prostitution in U.S.–Korea Relations* (New York: Columbia University, 1997), chap. 1.

29. *Munhwa Ilbo,* May 30, 2000.

30. *Daehan Maeil Sinmun,* May 24, 2000.

31. Republic of Korea National Assembly, Bill #16102, Migun kongyo chiyok chiwon mit chumin kwon-ik poho e kwanhan pomlyullan [Legislative bill on support to the USFK regions and protection of the rights and interests of residents], www.assembly.go.kr (March 27, 2003).

32. Iguchi, "Complication," 79.

33. See www.worldpress.org/article_model.cfm?article_id=501&dont=yes [accessed November 19, 2003].

34. See www.globalsecurity.org/military/library/news/2002/03/mil-020301ss02 .htm [accessed November 19, 2003].

35. Washington Post Foreign Series, January 28, 2002, www.mcsm.org/filipino01 .html (accessed November 19, 2003).

36. *Stars and Stripes* (Pacific edition), March 1, 2002, www.globalsecurity.org /military/library/news/2002/03/mil-020301-ss02.htm (accessed November 19, 2003).

37. Yamamoto, *Globalism, Regionalism, and Nationalism*, 104.

38. Kim, "State and Civil Society in Transition," 603.

39. Yoshida, "Rethinking the Public Interest in Japan," 42.

40. George, "Local Governance," 228.

41. George, "Local Governance," 227.

42. For details, see George, "Local Governance," 225.

43. George, "Local Governance," 227.

44. Yonghan Kim, "Okinawa migun kichi banhwan undong e seo baeunda" [Learning from the Return of the U.S. Military Base Movement in Okinawa], *Wolgan Mal* [Monthly Mal Magazine], September 1996, 92–95.

45. *Hankyore sinmun*, August 2, 2000, www.hani.co.kr/section-00300 . . . /0030040 11200008022127001.htm (accessed March 4, 2002).

46. *Hankyore sinmun*, August 6, 2000, www.hani.co.kr/section-00300 . . . /0030040 11200008062303001.htm (accessed March 4, 2002).

47. *Saram i saram ege* (October–November, 2000), 25.

48. Base21 (www.base21.0rg/show/show/php?p_cd=0&p_dv=0&p_docnbr =21475) (accessed October 2, 2002).

49. Amitav Acharya, "Democratisation and the Prospects for Participatory Regionalism in Southeast Asia," *Third World Quarterly* 24, no. 2 (2003): 381.

50. Acharya, "Democratisation," 384.

51. Koichi Iwabuchi, *Recentering Globalization: Popular Culture and Japanese Transnationalism* (Durham, N.C.: Duke University Press, 2002).

52. G. John Ikenberry, "Anti-Americanism in the Age of American Unipolarity," in *Korean Attitudes toward the United States: Changing Dynamics*, ed. David I. Steinberg (Armonk, N.Y.: M. E. Sharpe, 2005), 4.

53. Samuel S. Kim, "Northeast Asia in the Local-Regional-Global Nexus: Multiple Challenges and Contending Explanations," in *The International Relations of Northeast Asia*, ed. Samuel S. Kim (Lanham, Md.: Rowman & Littlefield, 2004), 27.

54. Larry Diamond, "Promoting Democracy in the 1990s: Actors, Instruments, and Issues," in *Democracy's Victory and Crisis*, ed. Alex Hadenius (Cambridge: Cambridge University Press, 1997), 352.

55. Tony Smith, "National Security Liberalism and American Foreign Policy," in *American Democracy Promotion*, ed. Michael Cox, G. John Ikenberry, and Takashi Inoguchi (New York: Oxford University Press, 2000), 100.

56. Diamond, "Promoting Democracy," 347.

57. Philip Shenon, "Philippine Senate Votes to Reject U.S. Base Renewal," *New York Times*, September 16, 1991.

58. Keith A. Nitta, "Paradigms," in *U.S.–Japan Relations in a Changing World*, ed. Steven K. Vogel (Washington, D.C.: Brookings Institution, 2002), 81.

59. Takashi Inoguchi, "Three Frameworks in Search of a Policy: U.S. Democracy Promotion in Asia-Pacific," in *American Democracy Promotion*, ed. Michael Cox, G. John Ikenberry, and Takashi Inoguchi (New York: Oxford University Press, 2000), 280.

60. Gerald L. Curtis, *The Logic of Japanese Politics: Leaders, Institutions, and the Limits of Change* (New York: Columbia University Press, 1999), 24.

61. Youngshik Bong, "Yongmi: Pragmatic Anti-Americanism in South Korea," *Brown Journal of World Affairs* 10, no. 2 (Winter–Spring 2004): 161.

62. Sook-Jong Lee, "The Rise of Korean Youth as a Political Force: Implications for the U.S.-Korea Alliance" (paper presentation, June 16, 2004. Available through the Center for Northeast Asia Policy Studies, Washington, D.C.: Brookings Institution), 20. Also see www.brookings.edu/fp/cnaps/events/20040616.htm (accessed July 5, 2004).

References

Acharya, Amitav. "Democratisation and the Prospects for Participatory Regionalism in Southeast Asia." *Third World Quarterly* 24, no. 2 (2003): 381.

Akaha, Tsuneo. "Three Faces of Japan: Nationalist, Regionalist and Globalist Futures." In *Globalism, Regionalism and Nationalism: Asia in Search of Its Role in the Twenty-first Century,* edited by Yoshinobu Yamamoto. Malden, Mass.: Blackwell, 1999.

Berger, Thomas U. "Norms, Identity, and National Security in Germany and Japan." In *The Culture of National Security: Norms, and Identity in World Politics,* edited by Peter J. Katzenstein. New York: Columbia University, 1996.

Bong, Youngshik. "Yongmi: Pragmatic Anti-Americanism in South Korea." *Brown Journal of World Affairs* 10, no. 2 (Winter–Spring 2004): 161.

Brown, Delmer M. *Nationalism in Japan: An Introductory Historical Analysis.* Berkeley: University of California, 1955.

Curtis, Gerald L. *The Logic of Japanese Politics: Leaders, Institutions, and the Limits of Change.* New York: Columbia University Press, 1999.

De Castro, Renato. "The Military and Philippine Democratization: A Case Study of the Government's 1995 Decision to Modernize the Armed Forces of the Philippines." In *Democratization: Philippine Perspectives,* edited by Felipe B. Miranda. Quezon City: University of the Philippines Press, 1997.

Diamond, Larry. "Promoting Democracy in the 1990s: Actors, Instruments, and Issues." In *Democracy's Victory and Crisis,* edited by Alex Hadenius. Cambridge: Cambridge University Press, 1997.

Furukawa, Shun'ichi. "Decentralization in Japan." In *Japan's Road to Pluralism: Transforming Local Communities in the Global Era,* edited by Shun'ichi Furukawa and Toshihiro Menju. Tokyo: Japan Center for International Exchange, 2003.

George, Terrence R. "Local Governance: People Power in the Provinces?" In *Noble Organizing for Democracy: NGOs, Civil Society, and the Philippine State,* edited by G.

Sidney Silliman and Lela Garner Noble. Honolulu: University of Hawaii, 1998.

Global Attitudes Project. *Views of a Changing World.* Washington, D.C.: Pew Research Center for the People and the Press, 2003.

Hill, Dilys M. *Democratic Theory and Local Government.* London: Allen & Unwin, Ltd., 1974.

Iguchi, Haruo. "Complication: American Military Presence in Okinawa and Enhancing the U.S.-Japan Alliance." In *United States–Japan Strategic Dialogue: Beyond the Defense Guidelines.* Honolulu: Center for Strategic and International Studies, Pacific Forum, 2001. www.csis.org/pacfor/us_japan_dialogue.pdf (accessed November 17, 2003).

Ikenberry, G. John. "Anti-Americanism in the Age of American Unipolarity." In *Korean Attitudes toward the United States: Changing Dynamics,* edited by David I. Steinberg. Armonk, N.Y.: M. E. Sharpe, 2005.

Inoguchi, Takashi. "Three Frameworks in Search of a Policy: U.S. Democracy Promotion in Asia-Pacific." In *American Democracy Promotion,* edited by Michael Cox, G. John Ikenberry, and Takashi Inoguchi. New York: Oxford University Press, 2000.

Iwabuchi, Koichi. *Recentering Globalization: Popular Culture and Japanese Transnationalism.* Durham, N.C.: Duke University Press, 2002.

Kamimura, Naoki. "Japanese Civil Society and U.S.-Japan Security Relations in the 1990s." *Medicine and Global Survival* 7, no. 1 (April 2001): 21.

Kim, Hyuk-rae. "The State and Civil Society in Transition: The Role of Non-Governmental Organizations in South Korea." *Pacific Review* 13, no. 4 (Winter 2000): 603.

Kim, Ilpyong J., and Eun Sung Chung. "Establishing Democratic Rule in South Korea: Local Autonomy and Democracy." *In Depth* 3, no. 1 (1993): 212.

Kim, Samuel S. "Northeast Asia in the Local-Regional-Global Nexus: Multiple Challenges and Contending Explanations." In *The International Relations of Northeast Asia,* edited by Samuel S. Kim. Lanham, Md.: Rowman & Littlefield, 2004.

Kim, Yonghan. "Okinawa migun kichi banhwan undong e seo baeunda" [Learning from the return of the U.S. military base movement in Okinawa]. *Wolgan Mal* [Monthly Mal Magazine], September 1996, 92–95.

King, Desmond, and Gerry Stoker, eds. *Rethinking Local Democracy.* London: Macmillan, 1996.

Lee, Jung-Hoon. "Globalization, Nationalism, and Security Options for South Korea." In *Democratization and Globalization in Korea: Assessments and Prospects,* edited by Chung-in Moon and Jongryn Mo. Seoul: Yonsei University, 1999.

Lee, Sook-Jong. "The Rise of Korean Youth as a Political Force: Implications for the U.S.-Korea Alliance." Brookings Institution Online. www.brookings.edu/fp/cnaps/events/20040616.htm (accessed July 5, 2004).

Moon, K. "Nationalism, Anti-Americanism, and Democratic Consolidation." In *Korea's Democratization,* edited by Samuel S. Kim. New York: Cambridge University, 2003.

Moon, Katharine H. S. "Resurrecting Prostitutes and Overturning Treaties: Gender Politics in the 'Anti-American' Movement in South Korea." *Journal of Asian Studies* (February 2007).

———. *Sex among Allies: Military Prostitution in U.S.–Korea Relations*. New York: Columbia University, 1997.

National Network to End the War against Iraq. "Anti-war protests begin in Asia-Pacific," October 15, 2002. www.endthewar.org/features/asiapacific/htm.

Nitta, Keith A. "Paradigms." In *U.S.-Japan Relations in a Changing World*, edited by Steven K. Vogel. Washington, D.C.: Brookings Institution, 2002.

Pew Global Attitudes Project. *What the World Thinks in 2002*. Washington, D.C.: Pew Research Center for the People and the Press, 2002.

Republic of Korea National Assembly. Bill #16102, Migun kongyo chiyok chiwon mit chumin kwon-ik po thing ho e kwanhan pomlyullan [Legislative bill on support to the USFK regions and protection of the rights and interests of residents]. (March 27, 2003). www.assembly.go.kr.

Rose, Fred. *Coalitions against the Class Divide: Lessons from the Labor, Peace, and Environmental Movements*. Ithaca, N.Y.: Cornell University Press, 2000.

Seong, Kyoung-Ryung. "Delayed Decentralization and Incomplete Democratic Consolidation." In *Institutional Reform and Democratic Consolidation in Korea*, edited by Larry Diamond and Doh Chull Shin. Stanford, Calif.: Hoover Institution Press, 2000.

Smith, Sheila A. "Challenging National Authority: Okinawa Prefecture and the U.S. Military Bases." In *Local Voices, National Issues: The Impact of Local Initiative in Japanese Policy-Making*, edited by Sheila A. Smith. Ann Arbor: University of Michigan Press, 2000.

Smith, Tony. "National Security Liberalism and American Foreign Policy." In *American Democracy Promotion*, edited by Michael Cox, G. John Ikenberry, and Takashi Inoguchi. New York: Oxford University Press, 2000.

Yoshida, Shin'ichi. "Rethinking the Public Interest in Japan: Civil Society in the Making." In *Deciding the Public Good: Governance and Civil Society in Japan*, edited by Tadashi Yamamoto. Tokyo: Japan Center for International Exchange, 1999.

8

Identity Politics, Nationalism, and the Future of Northeast Asian Order

Chung-in Moon and Seung-Won Suh

THE SUCCESSFUL LAUNCHING OF THE European Union and the amazing resilience of the North Atlantic Treaty Organization (NATO) in the post–Cold War era have renewed scholarly and policy interest in regionalism. Northeast Asia is no exception to this general trend. Dissolution of the bipolar Cold War structure, growing intraregional economic interdependence, and dense social and cultural networks among countries in the region have heightened expectation for a new Northeast Asian regional order based on multilateral security cooperation, collective security, and economic regionalism. Changing structural parameters as well as new waves of globalization and regionalization are believed to have dismantled the old regional order framed around finite deterrence, collective defense, and mercantile competition.[1]

But such liberal, optimistic anticipation seems rather premature. As Paul Bracken succinctly observes, "The post–Cold War never came to Asia. It was a Western conceit."[2] While the structure of finite deterrence embedded in East Asian geopolitics still persists,[3] the tragedy of great power politics haunts the region.[4] Aaron Friedberg even predicts that "Europe's past could be Asia's future."[5] Realists' pessimistic projections are not unfounded. As theorists of power transition expound, China's ascension and increasing dissatisfaction with its status in regional politics could pose a direct challenge to the American hegemonic position, undermining strategic stability and deepening conflict potential with the United States.[6] American disengagement from the region could further complicate its strategic outlook. A sequential development of American disengagement, Japanese remilitarization, Chinese hegemonic ambition, and a South Korean defensive posture could all contribute to reviving the nightmarish memory of the late-nineteenth-century anarchical order. What is dreadful is that Northeast Asian countries possess or have the potential of possessing daunting new military capabilities, such as weapons of mass destruction, to inflict considerable damage to outside powers. Such strategic uncertainty could dampen intraregional economic cooperation, significantly delaying the process of regional integration.

What drives the security dilemma in Northeast Asia? The Northeast Asian security dilemma is not solely a product of power politics. Distribution of power and subsequent relative gains and losses matter in shaping the region's strategic calculus, but serve only as a necessary, yet insufficient, condition. More critical is national identity and the politics of nationalism, which are closely intertwined with collective memory of history. National identity is important because it is responsible for shaping shared norms, interests, and images of countries in the region, eventually affecting mutual policy behavior. Northeast Asian countries have not yet cultivated a regional identity capable of reducing mutual distrust and suspicion and building a regional order for common security and prosperity in the region. The unresolved clash of identity politics has reinforced the security dilemma, clouding the future of the Northeast Asian regional order.

Against the backdrop of the above observations, this chapter attempts to elucidate how national identity and nationalism affect the formation of regional order in Northeast Asia. The first part of the chapter presents contending views of regional order by paying attention to power, interests, and identity. The second part examines old and new patterns of nationalism in Northeast Asia. The third part of the chapter attempts to understand the impact of nationalism on the shaping of regional order by analyzing survey data on mutual perceptions among Northeast Asian countries. The concluding part suggests ways of overcoming the dilemma of nationalist identity politics and facilitating a new regional order in Northeast Asia.

Power, Interests, Identity, and Regional Order: Analytical Notes

Regional order can be defined as "a formal or informal arrangement that sustains rule-governed interactions among states in their pursuit of individual and collective goals" in a specific region.[7] This definition of regional order presupposes three elements. The first element is the idea of patterned regularity.[8] Formal or informal arrangements of principles, rules, habits, and institutions facilitate countries in the region to behave in patterned ways. And the anticipation of patterned behavior in turn generates reciprocal reactions by other actors in the region. Such patterned regularity reduces chances for disorder and uncertainty. Second, reciprocal interactions and resulting patterned regularity are by and large a product of rule-governed behavior. Patterns of regularity would be inconceivable without corresponding rule-governed behavior. Compliance with principles, norms, and rules not only prevents any deviant behavior but also creates and enhances purposive order.[9] Finally, the purposive regional order is in turn predicated on the satisfaction of normative conditions for coexistence of actors in the region. They involve, not only the reduction of the likelihood of regional violence, but also the creation of minimally acceptable conditions of economic well-being, social justice, ecological stability, and participation in decision making in the region.[10]

How to achieve regional order? Pathways to regional order also differ among contending theoretical perspectives.[11] Realists argue that regional order is a function of power.[12] Depending upon the configuration of power, regional order can take several forms: anarchical, hierarchical, balance of power, consortium, or hegemonic. Anarchical regional order, which resembles the Hobbesian world of all against all, is rather rare in reality. However, diffused power; deformed governance structure; and individual maximizing behavior for power, wealth, and status can often lead to anarchical regional order. The only viable rule under the anarchical order is survival of the fittest. Actors in the region can avoid the violence and instability associated with anarchical order by resorting to a balance of power. However, a balance of power cannot guarantee stable peace either, because of the fluidity of power and the dynamics of alliance politics.[13]

The hierarchical form of regional order involves a differential arrangement of regional actors, depending upon their power and influence. A tributary system and patron-client relationships are classical examples of hierarchical regional order. Although the tributary system no longer exists, hierarchical structure of patron-client relationships can be found in various forms of alliances. The consortium form of regional order refers to collective management of regional security and economic order by major powers. As the Concert of Power in the post-Napoleonic era illustrates, such a regional arrangement can be undertaken through mutual consultation and consensus among major powers. Finally, a hegemonic order can be envisaged. It can be either benign or malignant. While a benign hegemonic regional order refers to regional security and economic arrangements in which a hegemonic leader provides collective goods for the survival and prosperity of regional actors, a malignant one can be defined as a regional order in which a hegemonic leader engages in the practice of domination and subjugation. The malignant hegemonic order often involves the imposition of imperial order on a regional scale.

Liberals and constructivists, however, suggest alternative views of regional order. Liberals argue that regional order can evolve into several diverse forms, depending upon the configuration of interests and norms, not power. Actors in the region can show rule-governed behavior, not only because of the salience of gain from patterned regularity and cooperation, but also because of norms, practices, and even institutional inertia.[14] Following the founding spirit of the United Nations, countries in a region can attempt to form a collective security system that can overcome the deficiencies of an alliance system. A collective security system, a regional order that is based on collective identity transcending parochial individual interests, can surely be conducive to building and sustaining a stable peace. Or regional regimes can be created and maintained in order to govern the security behavior of regional actors. Recent debates on the creation of multilateral security cooperation regimes at the regional level exemplify this aspect. Although regional security regimes might be weaker than a collective security system in the enforcement of common security and peace, they can be more desirable options than military deterrence and alliance politics in making and building peace. Some liberals would go beyond this. According to them, viable and sustaining regional order cannot be achieved without inducing the internal transformation of regional actors. In this regard, adoption of a market economy and democracy becomes an essential element in forming a community of security.[15] The ultimate liberal vision is the creation of total regional integration evolving from a free-trade area, common market, economic union, and currency union into the total political integration that would accompany a collective security system.

Internal structural transformation, provision of liberal trends, and subsequent regional arrangement of liberal institutions are important prerequisites for the creation of a viable regional order. As constructivists argue, however, institutions are nothing but a reflection of interests and identity in their social totality.[16] Failure to address identity and intersubjective understanding of its historical formation and behavioral manifestation is bound to yield a lack of authentic cooperation among regional actors, for identity is as important as power and interests in shaping and sustaining regional order. Identity and collective memory of the past are crucial variables in forging shared values and common goals vital to the formation of a community of security, simply because most countries in a given region are usually inflicted with pain from their fractured past. It is virtually inconceivable for them to engage in practices of cooperation without first healing the pain and then recognizing and respecting the identity of others.[17]

Central to the constructivist perspective is identity, which is socially constructed through knowledge and social interactions. Identity as a social construct shapes the rules, norms, and institutions that in turn affect the purpose, intention, and interests of agents. It is through identity that an agent defines one's own perception of and behavior toward the outside world, and its perception of, and the reactions it receives from, the outside world subsequently contribute to forming an agent's own identity. Identity also exists in a collective form. Collective identity emanates from a construction of nationhood or statehood that is based on interdependence, common fate, and homogeneity among members of a community.[18] Collective national identity is manifested through nationalism. Thus, nationalism offers an important clue to understanding national identity and its behavioral manifestations, such as approaches to regional cooperation and integration.[19]

What analytical perspective is then most ideal in accounting for and predicting a Northeast Asian regional order? As Peter J. Katzenstein and Rudra Sil suggest, an analytical eclecticism seems most suitable because power, interests, and norms, or identity alone cannot fully explain and predict the emerging nature of a regional order.[20] Patterns of regional order are by and large contingent upon the dynamic interplay of power, interests, and identity. The dynamics of power transition between the United States and China appears to be an important factor affecting a regional contour, but it does not seem to be deterministic. In a similar vein, growing economic interdependence and cultivation of dense social and human networks do not necessarily guarantee a liberal transition in the region based on the expansion of a market economy, proliferation of democracy, and the formation of an economic and security community. Liberal optimism is more than often counterbalanced by the logic of power politics. Moreover, identity and its behavioral manifestation through nationalism do not unilaterally dictate the course of a regional order either.

There are a number of scenarios that could play out in the region, depending on the combination of power, interests, and identity. If traumatic power transition is complicated with assertive nationalism, the Northeast Asian regional order could face a nightmarish outlook. For hegemonic rivalry for power and domination among regional actors, which is inspired by parochial nationalist zeal, is bound to bring about an anarchical regional order characterized by survival of the fittest. Peace and common prosperity cannot be anticipated under this setting. However, if liberal transition is combined with, and fostered by, a shared regional identity that transcends parochial nationalism, a viable and harmonious regional order and ultimately a community of peace and prosperity can be followed. This is because a complementarity of interests as well as shared norms and values, coupled with a common regional identity, can facilitate the process of regional cooperation and integration.

Two other scenarios are also feasible. One involves a situation in which the region undergoes a liberal transition amid the entanglement of parochial nationalism, whereas the probability of grand conflict resulting from power transition is relatively low. Such a scenario is likely to delay the process of community building in the region, but it would mitigate the potential of major military conflicts. The other scenario is predicated on the combination of a greater chance for power transition and a shared regional collective identity. This implies a situation where China, Japan, and South Korea are able to forge greater regional cooperation and integration through a collective regional identity, but China and the United States enter a hegemonic power rivalry. Given the pivotal role of the United States in the region, this scenario is less likely, but its plausibility cannot be ruled out.

In view of the above, there are two grand competing trends in Northeast Asia. One is power transition, and the other is liberal transition. Both are profoundly influenced by national identity and nationalism. Identity politics and nationalism can be seen as powerful wild cards that not only affect parameters underlying power and interests but also shape the ultimate landscape of a Northeast Asian regional order. Against this backdrop, we will attempt to elucidate the evolving nature of national identity and nationalism in Northeast Asian countries.

Collective Identity and Varieties of Northeast Asian Nationalism

Nationalism as a social construct of collective identity of nation or statehood influences patterns of state behavior.[21] The impact of nationalism on foreign policy behavior appears to be especially profound in Northeast Asia. What then are the old and newly emerging patterns of nationalism in Japan, South Korea, and China? What factors are responsible for its resuscitation? How do they affect the formation of a viable regional order for cooperation and integration?

The Resurgence of Neonationalism in Japan

Burdened by the defeat in the Pacific War and the shadow of American influence, Japan has long suffered from an ambiguous national identity.[22] There has been no immediate replacement to the Japanese nationalism that was deeply ingrained in the imperial system and national entity (*kokutai*). The Tokyo War Tribunal and the Peace Constitution were a constant reminder of crimes committed in the name of Japanese nationalism, and the scarlet letter of shame that it wore was effective in suppressing the revival of offensive Japanese nationalist zeal. Postwar Japan was a classical example of "compromised sovereignty" as evidenced by the Peace Constitution, which prohibits military sovereignty.[23] While the burden of history has forced the Japanese to constantly engage in an apologetic attitude toward neighboring countries, Japan also relied too heavily on the United States to be autonomous and independent. The United States was Japan's window to the world. Japan was a part of East Asia, but its Asian identity evaporated with its rush to the world and the West.[24] The burden of history, the moral imperative of pacifism, and its conformity with the United States overshadowed the formation of a distinct national identity in postwar Japan.

Since the early 1980s, however, two waves of nationalist revival have surfaced. The first wave was a revival from above. Japan's remarkable economic recovery and new status as one of the economic superpowers drove its right-wing political elite to search for Japan's own identity. Nakasone Yasuhiro took the lead, urging the Japanese to reestablish Japan's new position in international society by overcoming the masochistic view of history nurtured by the Tokyo War Tribunal. He stirred the nationalist revival by not only paying tribute to the Yasukuni Shrine, which enshrines Class A war criminals, but also campaigning for the "internationalization of Japan."[25] A number of conservative politicians followed Nakasone's lead. Ozawa Ichiro called for the creation of *futsu no kuni* ("normal state") through the flexible interpretation of the Peace Constitution.[26] Along with this, he justified the dispatch of the UN Peacekeeping Operation forces to Cambodia. Underlying the first revival of Japanese nationalist sentiments was the realignment of Japan's international political status to befit its economic power.

The second wave of nationalist revival emerged in the mid-1990s. Ishida and others identify four variants of this neonationalism.[27] The first is the historical revisionist movement, led by the Society for the Study of Liberal Historical View and the Society for Making New History Textbooks, among others. According to them, contemporary Japanese history was gravely distorted by the United States in order to implant an anti-Japanese masochistic view of history in the minds of the Japanese.[28] Their revisionist history includes the following: the Pacific War was initiated to liberate Asia from Western imperial domination; the Rape of Nanking is an outright fabrication by the Chinese; the existence of comfort women is fictional. This ultraconservative movement is supported by such right-wing media as *Seiron, Shokun,* and *SAPIO,* and 150 members of the Japanese Diet have formed the "Diet Members League for Shining Japan" to support the grassroots movement's effort to revise existing history textbooks.[29]

The second variant is what Ishida and others term parasite nationalism.[30] It can be seen as a conscious move by Japanese elites to promote their nationalist agenda by bandwagoning on the United States. Adoption of legislative and policy measures such as the new Defense Guidelines, overseas dispatch of noncombat forces, and the Emergency-Related Act was designed to accommodate American demands in its foreign and national security policy. But the compliance with American demands was tantamount to fostering Japan's own transformation into a normal state. John Dower dubs this version of nationalism a SCAPanese model (a punning combination of U.S. Supreme Command of Asia-Pacific [SCAP] and Japanese nationalism) in the sense that Japan has been taking advantage of the United States in realizing its nationalist goals, such as the recovery of military sovereignty.[31] Shintaro Ishihara, the controversial Tokyo governor, also belongs to this category. He was recognized as a staunch anti-American Japanese nationalist with the coauthoring of the book "*Japan That Can Say 'No,'*" meaning "no" to the United States.[32] But he has shifted his position from anti-American to anti-Chinese nationalism by arguing that in order to cope with threats from China, North Korea, and global terrorists, Japan should strengthen its alliance with the United States.[33]

Third, revival of a primordial form of nationalism is also nascent. This variant of neonationalism attempts to revive Japanese national identity through the resuscitation of the imperial system.[34] Traditional Japanese nationalism was rooted in its imperial system in which the deified emperor served as the essence of the Japanese national entity. But the postwar constitution, which was introduced by General Douglas MacArthur's occupation government, demoted the Japanese emperor to only a symbolic figure.[35] Its proponents strive to enhance the internal cohesion and unity of Japan by resorting to the essence of national identity manifested through the emperor. Former prime minister Mori Yoshiro's remark that "Japan is a *Kami no Kuni* (a divine country) with the Emperor at its center" well underscores this primordial sentiment.[36] Extreme ultraconservative nationalists have been pushing for this line of thought.[37]

Finally, neonationalism has increasingly taken the form of xenophobic populism reminiscent of the aftermath of the Kanto Great Earthquake in the 1920s, during which the Japanese massacred Korean residents in the Kanto area by spreading the rumor that Koreans engaged in arson and thefts. Racism has become the driving force of this populist nationalism. Ishihara Shintaro's recent remarks attributing an increase in crime to Chinese and other foreign, mostly Asian, residents in Japan exemplify this trend in Japan. He argues that Tokyo is full of *daisankokunin* (people of third countries) such as Korean and Taiwanese residents and illegal migrant foreigners, who would commit atrocious crimes if given the chance. When disasters strike Tokyo, it would be possible for them to set off a civil disturbance that the police force alone cannot control.[38] This kind of xenophobic populism seems to be broadly shared by the Japanese masses, who are often exposed to anti-Korean and anti-Chinese publications.[39]

Why the sudden resurgence of nationalist sentiment in Japan? Several factors account for it. First, the dissolution of the grand conservative ruling coalition under the Liberal Democratic Party has heightened political uncertainty. One way of coping with it has been to appeal to nationalist sentiments such as territorial integrity, national defense, promotion of national consciousness, and enhancement of patriotism.[40] Second, the new trend can be explained in part as a challenge by grassroots movements to the structural rigidity of the existing political system. Lack of political action by existing politicians has precipitated the rise of the popular nationalist movements. Third, neo-nationalism might be a response to the breakdown of Japan's economic and social system. While the *Heisei* recession followed by the bubble economy significantly depressed the Japanese economy, a series of social and natural disasters such as a surge in youth crime, the sarin gas attack in the Tokyo subway, a major accident at the Tokaimura uranium reprocessing plant, and the Kobe earthquake have heightened people's fear. Resurgence of nationalist sentiments among the Japanese can be seen as a desperate defense mechanism to console themselves over the social meltdown. Lastly, Tatsuo Inoue argues that the rise of neonationalism can be ascribed to the collapse of the existing Japanese system, which was characterized by the triad of order composed of the state, market, and community.[41] The weakening of community institutions (e.g., firms, bureaucracies, and schools), which functioned as healthy intermediate organizations linking the state to the market, may have encouraged Japanese to seek nationalism as an alternative to community.

Neonationalism has now become one of the major driving forces behind Japan's foreign and domestic policy. While the grassroots's push for revisionist history has produced some visible results, such as the publication of new history textbooks, Japan has been steadily preparing to become a normal state through legislative changes and the strengthening of its overall defense posture. Nuclear and missile threats from North Korea provide Japan with an ideal public rationale for the realignment. More importantly, former prime minister Koizumi Junichiro and the ruling Liberal Democratic Party have initiated a new move to amend the Peace Constitution's Article 9 to allow the possession of regular armed forces in Japan, while keeping its renunciation of war intact.[42] Former prime minister Nakasone justified it by stating "The first constitution in Japan (the Meiji constitution) was given by the emperor. General MacArthur gave the second constitution. It is time for the Japanese people to make their own constitution."[43] Koizumi's successor, Abe Shinzo, has also been capitalizing on the issue of constitutional amendment for his own political gains.

Japan's quest for national identity through assertive nationalism can negatively affect Northeast Asian regionalism in several ways. For Northeast Asian countries, the revival of right-wing nationalism in Japan is closely associated with the memory of Japanese colonial expansion and *Daitoa Kyoeiken.* Such perceptual association will make it harder to enhance regional cooperation with Japan and accept its regional leadership. The resurgence of national-ist sentiments has also led to a new domestic political geography in which "doves" (*hato ha*) have lost their power and influence, whereas "hawks" (*taka ha*) have taken a new commanding height.[44] Such a realignment bears negative implications for regional cooperation since "doves" have tradition-ally valued close ties with China and South Korea and promoted the idea of Northeast Asian regionalism. Meanwhile, "hawks" have been skeptical of it by taking a confrontational foreign policy on neighboring countries, and have successfully exploited suspicion of regionalism for domestic political gains.[45] Although Abe's assertive Asian diplomacy, as exemplified by his visit to Beijing and Seoul immediately after his election as the new prime minister of Japan in October 2006, has helped improve his "hawkish" image, his political agenda, such as the constitutional amendment (though not renewed visits to the Yasukuni Shrine[46]) is likely to invite opposition from neighboring countries, further deteriorating Japan's bilateral relations with China and South Korea.

Japan's pursuit of detour regionalism in Southeast Asia is also likely to undercut the process of regionalism in Northeast Asia. Geographic proximity is usually seen as the basic requirement for regional cooperation and integra-tion. Accordingly, it would seem natural for Japan to seek cooperation with its neighboring countries in Northeast Asia. But Japan has been giving greater emphasis to Southeast Asia in its pursuit of East Asian regionalism. This was evident in former prime minister Koizumi's proposal of establishing an East Asian community on the occasion of his visit to Southeast Asian countries in January 2002. It was the first time that the Japanese government officially mentioned the concept of an East Asian community, but its scope was limited to Southeast Asian countries, Australia, and New Zealand, with Northeast Asian countries excluded from this initiative.[47] Japan's tilt toward Southeast Asia has become further visible through the adoption of the Tokyo Declara-tion between Koizumi and ASEAN (Association of South East Asian Nations) leaders in December 2003, which reaffirmed the strengthened bilateral ties be-tween Japan and ASEAN. Such policy orientation toward detour regionalism has produced adverse effects on regional cooperation in Northeast Asia.

Finally, since the inauguration of the Koizumi cabinet, Japan has taken a staunchly pro-American policy line. Given the rise of China and North Korea's nuclear and missile threat, the policy shift could have been expected. However, promotion of neonationalism by bandwagoning on the United States has alarmed neighboring countries about Japan's intentions. Equally troublesome is that Japan has begun to relinquish its traditional regional leadership role as it has intensified adherence to its pro-American stance.[48] Japan is one of the few countries that can play a crucial leadership role in promoting regional cooperation and integration, as shown through its proposal on the Asian Monetary Fund and the Miyazawa Initiative. But its defection to the United States by "getting out of Northeast Asia" could not only damage its long-term national interests but also severely impede the process of building a stable regional order. The new prime minister, Abe Shinzo, has been trying to reverse such an image by undertaking an Asian diplomacy initiative, but its effectiveness is yet to be seen.

Unfailing Nationalist Zeal in South Korea

As in Japan, South Korea is also witnessing a resurgent fever of nationalism that defies the forces of globalization and regionalization. The sea of shirts with "red devil" prints (the South Korean soccer players were nicknamed "red devils") during the 2002 World Cup was the most outstanding testimonial of the revival of nationalist zeal, as millions of Koreans flooded the streets of Seoul to cheer and celebrate the Korean soccer team. Their awesome display of support alarmed the entire world. But their nationalist sentiments born of the sporting event were soon transposed into the political arena, with massive anti-American candlelight demonstrations in protest of the accidental killing of two middle-school girl students by American soldiers, which can be seen as an extension of the nationalistic enthusiasm formed during the World Cup. Koreans have also manifested hysterical responses to the revival of Japanese neonationalist movements. Although Koreans have been concerned about China's rise, the intensity of anti-Chinese sentiment has been significantly less than that of anti-Japanese and anti-American sentiments. South Koreans' militant role in aborting the Cancun WTO meeting as well as organizing opposition to liberalization of rice markets and bilateral free-trade agreements (FTAs) reveals another dimension of ascending economic nationalism. The specter of nationalism is indeed alive and well in South Korea.

Three contending variants of nationalism in Korea are in our purview: primordial, instrumentalist, and postmodernist.[49] The primordial perspective argues that Korean national identity is intrinsic through a common ancestry (*Dangun*), history, language, and culture.[50] Koreans, being descendants of Dangun, are the chosen people by heaven, and they are believed to benefit the world. To its proponents, the Dangun legend is not mythology, but a historical reality, and the blood ties originating from the same ancestry make all Koreans part of one extended family.[51] The primordial nationalism is founded on an organic view of the Korean nation, reinforced by religion and educational doctrine. Most elementary schools in South Korea have a statue of Dangun on campus and offer courses on Dangun and the Korean nation that emphasize the unity of Korean people as an organic entity. Primordial nationalism has been socialized through elementary education in South Korea. North Korea has been much more assertive in championing this form of nationalism by claiming the discovery of the original royal tomb of Dangun in a suburb of Pyongyang in the mid-1990s and declaring it the holiest site of the Korean nation.[52] The organic, primordial view has been inspired by such pioneering nationalist historiographers such as Shin Chae-ho and Park Eun-sik, who reconceptualized state history not as a dynastic history, but as a history of the nation (*minjok*). According to Shin, "Without the minjok, there is no history; without history, the minjok cannot have a clear perception of the state. . . . A state is an organic entity formed from the national spirit" (*minjok cheongshin*).[53]

The instrumentalist perspective asserts that nationalism is a foreign concept borrowed from Europe, and that it was formed and sustained with modernization and the birth of the nation-state.[54] Its proponents concur with the primordial view of the Korean nation as an a priori, homogeneous ethnic entity. But they differ from it in the sense that nationalism as an ideology emerged as an instrument to resist foreign penetration and domination, to foster the process of modernization, and to consolidate national sovereignty and unification. According to their view, Korean nationalism has evolved through three different forms. The first is the advent of an anti-imperial nationalism of self-preservation during the Japanese colonial period, which aimed at liberating Korea from Japanese colonial domination and restoring state sovereignty. It served as a backbone of the independence movement by enhancing national consciousness.

The second involves a modernizing nationalism. Upon gaining independence in 1945, Korea was left with two major national mandates, modernization and state building on the one hand, and unification of the divided country on the other. In order to expedite the process of modernization and state building, the South Korean government devised an official nationalism as a vehicle of mobilizing people and resources and consolidating state power and authority. Park Chung-Hee utilized this form of official nationalism to justify authoritarian state corporatism and exclusion of the popular sector, which in turn triggered the rise of popular nationalism (*minjung minjokjuui*). Popular nationalism developed into an ideological movement to challenge the legitimacy of Park's modernizing nationalism as well as to bring people's attention to democracy, equality, and a more self-reliant economy.[55] Dialectal interactions between official and popular nationalism shaped the discursive landscape of Korean nationalism in the 1970s and 1980s.

Finally, Korean nationalism has been closely associated with the realization of national unification. Since South Korea has attained modernization, it seems quite natural that Korean nationalism is now focused on national unification. Hak-joon Kim claims that "overcoming national division, namely national unification, is the very ideology and ideal of Korean nationalism. But Korea still remains divided, and, therefore, Korean nationalism encounters a major setback. Self-actualization of Korean nationalism can be achieved only through national unification."[56] Having set the unity of the divided Korean nation as the ultimate goal, the instrumentalists view Korean nationalism as a powerful means to carry out the incomplete task of national unification.

Most recently, both primordial and instrumentalist perspectives have been subject to intense critiques by postmodernists.[57] They contend that national-ism in Korea is nothing but a modern social construct to bind Koreans to an imagined community through cultural identity and shared memory of the historical past. Henry H. Em refutes the primordial and instrumental views of Korean nationalism by stating that "narratives on 'Korean' identity did not simply accumulate over time; not all such narratives got transmitted, and even those that were, were invariably translated (reinvented) for use in the present."[58] Underlying motives of these narratives are to legitimate state power, enhance social integration, and maintain order in postcolonial nation building through a selective interpretation for discourses on political power rather than to establish and acknowledge an objective reality. As Carter Eck-ert succinctly puts it, "nationalist paradigms have so dominated intellectual life in Korea that they have obfuscated, subsumed, or obliterated virtually all other possible modes of historical interpretation."[59] Thus, postmodernists believe that it is time for Koreans, especially Korean intellectuals, to escape from looking through a myopic nationalist lens and to resort to postmodern, postnationalist, and pluralist discourses.

Postmodern critiques notwithstanding, nationalism exists and thrives as a social reality by having evolved into concrete ideas, norms, actions, and movements affecting public attitudes as well as policy behavior. The failed and incomplete tasks of nationalism have made it all the more relevant and appealing.[60] Overcoming national division and achieving national unifica-tion constitute the top nationalist agenda. Some Korean nationalists have been calling for the recovery of military sovereignty by regaining wartime operational control of ROK (Republic of Korea) forces, which is currently under American military command. Having suffered from Japanese colonial domination, Koreans are extremely sensitive to the issue of territorial integ-rity. Korea's sovereign entitlement to Dokdo, a tiny island in the East Sea, and nationalist claims over the recovery of lost territory along the border with China underscore its importance. Nationalism has been extended to the economic domain too, where nationalists have been justifying the protection of the agricultural sector under the slogan of "body and soil are one" (*shinto bulyi*). Some hard-line nationalists even suggest that a unified Korea should emerge as a middle power with nuclear capabilities.

South Korea's search for national identity through nationalism reveals several inherent contradictions that can bring about harmful consequences for building a harmonious regional order.[61] First is a contradiction between nationalism and regionalism/globalism. The South Korean government has been pushing for regionalization and globalization, but such efforts have been undercut by nationalist sentiments and movements, as evidenced by delayed negotiations over free-trade agreements with Japan and China. Second, assertive nationalist sentiments have instilled a rather ambivalent perception of neighboring countries among Koreans. Improving economic and social ties have not ameliorated the Koreans' feeling of suspicion and distrust over Japan and China. Disputes over Dokdo, revision of Japanese history textbooks, and Prime Minister Koizumi's tributes to the Yasukuni Shrine have critically impaired Seoul-Tokyo ties, which were improved by the Kim-Obuchi Joint Declaration on Future Partnership in 1998 as well as the joint hosting of the 2002 World Cup. The same can be said of China–South Korea relations, where Chinese historical distortion of the Koguryo dynasty through the Northeast Project (*Dongbei Gongting*) has radically deteriorated South Korea's image of China.[62]

Finally, Korean nationalism has favored a vision of regional order different from that of other regional actors. For South Korean nationalists, the formation of a Korean commonwealth (*hanminjok gongdongche*) is preferred to any other form of regional community. The preference originates from Korea's historical experiences. South Korean nationalists strongly believe that Korean division was a product of the power politics of divide and rule among major powers, and that China, Japan, Russia, and the United States do not favor Korean unification for their own national interests. Thus, they feel that any meaningful discussion of regional order should occur only after Korean unification is achieved. Such an attitude can negatively influence South Korea's approach to regional cooperation and integration.

China: Between Popular and Positive Nationalism

At the Sixteenth Chinese Communist Party (CCP) Congress, which began on November 8, 2002, Jiang Zemin submitted a political report filled with such words as "national spirit" (*minzhu jingshen*), "patriotism" (*aiguozhuyi*), and "the Chinese civilization" (*zhonghuo wenming*). The report urged Chinese people to improve civic morality, patriotism, collectivism, honesty, family virtues, and professional ethics, which are all regarded as a core of Asian values spread by Chinese culture and civilization.[63] Although the report emphasized the connection of these values to a socialist ideological and ethical system, his remarks implied an ideological transition from socialism to nationalism. It became further evident when the PLA (People's Liberation Army) and party cadres touted his remarks as "a declaration of the resurrection of the Chinese people" (*zhonghua minzhu fuxing de xuanyanshu*). China's nationalist resurgence has become all the more pronounced since the publication of "China That Can Say 'No'" (*Zhongguo keyi shuo bu*) in 1996.[64] When the Chinese embassy in Belgrade was mistakenly bombed by NATO forces in May 1999, more than 170,000 Chinese held fierce anti-American demonstrations throughout China, the largest since the Cultural Revolution. Neither the socialist ideological template nor the democratic values increasingly shared among Chinese intellectuals could prevent the rise and diffusion of a new popular nationalism in China.

Chinese nationalism is not fixed, but varies over time, depending on circumstances. James Townsend classifies Chinese nationalism into four discernible categories: state nationalism, Han nationalism, Greater China nationalism, and transnational Chinese nationalism.[65] State nationalism has been dominant from the early days of the founding of the Republic of China by Sun Yat-sen in 1911 to the current communist state. As Friedrich Hegel envisaged, the state was seen as a completion of nationalist projects, and state nationalism was a valuable instrument for independence, nation building, and modernization. Meanwhile, Han nationalism is rooted in the ethnic origins of the Han race, such as shared history, language, and culture, through which the Han Chinese believe that they are superior to the outside world.[66] Whereas Greater China nationalism is predicated on the concept of an extended territoriality that includes not only mainland China, but also Hong Kong, Macao, and Taiwan, transnational Chinese nationalism is the most encompassing idea, since it includes overseas Chinese as an integral part of China.[67] These four categories of nationalism are not mutually exclusive, but overlap through the convergence of culturalism, statism, organic corporatism, and territoriality.

Zhimin Chen and Junbo Jian have also suggested three more recent versions of Chinese nationalism as they are related to foreign policy.[68] The first is positive nationalism, which Hu Yaobang conceived in 1982, and which still constitutes the mainstream form of nationalism in China. Chen and Jian argue that it is an enlightened or benign nationalism, which attempts not only to overcome the revolutionary, self-reliant nationalism of the past but also to seek harmonious and compromising relations with the international community. It is moderate and conservative by emphasizing peace and stability in international society as well as seeking international recognition and respect. Internally, positive nationalism aims at mobilizing Chinese people for modernization, economic development, and national integration. The second variant of Chinese nationalism is an official patriotism that emerged in the wake of the Tienanmen incident and the demise of the Cold War system. It places a greater importance on national symbols, such as the national flag and national anthem, through a systematic education of Chinese youths. It can be seen as an official doctrine of state nationalism by the CCP in order to consolidate state power, ensure political stability, and promote national integration by emphasizing the primacy of the nation-state. The final form is popular nationalism, which is founded on three cardinal tenets: traditionalism (Confucianism, cultural nationalism), neoconservatism (primacy of central authority), and *shuo bu zhuyi* (say "no"-ism).[69] Whereas official patriotism is nationalism from above, mass nationalism is from below. Chen and Jian contend that the future of Chinese nationalism depends on how to incorporate these two contending forms, official and defensive versus popular and offensive, into a dialectical synthesis of positive nationalism.

In spite of opening, reform, and the pressures of globalization, nationalist sentiments are on the rise in China. What explains this? First is the rekindling of national identity in the context of China's lingering collective memory of the past, such as the humiliating subjugation to Japan and Western powers and delayed modernization.[70] Victimization narratives associated with a century of national humiliation have long governed the Chinese national psyche, beginning with the first Opium War in the mid-nineteenth century. With the rediscovery of China's rich cultural heritage and new national potential, Chinese nationalism, regardless of its form, has become a persuasive instrument to enhance national pride, cement national cohesion and unity, and strengthen national power. Moreover, Chinese nationalism is an expression of China's regained confidence in the glory of its past history and contemporary performance.

The second factor lies in the gap between power and status. Since its opening and reform in the early 1980s, China has undergone a remarkable economic transformation. In 2005, China became the third-largest trading nation ($1.4 trillion), in the world only trailing the United States and Germany. Its gross domestic product is the sixth largest in the world, while its foreign currency reserve ($800 billion) is the second largest next to Japan. At the same time, China enjoyed a trade surplus of $162 billion with the United States in 2004, and it holds $500 billion worth of U.S. government and corporate bonds. China has transformed itself into one of the most dynamic and powerful economies in the world in a relatively short time. In addition, China has been pursuing a more assertive diplomatic posture in bilateral and multilateral relationships. As Pan Wei of Beijing University puts it, "China will never have the capacity to be the world's leader, but it has more than enough capacity to pull the world's leader down from the stage."[71] Notwithstanding this tremendous transformation, China has not been able to enjoy an international standing commensurate to its economic power. As the recent campaign for a peaceful rise (*heping jueqi*) illustrates, a new form of positive nationalism has come to the forefront of Chinese discourse to narrow the gap between its power and international status.[72]

Third, recent Chinese nationalism represents a reactive move to a series of external events that have interfered with its territorial and political sovereignty and national pride, as the trajectory of nationalist resurgence in China has been delicately intertwined with external events. The 1989 Tienanmen incident and economic sanctions by the West, American and French sales of advanced weapons to Taiwan, the NATO bombing of the Chinese embassy in Belgrade in 1999, territorial disputes with Japan, the 2001 midair collision of a Chinese fighter plane with an American reconnaissance plane, and Western opposition to Beijing's bid for the international Olympics in 2000 were responsible for precipitating massive nationalist sentiment in China. Concurrently, any Western actions that interfere with China's political and territorial sovereignty, such as the Taiwan and Tibet issues as well as human rights, have precipitated offended nationalist responses in China.

Fourth, the resurgence can also be partly attributed to the Western construction of a China threat thesis.[73] Beginning in the mid-1990s, conservatives in the United States began to portray China as a major challenger, or even threat, to U.S. hegemony.[74] The inauguration of the Bush administration and the rise of neoconservatives in the United States have further amplified the China threat thesis. Its logic is rather simple and straightforward. Coming conflict with China is inevitable, not only because China has been catching up with the United States in terms of national power, but also because China is increasingly dissatisfied with its international and regional status. The only way to avoid the conflict is to slow the pace of growth of China's national power, while pushing for a further deepening of the capitalist system and a democratic reform.[75] A containment or encirclement of China leads to the logical outcome of power transition and grand conflict. The fear of rising Chinese power in the United States and Japan has in turn triggered "a process of malign amplification" where "cooperative actions are discounted and conflictual behavior becomes the focus of analysis."[76] China's response to this has been varied, ranging from the moderate "peaceful development" (*heping fazhan*) and "peaceful rise" (*heping jueqi*) to a more hard-line "preservation of sovereignty." But it has become clear that outside pressure in the form of a China threat has profoundly contributed to enhancing more assertive nationalist sentiments that justify a greater Chinese military power buildup.[77]

Finally, both positive nationalism and official patriotism have been encouraged by the Chinese political leadership as an ideological alternative to the socialist governing ideology, which has been subject to the law of diminishing returns.[78] Chinese market socialism through opening and reform was a great success. However, it was that very success that began to erode the legitimacy of socialist governance and the CCP. Whereas the Tienanmen incident revealed the CCP's political limits, polarization of the Chinese economy and society in terms of income and wealth, the coast and the hinterland, urban and rural areas, and gender gaps, as well as rampant corruption, had severely undercut the CCP's political and social standing. Official patriotism, which was initiated by Jiang Zemin on the occasion of the return of Hong Kong in 1997, was a well-calculated political and ideological move to supplement a waning socialist ideology.[79]

What then are the implications of the nationalist resurgence in China for the future of a Northeast Asian order?[80] If China chooses a positive or enlightened nationalism, no profound conflict is envisaged. Under the "peaceful development" policy line, China will seek a more accommodating regional policy through cooperative bilateral relations, open regionalism, and compliance with multilateralism. The Chinese government could be quite effective in pacifying offensive and parochial nationalist sentiments, while pursuing pragmatic goals of economic growth and regional strategic stability. But if China fails to harness unruly nationalist fever, worrisome consequences will follow. If the Chinese government tolerates popular nationalism in the name of "patriotism is not guilty," as shown in its silence over massive violent anti-Japanese riots (e.g., attacks on the Japanese embassy in Beijing and consulate office in Shanghai as well as the boycott of Japanese products) in March 2005, a Northeast Asian regional order based on cooperation and integration is highly unlikely, for such hostile attitudes can negatively affect its relations not only with Japan but also with South Korea and the United States.

China's pursuit of detour regionalism can pose another challenge to the formation of a viable Northeast Asian regional order. According to geographic proximity, economic interdependence, and economies of scale, it seems quite natural for China to explore ways of institutionalizing economic and security cooperation with Japan and South Korea. But China has shown a rather lukewarm attitude toward fostering subregional cooperation in Northeast Asia. In contrast, like Japan, it has been very active in seeking bilateral cooperation with ASEAN countries by signing a Framework Agreement for Comprehensive Economic Cooperation with ASEAN in November 2001, which aims at finalizing a China-ASEAN FTA by 2015, and also by signing the ASEAN Treaty of Amity and Cooperation in 2003. China's tilt toward ASEAN is understandable, when one considers its motives to diversify economic ties and to expand diplomatic influence.[81] Nevertheless, such a detour regionalism, when combined with the economic power of overseas Chinese who are concentrated in Southeast Asia, could derail the process of building an open regionalism in Northeast Asia by tempting China to seek its own economic zone. At the same time, the expansion of popular nationalism can easily make China retreat into a mercantilist posture, jeopardizing a new regional economic order in Northeast Asia.

The most worrisome aspect comes from the correlates of assertive nationalism and China's strategic positioning. As long as China adheres to its traditional policy of peaceful coexistence with neighboring countries, China can continue to play a constructive role in shaping a new regional order. However, if and when China turns into a regional spoiler due to nationalist drives, the geopolitical and geoeconomic contour in Northeast Asia could face a traumatic shift. China could become the spoiler under two circumstances. One is a growing encirclement or containment of China by the United States and Japan in fear of China's rising power. This could be the negative outcome of the China threat thesis promoted by ultraconservatives in Japan and the United States. The other is a state of internal fragmentation and subsequent unrest in China that could result from the combination of faltering economic performance, societal and regional polarization, and the political incompetence of the CCP. The first will serve as the pull factor by precipitating popular nationalism and making China adopt more confrontational security and economic policies. The last will function as the push factor that would force Chinese leadership to invoke official patriotism and a scapegoat theory, inducing it to undertake a military adventure as it did through the invasion of Vietnam in the early 1980s. Such scenarios no longer seem fictional in military terms. Although meager by American standards, China's defense spending has been growing more than 10 percent per year since 1990, and China's progress in science and technology has also greatly enhanced its military potential.[82] And China's economic power has become even more formidable than its military power. Thus, nationalism-driven hardline confrontation can readily endanger the region's strategic and economic outlook. It may well be said that the future direction of Chinese nationalism is the wild card in determining the shape of Northeast Asia's regional order.

Nationalism, Domestic Politics, and Regional Order

It was postulated in the previous section that resurgent parochial nationalism in Japan, South Korea, and China could become a major hindrance to the formation of a viable and harmonious regional order in Northeast Asia. How has the resurgence of nationalism affected these countries' mutual cognitive dynamics and their actual policy behavior? What factors have been aggravating mutual suspicion and distrust among them? How has domestic politics factored into the negative amplification of nationalist sentiments across national boundaries?

Several opinion surveys indicate the deplorable state of mutual perception among the three countries. According to an opinion survey by the Japanese Cabinet Public Relations Office in 2004, 71.2 percent of Japanese respondents answered that they view the United States as a friendly nation.[83] But the figures for China and Korea are 37.6 and 56.7 percent respectively. What is interesting is that Japanese friendly perception of China radically deteriorated from 78.6 percent in 1980 to 52.3 percent in 1990, 45.6 percent in 2002, and 37.6 percent in 2004, whereas the figures for South Korea improved from 34.5 percent in 1981 to 54.2 percent in 2002 and 56.7 percent in 2004. In view of this, Japanese people appear to prefer the United States to China, and South Korea to China.

Another joint survey conducted by *Donga Ilbo* (South Korea), *Asahi Shimbun* (Japan), and the Chinese Academy of Social Science (China) in 2005 reveals a much worse situation.[84] Of South Korean respondents (sample size 1,500), 24.4 percent answered that they did not like China, whereas 20 percent liked China; 63.4 percent responded that they they did not like Japan, while only 7.8 percent gave a positive view of Japan. As to Japanese, 27.6 percent of respondents (sample size 1,781) answered that they did not like China, whereas only 9.9 percent said they like China. South Korea fared better than China among Japanese: 21.5 percent answered that they disliked South Korea, while 15.5 percent responded that they liked South Korea. Of Chinese respondents (sample size 2,160), 64.1 percent said that they did not like Japan, and only 7.8 percent gave a positive response. Meanwhile, 46.5 percent of Chinese respondents answered that they liked South Korea, and only 7.3 percent disliked South Korea. What is worse is people's perception of bilateral relations: 94 percent of South Korean respondents and 61 percent of Japanese respondents believed that Japan–South Korea relations were worsening. Compared to the same survey conducted in 2001, in which only 34 percent of South Koreans and 35 percent of Japanese responded that Japan–South Korea relations were getting worse, such a response indicates a sharp deterioration of bilateral perceptions. 75 percent of Chinese respondents and 61 percent of Japanese respondents also viewed China-Japan relations as worsening. In 2001, the figures were 62 percent for Chinese and 43 percent for Japanese. In contrast, China–South Korea relations seem to fare better. Of Chinese respondents, 82 percent thought that China–South Korea relations were good, but only 51 percent of South Koreans responded that their bilateral relations were good.

A 2001 joint survey by *Asahi Shimbun* and *Donga Ilbo,* conducted in China, Japan, South Korea, and the United States, reveals much more interesting empirical findings on regional cooperation.[85] The survey asked whether East Asia can achieve a regional integration comparable to the European Union. Only 33 percent of the respondents in South Korea, 12 percent in Japan, and 32 percent in China believed that such regional cooperation is possible. An absolute majority (67 percent in South Korea, 71 percent in Japan, and 66 percent in China) answered that a European Union type of regional integration is not possible in East Asia. The survey also asked a series of questions regarding obstacles to intraregional cooperation. In South Korea 85 percent of respondents, 58 percent in Japan, 51 percent in the United States, and 49 percent in China pointed out that military security in East Asia is still unstable, posing a major barrier to regional cooperation. Also, Northeast Asian countries appear to perceive each other as major economic rivals, with South Koreans (56 percent), Japanese (53 percent), and Americans (61 percent) answering that China would be a major economic rival, rather than a partner, in the coming decade.

But the most serious obstacle to intraregional cooperation in surveys turned out to be the Japanese attitude to history, such as the revision of history textbooks and Prime Minister Koizumi's tribute to the Yasukuni Shrine. It was pointed out by 90 percent of South Korean respondents, 87 percent of Chinese respondents, and 67 percent of Japanese respondents that the history issue has become a major impediment to regionalism. South Koreans appear to be most pessimistic about the resolution of history issues, as 82 percent of South Korean respondents answered that it would be extremely difficult to resolve the past history issues. However, Japanese and Chinese seem to be more optimistic, with only 40 percent of Japanese and 42 percent of Chinese respondents believing that past history issues cannot be resolved easily.

Mutual perceptions among Northeast Asian countries and their perceptions of regional cooperation appear to be quite negative. What factors have precipitated such a trend? We argue that domestic political abuse and misuse of nationalist sentiment and a coalition of adversaries formed through an amplifying negative feedback mechanism among China, Japan, and South Korea have become the most devastating obstacles to the process of intraregional cooperation and institutionalization. The origin of the chain reactions has always been Japan. Japanese right-wing politicians' intentional and sporadic provocations on history issues for domestic political purposes have facilitated nationalists in China and South Korea in exploiting them for their own domestic political gains by mobilizing the masses, reaffirming nationalist zeal, and agitating an anti-Japanese stance as a salient political issue. It is this unintended coalition of mutually hostile nationalist forces in China, Japan, and South Korea that has obstructed regional cooperation.

Let us examine the case of Japan–South Korea bilateral relations. Since diplomatic normalization in 1965, bilateral ties between Seoul and Tokyo have widened and deepened in all areas. Such interconnectedness, however, has not produced concurrent perceptual changes. Japan–South Korea relations have fluctuated extremely, depending on the national mood. For example, following the inauguration of the Kim Dae-jung government, Seoul–Tokyo ties reached a peak when the two countries adopted the Declaration on Future Partnership in October 1998.[86] Moreover, the cohosting of the World Cup in 2002 and the Korean culture boom in Japan further contributed to strengthening bilateral relations. But the advent of the Koizumi cabinet and its moves toward a nationalist stance shattered the congenial perception previously formed. Japan's ultraconservative historians' subsequent attempts to revise and distort (according to South Koreans) the contents of its middle school history textbooks, as well as Koizumi's tribute to the Yasukuni Shrine, turned the most amicable relationship in Northeast Asia into one of the worst.

President Roh Moo-hyun, who was inaugurated in February 2003, initially maintained a posture similar to that of Kim Dae-jung, by pledging not to politicize history issues in dealing with Japan. But the situation radically altered in 2005, which was designated as the "year of friendship" in 2001 in order to celebrate the fortieth anniversary of diplomatic normalization. In February 2005, the Shimane Prefectural Council in Japan adopted an act declaring February 22 as "the Takeshima Day," urging the Japanese government to recover the island from South Korea's illicit occupation. What further angered South Koreans was a remark by Toshiyuki Takano, Japanese ambassador to Seoul, who stated in an official press conference that Takeshima is a part of Japanese territory. In addition to the history textbook issue and the Yasukuni Shrine polemic, the territorial dispute has emerged as another burning issue. President Roh's reaction was furious. In a letter to the nation, he pointed out that "Japan annexed Dokdo after a victory in the Russo-Japanese War in 1905. It was an annexation by force. February 22, which the Shimane Prefecture declared as 'the Takeshima Day,' is the very day Japan forcefully incorporated Dokdo into its territory 100 years ago. This is an act to justify its past invasion as well as to deny the independence of the Republic of Korea." He acknowledged that Japanese leaders apologized and repented for Japan's past historical mistakes, yet he doubted their sincerity by arguing that "repentance and apology should be followed by concurrent actions and practices. Former prime minister Koizumi's tribute to the Yasukuni Shrine damaged the authenticity of repentance and apology made by previous Japanese leaders."[87] Roh's attitudes were widely shared by South Koreans, and his popularity soared. Nevertheless, Koizumi downplayed such developments by stating that "President Roh's remarks are motivated by domestic political considerations."[88]

Moves to revise history textbooks, the tributes to Yasukuni, and resurrection of territorial claims over Dokdo reflected the conscious efforts by Japan's ultraconservatives to garner domestic political support. But those domestic political gains resulted in diplomatic losses. The South Korean government not only withdrew its earlier position in support of Japan's permanent membership in the UN Security Council but also initiated a diplomatic campaign to block its entry. In the two summit talks held in June and November 2005, history, the Yasukuni Shrine, and territorial issues dominated the agenda, but the talks ended without any tangible outcomes, except reaffirming Japan's and South Korea's different attitudes on those three issues. The following summit talk, which was scheduled for December, was ultimately canceled, and negotiations over a Japan–South Korea FTA have been suspended since November 2004. The "year of friendship" ended up being one of the worst years in Japan–South Korea relations. A series of Koizumi's moves contributed to further worsening the bilateral relations. The clash of past history and national identity so deeply anchored in domestic politics virtually derailed the otherwise congenial Seoul–Tokyo relationship.

The roller-coaster dynamics evidenced between Japan and South Korea has been less pronounced in China–Japan relations, though they too have been sliding downward. From the early 1970s to the mid-1980s, China and Japan drew much closer through the cultivation of various forms of exchange and cooperation. Since the early 1990s, however, their relationship has steadily deteriorated. The causes of the uneasy relationship do not simply arise from conflicts over power and interests, but also from differences in the recognition of historical issues pertaining to past invasions and atrocities. As with South Korea, Japan's attempt to whitewash past crimes and mistakes by revising history textbooks, the lack of Japanese apologies over the atrocity committed in the city of Nanking in 1937, tributes to the Yasukuni Shrine by Prime Minister Koizumi, and unrepentant political remarks to distort and glorify its historical past as well as to demean China and the Chinese, have fueled sweeping anti-Japanese sentiment in China.

It is interesting to note that the anti-Japanese sentiment that erupted in South Korea throughout March quickly spread to China. April 2005 saw the violent outpouring of anti-Japanese rage in China.[89] Angry Chinese physically attacked the Japanese embassy and consulate offices as well as businesses in Beijing, Shanghai, and other cities, and a large number of Chinese began to participate in a nationwide campaign to boycott Japanese products. Products of Japanese firms that sponsored the right-wing organizations established to promote the revision of history textbooks were primary targets. Around that time, the Chinese government officially announced its opposition to Japan's bid to join an expanded UN Security Council by arguing that "Only a country that respects history . . . [and] wins over the trust of people in Asia and the world can take greater responsibilities in the international community."[90] Anti-Japanese sentiments escalated from history issues to other sensitive issues such as the territorial dispute over Diaoyudao (Senkaku Island) and Japan's interference over the issues of Taiwan and human rights. In May, China's deputy premier, Wu Yi, canceled her scheduled meeting with Prime Minister Koizumi in protest of his tribute to Yasukuni. Subsequently, China has intentionally avoided holding a bilateral summit with Japan since the Hanoi Asia-Europe Meeting (ASEM) in October 2004. During the APEC (Asia-Pacific Economic Cooperation) summit in November 2005, the China-Japan summit talk was not held, and during the Kuala Lumpur East Asian Summit in December 2005, both the China–Japan bilateral summit and China–Japan–South Korean summit were aborted. Diplomatic ties between Beijing and Tokyo hit rock bottom.

China–Japan relations have worsened much more than those between Japan and South Korea. In a sense, China and Japan have entered a game of chicken in which neither country can back out, and it is precisely a result of entanglement with domestic politics. The key issue here is Koizumi's tribute to Yasukuni. The Chinese government made it clear that unless Prime Minister Koizumi suspends his tributes to the Yasukuni Shrine, there will be no improvements in bilateral diplomatic ties. However, for Koizumi, accommodating Beijing's demand will be seen as an appeasement to China's pressure, which could in turn mean political suicide in Japan, especially because anti-China sentiments are widely shared among Japanese, who are fearful of China's rise amid resurgent nationalism. As to the Chinese leadership, compromise is highly unlikely, because anti-Japanese sentiments in China are a joint product of official patriotism and popular nationalism. Compromise cannot only mean the abandonment of official patriotism but also provoke immense political grievance from below, which can easily escalate into popular opposition to the leadership of the CCP. The diplomatic debacle is not likely to be resolved with the end of the Koizumi tenure, as Abe Shinzo, who has publicly pledged to pay tributes to the Yasukuni Shrine, has succeeded him.

Finally, China–South Korean relations are not necessarily congenial either. It is true that China and South Korea have become much closer, owing to an increasing economic interdependence and a shared policy view on the peaceful resolution of the North Korean nuclear issue. Until recently, the majority of South Koreans viewed China as one of their most favored countries. However, in early 2004, Beijing–Seoul ties soured with the publicization of the Chinese government's Northeastern Project (*Dongbei Gongting*). The project aims to rewrite the ancient history of China's Northeastern area under the official endorsement and sponsorship of the central and provincial governments. What outraged South Koreans was its attempt to reinterpret the Koguryo dynasty (37 BC–AD 668) as China's peripheral kingdom, making it part of Chinese history. For Koreans, Koguryo is a proud part of its ancient history, ruling over the northern part of the Korean Peninsula and most of Manchuria during the period of the Three Kingdoms, and treating it as part of China's peripheral kingdom is believed by them to deny Korean history and identity. It triggered a war of words over history between China and South Korea, straining bilateral relations. Intervention by the political leadership of both countries led to a compromise in which China has agreed to respect Korea's historical sovereignty (i.e., recognition of Koguryo as part of Korean history), whereas South Korea has agreed to respect China's territorial sovereignty over Manchuria. However, the issue is yet to be resolved. It can explode at any time, clouding the future of China–South Korean relations.

Conclusion

Building a viable regional order for peace, prosperity, and harmony in Northeast Asia seems a daunting journey. This is not only because of the strategic uncertainty embodied in the dynamics of power transition but also because of the incomplete stage of liberal transition in which the actors lack common values, norms, and interests. What is more troublesome is the resurgence of a nationalist identity politics, which fuels a vicious circle of suspicion and distrust among peoples and governments in the region. The specter of parochial and often offensive nationalism complicates the tragedy of great power politics and impedes a possible liberal transition. The "masses" can be mobilized at any instant under the banner of nationalism to denounce another country, undermining the chance for community building in the region. Thus, it would be quite unthinkable to establish and sustain a new regional order of coexistence and harmony without first tackling the problem of identity politics and nationalism.

What should be done? The most important task is to prevent nationalism from being misused and abused in the name of domestic political gains and power struggles. The task requires not only the prudence, self-restraint, and integrity of politicians, but also the practice of universal civic virtues and the vigilance of grassroots citizens. The pursuit of parochial nationalism at the expense of regional cooperation and integration is tantamount to commiting the fallacy of a Faustian bargain. Equally important is how to avoid a negatively reinforcing amplification of vicious nationalism across national boundaries. This task can be accomplished by cultivating transnational solidarity among liberal forces in the region as well as confronting and breaking down an unintended, inadvertent ultraconservative alliance, which earns political capital from a nationalist war of attrition. As demonstrated by successful public campaigns to block the adoption of revised history textbooks in Japan, a new transnational liberal coalition can work as a powerful social force to counterbalance conservative programs and actions.

Countries in the region should also work together to develop joint programs to cultivate a new regional identity of coexistence, harmony, and cooperation. Despite bitter historical memories of domination and subjugation, Northeast Asian countries share common cultural and historical heritages, and these should be emphasized as much, if not more than, contentious historical issues. And as Europe has shown in the early phase of its regional integration, Northeast Asia also needs to have new visionary leadership, which can put forward and implement a constructive agenda of regional cooperation and integration. Northeast Asia and Europe are different in many aspects, but the former has much to learn from the latter in terms of the role that visionary leadership can play in overcoming domestic political opposition and shaping a common vision of a regional community.

Notes

1. Muthiah Alagappa, ed., *Asian Security Order: Instrumental and Normative Features* (Stanford, Calif.: Stanford University Press, 2003); G. John Ikenberry and Michael Mastanduno, eds., *International Relations Theory and the Asia-Pacific* (New York: Columbia University Press, 2003).

2. Paul Bracken, *Fire in the East* (New York: Harper Collins, 1999), 148.

3. James R. Kurth, "The Pacific Basin versus the Atlantic Alliance: Two Paradigms of International Relations," *Annals of the American Academy of Political and Social Sciences,* no. 505 (September 1989): 34–45.

4. John Mearsheimer, *The Tragedy of Great Power Politics* (New York: W. W. Norton, 2001).

5. Aaron L. Friedberg, "Ripe for Rivalry: Prospects for Peace in a Multipolar Asia," *International Security* 18, no. 3 (Winter 1993–1994): 7.

6. See Woo Sang Kim, "Power Transition and Strategic Stability in East Asia," *Asian Perspective* 21, no. 1 (Spring–Summer 1997): 153–70.

7. M. Alagappa, "The Study of International Order: An Analytical Framework," in *Asian Security Order,* ed. M. Alagappa, 39–41.

8. Hedley Bull, *The Anarchical Society* (New York: Columbia University Press, 1977), 20–22.

9. Robert W. Cox with Timothy J. Sinclair, *Approaches to World Order* (New York: Cambridge University Press, 1996).

10. Stanley Hoffmann, ed., *Conditions of World Order* (New York: Simon and Schuster, 1968), introduction. Also refer to Raymond Aron's chapter "The Anarchical Order of Power" in the same volume, 25–48. For extended normative conditions, see Richard Falk, *The End of World Order* (New York: Holmes and Meier, 1983), 35–69.

11. For a succinct overview of contending analytical perspectives in the East Asian context, see J. J. Suh, Peter J. Katzenstein, and Allen Carlson, *Rethinking Security in East Asia: Identity, Power, and Efficiency* (Stanford, Calif.: Stanford University Press, 2004), chap 1.

12. John J. Mearsheimer, "The False Promise of International Institutions," *International Security* 19, no. 3 (Winter, 1994–1995): 5–49; Kenneth Waltz, *Theory of International Politics* (Reading, Mass.: Addison-Wesley, 1979).

13. Greg Cashman, *What Causes War? An Introduction to Theories of International Conflict* (New York: Lexington Books, 1993), 224–52.

14. Robert O. Keohane, *After Hegemony: Cooperation and Discord in the World Political Economy* (Princeton, N.J.: Princeton University Press, 1984); Hedley Bull and Adam Watson, eds., *The Expansion of European Society* (London: Oxford University Press, 1984).

15. Emanuel Adler and Michael Barnett, ed., *Security Communities* (New York: Cambridge University Press, 1998); Ethel Solingen, *Regional Orders at Century's Dawn* (Princeton, N.J.: Princeton University Press, 1998).

16. Alexander Wendt, "Collective Identity Formation and the International State," *American Political Science Review* 88, no. 2 (June 1994): 384–96; Alexander Wendt, *Social Theory of International Politics* (New York: Cambridge University Press, 1999); Nicholas G. Onuf, *World of Our Making: Rules and Rule in Social Theory and International Relations* (Columbia: University of South Carolina Press, 1998).

17. Consuelo Cruz, "Identity and Persuasion: How Nations Remember Their Pasts and Make Their Future," *World Politics* 52, no. 3 (April 2000): 276.

18. Wendt, *Social Theory of International Politics*, 343–63.

19. Peter J. Katzenstein, "Introduction: Alternative Perspectives on National Security," in *The Culture of National Security: Norms and Identity in World Politics*, ed. Peter Katzenstein, 1–32 (New York: Columbia University Press, 1996).

20. Peter J. Katzenstein and Rudra Sil, "Rethinking Asian Security: A Case for Analytical Eclecticism," in *Rethinking Security in East Asia: Identity, Power and Efficiency*, ed. J. J. Suh, Peter Katzenstein, and Allen Carlson (Stanford, Calif.: Stanford University Press, 2004), chap. 1.

21. Katzenstein, *Culture of National Security*; Richard Higgot, "Ideas and Identity in the International Political Economy of Regionalism: The Asia-Pacific and Europe Compared," *Kokusai Seiji* [International Politics], 114 (March 1997): 14–48; Peter J. Katzenstein, "Regionalism and Asia," *New Political Economy* 5, no. 3 (November 2000): 353–68.

22. On causal links between nationalism and foreign policy in Japan, see Masaru Tamamoto, "On Japanese Nationalism and Foreign Policy," *Global Asia* 1, no. 2 (March 2007); Masaru Tamamoto, "Ambiguous Japan: Japanese National Identity at Century's End," in Ikenberry and Mastanduno, *International Relations Theory and the Asia-Pacific*, 190–212.

23. Moon and Chun, "Sovereignty," 122.

24. Makoto Iokibe, "21 Seiki no nashonarizumu" [Nationalism in the Twenty-first Century], *Chuo Koron* (June 1995): 300–301.

25. See Yasuhiro Nakasone, "Sengo no sokessan kara 21 seiki sekai no Nihone" [From Complete Evaluation of the Postwar Period to Twenty-first-Century Japan],

Jiyu Minshu (March 1984): 30; Sekai Heiwa Kenkyusho, ed., *Nakasone Naikakushi: Rinen to seisaku* [History of Nakasone Cabinet: Philosophy and Policy] (Tokyo: Marunouchi Shuppan, 1995).

26. Ozawa Ichiro, *Nihon kaizo keikaku* [Japan Reform Plan] (Tokyo: Kodansha, 1993); Ozawa Ichiro, "Kokusai shakai ni okeru Nihon no yakuwari" [Japan's Role in International Society], *Bungei Shunju* (April 1992): 132–45.

27. Hidetaka Ishida, Satoshi Ukai, Yoichi Komori, and Tetsuya Takahashi, "Datsu parasato nashonarizumu [Getting Rid of Parasite Nationalism]," *Sekai* (August 2000): 189–208; Sekai Henshubu, ed., *21 seiki no manifesto* [A Manifesto of the Twenty-first Century] (Tokyo: Iwanami Shoten, 2001), chap. 2. On the other hand, Brian McVeigh categorizes Japanese nationalism into two types. The first includes the state and official nationalisms such as economic, educational, ethnos, and state cultural nationalism. The second includes the popular and nonofficial nationalisms: popular cultural, postimperial ethnos, gendered, mainstream, and marginal nationalism. Brian J. McVeigh, *Nationalisms of Japan: Managing and Mystifying Identity* (Oxford: Rowman and Littlefield, 2004).

28. Atarashi Rekishi Kyokasho wo Tsukurukai [The Society for Making New History Textbook], ed., *Nihon no Bijon* [Vision of Japan] (Tokyo: Fusosha, 2003); Rekishi Kento Inkai, ed., *Daitoa Senso Sokatsu* [Blanket View on the Great East Asia War] (Tokyo: Tendensha, 1995).

29. On Japanese domestic debates on how to view its past history, see Tetsuya Takahashi, ed., *Rekishi ninshiki ronso* [Debates over the Historical View] (Tokyo: Sakuhinsha, 2002).

30. Ishida et al., "Getting Rid of Parasite Nationalism," 189–208.

31. John W. Dower, *Embracing Defeat: Japan in the Wake of World War II* (New York: W. W. Norton and Company, 1999), epilogue.

32. Shintaro Ishihara and Akio Morita, *Japan That Can Say "No"* (Tokyo: Kobunsha, 1989).

33. Shintaro Ishihara, "Ima koso America no Tomoe" [Now Japan Should Be a Real Friend of America], *Shokun* (December 2001): 36–49.

34. Sang-jung Kang, *Nashonarizumu* [Nationalism] (Tokyo: Iwanami Shoten, 2001); Sang-jung Kang and Hiroshi Morris, *Nashonarizumu no Kokufuku* [Overcoming the Nationalism] (Tokyo: Shueisha Sinsho, 2002).

35. On the establishment and role of the postwar emperor system, refer to Kenneth J. Ruoff, *The People's Emperor: Democracy and the Japanese Monarchy, 1945–1995* (Cambridge, Mass.: Harvard University Asia Center, 2001).

36. The whole statement by Yoshiro Mori can be seen at the *Jinja* Online Network Association website: jinja.jp/jikyoku/kaminokuni/kaminokuni2.html.

37. Tagao Sakamoto, *Shocho tennosei to Nihon no raireki* [Symbolic Emperor System and Japan's Origin] (Tokyo: Toshishuppan, 1995); Uzuhiko Ashizu, *Kokka Shinto towa nandattanoka* [What Was the State Shinto] (Tokyo: Jinjashinposha, 1987).

38. *Asahi Shimbun*, April 10 and April 12, 2000.

39. In the fall of 2005, a comic book titled *Kenkanryu* [Hate the Korean Culture boom] sold more than 300,000 copies within one month of its publication.

40. Soichiro Tahara, Susumu Nishibe, and Sang-jung Kang, *Aikokushin* [Patriotism] (Tokyo: Kodansha, 2003), 32.

41. Tatsuo Inoue, *Jiyu, Kenryoku, Yutopia* [Liberty, Power, and Utopia] (Tokyo: Iwanami Shoten, 1998).

42. *New York Times*, February 7, 2005.

43. Nakasone's remark was made during an interview with KBS (Korea Broadcasting System), November 16, 2003.

44. Yoshibumi Wakamiya, "Hatoha no fuyu" [The Dove's Winter], *Asahi Shimbun*, February 29, 2004.

45. Takashi Sasaki, "Nashonarizumu no jidai wo yom" [Reading the Age of Nationalism], *Tokyo Shimbun*, June 12, 2005.

46. Prime Minister Abe has taken a rather strategic ambiguity on the issue of his tribute to the Yasukuni Shrine. For example, he paid a visit to the Meiji Shrine, not Yasukuni, in January 2007. It seems quite unlikely for him to pay a visit to Yasukuni during his tenure.

47. Susumu Yamakage, ed., *Higashi ajia chiikishugi to Nihon gaiko* [East Asian Regionalism and Japan's Diplomacy] (Tokyo: Nihon Kokusai Mondai Kenkyujo, 2003), 6.

48. Edward Lincoln, *East Asian Economic Regionalism* (Washington, D.C.: Brookings Institution Press, 2004), 248.

49. Jae-ho Cheon, "Minjokjuui Yongu ui Hyunhwang" [Present Status of Study of Nationalism], *Tongil Munje Yongu* 23 (May 1995): 230–46; Duk-kyu Jhin, ed., *Hankuk ui Minjokjuui* [The Nationalism of Korea] (Seoul: Seoul Sasangsa, 1976).

50. Young-hun Chung, *"Dangun Minjokjuui" wa Keu Cheongshin Sasangsajeok Seongkyuk e kwanhan Yongu* [A Study of the "Dangun Nationalism" and Its Characteristics of Political Philosophy] (Ph.D. dissertation, Graduate School of Politics and Diplomacy, Dankuk University, Seoul, 1993).

51. Sung-jo Han, *Hankuk Minjujui—Irongwa Silje* [Korean Democracy: Theory and Practice] (Seoul: Hyunsul Chulpansa, 1984), 341–42; Ho-sang Ahn, *Minjok Jungron* [Right Thesis on Nation] (Seoul: Sarimwon, 1982).

52. Jong-seok Lee, "Juche Sasang gwa Minjokjuui: Kue Yonkwanseong e Kwanhan Yongu" [Juche Ideology and Nationalism: A Study on Its Relationship], *Tongil Munje Yongu* 21 (July 1994): 65–96, esp. 61–72; Chae-wan Im, "Bukhan ui Minjokjuui Iron gwa kue Byunhwa Chuyi" [Theories of North Korean Nationalism and Its Changes], *Cheongshin Munhwa Yongu* 17, no. 2 (June 1994): 37–52.

53. Requoted from Henry H. Em, "Minjok as a Construct," in *Colonial Modernity in Korea*, ed. Gi-Wook Shin and Michael Robinson (Cambridge, Mass.: Harvard University Press, 1999), 343.

54. Yong-hee Lee, "Hankuk Minjokjuui ui Je Munje [The Issues of Korean Nationalism]," in *Hankuk ui Minjokjuui* [Nationalism of Korea], ed. Yong-hee Lee et al. (Seoul: Hankuk Ilbosa, 1967) (cited in Hak-joon Kim, "Tongil Inyum euroseoui Hankuk Minjokjuui" [Korean Nationalism as a Unification Philosophy], *Tongil Munje Yongu* 21 (July 1994): 43); Ki-byuk Cha, *Hankuk Minjokjuui ui Inyum gwa Shiltae* [Philosophy and Circumstances of Korean Nationalism] (Seoul: Kachi 1978); Hong-gu Lee, "Hankuk Minjokjuui reul boneun Sae Shigak ui Mosaek" [Searching for a New Perspective on Korean Nationalism], *Asea Yongu* 27, no. 1 (January 1984): 38–62.

55. Hyun-chae Park et al., eds., *Hankuk Minjok Undong ui Inyum gwa Yoksa* [Philosophy and History of Korean Nationalism Movements] (Seoul: Hangilsa, 1987);

Ul-bung Chang, *Uri Shidae Minjok Undong ui Kwaje* [Challenges of the Current Nationalism Movements] (Seoul: Hangilsa, 1987).

56. Hak-joon Kim, "Tongil Inyum euroseoui Hankuk Minjokjuui" [Korean Nationalism as a Unification Philosophy], *Tongil Munjae Yongu*, 21 (July 1994): 50.

57. See Em, *Colonial Modernity in Korea*; Jie-hyun Lim, "Minzokjuui: Cheontong gwa Keundae ui Byunjeungbeop?" [Nationalism: A Dialectic of Tradition and Modernity?], *Sungkyunkwan Inmunkwahak* 30 (February 2000): 357–70; Jie-Hyun Lim, *Jokdaejok Gongbumjadeul* [Adversarial Accomplices] (Seoul: Sonamu, 2004).

58. Henry H. Em, "Minjok as a Modern and Democratic Construct: Shin Ch'aeho's Historiography," in Shin and Robinson, *Colonial Modernity in Korea*, 336.

59. Carter Eckert, "Epilogue: Exorcising Hegel's Ghosts: Toward a Postnationalist Historiography of Korea," in *Colonial Modernity in Korea*, ed. Gi-Wook Shin and Michael Robinson (Cambridge, Mass.: Harvard University Press, 1999), 366.

60. Young-hun Chung, "Keundae Hankuk Minjokjuui ui Teukjing: Minjok itneun Minjokjuui' ui Shilpae" [The Characteristics of the Mondern Korean Nationalism: Failure of the "Nationalism" with Nation], *Cheongshin Munhwa Yongu* 17, no. 2 (1994): 15–36; Ki-pyok Cha, "Minjokjuui jeok Shigak eseo bon Hanbando Tongil" [The Problem of Korean Unification Considered from the Perspective of Nationalism], *Daehanminguk Haksulwon Nonmunjip* 29 (December 1990): 339–72; Yun-hwan Kim, "Tongil Hankuk ui Miraesang" [The Future Figure of a Unified Korea], *Tongil Cheongchaek* 5, no. 4 (1979).

61. See Roh Moo-hyun, "History, Nationalism, and Community-building in Northeast Asia," *Global Asia* 1, no. 2 (March 2007); Yong-duck Kim, "History, Nationalism, and Foreign Policy in South Korea," *Global Asia* 1, no. 2 (March 2007).

62. Although the Koguryo dynasty is integral part of Korean history, some Chinese historians have been undertaking a massive historical project that attempts to interpret it as a part of China's peripheral history. For details, see Koguryo Research Foundation, *Jungkukui "Dongbuk Gonjung"—Keu Shilche wa Heogusung* [China's "Northeast Project"—Its Reality and Fiction] (Seoul: Koguryo Reseach Foundation, 2004).

63. A summary of Jiang Zemin's political report to the Sixteenth National Congress of the Communist Party of China (CPC) can be seen at the *People's Daily Online* at english.people.com.cn/200211/08/eng20021108_106503.shtml.

64. Qiang Song, Cang-cang Zhang, Zheng-yu Tang, Qing-sheng Gu, and Bian Chao, *Zhungguo Keyi Shuobu* [China That Can Say "No"] (Beijing: Zhongguo Gongshang Lianho Chubanshe, 1996).

65. James Townsend, "Chinese Nationalism," *Australian Journal of Chinese Affairs*, no. 27 (January 1992): 97–130, esp. 128.

66. Prasenjit Duara, "De-constructing the Chinese Nation," *Australian Journal of Chinese Affairs*, no. 30 (1993): 1–26.

67. According to a 1994 survey in Guangdong Province, 84 percent of respondents identified the Chinese people (*Zhonghua Minzu*) with the total sum of 1.1 billion mainland and overseas Chinese. Those who identified it with the Han race (*Hanzu*) was 3.5 percent, and those who identified it with mainland Chinese was 12.5 percent. Kazuko Mori, "Chuka Sekai no Aidentiti no Henyo to Sai Chuzo" [Transformation and Recasting of Identity in the Chinese World], in *Chuka sekai: Aidentiti no saihen*

[Chinese World: Reorganization of Identity], ed. Kazuko Mori, 30–32 (Tokyo: Tokyo University Press, 2001).

68. Zhimin Chen and Junbo Jian, "Lijie Zhongguo waijiao zhengce: Yi minzuzhuyi wei xiansuo" [Understanding Chinese Foreign Policy: With Reference to Nationalism], *Guoji Wenti Rundan*, no. 36 (Fall 2004), irchina.org/news/view.wp?

69. For a rich discussion of mass nationalism, refer to Peter Hays Gries, *China's New Nationalism: Pride, Politics, and Diplomacy* (Berkeley: University of California Press, 2004).

70. Ge Sun and Hiroko Sakamoto, "Sozoryoku no hinkon to shiso no tetsuzuki" [Poverty of Creativity and Procedure of Philosophy], *Gendai Shiso* 29, no. 4 (March 2001): 42–55; Gries, *China's New Nationalism*; Shigeo Nishimura, ed., *Gendai Chugoku no kozo hendo 2: Nashonarizumu* [Structural Change in Contemporary China 2: Nationalism] (Tokyo: Tokyo University Press, 2000).

71. Requoted from David Lague, "Coming to Terms with China's Ascent," *International Herald Tribune*, November 7, 2005, 15.

72. Bijian Zheng, "China's 'Peaceful Rise' to Great-Power Status," *Foreign Affairs* 84, no. 5 (September–October 2005): 18–24; Jisi Wang, "China's Search for Stability with America," *Foreign Affairs* 84, no. 5 (September–October 2005): 39–48.

73. See David Shambaugh, "China's Fragile Future," *World Policy Journal* 11(Fall 1994): 41–45; Denny Roy, "Hegemon on the Horizon: China's Threat to East Asian Security," *International Security* 19, no. 1 (Summer 1994): 149–68; Alstair I. Johnston, "Is China a *Status Quo* Power?" *International Security* 27, no. 4 (Spring 2003): 5–56.

74. See Bill Gertz, *The China Threat* (Washington, D.C.: Regency, 2002).

75. John Mearsheimer, *The Tragedy of Great Power Politics* (New York: Norton, 2001).

76. A. I. Johnston, "Beijing's Security Behavior in the Asia-Pacific: Is China a Dissatisfied Power?" in *Rethinking Security in East Asia: Identity, Power, and Efficiency*, ed. J. J. Suh, Peter J. Katzenstein, and Allen Carlson (Stanford, Calif.: Stanford University Press, 2004), 67.

77. See Xue-Tong Yan, "Qiangdajunli caineng baozheng heping jueqi" [Strong military power can only guarantee peaceful rise], *Huan Qiu (Globe)*, no. 17 (September 1, 2005); Yongnian Zheng, *Discovering Chinese Nationalism in China: Modernization, Identity, and International Relations* (Cambridge: Cambridge University Press, 1999), 108–9.

78. Yongnian Zheng, *Discovering Chinese Nationalism*, chap. 5.

79. Guangqiu Xu, "Anti-Western Nationalism in China, 1989–1999," *World Affairs* 163, no. 4 (Spring 2001): 151–62.

80. See Weishi Yuan, "Nationalism in a China Transforming," *Global Asia* 1, no. 2 (March 2007).

81. Christopher R. Hughes, "Nationalism and Mulateralism in Chinese Foreign Policy: Implications for Southeast Asia," *Pacific Review* 18, no. 1 (March 2005): 119–35.

82. Ikuo Kayahara, "Chugoku no kokubo kindaika to Ajia no kincho" [China's Defense Modernization and Asia's Tension], *Chuo Koron* (May 2005): 204–15.

83. See Japanese Cabinet Public Relations Office, "Survey on Diplomacy" (October 2004), www8.cao.go.jp/survey/h16-gaiko/index.html.

84. *Donga Ilbo*, April 26, 2005.
85. *Asahi Shimbun* and *Donga Ilbo* Joint Survey (November 2001), www.donga .com/fbin/output?code=ap_&n=200112240204&curlist=30.
86. See Chung-in Moon and Seung-won Suh, "Security, Economy, and Identity Politics between Japan and South Korea under the Kim Dae-jung Government," *Korea Observer* 36, no. 4 (Winter 2005): 561–602.
87. For these quotes, see www.president.go.kr/cwd/kr/archive.
88. *Asahi Shimbun*, April 2, 2005.
89. *Time*, April 25, 2005; *Asahi Shimbun*, April 18, 2005.
90. A statement by China's premier Wen Jiabao, cited in *Time*, April 25, 2005.

References

Adler, Emanuel, and Michael Barnett, ed. *Security Communities.* New York: Cambridge University Press, 1998.
Ahn, Ho-sang. *Minjok Jungron* [Right Thesis on Nation]. Seoul: Sarimwon, 1982.
Alagappa, Muthiah. "The Study of International Order: An Analytical Framework." In Alagappa, *Asian Security Order.*
Alagappa, Muthiah, ed. *Asian Security Order: Instrumental and Normative Features.* Stanford, Calif.: Stanford University Press, 2003.
Asahi Shimbun and *Donga Ilbo* Joint Survey, November 2001, www.donga.com/fbin/ output?code=ap_&n=200112240204&curlist=30/.
Ashizy, Uzuhiko. *Kokka Shinto towa nandattanoka* [What Was the State Shinto]. Tokyo: Jinjashinposha, 1987.
Atarashi Rekishi Kyokasho wo Tsukurukai [The Society for Making New History Textbook], ed. *Nihon no Bijon* [Vision of Japan]. Tokyo: Fusosha, 2003.
Bracken, Paul. *Fire in the East.* New York: Harper Collins, 1999.
Bull, Hedley. *The Anarchical Society.* New York: Columbia University Press, 1977.
Bull, Hedley, and Adam Watson, eds. *The Expansion of European Society.* London: Oxford University Press, 1984.
Cashman, Greg. *What Causes War? An Introduction to Theories of International Conflict.* New York: Lexington Books, 1993.
Cha, Ki-byuk. *Hankuk Minjokjuui ui Inyum gwa Shiltae* [Philosophy and Circumstances of Korean Nationalism]. Seoul: Kachi, 1978.
Cha, Ki-pyok. "Minjokjuui jeok Shigak eseo bon Hanbando Tongil" [The Problem of Korean Unification Considered from the Perspective of Nationalism]. *Daehanminguk Haksulwon Nonmunjip* 29 (December 1990): 339–72.
Chang, Ul-bung. *Uri Shidae Minjok Undong ui Kwaje* [Challenges of the Current Nationalism Movements]. Seoul: Hangilsa, 1987.
Chen, Zhimin, and Junbo Jian. "Lijie Zhongguo waijiao zhengce: Yi minzuzhuyi wei xiansuo" [Understanding Chinese Foreign Policy: With Reference to Nationalism]. *Guoji Wenti Rundan*, no. 36 (Fall 2004). irchina.org/news/view.wp?/
Cheon, Jae-ho. "Minjokjuui Yongu ui Hyunhwang" [Present Status of Study of Nationalism]. *Tongil Munje Yongu* 23 (May 1995): 230–46.

Chung, Young-hun. *"Dangun Minjokjuui" wa Keu Cheongshin Sasangsajeok Seongkyuk e kwanhan Yongu* [A Study of the "Dangun Nationalism" and Its Characteristics of Political Philosophy]. Ph.D. dissertation, Graduate School of Politics and Diplomacy, Dankuk University, Seoul, 1993.

———. "Keundae Hankuk Minjokjuui ui Teukjing: Minjok itneun Minjokjuui' ui Shilpae" [The Characteristics of the Modern Korean Nationalism: Failure of the "Nationalism with Nation"]. *Cheongshin Munhwa Yongu* 17, no. 2 (1994): 15–36.

Cox, Robert W., with Timothy J. Sinclair. *Approaches to World Order.* New York: Cambridge University Press, 1996.

Cruz, Consuelo. "Identity and Persuasion: How Nations Remember Their Pasts and Make Their Future." *World Politics* 52, no. 3 (April 2000): 276

Dower, John W. *Embracing Defeat: Japan in the Wake of World War II.* New York: W. W. Norton and Company, 1999.

Duara, Prasenjit. "De-constructing the Chinese Nation." *Australian Journal of Chinese Affairs,* no. 30 (1993): 1–26.

Eckert, Carter. "Epilogue: Exorcising Hegel's Ghosts: Toward a Postnationalist Historiography of Korea," In *Colonial Modernity in Korea,* edited by Gi-Wook Shin and Michael Robinson, Cambridge, Mass.: Harvard University Press, 1999.

Em, Henry H. "Minjok as a Construct." In *Colonial Modernity in Korea,* edited by Gi-Wook Shin and Michael Robinson. Cambridge, Mass.: Harvard University Press, 1999.

———. "Minjok as a Modern and Democratic Construct: Shin Ch'aeho's Historiography." In *Colonial Modernity in Korea,* edited by Ji-Wook Shin and Michael Robinson. Cambridge, Mass.: Harvard University Press, 1999.

Falk, Richard. *The End of World Order.* New York: Holmes and Meier, 1983.

Friedberg, Aaron L. "Ripe for Rivalry: Prospects for Peace in a Multipolar Asia." *International Security* 18, no. 3 (Winter 1993–1994).

Gertz, Bill. *The China Threat.* Washington, D.C.: Regency, 2002.

Gries, Peter Hays. *China's New Nationalism: Pride, Politics, and Diplomacy.* Berkeley: University of California Press, 2004.

Han, Sung-jo. *Hankuk Minjujui—Irongwa Silje* [Korean Democracy: Theory and Practice]. Seoul: Hyunsul Chulpansa, 1984.

Henshubu, Sekai, ed. *21 seiki no Manifesto* [A Manifesto of the Twenty-first Century]. Tokyo: Iwanami Shoten, 2001.

Higgot, Richard. "Ideas and Identity in the International Political Economy of Regionalism: The Asia-Pacific and Europe Compared." *Kokusai Seiji* [International Politics], 114 (March 1997): 14–48.

Hoffmann, Stanley, ed. *Conditions of World Order.* New York: Simon and Schuster, 1968.

Hughes, Christopher R. "Nationalism and Multilateralism in Chinese Foreign Policy: Implications for Southeast Asia." *Pacific Review* 18, no. 1 (March 2005): 119–35.

Ikenberry, G. John, and Michael Mastanduno, eds. *International Relations Theory and the Asia-Pacific.* New York: Columbia University Press, 2003.

Im, Chae-wan. "Bukhan ui Minjokjuui Iron gwa kue Byunhwa Chuyi" [Theories of

North Korean Nationalism and Its Changes]. *Cheongshin Munhwa Yongu* 17, no. 2 (June 1994): 37–52.

Inoguchi, Takashi. "Kokusai shakai ni okeru Nihon no yakuwari" [Japan's Role in International Society]. *Bungei Shunju*, April 1992, 132–45.

Inoue, Tatsuo. *Jiyu, Kenryoku, Yutopia* [Liberty, Power, and Utopia]. Tokyo: Iwanami Shoten, 1998.

Iokibe, Makoto. "21 Seiki no Nashonarizumu" [Nationalism in the Twenty-first Century]. *Chuo Koron* (June 1995): 300–301.

Ishida, Hidetaka, Satoshi Ukai, Yoichi Komori, and Tetsuya Takahashi. "Datsu para-sato nashonarizumu" [Getting Rid of Parasite Nationalism]. *Sekai*, August 2000, 189–208.

Ishihara, Shintaro. "Ima koso America no Tomo e" [Now Japan Should Be a Real Friend of America]. *Shokun*, (December 2001): 36–49.

Ishihara, Shintaro, and Akio Morita. *Japan That Can Say "No."* Tokyo: Kobunsha, 1989.

Japanese Cabinet Public Relations Office. "Survey on Diplomacy," October 2004. www8.cao.go.jp/survey/h16-gaiko/index.html.

Jhin, Duk-kyu, ed. *Hankuk ui Minjokjuui* [The Nationalism of Korea]. Seoul: Seoul Sasangsa, 1976.

Johnston, A. I. "Beijing's Security Behavior in the Asia-Pacific: Is China a Dissatisfied Power?" In *Rethinking Security in East Asia: Identity, Power, and Efficiency*, edited by J. J. Suh, Peter J. Katzenstein, and Allen Carlson, 67. Stanford, Calif.: Stanford University Press, 2004.

Johnston, Alstair I. "Is China a *Status Quo* Power?" *International Security* 27, no. 4 (Spring 2003): 5–56.

Kang, Sang-jung. *Nashonarizumu* [Nationalism]. Tokyo: Iwanami Shoten, 2001

Kang, Sang-jung, and Hiroshi Morris. *Nashonarizumu no Kokufuku* [Overcoming the Nationalism]. Tokyo: Shueisha Sinsho, 2002.

Katzenstein, Peter J. "Introduction: Alternative Perspectives on National Security." In *The Culture of National Security: Norms and Identity in World Politics*, edited by P. Katzenstein. New York: Columbia University Press, 1996.

———. "Regionalism and Asia." *New Political Economy* 5, no. 3 (November 2000): 353–68.

Katzenstein, Peter J., and Rudra Sil. "Rethinking Asian Security: A Case for Analytical Eclecticism." In *Rethinking Security in East Asia*, edited by J. J. Suh, Peter Kaztenstein, and Allen Carlson. Stanford, Calif.: Stanford Unversity Press, 2004.

Kayahara, Ikuo. "Chugoku no kokubo kindaika to Ajia no kincho" [China's Defense Modernization and Asia's Tension]. *Chuo Koron* (May 2005): 204–15.

Kenkyusho, Sekai Heiwa, ed. *Nakasone Naikakushi: Rinen to seisaku* [History of Nakasone Cabinet: Philosophy and Policy]. Tokyo: Marunouchi Shuppan, 1995.

Keohane, Robert O. *After Hegemony: Cooperation and Discord in the World Political Economy.* Princeton, N.J.: Princeton University Press, 1984.

Kim, Hak-joon. "Tongil Inyum euroseoui Hankuk Minjokjuui" [Korean Nationalism as a Unification Philosophy]. *Tongil Munjae Yongu* 21 (July 1994): 50.

Kim, Woo Sang. "Power Transition and Strategic Stability in East Asia." *Asian Perspective* 21, no. 1 (Spring–Summer 1997): 153–70.

Kim, Yong-duck. "History, Nationalism, and Foreign Policy in South Korea." *Global Asia* 1, no. 2 (March 2007).

Kim, Yun-hwan. "Tongil Hankuk ui Miraesang" [The Future Figure of a Unified Korea]. *Tongil Cheongchaek* 15, no. 4 (1979).

Koguryo Research Foundation. *Jungkukui "Dongbuk Gonjung"—Keu Shilche wa Heogusung* [China's "Northeast Project"—Its Reality and Fiction]. Seoul: Koguryo Research Foundation, 2004.

Kurth, James R. "The Pacific Basin versus the Atlantic Alliance: Two Paradigms of International Relations." *Annals of the American Academy of Political and Social Sciences*, no. 505 (September 1989): 34–45.

Lague, David. "Coming to Terms with China's Ascent." *International Herald Tribune,* November 7, 2005.

Lee, Hong-gu. "Hankuk Minjokjuui reul boneun Sae Shigak ui Mosaek" [Searching for a New Perspective on Korean Nationalism]. *Asea Yongu* 27, no. 1 (January 1984): 38–62.

Lee, Jong-seok. "Juche Sasang gwa Minjokjuui: Kue Yonkwanseong e Kwanhan Yongu" [Juche Ideology and Nationalism: A Study on Its Relationship]. *Tongil Munje Yongu* 21 (July 1994): 65–96.

Lee, Yong-hee. "Hankuk Minjokjuui ui Je Munje" [The Issues of Korean Nationalism]." In *Hankuk ui Minjokjuui* [Nationalism of Korea], edited by Yong-hee Lee et al.. Seoul: Hankuk Ilbosa, 1967. Cited in Hak-joon Kim. "Tongil Inyum euroseoui Hankuk Minjokjuui" [Korean Nationalism as a Unification Philosophy]. *Tongil Munje Yongu* 21 (July 1994): 43.

Lim, Jie-hyun. *Jokdaejok Gongbumjadeul* [Adversarial Accomplices]. Seoul: Sonamu, 2004.

———. "Minzokjuui: Cheontong gwa Keundae ui Byunjeungbeop?" [Nationalism: A Dialectic of Tradition and Modernity?] *Sungkyunkwan Inmunkwahak* 30 (February 2000): 357–70.

Lincoln, Edward. *East Asian Economic Regionalism.* Washington, D.C.: Brookings Institution Press, 2004.

McVeigh, Brian J. *Nationalisms of Japan: Managing and Mystifying Identity.* Oxford: Rowman and Littlefield, 2004.

Mearsheimer, John J. "The False Promise of International Institutions." *International Security* 19, no. 3 (Winter 1994–1995): 5–49.

Mearsheimer, John. *The Tragedy of Great Power Politics.* New York: W. W. Norton, 2001.

Moon, Chung-in, and Seung-won Suh. "Security, Economy, and Identity Politics between Japan and South Korea under the Kim Dae-jung Government." *Korea Observer* 36, no. 4 (Winter 2005): 561–602.

Mori, Kazuko. "Chuka Sekai no Aidentiti no Henyo to Sai Chuzo" [Transformation and Recasting of Identity in the Chinese World]. In *Chuka sekai: Aidentiti no saihen* [Chinese World: Reorganization of Identity], edited by Kazuko Mori. Tokyo: Tokyo University Press, 2001.

Mori, Yoshiro. At the *Jinja* Online Network Association, jinja.jp/jikyoku/kaminokuni/ kaminokuni2.html/.

Nakasone, Yasuhiro. "Sengo no sokessan kara 21 seiki sekai no Nihone" [From Complete Evaluation of the Postwar Period to Twenty-first-Century Japan]. *Jiyu Minshu,* March 1984, 30.

Nishimura, Shigeo, ed. *Gendai Chugoku no kozo hendo 2: Nashonarizumu* [Structural Change in Contemporary China 2: Nationalism]. Tokyo: Tokyo University Press, 2000.

Office of the President of ROK, www.president.go.kr/cwd/kr/archive/.

Onuf, Nicholas G. *World of Our Making: Rules and Rule in Social Theory and International Relations.* Columbia: University of South Carolina Press, 1998.

Ozawa Ichiro. "Kokusai shakai ni okeru Nihon no yakuwari" [Japan's Role in International Society], *Bungei Shunju* (April 1992): 132–45.

———. *Nihon kaizo keikaku* [Japan Reform Plan]. Tokyo: Kodansha, 1993.

Park, Hyun-chae et al., eds. *Hankuk Minjok Undong ui Inyum gwa Yoksa* [Philosophy and History of Korean Nationalism Movements]. Seoul: Hangilsa, 1987.

Rekishi Kento Inkai (Committee on Historical Examination), ed. *Daitoa senso sokatsu* [Overview of the Great East Asia War]. Tokyo: Tendensha, 1995.

Roh, Moo-hyun. "History, Nationalism, and Community-building in Northeast Asia." *Global Asia* 1, no. 2 (March 2007).

Roy, Denny. "Hegemon on the Horizon: China's Threat to East Asian Security." *International Security* 19, no. 1 (Summer 1994): 149–68.

Ruoff, Kenneth J. *The People's Emperor: Democracy and the Japanese Monarchy, 1945–1995.* Cambridge, Mass.: Harvard University Asia Center, 2001.

Sakamoto, Tagao. *Shocho tennosei to Nihon no raireki* [Symbolic Emperor System and Japan's Origin]. Tokyo: Toshishuppan, 1995.

Sasaki, Takashi. "Nashonarizumu no jidai wo Yomu" [Reading the Age of Nationalism]. *Tokyo Shimbun,* June 12, 2005.

Shambaugh, David. "China's Fragile Future." *World Policy Journal,* 11, no. 3 (Fall 1994),

Solingen, Ethel. *Regional Orders at Century's Dawn.* Princeton, N.J.: Princeton University Press, 1998.

Song, Qiang, Cang-cang Zhang, Zheng-yu Tang, Qing-sheng Gu, and Bian Chao. *Zhungguo Keyi Shuobu* [China That Can Say "No"]. Beijing: Zhongguo Gongshang Lianho Chubanshe, 1996.

Suh, J. J., Peter J. Katzenstein, and Allen Carlson, eds. *Rethinking Security in East Asia: Identity, Power, and Efficiency.* Stanford, Calif.: Stanford University Press, 2004.

Sun, Ge, and Hiroko Sakamoto. "Sozoryoku no hinkon to shiso no tetsuzuki" [Poverty of Creativity and Procedure of Philosophy]. *Gendai Shiso* 29, no. 4 (March 2001): 42–55.

Tahara, Soichiro, Susumu Nishibe, and Sang-jung Kang. *Aikokushin* [Patriotism]. Tokyo: Kodansha, 2003.

Takahashi, Tetsuya, ed. *Rekishi ninshiki ronso* [Debates over the Historical View]. Tokyo: Sakuhinsha, 2002.

Tamamoto, Masaru. "On Japanese Nationalism and Foreign Policy." *Global Asia* 1, no. 2 (March 2007).

———. "Ambiguous Japan: Japanese National Identity at Century's End." In *Inter-*

national Relations Theory and the Asia-Pacific, edited by J. Ikenberry and M. Mastanduno.

Townsend, James. "Chinese Nationalism." *Australian Journal of Chinese Affairs,* no. 27 (January 1992): 97–130, esp. 128.

Wakamiya, Yoshibumi. "Hatoha no fuyu" [The Dove's Winter]. *Asahi Shimbun,* February 29, 2004.

Waltz, Kenneth. *Theory of International Politics.* Reading, Mass.: Addison-Wesley, 1979.

Wang, Jisi. "China's Search for Stability with America." *Foreign Affairs* 84, no. 5 (September–October 2005): 39–48.

Wendt, Alexander. *Social Theory of International Politics.* Cambridge: Cambridge University Press, 1999.

———. "Collective Identity Formation and the International State." *American Political Science Review* 88, no. 2 (June 1994): 384–96.

Xu, Guangqiu. "Anti-Western Nationalism in China, 1989–1999." *World Affairs* 163, no. 4 (Spring 2001): 151–62.

Yamakage, Susumu, ed. *Higashi ajia chiikishugi to Nihon gaiko* [East Asian Regionalism and Japan's Diplomacy]. Tokyo: Nihon Kokusai Mondai Kenkyujo, 2003.

Yan, Xue-Tong. "Qiangdajunli caineng baozheng heping jueqi" [Strong Military Power Can Only Guarantee Peaceful Rise] *Huan Qiu* (Globe), no. 17 (September 1, 2005).

Yasuhiro, Nakasone. Interview, KBS (Korea Broadcasting System), November 16, 2003.

Yuan, Weishi. "Nationalism in a China Transforming." *Global Asia* 1, no. 2 (March 2007).

Zheng, Bijian. "China's 'Peaceful Rise' to Great-Power Status." *Foreign Affairs* 84, no. 5 (September–October 2005).

Zheng, Yongnian. *Discovering Chinese Nationalism in China: Modernization, Identity, and International Relations.* Cambridge: Cambridge University Press, 1999.

9

Managing the North Korean Nuclear Quagmire
Capability, Impacts, and Prospects

Chung-in Moon

P ROFOUND TRANSFORMATION IN THE GLOBAL security landscape following
the end of the Cold War era has heightened expectations of peace and
stability in Northeast Asia. But such anticipation still appears premature as
the region continues to suffer from volatile security dilemmas. The North
Korean–South Korean conflict, cross-strait relations, unresolved territorial
disputes, and the rise of China and its strategic uncertainty underscore the
precarious nature of the Northeast Asian security complex. Beginning in
2002, however, the North Korean nuclear problem has emerged as a new flash
point, further complicating the regional security dilemma.

The North Korean nuclear quagmire is not a new phenomenon. Its origin
dates back to the early 1990s, when North Korea threatened to withdraw
from the Nuclear Nonproliferation Treaty (NPT) and to reprocess spent
fuel rods for the manufacturing of plutonium. The United States was on the
verge of commencing military action to block North Korea's nuclear venture,
precipitating a major crisis escalation on the Korean Peninsula. Ultimately, the
first nuclear crisis was defused and settled with the signing of the Geneva Agreed
Framework between North Korea and the United States in October 1994.

However, the issue resurfaced in October 2002. The latest round of the nuclear
crisis was triggered by North Korea's alleged admission of a highly enriched
uranium (HEU) program in October 2002 and escalated with the subsequent
tit for tat between North Korea and the United States. North Korea's declaration
of its possession of two nuclear warheads and its reprocessing of eight thousand
spent fuel rods for the manufacturing of plutonium during the Beijing three-
party talks in April 2003 further aggravated the nuclear standoff. Although North

Korea and the United States have since participated in six-party talks through China's mediation, the first three rounds did not yield any tangible results. A major breakthrough came during the fourth round of the six-party talks, held in Beijing in September 2005, at which the September 19 Joint Statement was adopted. Nevertheless, negotiations over the North Korean nuclear problem have stalled once again as the North refuses to participate in the six-party talks in protest of the freezing of its bank accounts in Macau, following U.S. accusations of its alleged involvement in counterfeit currency and money laundering. The situation worsened when North Korea methodically test-launched its missiles and undertook underground nuclear testing in 2006. After more than a year of stalemate, confrontation, and crisis, the third session of the fifth round of the six-party talks, held this year in Beijing on February 8–13, reversed the trend by producing an agreement on "Initial Actions for the Implementation of the Joint Statement." Although uncertainty remains as to whether the agreed implementation will be realized or not, a negotiated settlement of the North Korean nuclear problem has become all the more clear.

Nonetheless, negotiations with the North are tough, and another nuclear standoff and crisis cannot be ruled out. Such developments cannot only jeopardize peace and stability on the Korean Peninsula by altering the balance of power between the two Koreas but also severely undermine strategic stability in the region by potentially triggering a nuclear domino effect. Furthermore, proliferation of nuclear materials through transfer to third parties by the North can threaten the very foundation of global security.

It is with this understanding that this chapter attempts to elucidate the complex nature of the North Korean nuclear problem as well as to explore viable alternatives for managing it. The first part examines North Korea's nuclear capabilities; its motives for nuclear ambition; and its peninsular, regional, and global security impacts. The second traces what went wrong with the North Korean nuclear crisis. The third looks into the three plausible scenarios for resolving the North Korean nuclear quagmire. Finally, the chapter explores prospects for negotiated settlement by making an in-depth analysis of the six-party talks process and draws some policy implications for the peaceful and diplomatic resolution of the nuclear problem.

Understanding the North Korean Nuclear Quagmire: Capabilities, Motives, and Impacts

North Korea's Nuclear Weapons Capabilities

With the undertaking of an underground nuclear test on October 9, 2006, North Korea officially declared that it is a nuclear weapons state. Can its claim be accepted? In order for a country to be recognized as a nuclear weapons state, it should satisfy at least four conditions: possession of nuclear warheads, demonstration of delivery capability, actual nuclear testing, and miniaturization of nuclear warheads to mount on missiles. Let's examine each of these components.

As to the possession of nuclear warheads, there are the past, present, and future dimensions.[1] The past dimension involves North Korea's acquisition of nuclear warheads before the signing of the 1994 Agreed Framework. It is generally believed that North Korea could have produced plutonium sufficient enough to manufacture one or two nuclear bombs before 1994. But given that the United States did not raise the issue during the negotiations of the Geneva Agreed Framework in 1994, the past nuclear dimension may not pose a serious threat.

The present dimension, which is much more serious, centers on the reprocessing of eight thousand spent fuel rods stored in a water pond, the reprocessing of additional spent fuel rods to be obtained from reactivation of its 5-megawatt (MW) and 50 MW reactors in Yongbyon and a 200 MW reactor in Taechun, the manufacturing and exporting of plutonium (Pu), and the production of additional nuclear warheads, all of which had previously been frozen according to the 1994 Agreed Framework. Estimates on North Korea's Pu bombs vary among different analysts, but it is estimated that the reprocessing of 8,060 spent fuel rods stored in a cooling pond should have yielded one or two bombs. Reactivation of the 5 MW reactor is believed to have produced 44–52 kg Pu, sufficient to manufacture five or six Pu warheads. The 50 MW reactor is not yet completed, but its completion and activation could yield about 56 kg Pu per year, which would be sufficient to manufacture eleven bombs. The 200 MW reactor is projected to produce 220 kg Pu per year for an annual yield of forty-four bombs. The 50 MW nuclear reactor is expected to be completed within two to five years, but the construction of the 200 MW nuclear reactor in Taechun would take much longer.

The third dimension is the future nuclear problem associated with the development of a HEU program. The United States claims that North Korea admitted its existence during the visit of its special envoy, James Kelly, to Pyongyang in early October 2002. Some projected that North Korea would be capable of producing 75 kg of HEU per year starting in 2005, which would be sufficient to manufacture three HEU weapons every year.[2] Despite wild speculations on North Korea's HEU-related programs, however, no hard evidence on acquisitions has yet been presented. It is generally believed that North Korea could have acquired some parts and components of a HEU program such as gas centrifuges and high-intensity aluminum tubes, but that it is short of acquiring complete HEU programs and actual bombs.[3] And previous intelligence estimates on North Korea's HEU program by the Bush administration have been increasingly subject to criticism.[4] Thus, it is highly unlikely that North Korea possesses actual HEU programs and bombs.

According to Jon B. Wolfsthal, a high-end estimate of North Korea's usable nuclear material production through 2010 is 253 nuclear weapons, which includes 235 Pu weapons and 18 HEU weapons, while a low-end estimate is 112 weapons (97 Pu weapons, 15 HEU weapons). A midrange estimate is 185 weapons, composed of 170 Pu weapons and 15 HEU weapons.[5] However, it should be noted that several observers have raised the question of the reliability of intelligence estimates on North Korea's nuclear capability. For example, Douglas Frantz of the *Los Angeles Times* reported that experts have questioned U.S. government claims about North Korea's nuclear abilities, warning that a confrontation based on dubious evidence could further damage trust.[6] Nevertheless, it seems undeniable that North Korea has acquired at least plutonium bombs, if not HEU bombs, satisfying the first precondition—the possession of nuclear warheads.

While possession of nuclear warheads is one thing, the capability to deliver them is an altogether different story. Unfortunately, North Korea is known to have credible delivery capability. It currently possesses several types of missiles: Scud B (range 320 km, payload 1,000 kg), Scud C (range 500 km, payload 770), and Nodong (range 1,350–1,500 km, payload 770–1,200 kg).[7] On August 31, 1998, North Korea alarmed the entire world by conducting a test launching of a Daepodong I missile (range 1,500–2,500 km, payload 1,000–1,500 kg). But it was known that the test launching was a failure. Another test launching of Daepodong II missiles (range 3,500–6,000 km, payload 700–1,000 kg) on July 6, 2006, is believed to have failed too. Thus, it might take more than a decade for the North to develop full-scale intercontinental ballistic missiles.[8] In view of this, North Korea has not yet developed long-range missiles capable of threatening the mainland United States, but it would be able to strike South Korea and Japan through its short- and medium-range missiles.

Departing from its usual opacity, the North Korean government announced that it had successfully undertaken underground nuclear testing on October 9, 2006. Despite North Korea's claim, most international nuclear experts believe that its nuclear testing failed because the explosive yield measured from the seismic analysis is estimated to be 0.5–0.8 kilotons. Given that the lowest explosive yield, which came from the Pakistani nuclear testing, was 19 kilotons, and that the nuclear bomb that destroyed Hiroshima on August 6, 1945, was roughly 15 kilotons, a yield of less than 1 kiloton cannot be considered successful. Thus, Jungmin Kang and Peter Hayes, leading observers of the North Korean nuclear issue, make the following evaluation: "The DPRK

[Democratic People's Republic of Korea] might believe that a half kiloton 'mininuke' still provides it with a measure of nuclear deterrence and compellence; but it could not rely on other nuclear weapons states to perceive it to have anything more than an unusable, unreliable, and relatively small nuclear explosive device."[9] Thus, North Korea's claim of a successful nuclear test needs to be scrutinized.

North Korea's possession of nuclear warheads, delivery capability, and reported nuclear testing are necessary but insufficient conditions for becoming a nuclear state. It should demonstrate the capability to miniaturize nuclear warheads and mount them on Nodong or Scud missiles for effective use. Most intelligence analyses indicate that North Korea is far short of developing such technology.

In sum, North Korea has nuclear warheads and delivery capabilities. But its nuclear testing was not successful, and its miniaturization capability seems doubtful. Judged on these factors, it appears rather premature to treat North Korea as a full-fledged nuclear weapons' state. North Korea should be seen as a dangerous country with enormous nuclear weapons capability, but not as a nuclear weapons state per se.

Why Nuclear Ambition?

By all accounts, North Korea is a failing, if not failed, state. A devastating famine in the 1990s is known to have killed millions, and a great majority of North Koreans still suffer from chronic food shortages and malnutrition.[10] Human catastrophe in the North has been further compounded by an acute energy shortage.[11] The lack of domestic energy resources as well as hard currency to import oil effectively paralyzed the North Korean economy by lowering its capacity utilization rates to below 20 percent, leading to a miserable quality of life in North Korea. A satellite photo showing complete darkness in the North Korean terrain presents a dramatic testimonial to its energy crisis. North Korea has failed to satisfy the most basic human needs of its own people, yet it has continued to pursue nuclear ambitions. Why such a discrepancy? What are the motives behind its pursuit of nuclear weapons?[12]

North Korea's official rationale is based on the logic of nuclear deterrence. For the North Korean leadership and even its citizens, the fear of an American nuclear attack is not contrived, but real. They believe that the United States has plans to stage nuclear attacks on the North, and that the only way to deter them is to arm itself with nuclear weapons for second-strike capability. North Korea's logic of nuclear deterrence has been further consolidated as a result of American actions since September 11. President Bush's labeling of North Korea as part of an axis of evil and a rogue nation reaffirmed North Korea's threat perception. In addition, U.S. adoption of the preemption doctrine; its announcement of the Nuclear Posture Review (NPR), which would allow the use of tactical nuclear weapons; and the invasion of Iraq appear to have led North Korean policymakers to rely on nuclear weapons as a deterrent force. The following passages from an editorial in *Nodong Shinmun,* the daily newspaper of the Korean Workers' Party, is a revealing account of the North's motives for nuclear weapons: "America's intention is to disarm us and to destroy us with nuclear weapons. . . . Whatever preemptive nuclear attacks the United States undertake, we are ready to meet them with powerful retaliatory strikes."[13]

Two factors further reinforce the deterrence motive. In the past, the North used to take the position of opaque deterrence, which is characterized by "absence of testing, denial of possession, eschewal of nuclear threats, and non-deployment."[14] However, as American pressure has increased, the North's deterrence posture has shifted from opaque to explicit, as it declares its possession of nuclear weapons. Although its nuclear possession needs to be verified through actual inspection or testing and deployment, the North has become much bolder in pursuing the strategy of nuclear deterrence. Another factor can be seen in the development of its delivery capability. Apart from short-range missiles, the North has developed medium-range missiles (Nodong 1 and 2) targeted at Japan and is also developing long-range missiles (Daepodong I and II) targeted at Guam and the U.S. mainland. The missile development strategy indicates that the North is deliberating on a strike capability aimed at American military personnel and assets in South Korea and Japan, as well as the mainland U.S. itself. Although it is quite doubtful whether its handful of nuclear bombs can deter the United States from mounting nuclear attacks on the North, the North has nevertheless been driven by such logic.

Deterrence is not the only rationale. North Korea's nuclear venture also seems to be closely associated with the domestic politics of legitimacy and coalition building.[15] Chairman Kim's legitimacy stems from his succession of political leadership from his father, Kim Il-sung, as well as from his role as the guardian of North Korea from the American military threat. Since his political ascension in 1994, Kim Jong-il has championed the slogan of *gangsung daeguk* (a strong and prosperous great nation) as the new governing ideology. That strong and prosperous great nation is to be materialized through *sungun jung-chi* (military first politics), which gives the military the preeminent position in North Korean politics.[16] Ahn Kyung-ho, a senior member of the Korean Workers' Party, made this point clear to the author by stating, "Why are we pursuing 'the military first politics'? American military threats are real and present. If the military cannot defend the motherland from American threats, there will be neither motherland nor the Korea Workers' Party. That is why we consider the military the most important, even transcending the party."[17]

Given these considerations, the nuclear ambition appears to satisfy several domestic political purposes. It not only enhances Kim Jong-il's political legitimacy by materializing the vision of a strong and prosperous great nation but also serves as a vehicle for consolidating his political power through the co-option of the military. With the added benefit of enhancing North Korea's international status and prestige by joining the elite group of nuclear states, the possession of nuclear weapons can strengthen Kim's domestic rule.

The nuclear ambition has another function, which is to balance the military equilibrium on the peninsula through the acquisition of asymmetric military capabilities. North Korea maintained military superiority over South Korea until the 1970s. However, the inter-Korean military balance began to shift in favor of the South beginning in the 1980s. Whereas the North's military followed a more labor-intensive force structure, South Korea was able to surpass the North by combining its enhanced defense industrial production with the acquisition of advanced foreign weaponry. The widening gap in conventional forces between the North and the South was an inevitable outcome of the rapidly growing disparity in economic and technological capabilities. While the South has emerged as the eleventh-largest economy in the world, greatly facilitating its defense buildup, the North's continued poor economic performance is reflected in its slower military buildup. In 2004, South Korea's economic size was thirty times larger than that of North Korea, and North Korea's defense spending in the same year is reported to be $5.5 billion, accounting for 25 percent of its GDP but only one-third the amount of South Korea's spending ($14.6 billion).[18] North Korea's attempt to possess nuclear weapons can be interpreted as a calculated move to make up for its weakness in conventional forces by pushing for a nonconventional, asymmetric force buildup via weapons of mass destruction (WMD) and missiles.[19] This provides a less expensive path of offsetting the growing gap in conventional forces.

Finally, North Korea appears to regard nuclear weapons as a valuable economic asset for two reasons. One is as bargaining leverage for economic gains and the other is as a tool for export earnings. As the 1994 Geneva Agreed Framework demonstrated, the North was able to win lucrative economic and energy concessions such as two light-water nuclear reactors, a supply of heavy oil, and other forms of economic assistance in return for freezing its nuclear activities and returning to the NPT. Although such concessions were not fully materialized, Pyongyang learned that the nuclear weapons card can be utilized as powerful bargaining leverage in obtaining economic and energy gains. And it should not be ruled out that the North may consider using nuclear weapons and related materials as a way of generating desperately needed hard currency. The latter possibility appears unlikely because of the hostile international environment against proliferators of WMD. Nevertheless, its track record on the export of missiles and other military weapons shows that Pyongyang is capable of and willing to transfer nuclear materials for export earnings.

Impacts on Peninsular, Regional, and Global Security

North Korea's test launching of its Daepodong missile on August 31, 1998, sent an enormous tremor through Japan, ultimately resulting in a major paradigm shift in Japan's national security culture. North Korea's nuclear testing on October 9, 2006, was more critically perceived than the "Daepodong Shock" of 1998. What then are the security implications of North Korea's nukes?

Implications for peninsular security are quite grave.[20] A nuclear North Korea is not compatible with the ideal of peace building on the Korean Peninsula, because it would not only pose formidable nonconventional threats to the South but also fundamentally alter the inter-Korean military balance and tempt the North to continue deliberation of its old strategy of communizing the South. No matter how rhetorical it might sound, nuclear armament seems to dovetail with North Korea's governing ideologies of *gangsung daekuk* and *sungun jungchi,* which emphasize military self-reliance and the unification of Korea on its own terms. Under these circumstances, peaceful coexistence between the two Koreas is highly unlikely, and conventional and nonconventional arms races between the two will intensify. What could be even more troublesome is that since North Korea's possession of nuclear weapons is bound to nullify the Joint Declaration on the Denuclearization of the Korean Peninsula, South Korea might also venture into the nuclear arms race. According to a recent survey in South Korea, 66.5 percent of respondents advocated that South Korea should also possess nuclear weapons to counter the North.[21]

Equally worrisome are the negative consequences of crisis escalation. If the North Korean nuclear problem cannot be resolved through peaceful means, use of coercive measures, including military options, might become unavoidable. Such developments would incur massive collateral damage to the South. Given the military force structure along the Demilitarized Zone (DMZ) and the massive deployment of conventional forces such as missiles, any preemptive North Korean military provocation or allied forces' military action and subsequent North Korean counterattacks on the South will certainly escalate into a major military conflict on the Korean Peninsula. Estimates of war casualities would exceed half a million at the initial stage of a full-scale war, as presented by William Perry and Ashton Carter.[22] If the North attacks South Korea with its nuclear weapons, the collateral damage would be much higher since most military facilities, including American military bases, are located in urban areas.[23]

North Korea's nuclear venture can easily precipitate a nuclear arms race with the South that bears nightmarish implications for regional security. Facing new threats from North Korea, Japan may well justify a move into becoming a nuclear power.[24] Japan has the financial and technological capability and has already amassed an inventory of 40.6 metric tons of plutonium.[25] Its transformation into a nuclear power could simply be a matter of time. Taiwan could join the nuclear camp too, which would in turn foster China's nuclear buildup. Charles Krauthammer, a leading conservative columnist in the United States, has even suggested playing "Japan's nuclear card" as an alternative for coping with the North Korean nuclear standoff.[26] The nuclear domino effect, set off by North Korea's nuclear ambition, could lead the entire Northeast Asian region into a perpetual security dilemma far worse than that of the late nineteenth century.

Finally, a nuclear North Korea can also threaten global security. The North is reported to be able to produce small nuclear bombs that are hard to detect and easy to sell to others. Given North Korea's past behavior, which includes the transfer of missiles and components as well as the smuggling of drugs, counterfeit currencies, and tobacco and alcohol, there is a growing concern regarding the transfer of nuclear materials, especially plutonium, to global terrorists and rogue states. As September 11 clearly demonstrated, worldwide proliferation of nuclear materials can endanger not only the United States and Europe, but also the entire world. In addition, failure to block the advent of a nuclear North Korea can critically damage the existing NPT regime by tempting other states such as Iran to follow suit.

What Went Wrong?: An Overview of Crisis Escalation

Since the end of the Korean War in 1953, North Korea has remained concerned with potential nuclear attacks by the United States, and it first began developing a nuclear reactor program for research purposes with the assistance of the Soviet Union in the 1960s. But its nuclear weapons venture came to the attention of the international community in the early 1980s. As early as April 1982, a U.S. intelligence satellite detected the construction of nuclear reactors in Yongbyon. By March 1986, the North had not only completed the construction of a 5 MW graphite reactor but also launched construction of an additional 50 MW nuclear reactor in Yongbyon. But before the completion of the 5 MW reactor, the North joined the NPT in 1985 under international pressure and signed the safeguard clause of the International Atomic Energy Agency (IAEA) in January 1992, which was ratified by its Supreme People's Congress in April 1992. North Korea's cooperative behavior was attributed in part to the withdrawal of American tactical nuclear weapons from South Korea in 1990 and in part to improved relations between North Korea and the United States. But North Korea's pledges lacked transparency, and its refusal to cooperate with IAEA for the inspection of its past and present nuclear activities and facilities immediately prompted a negative spiral of suspicion and antagonism. When the IAEA and the United States challenged the North with compelling evidence of the construction of nuclear reactors (e.g., satellite photos of the Yongbyon facilities), North Korea responded by withdrawing its membership from the NPT on March 12, 1993. North Korea and the United States then entered a tense and protracted confrontation from March 1993 to June 1994.[27]

The crisis was defused through the mediating role of Jimmy Carter and the subsequent signing of the Geneva Agreed Framework between the United States and North Korea in October 1994. North Korea decided to freeze its nuclear programs and rejoin the NPT in return for the construction of two light-water nuclear reactors, supply of heavy oil (50,000 tons per year until the completion of the reactors), negative security assurances, exchange of liaison offices, and ultimately, diplomatic normalization.[28] Despite the sporadic eruption of disputes such as the test launching of the Daepodong missile in 1998 and the discovery of a suspected nuclear site in Kumchangri in 1999, as well as delayed implementation of the mutual agreement terms, the Agreed Framework and the Perry process succeeded in keeping North Korea's nuclear programs frozen, easing tension on the Korean Peninsula.[29] Pyongyang–Washington relations improved further with Vice Marshal Cho Myongrok's visit to the United States on October 12, 2000, and the adoption of the Albright-Cho Joint Communiqué on nonhostile intent, mutual respect of sovereignty, and the principle of noninterference, as well as then secretary of state Madeleine Albright's return visit to North Korea in November 2000.

However, bilateral relations began to deteriorate with the inauguration of the Bush administration in January 2001. President Bush's personal distrust and dislike of Chairman Kim Jong-il, the September 11 tragedy, and the ascension of neoconservatives in the U.S. foreign policymaking community, coupled with the Bush administration's ABC (Anything But Clinton) stance, abruptly suspended the Clinton administration's policy on North Korea, which was based on negotiated settlement and engagement. The Bush Doctrine, which is framed around the primacy of WMD and global terrorism in its national security agenda, moral absolutism, hegemonic unilateralism, and offensive realism, made North Korea one of the Bush administration's prime targets. North Korea was depicted as a rogue state and a member of an axis of evil to be contained and crushed.[30] Although the United States announced its intention to meet with North Korean officials at "any time, any place, without any preconditions" on June 6, 2001, official contact between the two countries was virtually frozen.

A major breakthrough came in April 2002, on the occasion of Lim Dong-won's visit to Pyongyang. Lim, who then served as national security advisor to President Kim Dae-jung, met with Chairman Kim and urged him to receive a special envoy from the United States. Chairman Kim agreed, and almost six months later, the United States sent a special envoy, Assistant Secretary of State James Kelly, to Pyongyang in early October 2002. Contrary to public expectation, Kelly's visit to Pyongyang was motivated more by the American desire to confirm the existence of North Korea's HEU program than by any intention to improve bilateral ties. His visit turned out to be a disaster, triggering the current North Korean nuclear standoff. According to Kelly, after two days of intense meetings, Kang Sok-joo, first vice foreign minister of the DPRK, admitted to him that North Korea possessed a highly enriched uranium program.[31]

The revelation outraged the Bush administration and amplified its distrust of North Korea. In retaliation, the Korea Energy Development Organization (KEDO) suspended the supply of heavy oil to North Korea on November 14, 2002, under heavy pressure from the United States, which argued that the clandestine development of a HEU program was an outright violation of the Geneva Agreed Framework. North Korea officially denied the program's existence and accused the United States of fabricating the fact. According to North Korea, Kang did not admit the existence of a HEU program but simply emphasized its sovereign entitlement to a nuclear weapons program. The North equated the suspension of heavy oil supply with the nullification of the 1994 Agreed Framework and responded with a sequence of methodical reciprocal measures. They included reactivation of a 5 MW nuclear reactor in Yongbyon (December 12), unsealing frozen nuclear facilities, removing monitoring cameras, expelling three IAEA inspectors (December 21), withdrawing from the NPT (January 10, 2003), and announcing the reprocessing of spent fuel rods (April 18, 2003).[32]

The United States advocated for hard-line measures, including the transfer of the North Korean case to the United Nations Security Council. Despite North Korea's strong appeals, the United States refused to have direct talks with the North, and tensions between the two deepened. In late March 2003, China was able to bring North Korea and the United States back to the negotiation table through a three-party-talk formula. But the situation only worsened, as North Korea admitted during the Beijing three-party talk on April 23–25, 2003, that it possessed nuclear weapons and that it had completed the reprocessing of spent fuel rods. The three-party talk between China, North Korea, and the United States failed, but a new modality of negotiations under a six-party-talk formula that included Japan, Russia, and South Korea resuscitated the possibility of peaceful and diplomatic resolution of the North Korean nuclear dilemma. China again mediated the six-party talks by accommodating the American demand for a multilateral solution to the North Korean nuclear problem, while persuading the North to attend. The first round of the six-party talks, which was held in Beijing on August 27–29, 2003, did not make any progress. The two successive rounds (second on February 25–28, third on June 23–26, 2004) also showed dismal results due to deep-rooted mutual distrust and differences in policy stances between North Korea and the United States. Whereas the United States called for a sequential approach of complete, verifiable, irreversible dismantling (CVID) of North Korea's nuclear weapons first, and resumption of energy and economic assistance and diplomatic normalization later, North Korea countered by proposing a simultaneous approach in which freezing, verifiable inspection, and dismantling should be tied to corresponding incentives. The hard adherence to these contrasting approaches proved too wide a chasm to bridge.

On the occasion of the fourth round of six-party talks in September 2005, however, North Korea and the United States, along with the other four countries (China, Japan, Russia, and South Korea), reached a basic agreement on how to resolve the North Korean nuclear problem through peaceful and diplomatic means. Yet elation from the breakthrough was short-lived, as another development contributed to the derailing of negotiations. The U.S. Treasury Department listed North Korea's suspicious illicit activities—involving counterfeit currency and money laundering at the Banco Delta Asia (BDA) in Macau—on the Federal Register on September 15, 2005, and the BDA subsequently froze fifty-two North Korean bank accounts under U.S. pressure. North Korea attended the fifth round of the six-party talks, held in Beijing in November 2005, and requested the United States to lift the sanction. When the United States did not accommodate its demand, North Korea refused further participation in the six-party talks, stalling the nuclear negotiations once again. Amid the stalemate, North Korea again began to engage in dangerous brinkmanship diplomacy by first test-launching short-, medium-, and long-range missiles on July 5, 2006, and then undertaking an underground nuclear test on October 9, 2006. It crossed most of the would-be red lines, such as possession of additional nuclear weapons through reprocessing of eight thousand spent fuel rods, reactivation of a 5 MW nuclear reactor and further production of spent fuel rods, test launching of long-range missiles, and ultimately nuclear testing. The only remaining red lines would be additional nuclear testing and the transfer of nuclear materials to third parties. Rigid policy stances, protracted mutual distrust between Pyongyang and Washington, and structural limits of multilateral negotiations portended a major catastrophic development. The impending crisis was narrowly defused by new diplomatic efforts, this time by the United States, which have yielded the February 13, 2007, agreement on Initial Actions for the Implementation of the Joint Statement in Beijing during the third session of the fifth round of the six-party talks.

Managing the North Korean Dilemma: Three Scenarios

How to manage the North Korean nuclear dilemma? With the new break-through in Beijing on February 13, 2007, the negotiated settlement option has become all the more plausible. Given past experiences, however, dramatic reversals are always possible, and the use of other options such as military actions and regime transformation through the isolation and containment of North Korea cannot be ruled out. Let's examine each of these options.[33]

Military Option and Catastrophe

The most worrisome scenario is the military option, designed to eliminate North Korea's nuclear arsenal through coercive measures. Some hard-liners in the United States have long advocated military actions against North Korea. Three options can be considered in this regard. The first is a preemptive surgical strike on nuclear facilities in Yongbyon and missile sites in Gilju. This option was deliberated on during the 1994 nuclear crisis and resurfaced on the occasion of North Korea's missile test launching on July 5, 2006, and after the underground nuclear test on October 9, 2006.[34] The second is the combination of a surgical strike and preemptive all-out attack on North Korea. The final option could involve a sequence of surgical attack, North Korea's retaliation, and counterattack. No matter what types of options are available or executed, any military action is likely to heighten the potential for major military conflicts. The combined forces of South Korea and the United States would eventually prevail over the North, but it would be achieved at the expense of enormous costs in human lives and economic prosperity.

The military option on North Korea is by and large framed around a preemption doctrine, which is predicated on the assumption that "we can-not let our enemies strike first," and that "America will act against emerging threats before they are fully formed."[35] Preemptive action now presupposes the possible use of tactical nuclear weapons. The NPR, which was submitted to Congress in January 2002, has pointed out the increasing value of mis-sile defense and the use of tactical nuclear weapons in coping with the new security environment of global terrorism and the proliferation of WMD. It suggested adopting the triad of an offensive strike system (both nuclear and nonnuclear), strengthened defenses (both active and passive), and a revitalized defense infrastructure. Central to this new strategic concept are offensive deterrence, namely preemption, and the tactical use of nuclear weapons.[36]

Several factors make these military options less feasible and desirable, however.[37] The most prominent is the rather weak rationale for undertaking military actions.[38] North Korea is still willing to talk with the United States and to accept the American request for verifiable inspection and dismantling of nuclear weapons. In return, it seeks security assurances in the form of termination of the United States' hostile intent and policy, recognition of its sovereignty, and normalization with the United States, as well as economic and energy assistance. There seems to be no reason why the United States should not consider these requests more seriously. It would be extremely difficult for the United States to win international support and legitimacy by disregarding North Korea's appeal to dialogue and negotiation and taking unilateral military actions, even if the North undertook further nuclear testing.

Geopolitics also matter. North Korea is different from Iraq in that China, Russia, and even Japan may strongly oppose American unilateral military actions. The United States cannot wage an effective war on North Korea without winning support from these neighboring countries and utilizing their ground bases. In the worst case, Chinese military involvement in North Korea cannot be ruled out, as was the case during the Korean War, because toleration of such aggressive American behavior could bear negative implications for China's own national security. South Korea's opposition will also pose another formidable deterrent. The inevitable devastation that would accompany military actions will make South Koreans vehemently opposed to American military action. U.S. preemptive military action without full consultation with the South Korean government could instantly jeopardize the ROK-U.S. military alliance, without which the United States cannot conduct effective military operations.

It also seems doubtful whether the United States would be able to achieve its political and military objectives through military actions. A surgical strike on the Yongbyon nuclear facilities cannot satisfy the American goal of destroying North Korea's nuclear capabilities completely. For though such a strike might be able to resolve the present nuclear problem (i.e., reprocessing of spent fuel rods and manufacturing of plutonium), it cannot root out the past nuclear issue (one or two nuclear bombs) and the future one (highly enriched uranium). It would achieve a very limited goal, with the overwhelming consequences of major conflict escalation and massive radioactive pollution over South Korea and Japan. A preemptive all-out attack seems questionable too. No matter how backward and ill-equipped, the North Korean military is still one of the largest in the world. At the same time, the ideology of "military first politics," widespread anti-Americanism deeply embedded in the North Korean people, hostile terrain, fortification of military bases, and asymmetric forces deployed along the DMZ would not yield an easy victory to the United States.

Finally, both rational calculus and domestic political considerations in the United States do not favor military initiatives. North Korea possesses neither oil nor other valuable natural resources, and American economic gains in the postwar era will be minimal, while the costs of war and postwar reconstruction will be prohibitively high. Moreover, the protracted conflict in Iraq and diminishing domestic support for overseas military ventures as well as concerns regarding an overextended force deployment across the globe will make it extremely hard for President Bush to undertake another war on the Korean Peninsula.

Hostile Neglect and Regime Transformation

Facing considerable constraints over the military option, those who sympathize with neocons have patronized a strategy of hostile neglect based on isolation and containment of North Korea and eventual transformation of the Kim Jong-il regime.[39] The hostile neglect option is predicated on several assumptions. The most important assumption is that the United States should "let North Korea go nuclear."[40] This assumption implies that there is no other option but to recognize North Korea as a nuclear power, either because of delayed dialogue and negotiation with the North, or because of North Korea's resolute intention to develop nuclear weapons both for survival and as bargaining leverage. Still, allowing the North to be a nuclear power would not pose any immediate nuclear threat to countries in the region, since it would require more time to emerge as a full-fledged nuclear power. Another fundamental assumption underlying this option is that the North Korean nuclear problem cannot be solved without toppling the current regime. As long as Kim Jong-il stays in power, North Korea will concurrently pursue both dialogue and the nuclear bomb. The belief is that removing him from power and creating a new regime in North Korea are the best and surest way to solve the North Korean nuclear dilemma,[41] while isolation and containment of North Korea through concerted international efforts are vital to the regime transformation.

Since North Korea has undertaken nuclear testing, this option has become all the more plausible. Most of all, in reaction to the nuclear testing, the United Nations Security Council passed Resolution 1718, calling for sanctions on conventional weapons, WMD, and luxury items as well as interdictions of any vessels suspected of transporting the above items from and to North Korea. And the United States has been strengthening the Proliferation Security Initiative (PSI), which President Bush proposed in Krakow, Poland, on May 31, 2003. The PSI is designed to "combat proliferation by developing new means to disrupt WMD trafficking at sea, in the air, and on land."[42] The United States and eighty-five participating countries are supposed to investigate, interdict, and confiscate illicit WMD-related transfers.[43] Some have interpreted the Bush administration's move to freeze North Korean bank accounts at BDA and elsewhere as part of this hostile neglect strategy.[44] At the same time, the United States has been putting bilateral pressure on China and South Korea to undertake effective sanctions against North Korea such as suspension of economic and energy assistance.

Nevertheless, the hostile neglect and eventual transformation of the Kim Jong-il regime through outside pressure are not likely to offer a viable solution to the current nuclear crisis, as a closer look at the approach reveals several serious limitations and constraints, along with the danger of a negative backlash. Such a move would worsen rather than improve the current nuclear standoff, leaving the North with fewer and fewer alternatives to actions that would eventually escalate into a major conflict on the Korean Peninsula. Moreover, the option seems to rely on faulty assumptions regarding the effectiveness of isolation and containment. It can easily become problematic if the Kim Jong-il regime does not quickly collapse, and North Korea becomes a true nuclear weapons state by crossing critical red lines. Such actions would only solidify Kim's power base, strengthen the strategic position of the military in North Korea, and extend his regime's survival, all the more so because of the intense and widespread anti-American sentiments in North Korean society that have resulted from both its people's long-lasting memory of American air raids during the Korean War and the ruling regime's systematic indoctrination.[45] And most importantly, China and South Korea would not join the United States in pursuing the strategy of isolation, containment, and transformation. American pressures notwithstanding, they refused to participate in the PSI and to suspend economic and energy assistance to the North, and the hard-line strategy would not be effectual without these two countries' active cooperation.

Negotiated Settlement and Engagement

Negotiated settlement through peaceful and diplomatic means and the gradual change of North Korea through engagement is the last of the three broad approaches to the North Korean nuclear issue.[46] The negotiated settlement and engagement scenario presupposes several common assumptions. First is a shared understanding of the urgency of an immediate freezing of North Korea's nuclear activities. Verifiable inspection of nuclear programs and their irreversible dismantling can come later. Time is on nobody's side. The failure to freeze activities and a prolonged stalemate could turn the North into a nuclear power, dramatically worsening the situation and making peaceful resolution radically more complicated. Thus, priority should be given to the immediate freezing of North Korea's nuclear activities.

Second, those who advocate this scenario assume that despite its past erratic and even deceptive behavior, the North Korean leadership is not irrational. Although the North is a tough bargainer, it is willing to cooperate if the proper mix of incentives is given. North Korea has always responded positively to positive reinforcement, and vice versa.[47] Recognition of its identity, provision of tangible incentives, and occasional face-saving treatment has yielded and can yield positive results. Negotiations over the Geneva Agreed Framework and the six-party talks reveal that North Korea's brinkmanship diplomacy has always resulted in negotiated settlements when its identity is recognized and proper incentives are given.

Third, it is also a widely shared view that the negotiation and engagement scenario is the most desirable and feasible development. Military options are too costly in all respects, whereas transformation through hostile neglect has the very probable risk that North Korea will become an outright nuclear power before progress is made, as well as the fact that the United States' aggressive posture can quickly escalate into military action. Thus, policy efforts should first be committed to negotiated settlement, and only in the event of its failure should other, more hard-line options be explored.

Its proponents argue that active engagement with the North in tandem with a negotiated settlement will certainly lead to opening, reform, and gradual changes in North Korea. Engagement will entail trust, the most indispensable element for dialogue and negotiation. Given that the current standoff resulted from mutual distrust (i.e., the American accusation of North Korea as a violator of the Agreed Framework and North Korea's fear of an American nuclear attack reminiscent of recent developments in Iraq), trust building should be the first step, which engagement will immediately facilitate. Trust building cannot be enhanced without mutual recognition of identity.[48] Recognition, positive reinforcement, and exchanges and cooperation through a process of engagement can foster major domestic structural changes, making the North a constructive member of the international community.

As Selig Harrison, Michael O'Hanlon and Mike Mochizuki, and the United States Institute of Peace report point out, the North Korean nuclear issue is also deeply embedded in the structure of the Korean conflict. North Korea claims its nuclear sovereignty because of American nuclear and conventional threats that exist partially due to the military confrontation along the DMZ. Thus, it might be difficult to completely resolve the nuclear issue without first transforming the current armistice agreement into a new peace treaty involving the North, the South, and the United States. Tying the nuclear issue into the overall peace regime in Korea could facilitate the very process of negotiation. The peaceful resolution of the nuclear issue will eventually cultivate new trust among concerned parties, and such trust can easily facilitate the resolution of other outstanding security and nonsecurity concerns. Thus, progress in nuclear negotiations can produce positive linkage effects on negotiations on the transformation of the armistice agreement into a new peace regime in Korea.

The Six-Party-Talks Process and Prospects for Negotiated Settlement

Of the contending options, negotiated settlement seems the most desirable and plausible. In this regard, adoption of the September 19 Beijing Joint Statement was a promising step toward the peaceful resolution of the North Korean nuclear problem.[49] According to the Joint Statement, North Korea committed to abandoning all nuclear weapons and existing nuclear programs, as well as to returning to the NPT and IAEA safeguards. American affirmation of nonhostile intent, mutual respect of sovereignty, peaceful coexistence, and eventual normalization was also refreshing and tremendously encouraging to the overall process. In particular, American commitment to refrain from attacking or invading North Korea with nuclear or conventional weapons reduces the risk of catastrophic military conflict on the Korean Peninsula.

The five other countries also assured North Korea that they are willing to help rebuild its failing economy by engaging in bilateral and multilateral economic cooperation in the fields of energy, trade, and investment. Such willingness sent an auspicious signal to a North Korea burdened by extreme economic hardship. The agreement produced two other positive peace dividends. One is the agreement to negotiate a permanent peace regime on the Korean Peninsula, and the other is that the six parties have committed to make joint efforts for lasting peace and stability in Northeast Asia by agreeing to explore ways and means to promote multilateral security cooperation. Both are vital to shaping a new peace and security architecture on the Korean Peninsula and in the region.

The agreement underscored the triumph of innovative diplomacy where everyone is a winner: security assurance as well as economic and energy assistance for North Korea, abandonment of North Korea's nuclear weapons and programs for the United States, and diplomatic success for China. South Korea was perhaps the greatest beneficiary of all, as the Joint Statement addressed most of the issues on its long-cherished wish list: a nonnuclear North Korea, no military action by the United States, resuscitation of the 1992 Joint Declaration of the Denuclearization of the Korean Peninsula, and multilateral security cooperation in the region. Japan and Russia must have shared similar satisfaction.

However, within months of the Joint Statement, the six-party-talks process became stalled again. The fifth round of the six-party talks, held in Beijing in late November 2005, failed to make any progress due to disputes over punitive measures by the United States against North Korea's money laundering and counterfeiting, which resulted in the freezing of the latter's bank accounts at BDA. Pyongyang has refused to show up to the six-party talks unless the U.S. government relaxes its position and unfreezes its bank accounts. Yet, the American position was firm, stating that the nuclear negotiations and counterfeit currency and money laundering are two separate issues and that since the latter involves criminal justice issues, they cannot be subject to political and diplomatic bargaining. At the same time, the United States has been intensifying pressures on the North by heightening its criticism of such issues as human rights violations, smuggling, drug trafficking, and ties with transnational crime organizations.[50] North Korea has perceived such moves as part of a calculated American effort to isolate and contain the North and transform its regime and responded by test-launching missiles and undertaking underground nuclear testing. The entire six-party talks became a captive of the BDA issue for more than a year.

However, the vicious circle of confrontation and crisis did not escalate into a full-blown catastrophe, owing to a new breakthrough during the third session of the fifth round of the six-party talks, which was held in Beijing on February 8–13, 2007. The six parties reached an agreement for Initial actions for the Implementation of the Joint Statement.[51] According to the agreement, North Korea pledged to "shut down and seal for the purpose of eventual abandonment of the Yongbyon nuclear facility, including the reprocessing facility," and "invite back IAEA personnel to conduct all necessary monitoring and verifications." And the North has also agreed to come up with "a list of all its nuclear programs as described in the Joint Statement, including plutonium extracted from used fuel rods." In return for these initial actions, the United States has agreed to start bilateral talks with North Korea aimed at "resolving pending bilateral issues" (i.e., removing North Korea from the list of state sponsors of terrorism and the termination of the application of the Trading with the Enemy Act on North Korea) and "moving toward full diplomatic relations." Japan agreed to resume bilateral talks aimed at taking steps to normalize its relations with the North. And five countries (the United States, China, South Korea, Japan, and Russia) agreed to make an initial shipment of 50,000 tons of heavy fuel oil (HFO) to the North within the next sixty days, contingent upon North Korea's implementation of its initial pledges.

The six parties have also established five working groups (denuclearization of the Korean Peninsula, DPRK-U.S. normalization, DPRK-Japan normalization, economy and energy cooperation, and Northeast Asia Peace and Security Mechanism) in order to carry out the initial actions and fully implement the Joint Statement. If North Korea makes a complete declaration of all nuclear programs and disables all existing nuclear facilities, including graphite-moderated reactors and reprocessing plants, then economic, energy, and humanitarian assistance up to the equivalent of one million tons of HFO, including an initial shipment equivalent to 50,000 tons, will be provided to North Korea. It is also interesting to note that "once the initial actions are implemented, the six parties will promptly hold a ministerial meeting to confirm implementation of the Joint Statement and explore ways and means for promoting security cooperation in Northeast Asia." The parties also agreed to hold the sixth round of the six-party talks on March 19, 2007 to hear reports of working groups and discuss actions for the next phase.

Although the February 13 agreement is nothing but a first step toward the fuller denuclearization of the Korean Peninsula, it deserves commendation for several reasons. First, in contrast to the Joint Statement, which is rather comprehensive and declaratory, the agreement is significant because it gives a very concrete picture of actions with a clearly defined timetable. Second, the agreement is also innovative in the sense that it effectively combines bilateral with multilateral approaches. Most interesting is the shifting U.S. position. The United States has become pragmatic enough to pursue bilateral contacts with the North, departing from previous adherence to multilateral contacts. It is particularly noteworthy that all five countries have pledged to share the costs of energy assistance to North Korea in accordance with the principle of equality and fairness. Third, both North Korea and the United States appear to have committed to the diplomatic resolution of the nuclear problem through the six-party-talks process by overcoming the inertia-driven behavior of the past. Immediately after signing the agreement, both parties started moving fast. Whereas the United States pledged to resolve the BDA problem within thirty days and invited Vice Foreign Minister Kim Gye-gwan, North Korea's chief delegate to the Beijing talks, to visit New York on March 1 to initiate bilateral talks on normalization, North Korea fades out also reciprocated by inviting Mohammed el-Baradei, head of the IAEA, to visit the North, which can be viewed as a pretext for the return of its inspectors. Finally, there appears to be a shared perception and unity of purpose among all parties, even including North Korea, that the breakdown of the agreement could lead to the collapse of negotiated settlement, portending a major disaster, and that no one wants to lose face by becoming a spoiler.

Nonetheless, several challenges await the six-party talks. The most crucial issue is the scope of nuclear activities and programs to be declared, inspected, and dismantled. Does "abandoning all nuclear weapons and existing nuclear programs" include the highly enriched uranium program? Obviously, the United States would think so, whereas the North may continue to deny that it even exists. Factual evidence should eventually resolve this issue. Verifiable inspections pose another daunting challenge. Would North Korea allow an intrusive inspection? Given the clandestine nature of North Korean society, its extraordinarily high national pride, and the powerful position of its military, it would be extremely difficult for outside inspectors to undertake a sweeping and intrusive inspection of nuclear facilities in the North. Even if North Korea showed a passively cooperative attitude, verifiable inspections may still prove difficult, with the Iraq experience an obvious testament to the dilemma of inspections.

Let's assume that North Korea fully cooperates with the verifiable dismantling. Such cooperative behavior is predicated on incentives, and bilateral and multilateral energy assistance, expansion of trade and investment, and other forms of assistance will be integral to the successful implementation of freezing, verifiable inspection, and irreversible dismantling of nuclear programs. Pooling financial resources for such a scope of assistance is another hurdle the parties involved must face. As it stands, it may fall to China and South Korea to spearhead such assistance. Russia has also become more proactive in extending assistance to the North. Considering other pending issues such as missile proliferation, human rights violations, and illicit drug and counterfeit currency trafficking, however, Japan and the United States may discover significant domestic political opposition to assuming the lion's share of the costs in assisting North Korea. Japan might not join such efforts unless the issue of abducted Japanese is resolved. Provision of incentives and engagement with North Korea might become less effectual without the participation of Japan and the United States. And from a logistical point of view, it would also be a formidable task to coordinate and steer five working groups simultaneously.

Likewise, the negotiated settlement of the North Korean nuclear dilemma will not be an easy affair, and impending challenges could undermine prospects for the six-party-talks process. But there seem to be no other realistic alternatives but the talks, and all parties should make serious efforts to make them successful.

Conclusion

Several implications can be drawn from the examination of the North Korean nuclear problem. The first implication is that North Korea is a dangerous country with nuclear weapons capability and that its possession of usable nuclear weapons should be blocked. Otherwise, peninsular, regional, and global peace and security can be profoundly jeopardized. In particular, nuclear domino effects in Northeast Asia, which might result from North Korea's nuclear ambition, can critically threaten regional peace and prosperity.

Second, neither military actions nor a hostile neglect strategy based on isolation, containment, and transformation can serve as a viable alternative to resolving the North Korean nuclear quagmire. The most feasible and desirable option is negotiated settlement through peaceful and diplomatic means. It is for this reason that the six-party-talks process should be highly valued. Freezing, verifiable inspection, and irreversible dismantling of North Korea's nuclear weapons as well as lifting sanctions and the PSI should be discussed bilaterally or multilaterally within the framework of the six-party talks.

Third, negotiated settlement needs to be prudently linked to engagement with North Korea. Engagement aims not only at promoting exchange and cooperation with North Korea but also at fostering the process of opening and reform. Ultimately, it will lead to institutionalization of the market economy, expansion of civil society, and the rise of a middle class, resulting in the gradual transformation of North Korea. Political changes can come from within, minimizing or preventing the pains and costs of implosion or abrupt collapse. Such changes can ensure irreversible dismantling of North Korea's nuclear weapons.[52] But engagement should start with recognition of mutual identity, which is essential for mutual trust building.

Fourth, as the Beijing Joint Statement properly acknowledges, the ultimate resolution of the North Korean nuclear problem cannot be separated from the issues of the transformation of the armistice treaty regime into a peace regime on the Korean Peninsula through the formal ending of the Korean War system and of the creation of a viable multilateral security cooperation regime in Northeast Asia. Thus, there must be renewed efforts to explore a peace regime in Korea and a multilateral security cooperation regime in the region.

Finally, participants in the six-party talks should treat each other as legitimate negotiation partners, and instrumental if not consummate trust should be extended among them. It should also be kept in mind that positive reinforcement is better than negative reinforcement in dealing with North Korea. Despite the suspicion of deception, North Korea has usually shown positive responses to engagement, which can ultimately bring about a virtuous, rather than vicious, cycle of interactions in dealing with North Korea.

Notes

1. See Institute of International and Strategic Studies (IISS), *North Korea's Weapons Programme: A Net Assessment* (London: IISS, 2004), 63–84; Jon B. Wolfsthal,

"Estimates of North Korea's Unchecked Nuclear Weapons Production Potential," Carnegie Endowment for International Peace, www.ceip.org/files/projects/npp/pdf/JBW/nknuclearweaponproductionpotential.pdf (accessed November 2, 2003); David Albright, "North Korean Plutonium Production," *Science and Global Security,* 5 (1994): 78; Monterey Institute's Center for Nonproliferation Studies, "North Korean Nuclear Capabilities," www.nti.org/db/profiles/dprk/msl/msl_overview.html (accessed November 2, 2003); *Yonhap News,* January 2.

2. Wolfsthal, "Estimates"; Fred McGoldrick, "The North Korea Uranium Enrichment Program: A Freeze and Beyond" (Working Papers of the Nautilus Institute for Security and Sustainability, no. 38, June 2003).

3. See David Albright, "North Korea's Alleged Large-Scale Enrichment Plant: Yet Another Questionable Extrapolation Based on Aluminum Tubes," *ISIS Report,* February 23, 2007, www.isis-online.org/publications/DPRK/DPRKenrichment22Feb.pdf.

4. See Dong-young Yoon, "Call for Re-examination on Intelligence Estimates on North Korea's HEU Program," *Yonhap News,* February 25, 2007 (in Korean).

5. Here, the high-end estimate assumes full production capability, construction or expansion of additional reprocessing capacity, and early operation of facilities, while the low-end one assumes late completion of reactors, no increase in reprocessing capabilities, and late completion of HEU capability. The midrange estimate assumes early completion of reactors, delayed completion of HEU production, and a slight increase in reprocessing capabilities. See Wolfsthal, "Estimates."

6. Douglas Frantz, "N. Korea's Nuclear Success Is Doubted," *Los Angeles Times,* December 9, 2003. Also refer to David Sanger, "Intelligence Puzzle: North Korean Bombs," *New York Times,* October 14, 2003.

7. See International Institute for Strategic Studies, *North Korea's Weapons Programmes,* 63–84.

8. Robert S. Nerris, Hans M. Kristensen, and Joshua Handler, "North Korea's Nuclear Program," *Bulletin of the Atomic Scientists* 59, no. 2 (March–April 2003): 76–77; David Albright, "Assessment of the North Korean Missile Threat," Nautilus Institute, www.nautilus.org/fora/security/0320A-%20Wright.html (accessed November 2, 2003).

9. Jungmin Kang and Peter Hayes, "Technical Analysis of the DPRK Nuclear Test," Nautilus Institute, www.nautilus.org/fora/security/0689HayesKang.html (accessed October 20, 2006), 1. Also see International Institute for Strategic Studies, "North Korea's Nuclear Test: Continuing Reverberations," *IISS Strategic Comments* 12, no. 8 (October 8, 2006).

10. See Hazel Smith, *Hungry for Peace: International Security, Humanitarian Assistance, and Social Change in North Korea* (Washington, D.C.: United States Institute of Peace, 2006); Stephan Haggard and Marcus Noland, *Hunger and Human Rights: The Politics of Famine in North Korea* (Washington, D.C.: U.S. Committee for Human Rights in North Korea, 2005).

11. Nautilus Institute, *Report Prepared for the Korea Energy Economics Institute,* September 13, 2002.

12. See Scott D. Sagan, "Why Do States Build Nuclear Weapons: Three Models in Search of Bomb," *International Security* 21, no. 3 (Winter 1996–1997).

13. *Nodong Shinmun,* September 21, 2005. This editorial appeared as a response to a *Washington Post* article that reported the Pentagon's proposed revision to its nuclear doctrine that "would allow commanders to seek presidential approval for using atomic arms against nations or terrorists who intend to use chemical, biological, and nuclear weapons against the U.S., its troops or allies." Walter Pincus, "Pentagon May Have Doubts on Preemptive Nuclear Moves," *Washington Post,* September 21, 2005.

14. Rajesh M. Basrur, *Minimum Deterrence and India's Nuclear Security* (Stanford, Calif.: Stanford University Press, 2006), 28.

15. Mun-hyung Huh, "Bukhanui Haekgaibal Gyoehoick Injunggwa Hyanghu Jungchaek Junmang" [North Korea's Admission of Nuclear Development Plan and Prospects of Future Policy], in *Bukhaek Munjeui Haebopgwa Junmang* [Solution and Prospects of the North Korean Nuclear Problem], ed. Jung-bok Lee (Seoul: Jungang M & B, 2003), 157–206.

16. Chung-in Moon and Hideshi Takesada, "North Korea: Institutionalized Military Intervention," in *Coercion and Governance,* ed. Muthiah Alagappa (Stanford, Calif.: Stanford University Press, 2001), 257–82.

17. Kyung-ho Ahn, Secretary General of the Committee for Peaceful Unification of Motherland, interview with the author, March 28, 2004, Pyongyang.

18. Institute of International Strategic Studies, *Military Balance, 2004–2005* (London: IISS, 2005).

19. Taik-young Hahm, "Nambukhan Gunbi Gyongjaengui Ihae" [Understanding North-South Korean Arms Race], in *Bundaui Dueolgul* [Two Faces of Division], ed. Seung-ryol Kim and Jubaek Shin (Seoul: Yoksa Bipyong, 2005), 106–7.

20. Bruce Bennett, "Avoiding the Peacetime Dangers of North Korean Nuclear Weapons," *IFANS Review* 13, no. 2 (December 2005): 30–37.

21. *Joongang Ilbo,* October 14, 2005.

22. Ashton Carter and William Perry, *Preventive Defense: A New Security Strategy for America* (Washington, D.C.: Brookings Institution Press, 1999), chap. 4. Also see Michael Schuman, "Peace and War," *Time,* March 3, 2003, 38.

23. Bennett, "Avoiding the Peactime Dangers," 32–34.

24. Former prime minister Nakasone Yasuhiro claims that Japan should deliberate on having nuclear weapons for defensive purposes. *Yonhap News,* January 7, 2004.

25. *Ohmynews,* February 3, 2006.

26. Charles Krauthammer, "The Japan Card," *Washington Post,* January 3, 2003.

27. See Don Oberdorfer, *Two Koreas: A Contemporary History* (Reading, Mass.: Addison-Wesley, 1997), 249–80.

28. For excellent accounts of the 1994 crisis, see Leon Sigal, *Disarming Strangers: Nuclear Diplomacy with North Korea* (Princeton, N.J.: Princeton University Press, 1998); Don Oberdorfer, *Two Koreas: A Contemporary History,* 249–368; Joel S. Witt, Daniel B. Poneman, and Robert L. Gallucci, *Going Critical: The First North Korea Nuclear Crisis* (Washington, D.C.: Brookings Institution, 2004).

29. The Perry process refers to American efforts to resolve the North Korean nuclear problem through negotiation and engagement that were coordinated by William J. Perry, former U.S. secretary of defense. See William J. Perry, *Review of United States*

Policy toward North Korea: Findings and Recommendations (Washington, D.C.: Office of the North Korea Policy Coordinator, October 12, 1999).

30. Chung-in Moon and Jong-yun Bae, "The Bush Doctrine and the North Korean Nuclear Crisis," *Asian Perspective* 27, no. 4 (2003): 9–45.

31. The South Korean government has been providing the United States with intelligence on North Korea's HEU program since early 1999. In early 1999, South Korea notified the United States of the dispatch of North Korean nuclear scientists to Pakistan. In March 1999, South Korea and the United States jointly aborted North Korea's efforts to purchase component parts for gas centrifuge systems from Japan. In March 2002, the South Korean government also provided the United States with intelligence on North Korea's purchase of high-intensity aluminum. But South Korea seems to have a somewhat doubtful view on the existence of an actual HEU program. This view has been shared by China too. See Glenn Kessler, "Chinese Not Convinced of North Korean Uranium Effort," *Washington Post,* January 7, 2004, A16.

32. For the chronology of the North Korean crisis escalation, see www .yonhapnews.co.kr/cgi-bin/naver/query_news.

33. For a comprehensive discussion of management strategies, see Victor D. Cha and David C. Kang, *Nuclear North Korea: A Debate on Engagement Strategies* (New York: Columbia University Press, 2003) and the debate between Henry Sokolski, "Treat North Korea as a Nuclear Proliferator," and Leon V. Sigal, "Try Engagement for a Change," *Global Asia* 1, no. 1 (September 2006): 42–57.

34. See William Perry, "The Case for a Preemptive Strike on North Korea's Missiles," *Time Magazine,* July 10, 2006.

35. White House, *The National Security Strategy of the United States of America,* September 2002, www.whitehouse.gov.

36. U.S. Department of Defense, *Nuclear Posture Review Report,* submitted to Congress on January 8, 2002, www.globalsecurity.org/wmd/library/policy/dod/npr .htm (accessed June 4, 2003), 7. Also see the testimony of John Bolton, undersecretary of state, before the House Committee on International Relations. "U.S. to eliminate WMD in all rogue states, by force if necessary," World-AFP, June 5, 2003.

37. For an excellent analysis of the limits of military options, see Donald G. Gross, "September 11, Iraq and North Korea: The Evolution of U.S. Policy," mimeo, June 2003.

38. Jeremy Brecher, "Terminating the Bush Juggernaut," FPIF Discussion Paper, May 2003, www.fpif.org/papers/juggernaut/index.html (accessed June 4, 2003); Leon V. Sigal, "North Korea Is No Iraq: Pyongyang's Negotiating Strategy," *Arms Control Today* 32, no. 10 (December 2002): 11–12.

39. Nicholas Eberstadt, *The End of North Korea* (Washington, D.C.: American Enterprise Institute, 1999); Henry Sokolski, "Let's Not Do It Again," *National Review Online* 24 (October 2002), www.nationalreview.com/comment; Victor Cha, "Isolation, Not Engagement," *New York Times,* December 29, 2002, D9; Henry S. Rowen, "Kim Jong-Il Must Go," *Policy Review* (October–November 2003): 15–16.

40. Sonni Efron, "U.S. Said to Be Resigned to a Nuclear Korea," *Los Angeles Times,* March 5, 2003; "Bush Shifts Focus to Nuclear Sales by North Korea," *New York Times,* May 5, 2003. Some suggest a more pessimistic scenario that North Korea will not give

up the nuclear bomb and that precautionary measures should be prepared to reduce the threats and risks coming from a nuclear North Korea. See Bennett Ramberg, "Why North Korea Will Not Give Up the Bomb," *International Herald Tribune*, January 6, 2006, 6.

41. See Rowen, "Kim Jong-Il Must Go," 15.

42. John Bolton, "Nuclear Weapons and Rogue States: Challenge and Response," remarks to the Conference of the Institute for Foreign Policy Analysis and the Fletcher School's International Security Studies Program, December 2, 2003, www.state.gov/t/us/rm/26786.htm (accessed December 10, 2003).

43. *JoongAng Ilbo*, June 2, 2003.

44. See Joel Brinkley, "U.S. Squeezes North Korea's Money Flow," *New York Times*, March 10, 2006.

45. For a critical view of the regime change option in North Korea, see Robert S. Litwak, *Regime Change: U.S. Strategy through the Prism of 9/11* (Washington, D.C.: Woodrow Wilson International Center, 2007), 245–91.

46. See Jung-Hoon Lee and Chung-in Moon, "The North Korean Nuclear Crisis Revisited: The Case for a Negotiated Settlement," *Security Dialogue* 34, no. 2 (June 2003): 135–51.

47. Chung-in Moon, "North Korea's Foreign Policy in Comparative and Theoretical Perspective," in *North Korea and the World: Explaining Pyongyang's Foreign Policy*, ed. B. C. Koh, 355–68 (Seoul: Kyungnam University Press, 2004); Joseph Cirincione and Jon Wolfsthal, "Dealing with North Korea," *Proliferation Brief* 6, no. 23 (December 19, 2003); Selig Harrison, *Turning Point in Korea: New Dangers and New Opportunities for the United States* (Washington, D.C.: Center for International Policy, 2003); United States Institute of Peace, "A Comprehensive Resolution of the Korean War," *Special Report* 106 (May 2003), 2; Council on Foreign Relations, *Meeting the North Korean Nuclear Challenge* (Washington, D.C.: Council on Foreign Relations, 2003). Michael O'Hanlon and Mike Mochizuki, *Crisis on the Korean Peninsula: How to Deal with a Nuclear North Korea* (New York: McGraw-Hill, 2003), 18–21.

48. J. J. Suh, "Producing Security Dilemma out of Uncertainty: The North Korean Nuclear Crisis," mimeo, November 2006.

49. See Chung-in Moon, "After Beijing Breakthrough, What Next?" *Korea Times*, September 23, 2005; Joseph Kahn, "North Korea Signs Nuclear Accord," *International Herald Tribune*, September 20, 2005.

50. See David Asher, "The North Korean Criminal State, Its Ties to Organized Crime, and the Possibility of WMD Proliferation," remarks to the Counter-Proliferation Study Group, Woodrow Wilson Center, Washington D.C., October 21, 2005.

51. For its full text, refer to www.mofat.go.kr/mofat/mk_a008/mk_b083/mk_c063.html. Also see "Faces Saved All Round," *Economist*, February 17, 2007, 28–30.

52. See Chung-in Moon, "Managing Collateral Catastrophe: Rationale and Preconditions for International Economic Support for North Korea," in *A New International Engagement: Framework for North Korea*, ed. Choong-young Ahn, Nicholas Eberstadt, and Young-sun Lee, 117–46 (Washington, D.C.: Korea Economic Institute of America, 2004).

References

Ahn, Choong-young, Nicholas Eberstadt, and Young-sun Lee, eds. *A New International Engagement: Framework for North Korea.* Washington, D.C.: Korea Economic Institute of America, 2004.

Ahn, Kyung-ho, secretary general of the Committee for Peaceful Unification of Motherland, interview by the author, March 28, 2004, Pyongyang.

Albright, David. "Assessment of the North Korean Missile Threat." Nautilus Institute. www.nautilus.org/fora/security/0320A-%20Wright.html (accessed November 2, 2003).

———. "North Korean Plutonium Production." *Science and Global Security* 5 (1994): 78.

———. "North Korea's Alleged Large-Scale Enrichment Plant: Yet Another Questionable Extrapolation Based on Aluminum Tubes." *ISIS Report,* February 23, 2007. www.isis-online.org/publications/DPRK/DPRKenrichment22Feb.pdf.

Asher, David. "The North Korean Criminal State, Its Ties to Organized Crime, and the Possibility of WMD Proliferation." Remarks to the Counter-Proliferation Study Group, Woodrow Wilson Center, Washington. D.C., October 21, 2005. www.mofat.go.kr/mofat/mk_a008/mk_b083/mk_c063.html.

Basrur, Rajesh M. *Minimum Deterrence and India's Nuclear Security.* Stanford, Calif.: Stanford University Press, 2006.

Bennett, Bruce. "Avoiding the Peacetime Dangers of North Korean Nuclear Weapons." *IFANS Review* 13, no. 2 (December 2005): 30–37.

Bolton, John. "Nuclear Weapons and Rogue States: Challenge and Response." Remarks to the Conference of the Institute for Foreign Policy Analysis and the Fletcher School's International Security Studies Program, December 2, 2003. www.state.gov/t/us/rm/26786.htm (accessed December 10, 2003).

———. "U.S. to eliminate WMD in all rogue states, by force if necessary." Testimony of the Undersecretary of State before the House Committee on International Relations. World-AFP, June 5, 2003.

Brecher, Jeremy. "Terminating the Bush Juggernaut." FPIF Discussion Paper, May 2003. www.fpif.org/papers/juggernaut/index.html (accessed June 4, 2003).

Brinkley, Joel. "U.S. Squeezes North Korea's Money Flow." *New York Times,* March 10, 2006.

Carter, Ashton, and William Perry, *Preventive Defense: A New Security Strategy for America.* Washington, D.C.: Brookings Institution Press, 1999.

Cha, Victor D., and David C. Kang, *Nuclear North Korea: A Debate on Engagement Strategies.* New York: Columbia University Press, 2003.

Cha, Victor. "Isolation, Not Engagement," *New York Times,* December 29, 2002.

Cirincione, Joseph, and Jon Wolfsthal. "Dealing with North Korea." *Proliferation Brief* 6, no. 23 (December 19, 2003).

Council on Foreign Relations. *Meeting the North Korean Nuclear Challenge.* Washington, D.C.: Council on Foreign Relations, 2003.

Eberstadt, Nicholas. *The End of North Korea.* Washington, D.C.: American Enterprise Institute, 1999.

Economist, "Faces Saved All Round," February 17, 2007.

Efron, Sonni. "U.S. Said to Be Resigned to a Nuclear Korea." *Los Angeles Times*, March 5, 2003.

Frantz, Douglas. "N. Korea's Nuclear Success Is Doubted." *Los Angeles Times*, December 9, 2003.

Gross, Donald G. "September 11, Iraq and North Korea: The Evolution of U.S. Policy." (mimeo, June 2003).

Haggard, Stephan, and Marcus Noland. *Hunger and Human Rights: The Politics of Famine in North Korea*. Washington, D.C.: U.S. Committee for Human Rights in North Korea, 2005.

Hahm, Taik-young. "Nambukhan Gunbi Gyongjaengui Ihae" [Understanding North-South Korean Arms Race]. In *Bundaui Dueolgul* [Two Faces of Division], edited by Seung-ryol Kim and Jubaek Shin. Seoul: Yoksa Bipyong, 2005.

Harrison, Selig. *Turning Point in Korea: New Dangers and New Opportunities for the United States*. Washington, D.C.: Center for International Policy, 2003.

Huh, Mun-hyung, "Bukhanui Haekgaibal Gyoehoick Injunggwa Hyanghu Jungchaek Junmang" [North Korea's Admission of Nuclear Development Plan and Prospects of Future Policy]. In *Bukhaek Munjeui Haebopgwa Junmang* [Solution and Prospects of the North Korean Nuclear Problem], edited by Jung-bok Lee. Seoul: Jungang M & B, 2003.

International Institute for Strategic Studies (IISS). *Military Balance, 2004–2005*. London: IISS, 2005.

———. "North Korea's Nuclear Test: Continuing Reverberations." *IISS Strategic Comments* 12, no. 8 (October 8, 2006).

———. *North Korea's Weapons Program: A Net Assessment*. London: IISS, 2004.

Kahn, Joseph. "North Korea Signs Nuclear Accord." *International Herald Tribune*, September 20, 2005.

Kang, Jungmin, and Peter Hayes. "Technical Analysis of the DPRK Nuclear Test." Nautilus Institute. www.nautilus.org/fora/security/0689HayesKang.html (accessed October 20, 2006)

Kessler, Glenn. "Chinese Not Convinced of North Korean Uranium Effort." *Washington Post*, January 7, 2004.

Koh, B. C. *North Korea and the World: Explaining Pyongyang's Foreign Policy*. Seoul: Kyungnam University Press, 2004.

Krauthammer, Charles. "The Japan Card." *Washington Post*, January 3, 2003.

Lee, Jung-Hoon, and Chung-in Moon. "The North Korean Nuclear Crisis Revisited: The Case for a Negotiated Settlement." *Security Dialogue* 34, no. 2 (June 2003): 135–51.

Litwak, Robert S., *Regime Change: U.S. Strategy through the Prism of 9/11*. Washington, D.C.: Woodrow Wilson International Center, 2007.

McGoldrick, Fred. "The North Korea Uranium Enrichment Program: A Freeze and Beyond." Working Papers of the Nautilus Institute for Security and Sustainability, no. 38 (June 2003).

Monterey Institute's Center for Nonproliferation Studies. "North Korean Nuclear Capabilities." *Yonhap News*, January 2, 2003, www.nti.org/db/profiles/dprk/msl/msl_overview.html (accessed November 2, 2003).

Moon, Chung-in. "After Beijing Breakthrough, What Next?" *Korea Times,* September 23, 2005.

———. "Managing Collateral Catastrophe: Rationale and Preconditions for International Economic Support for North Korea." In *A New International Engagement: Framework for North Korea,* edited by Choong-young Ahn, Nicholas Eberstadt, and Young-sun Lee, 117–46. Washington, D.C.: Korea Economic Institute of America, 2004.

———. "North Korea's Foreign Policy in Comparative and Theoretical Perspective." In *North Korea and the World: Explaining Pyongyang's Foreign Policy,* edited by B. C. Koh, 355–68. Seoul: Kyungnam University Press, 2004.

Moon, Chung-in, and Jong-yun Bae. "The Bush Doctrine and the North Korean Nuclear Crisis." *Asian Perspective* 27, no. 4 (2003): 9–45.

Moon, Chung-in, and Hideshi Takesada. "North Korea: Institutionalized Military Intervention." In *Coercion and Governance,* edited by Muthiah Alagappa. Stanford, Calif.: Stanford University Press, 2001.

Nautilus Institute. *Report prepared for the Korea Energy Economics Institute,* September 13, 2002.

Nerris, Robert S., Hans M. Kristensen, and Joshua Handler. "North Korea's Nuclear Program." *Bulletin of the Atomic Scientists* 59, no. 2 (March–April 2003): 76–77.

New York Times, "Bush Shifts Focus to Nuclear Sales by North Korea," May 5, 2003.

Oberdorfer, Don. *Two Koreas: A Contemporary History.* Reading, Mass.: Addison-Wesley, 1997.

O'Hanlon, Michael, and Mike Mochizuki. *Crisis on the Korean Peninsula: How to Deal with a Nuclear North Korea* (New York: McGraw-Hill, 2003), 18–21.

Perry, William. "The Case for a Preemptive Strike on North Korea's Missiles." *Time Magazine Online,* July 10, 2006.

Perry, William J. *Review of United States Policy toward North Korea: Findings and Recommendations.* Washington, D.C.: Office of the North Korea Policy Coordinator, October 12, 1999.

Pincus, Walter. "Pentagon May Have Doubts on Preemptive Nuclear Moves." *Washington Post,* September 21, 2005.

Ramberg, Bennett. "Why North Korea Will Not Give Up the Bomb." *International Herald Tribune,* January 6, 2006.

Rowen, Henry S. "Kim Jong-Il Must Go." *Policy Review* (October–November 2003): 15–16.

Sagan, Scott D. "Why Do States Build Nuclear Weapons: Three Models in Search of Bomb." *International Security* 21, no. 3 (Winter 1996–1997).

Sanger, David. "Intelligence Puzzle: North Korean Bombs," *New York Times,* October 14, 2003.

Schuman, Michael. "Peace and War." *Time,* March 3, 2003.

Sigal, Leon. *Disarming Strangers: Nuclear Diplomacy with North Korea.* Princeton, N.J.: Princeton University Press, 1998.

Sigal, Leon V. "North Korea Is No Iraq: Pyongyang's Negotiating Strategy." *Arms Control Today* 32, no. 10 (December 2002): 11–12.

———. "Try Engagement for a Change." *Global Asia* 1, no. 1 (September 2006): 50–57.

Smith, Hazel. *Hungry for Peace: International Security, Humanitarian Assistance, and Social Change in North Korea.* Washington, D.C.: United States Peace Institute, 2006.

Sokolski, Henry. "Let's Not Do It Again," *National Review Online,* October 24, 2002. www.nationalreview.com/comment.

———. "Treat North Korea as a Nuclear Proliferator." *Global Asia* 1, no. 1 (September 2006): 42–49.

Suh, J. J. "Producing Security Dilemma out of Uncertainty: The North Korean Nuclear Crisis." (November 2006, mimeo).

United States Institute of Peace. "A Comprehensive Resolution of the Korean War." *Special Report* 106 (May 2003).

U.S. Department of Defense. *Nuclear Posture Review Report:* Submitted to Congress on January 8, 2002. www.globalsecurity.org/wmd/library/policy/dod/npr.htm (accessed June 4, 2003).

White House. *The National Security Strategy of the United States of America.* September 2002, www.whitehouse.gov.

Witt, Joel S., Daniel B. Poneman, and Robert L. Gallucci. *Going Critical: The First North Korea Nuclear Crisis.* Washington, D.C.: Brookings Institution, 2004.

Wolfsthal, Jon B. "Estimates of North Korea's Unchecked Nuclear Weapons Production Potential." Carnegie Endowment for International Peace. www.ceip.org/files/projects/npp/pdf/JBW/nknuclearweaponproductionpotential.pdf (accessed November 2, 2003).

Yoon, Dong-young. "Call for Re-examination on Intelligence Estimates on North Korea's HEU Program." *Yonhap News,* February 25, 2007 (in Korean).

Part III
DESIGNING NEW ORDER

10

Hegemonic Order, September 11, and the Consequences of the Bush Revolution

Michael Mastanduno

THE END OF THE COLD WAR brought forth a systemic change in world politics, from an international system dominated by two superpowers to a system dominated by one. This systemic shift is profound, and it implies new patterns of interaction among states. It leads states, particularly major powers, to reconsider and possibly redirect their foreign policies. Systemic change also has consequences for order and stability in key regions of the world.

The defining feature of the new international system is the dominance of the United States.[1] The United States faces no challengers or peer competitors in the traditional sense of great power politics. It is dominant militarily and economically, and its core ideological preferences are shared in many parts of the world. No other state can balance the United States, and no effective combination of balancers is plausibly on the horizon. In this context, a key strategic priority of the United States has been to preserve its preponderant position. The United States has sought since the end of the Cold War to maintain its primacy globally and to shape international order in key regions, including Europe, the Middle East, and East Asia.[2]

This article advances three main arguments. First, the United States, in response to the opportunity presented by its dominant power position, has pursued a hegemonic strategy for the maintenance of order in East Asia. A hegemonic strategy means the United States does not aspire simply to dominate other states; it seeks instead to gain their acceptance for an international order shaped by the United States and consistent with its interest and values. I argue that U.S. hegemony has provided public goods and made important contributions to East Asian order but remains incomplete in that it is accepted only partially by other major states in the region.

Second, I argue that the events of September 11 have had a profound impact on U.S. foreign policy. The terrorist attacks refocused the perceptions of threat and security in the United States. They have led to a U.S. foreign policy that is more moralistic, more risk acceptant, and less wedded to particular institutional arrangements. These changes have not led the United States to abandon its hegemonic strategy. But they have complicated significantly the application and implementation of that strategy. Although it is not the intention of the United States, the ultimate result of these foreign policy changes, in combination with other developments, may be the transformation of the East Asian security architecture that emerged during the Cold War and persisted in essentially the same shape during the initial post–Cold War decade of the 1990s. We cannot take for granted that the "hub and spoke" system, with the United States at the center of a specific set of bilateral alliances and serving as regional stabilizer, will survive in the same manner as it has for the past several decades.

Third, I argue that there is a vital economic dimension to the U.S. hegemonic strategy. Economic liberalization and interdependence are key components of U.S. hegemony and regional order. I suggest, however, that the management of economic relations will become increasingly difficult. The United States served during the 1990s as a key engine of growth for the world economy. But the strategies it has pursued since September 11 will continue to generate sizable fiscal and external deficits. The stage is set for international economic conflict in the years ahead, particularly if China continues to rise and if the U.S. economy experiences a period of slower growth. Economic conflicts will complicate further the efforts of U.S. officials to maintain the existing East Asian security order.

The United States will retain its preeminent power position in the years ahead. Nonetheless, the task of maintaining and completing hegemony in East Asia will become more difficult. The United States will face the twin challenges of conducting the global war on terror while simultaneously managing the rise of China. As a consequence, the prospects for order in East Asia will remain uncertain and problematic.

U.S. Hegemony in East Asia: Contributions and Limitations

Although political scientists sometimes use the terms interchangeably, hegemony and unipolarity should be distinguished analytically. Unipolarity refers to a distribution of material capabilities—one that overwhelmingly favors a single state.[3] Hegemony has both material and nonmaterial components; it pertains both to power and to social relations. Hegemony means that one actor has the power to shape the rules of international politics according to its own interests.[4] But it also means that there is a reasonable degree of acquiescence on the part of other major states in the system.[5] A durable hegemonic order requires some consensus on the desirability of the dominant state's leadership and on the social purposes that it promotes. Hegemony, in this sense, is not simply domination but involves the legitimate exercise of power. A hegemonic order thus should also be distinguished from an empire or imperial order, which implies the formal rule of one political entity over another.[6]

By the middle of the 1990s, the United States was clearly in pursuit of a hegemonic strategy in East Asia. It sought a special role for itself as the principal guarantor of regional order. After the Cold War, U.S. officials could have pursued other strategies. They could have withdrawn from the region, allowed a local balance of power to emerge, and taken on the role of "offshore balancer."[7] They could have attempted to build multilateral security institutions as the primary foundation of regional order.[8] They could have sought to organize one set of states in opposition to another by focusing on the containment of China. U.S. officials chose instead the hegemonic path, and they have sought support for a U.S.-centered regional order.

There are two key institutional features of the U.S. hegemonic strategy. First, the United States has relied on bilateral relationships with other key states. The principal bilateral ties have been with Japan and South Korea, reflecting a U.S. preference for continuity in arrangements that developed during the Cold War. Similarly, the United States has reaffirmed its close partnership with Australia. In relations with China the United States has pursued engagement rather than containment. Despite initial misgivings, the Bush administration has continued the pursuit of a partnership with China. It also began to develop a closer bilateral relationship with Asia's other emerging power, India. The overall U.S. approach to regional order is aptly described in terms of "hub and spokes," with Washington seeking to assure key players that their relationship with the United States is primary and indispensable.[9]

U.S. officials have been receptive to multilateral security initiatives in the region, such as the ASEAN Regional Forum and the Northeast Asian Cooperation Dialogue. But they clearly view multilateral or minilateral arrangements as complements to, rather than as substitutes for, a primary set of bilateral relationships.[10]

The other institutional feature of hegemony has been the forward U.S. military presence. By 1995, U.S. officials had made clear their intention to maintain a political and military commitment to East Asia that would be of indefinite duration.[11] This commitment included the stabilization of the U.S.

troop presence at approximately 100,000 and the maintenance of a dominant naval presence. In Northeast Asia, the U.S. naval presence is secured by alliances with South Korea and Japan. In Southeast Asia, it is secured through a series of naval agreements with states, including Indonesia, Singapore, Malaysia, and the Philippines.

The U.S. hegemonic strategy has provided public goods and contributed to regional order in several ways. The U.S. presence has helped to deter major powers from developing or intensifying dangerous rivalries. Japan and China, most obviously, have a history of antagonism and mutual recrimination. Negative sentiment is not far from the surface even some sixty years after the Second World War.[12] Ideally for China, the U.S. presence constrains Japan, serving as the "cork in the bottle" to suppress possible Japanese aggression.[13] Similarly, for Japan the U.S. presence deters China from a bid for regional dominance commensurate with its growing economic power and political influence.

U.S. officials have also worked to manage regional conflicts with the potential to escalate to local and even broader wars. The United States took the initiative throughout the 1990s to stabilize security crises through diplomacy and the implied threat of military force. The critical U.S. role was evident in the China-Taiwan crisis of 1996, the North Korean nuclear crisis of 1994, and the India-Pakistan crises over Kashmir in 1998 and again in 2001.

Finally, the United States has worked to discourage the nationalist economic competition that often results when states find themselves in economic distress. U.S. officials have pushed an economically troubled Japan to reform domestically and continue to open its markets. They have sought to integrate China into a globalizing world economy. After the Asian financial crisis, U.S. officials tried to discourage beggar-thy-neighbor responses by keeping open its own large market and ensuring continued sources of global liquidity.

It is important to recognize the contributions of hegemony to order, but also to note its limitations. The U.S. hegemonic strategy has sought to manage relationships and crises and avoid major conflicts. It has not brought any fundamental resolution to long-standing problematic relationships such as those between China and Taiwan, North and South Korea, Japan and China, or Japan and Korea. The U.S. strategy has been more of a holding action, an effort to keep relations from deteriorating, than a progressive attempt at final resolution.

U.S. hegemony is also incomplete. If hegemony requires an acceptance by other states of the dominant state's vision for order, then the United States has been only partially successful. Japan, for example, perceives the dominant role of the United States as constructive and legitimate. This is not to say that the United States can take Japan for granted—only that to date Japan has anticipated greater benefit from cooperating with rather than challenging U.S. hegemony. The same is true for Australia. China, of course, is less certain. On the one hand it desires the benefits of integration; on the other, it is uncomfortable in a world and region dominated by one power, and it may have system-shaping or region-shaping aspirations of its own. India, like China, perceives itself as a rising power with legitimate security concerns and an eventual claim to great-power status. The United States made minimal effort to cultivate a meaningful relationship with India until President Clinton's visit in 1998. The Bush administration similarly has recognized India's importance and has sought to redress previous U.S. inattention.

In summary, U.S. hegemony is by no means an ideal pathway to regional order. It is limited and incomplete, and to have one power so dominant makes other states uneasy. But hegemony does contribute significantly to order in what most agree is a potentially unstable region of the world.[14] Other states may resent U.S. power and be critical of particular U.S. policies. But, after the first post–Cold War decade, most would probably have agreed that regional order was better served with the United States engaged in the region rather than withdrawn from it.

September 11 and the Transformation of U.S. Foreign Policy

The events of September 11, 2001, may not have changed the international system, but they did transform U.S. foreign policy. These attacks were unprecedented in the U.S. experience. The comparison typically drawn has been to the Japanese attack on Pearl Harbor, but that attack was on an American outpost by an adversary the United States anticipated it would eventually engage in war. The September 11 attack achieved greater surprise, involved two of America's most important cities, and was directed at the prominent symbols of U.S. military preponderance, the Pentagon, and U.S. economic dominance, the World Trade Center in New York's financial district. Although these attacks and the U.S. response are recent, we can begin to discern their impact on U.S. foreign policy generally and on the U.S. strategy for East Asia.[15]

There are five major impacts on U.S. foreign policy. First, the terrorist attacks refocused the perception of threat and the core national security concerns of the United States. U.S. foreign policy after the defeat of the Soviet Union seemed at times to be in search of the next great threat. For a short time as the Cold War ended, Japan was the center of U.S. attention, for economic rather than military reasons. Then a rising China, with the long-term potential to challenge U.S. preponderance, began to attract considerable interest during the 1990s. The first major foreign policy conflict of the new Bush administration in 2001 involved an aerial conflict off the coast of China.

The attacks of September 11 turned the U.S. foreign policy community in a different direction. Policymakers have determined that the central challenge to U.S. national security is found at the intersection of terrorism of global reach, rogue states, and weapons of mass destruction (WMD). The perception of threat is articulated most clearly in the Bush administration's National Security Strategy of September 2002.[16] This document has been aptly compared to NSC-68, which played a similar role, at the outset of the Cold War, in laying out the challenges of a new world faced by the United States in the aftermath of a previous great conflict.

The new cluster of threats has highlighted the importance of homeland defense. The protection of the homeland, arguably always a vital interest, faded into the background after the collapse of the Soviet threat. This concern returned with a great sense of urgency after September 11. Homeland security has taken its place alongside the preservation of U.S. primacy as a central objective of U.S. national security policy. The creation of a new institutional infrastructure, organized around the Department of Homeland Security, reflected the elevation of this renewed national security priority—just as the National Security Act of 1947 symbolized the reordering of U.S. priorities in the new era of the Cold War.

Second, U.S. foreign policy after September 11 has been framed more explicitly in terms of morality. U.S. officials have cast the struggle against global terrorism in binary terms, as a struggle of good against evil. In mobilizing support, U.S. officials stressed that other states are either "for us" or "against us." President Bush's identification of Iran, Iraq, and North Korea as an "axis of evil" served to remind Americans that rogue states and stateless terrorists constituted a common enemy. The Bush administration recognizes the value of framing conflicts in terms of morality for the mobilization of U.S. public opinion. Ronald Reagan cast his struggle against the "evil empire" of the Soviet Union, and an earlier generation of U.S. leaders depicted the wartime struggle against fascism as a struggle against evil.

U.S. officials have framed the moral agenda in terms of opportunity as well as threat. The National Security Strategy calls explicitly for the overseas projection of U.S. values and institutions as a national security priority. It goes as far as to assert the existence of a "single sustainable model for national success: freedom, democracy, and free enterprise."[17] President Bush frequently has spoken of the extension of freedom as a moral obligation on the part of the United States.

Third, in the aftermath of the attacks U.S. foreign policy has become more risk acceptant. During the 1990s U.S. officials pursued hegemony cheaply and quietly. They intervened in Somalia but departed as soon as casualties mounted. They tried to avoid direct involvement in Bosnia and intervened only when the stability and viability of the North Atlantic Treaty Organization (NATO) were at stake. They intervened in Kosovo using military power at high altitudes in order to avoid even minimal casualties. The maintenance of international order and preservation of U.S. primacy were combined with risk avoidance—in part because, for an uncontested United States, most interventions were optional, and in part because U.S. officials perceived that the U.S. Congress and public would not tolerate a foreign policy that was costly in terms of American lives or resources.

After the attacks, U.S. officials proved more inclined to take risks. They intervened and overthrew the Taliban despite ominous warnings that history was not kind to great powers who took on Afghanistan. The 2003 intervention in Iraq was more discretionary and considerably bolder. That war could have led to the destruction of oil fields and consequent global financial instability. It could have spilled over into a more general Arab-Israeli war and led to political upheaval against friendly but fragile regimes in the region. These dire consequences have been avoided—at least as of 2007. But the Iraq adventure has involved the United States in a politically controversial war of attrition in which the costs in terms of the national treasury and military casualties have mounted significantly. The preventive, now counterinsurgent war in Iraq is precisely the type of conflict U.S. officials made sure to avoid during the 1990s. U.S. officials have accepted these risks and consequences on the presumption that rogue states with potential WMD capacity pose an unacceptable threat to U.S. security. They also perceived, ambitiously, the opportunity to use intervention in Iraq as the starting point for a more general transformation of the Middle East—a transformation that ideally would lead states and peoples in the region to embrace U.S. institutions and values.

Fourth, the United States has become less wedded to particular institutional arrangements. It would be inaccurate to characterize this shift as one from multilateralism to unilateralism. There were strong elements of unilateralism in U.S. foreign policy before September 11, and a commitment to multilateralism in a variety of areas (e.g., international trade and finance) persists after September 11. What is different is that the United States feels less compelled than before to use or defend any particular international institution. Secretary of Defense Donald Rumsfeld's oft-quoted phrase that "the mission determines the coalition, rather than vice versa" aptly captures the shift. During the 1990s, U.S. officials turned to the United Nations as a first resort in the Persian Gulf War, Somalia, and Bosnia, and to NATO in the absence of UN Security Council support in Kosovo. After September 11, the United States took on Afghanistan largely on its own, despite the fact that NATO took the historic step of invoking Article 5 in defense of the United States. In the Iraq War, U.S. officials went forward with an ad hoc "coalition of the willing" in defiance of strong opposition from key members of both the UN Security Council and the NATO alliance.

Fifth, U.S. officials have affirmed U.S. primacy publicly and self-consciously. During the 1990s, defenders of the Clinton administration's more tentative foreign policy viewed it as appropriately restrained, while critics argued that U.S. policy failed to recognize and match U.S. power. President Bush, prior to September 11, emphasized that U.S. foreign policy needed to be humble and non-threatening. Initial signals from his administration suggested that the United States would scale back rather than expand international commitments. After September 11, the restraints were lifted in both rhetoric and policy. In 1992, when the Pentagon's call for the United States to discourage peer competitors was leaked to the press, the first Bush administration disavowed it. Ten years later, the second Bush administration proudly and publicly asserted that "our forces will be strong enough to dissuade potential adversaries from pursuing a military build-up in hopes of surpassing, or equaling, the power of the United States."[18] The pointed challenge to other states to decide whether they are for or against the United States reflects the U.S. attitude that others need the United States more than the United States needs them. The administration that warned prior to September 11 against the dangers of nation building, afterward not only engaged in it, but sought to manage the broader transformation of one of the world's most troubled regions. The United States, in short, after September 11 began to act as a revisionist power, with the intention of transforming international relations, rather than as a conservative power interested primarily in the perpetuation of the international status quo.

The Bush Revolution and U.S. Asia Strategy

What impact do these broad changes have on the U.S. strategy for hegemonic order in East Asia? The best *intentions* of U.S. officials have been to continue the strategic approach set out in the 1990s, centered on forward defense, bilateral alliances and partnerships, and a U.S. role as regional stabilizer. Bush administration officials might even view the task as somewhat easier, because they believe that all the major powers are aligned on the same side in the war on terrorism. Ultimately, however, September 11 and the consequent changes in U.S. foreign policy will greatly complicate the U.S. hegemonic strategy that evolved during the 1990s.

On the surface, the overall U.S. strategy for East Asia remains intact. What Joseph Nye termed "deep engagement" during the 1990s continues, after

September 11, to characterize the fundamental thrust of U.S. strategy.[19] Deep engagement depends on the forward deployment of U.S. land, naval, and air forces, based in friendly states in the region. U.S. officials continue to view the American presence as a stabilizing force in a part of the world characterized by unresolved historical resentments, a diversity of regime types and levels of economic development, and long-standing conflicts that could serve as flashpoints for broader regional conflict.

At least in the short run, September 11 and its aftermath may have facilitated and reinforced the U.S. hegemonic strategy. U.S. strategy during the 1990s was to cultivate a series of special relationships with major regional powers, designed to reassure potential challengers of the desirability of a U.S.-centered order and of the mutual benefits of cooperation with the United States. By the end of the 1990s, relations with Russia and China had deteriorated significantly. But right after September 11, Russian president Vladimir Putin seized the opportunity presented by the terrorist attacks to change direction and develop a closer partnership with the United States, centered on a common response to the shared threat of terrorism. China, albeit with less enthusiasm, similarly viewed the war on terrorism as an opportunity to cooperate with rather than defy the United States. Japan, for its part, used the September 11 crisis to reaffirm its stance as a loyal ally of the United States—one that even fights side by side with the United States, within the constraints and limitations imposed by Japan's constitutional and political realities.

U.S. officials clearly welcomed this opportunity to strengthen relations with other major powers. They went even further, proclaiming that after September 11 the world's major powers are "on the same side—united by common dangers of terrorist violence and chaos." The 2002 National Security Strategy goes on to assert that the United States and other major powers—including China and Russia—are increasingly united by common values. In short, "the events of September 11, 2001, fundamentally changed the context for relations between the United States and other main centers of global power, and opened vast, new opportunities."[20]

This celebration is premature. In the short term, there may be little conflict between the hegemonic strategy the United States developed for East Asia during the 1990s and the new U.S. commitment to homeland security through the global war on terrorism. Over time, however, the continued pursuit of the war on terrorism is likely to complicate America's East Asian strategy. September 11 refocused U.S. priorities and behavior. Yet other states are not simply standing by as the United States turns its attention to terrorist threats and homeland security. As the changes in U.S. priorities and behavior interact with developments in the region, U.S. officials will find it even more difficult to complete their hegemonic strategy.

First, the shift in core U.S. priorities has diplomatic consequences. U.S. officials gave highest priority to Europe and Northeast Asia during the first post–Cold War decade as they focused on the preservation of a dominant U.S. position. Potential challengers are found in these key regions, leading U.S. officials to pay particular attention to the U.S. role as provider of regional security. September 11 deflected or distracted U.S. attention in two ways. It prompted U.S. officials to worry less about preserving preeminence, because they took both U.S. dominance and the cooperation of other great powers for granted. Equally important, September 11 shifted U.S. attention from Europe to the Middle East and Southwest Asia, and from Northeast Asia to Southeast Asia. If the war on terrorism is the principal objective, then U.S. foreign policy must give priority to where the action is. This is not to suggest that the United States will abandon or ignore Northeast Asia, only that the particular concerns of order in this challenging region will compete for U.S. attention with the pressing concerns of the war on terror.

This shift is especially apparent in the allocation of U.S. military assets. The 1990s strategy of preserving preponderance created incentives to station a particular level of forces in Europe and Northeast Asia, in order to reassure other major powers and to provide a tangible signal of the U.S. commitment to regional stability. The war on terror has created a different incentive, for more flexible and mobile military assets. The movement of U.S. forces away from the South Korean central front, no matter how U.S. officials attempt to spin it, reflects this reorientation of priorities. In the words of the U.S. Defense Department, both the United States and its allies must be prepared for "everything to move everywhere" in terms of U.S. military forces.[21] They must also face the simple fact that U.S. military resources, notwithstanding the United States' position of global dominance, are not infinite. Forces tied up for the long haul in Iraq and Afghanistan necessarily imply that fewer will be available for the possibility of stabilizing regional conflict in Northeast Asia.

Second, the United States may no longer be prepared to stabilize regional conflicts as consistently and predictably as it did during the 1990s. In the first post–Cold War decade, the U.S. imposed upon itself the task of primary regional stabilizer. Its approach was fairly cautious. U.S. officials sought less to *resolve* regional crises, and instead tried to manage them so as to avoid immediate military conflict in the hope that over time a resolution might present itself. In other words, the United States favored the status quo and believed time was on its side. In 1994, the Clinton administration bought off a belligerent North Korea with the promise of economic concessions. In 1996, it resorted to calculated ambiguity to discourage provocative Chinese acts against Taiwan.

Whether the United States will take a similar approach to regional crises in the years ahead is questionable. The Korean situation is instructive. North Korea is a consistent practitioner of coercive diplomacy. It drives its bargaining partners to the brink, both because it does not wish to appear weak and because it believes it can extract concessions that it desperately needs, especially in the economic realm. The U.S. approach during the 1990s was essentially to placate North Korea, on the assumption that war avoidance was a prudent outcome and that time was not working in favor of the North Korean regime.

As a consequence of September 11, there is likely to be greater variability and less predictability in the U.S. response to regional crises. On the one hand, the United States might be tempted to seize the initiative and, as in Iraq, try to solve intractable problems once and for all. The United States itself is more risk prone, opening the possibility that neither the United States nor North Korea will back down in deference to the other. U.S. officials are also less likely to believe that time is on their side. In their view, the marriage of rogue states and WMD poses an urgent security problem that must be solved sooner rather than later. To play for time in the hope that the situation will resolve itself is a luxury that U.S. policymakers enjoyed during the 1990s, but now might no longer believe they can afford. This thinking may lead, as in the case of Iraq, to risky military strategies of preemption or prevention.

On the other hand, the United States might migrate to the other extreme and "pass the buck" of the management of regional conflicts to others. Facing more pressing problems elsewhere, the United States might defer to other players in the region rather than serve as primary stabilizer itself. China has taken the diplomatic initiative since 2003 in negotiations over the North Korean nuclear program. China clearly has its own reasons to engage, but it may also be filling the vacuum left by a United States that is more preoccupied elsewhere. The United States, for its part, may be more willing now than in the past to defer its leadership role to China on the assumption that the major powers are "on the same side" and share common interests. This is not to suggest that China's contribution is necessarily unhelpful, only that the role of the United States in regional conflicts is likely to be less consistent and predictable. Diplomatic deference to China also raises questions in Asian capitals regarding the durability of the U.S. regional commitment.

Third, the U.S. response to September 11 has complicated its relations with other major players in the region. During the 1990s, U.S. officials believed that other states in the region, supporters as well as potential challengers, needed to be reassured that U.S. intentions were benign and that benefits would flow from participation in a U.S.-centered order.[22] September 11, however, has created a dual problem—it has created incentives for U.S. officials to take for granted that other powers will cooperate with the United States, at precisely the moment that U.S. behavior has become less reassuring and more alarming in the international system.

It is a mistake for the United States to take for granted cooperation among the major powers, much less to assume a new great-power concert is falling into place. The war on global terror has the potential to divide as well as to unite major powers. This was evident in the 2003 Iraq War, which found the United States at odds, in varying degrees, with Russia, China, France, and Germany. It is not difficult to imagine a similar outcome over how to deal with North Korea, or with Iran, depending on the course the United States feels it must take to protect its national security. The fact that the current administration is prone to view such conflicts in "for us or against us" terms makes it more difficult to finesse major power disagreements. The U.S. dispute with France and Germany over Iraq in 2003 was far more intense than most prior conflicts, with the discontent reaching deeply into the domestic politics of each side.[23] The vigor with which the United States is pursuing its homeland security objective will continue to raise anxiety, in the capitals of other major powers, about the desirability of a world dominated by one unrestrained superpower.

It is ironic that the United States perceives a condominium of interests at precisely the time that other states in the international system see the United States as more threatening. In a world of sovereign states, dominant powers always create anxiety for other states, even if the intentions of the dominant state appear benign. However one characterized the United States prior to September 11, it seems clear that after that event the United States appears less benign. By publicly touting its primacy, acting unilaterally, and undertaking ambitious military operations, the United States has taken on a more nationalist and "imperial" demeanor, whether this is intentional or not.[24] Prior to September 11, smaller powers in East Asia could reasonably believe that the United States was a dominant power without revisionist ambitions. After September 11, they cannot be so sure. The United States attacked and made clear its plan to occupy Iraq. It placed North Korea and Iran in the same category as Iraq. It invaded Afghanistan and overthrew its regime on the presumption that terrorists and states that harbor them are essentially the same. States in the region have little choice but to question the ambitions and next steps of what has abruptly appeared to be a dominant state with minimal external restraints.

These changes in U.S. priorities and behavior must be viewed in the context of developments elsewhere in East Asia. The region is not standing still while the United States reorders its priorities and sorts out its strategies. Consider first the position of China and U.S.–Chinese relations. September 11 delayed, but did not resolve, the potential Chinese challenge to U.S. hegemony in Asia. Recall that prior to September 11, the new Bush administration contemplated moving away from a strategy of engagement and taking a harder line in relations with China. Eventually, the question of how to deal with China will return to the forefront of U.S. foreign policy.[25] China, for its part, may have some degree of common interests with the United States, but it must also confront the question of whether and how to manage a United States that has grown increasingly powerful, assertive, and confident—as China grows more powerful and confident itself. The war on terrorism has already brought a U.S. military presence into close proximity with what China considers its immediate neighborhood—Central Asia and the South Pacific.

The potential for conflict is driven by the fact that the two sides have differing conceptions of their fundamental relationship. For the United States, China ideally will evolve as an important "spoke" to the U.S. "hub." China, that is, should be a supportive partner in a U.S.-centered world order. China, however, is unlikely to be content as a spoke in another power's wheel. China refused, during the early Cold War, to be a junior partner in the Communist order constructed by the Soviet Union. Later in the Cold War, it resisted being a "card" to be played by the United States in its efforts to balance Soviet power after the Vietnam War. As China progresses economically and militarily, and sees itself more as a great power than as a developing nation, it is all the more unlikely to be content in a subordinate role in a part of the world in which historically it has been the dominant political and cultural actor.[26]

The potential for conflict is similarly apparent in U.S. relations with South Korea. South Korea has become more advanced economically, more democratic, and more confident diplomatically. These are developments that are welcomed by the United States, but that nonetheless complicate the relationship. As the United States experienced with Turkey during the Iraq War, as allies become more democratic they also become more assertive of their own interests, even when those interests conflict with those of their great-power ally.

South Korea has become more assertive at precisely the time that its relationship with the United States has become less predictable. Put another way, for South Korea the twin alliance fears of entrapment and abandonment are on the table simultaneously. A more assertive United States might conclude that its interests regarding North Korea are best served by coercive disarmament or regime change. This alarms South Korea, which fears the consequences of any North Korean collapse and prefers a longer-term strategy of economic engagement and gradual transformation. Yet, South Korea may also be alarmed by U.S. troop redeployments after decades of a predictable U.S. presence. To the United States, troop redeployment makes good sense in

terms of global strategy and does not necessarily imply a diminution of the
U.S. commitment to South Korea. To South Korea, the move may reinforce the
concern that for better or for worse South Korea must begin to chart a foreign
policy course that is more independent of the United States.

The potential for conflict is least likely in U.S.–Japan relations, but it still
exists, and with a very different dynamic. The temptation for the United
States, after September 11, is to take its durable and loyal ally in the Pacific
for granted. Japan and the United States, after all, are on the same side in the
war on terrorism. Japan, however, will likely expect not only some baseline
level of U.S. attention but an even deeper U.S. commitment to the bilateral
relationship as well. The greater the uncertainty in the region, and the more
preoccupied the United States outside the region, the more Japan will require
tangible evidence that its relationship with the United States is indeed a special one. The risk and problem to be managed is not clash and divorce, but
drift and disappointment.[27] Japan's intention to transform itself into more
than merely a great economic power is increasingly clear. It is building its military capabilities and seeking a permanent seat on the UN Security Council.[28]
These changes are consistent with a more expansive and ambitious U.S.-Japan
bilateral alliance. But they also provide Japan with options it did not have during the Cold War and immediately thereafter, in the event the United States
turns its attention elsewhere.

The Economic Dimension of Hegemony and Order

By 1990, Japan appeared to pose a formidable trade and technological challenge to the United States. U.S. officials, freed from the security burdens of
the U.S.-Soviet rivalry, turned their attention to the protection of national
economic interest. Both the first Bush and Clinton administrations practiced
aggressive unilateralism in an effort to pry open Japanese and other Asian
markets to U.S. exports of goods, services, and capital. This effort was popular
with business interests at home yet created diplomatic friction in U.S. relations with Asian trade partners.

By the middle of the 1990s, U.S. foreign economic policy was shifting to
reinforce the U.S. security strategy of preserving a U.S.-centered international
order by reassuring and integrating other major powers. Following the Korean
crisis of 1994 and the Taiwan Straits crisis shortly thereafter, U.S. officials
viewed the security environment in East Asia as increasingly problematic.
The 1996 Clinton-Hashimoto Summit signaled a shift in U.S. priorities from
bilateral economic conflicts to bilateral security cooperation. The continued
stagnation of the Japanese economy reinforced this U.S. shift and led U.S. of-

ficials to the view that it was not Japan's economic strength but its economic weakness that posed a greater danger to U.S. security.

From the perspective of the United States the solution was then and still is found in the deregulation and liberalization of the Japanese domestic economy. As financial crisis spread across East Asia during the latter part of the 1990s, this same message was conveyed by the United States, working in tandem with the International Monetary Fund, to Thailand, Malaysia, South Korea, and Indonesia. China managed to avoid the Asian crisis, but to U.S. officials it nevertheless required a similar prescription. The U.S. strategy of engagement promised China the economic benefits of integration into the capitalist world economy, on the condition that China continue to undertake meaningful economic reform, including the liberalization of trade and financial markets, the privatization of the state sector, and the transformation of the troubled Chinese banking sector.

In short, the economic component of U.S. hegemonic strategy calls for East Asian states to liberalize foreign economic policies and transform domestic institutions to make them more similar to, and more compatible with, U.S. policies and institutions. The overall objective is the deepening of regional and global economic interdependence. Deeper interdependence, in turn, generates greater prosperity and, of direct relevance in the context of U.S. relations with China, creates incentives for more accommodating foreign policies. For U.S. officials, all good things go together. Economic liberalization, interdependence, prosperity, domestic stability, and cooperative foreign policies prove mutually reinforcing. This virtuous cycle serves U.S. economic interests, since the large and dynamic U.S. economy benefits most from the free movement of goods, services, capital, people, and ideas. The open world economy is also essential to U.S. security strategy. U.S. officials believe that interdependence reinforces peace, and that states that share U.S. economic institutions and values are likely to share U.S. security values and priorities as well.

The 2002 National Security Strategy explicitly recognizes this economic dimension of U.S. hegemony and security. It asserts that there is now a "single sustainable model for national success," which, not surprisingly, is the American model of individual liberty and free enterprise.[29] National economic success elsewhere does not pose a threat to the United States—the United States is too powerful to be threatened by advanced capitalist states, and advanced capitalist states will share U.S. security values in any event. The National Security Strategy asserts that strong economic growth in Europe and Japan is vital to U.S. national security interests. It goes on to say that "we want our allies to have strong economies for their own sake, for the sake of the global economy, and for the sake of global security." Later, it states that "we welcome the emergence of a strong, peaceful and prosperous China."[30]

The United States has positioned itself as the key player in this virtuous cycle of liberalization, interdependence, and peace. It has led by example, and its large open market has served as an engine of global economic growth. This is especially important to export-oriented Asian economies, and all the more so to the newest Asian export tiger, China. The strength of the U.S. economy has attracted large flows of foreign capital and has encouraged others to hold U.S. dollar assets in reserve. These capital account inflows, in turn, have helped to finance U.S. current account deficits.

It is not surprising that U.S. officials pushed the idea of the virtuous cycle enthusiastically during the 1990s. The U.S. economy grew rapidly in this first post–Cold War decade, and the United States was among the greatest beneficiaries of globalization. The challenge for the United States in the current decade will be to maintain the commitment to liberalization—at home and abroad—during a likely era of slower growth. The second decade after the Cold War poses greater challenges, both for U.S. economic strategy and for the ability of economic strategy to reinforce U.S. security strategy.

Although the U.S. economy often defies expectation, it is reasonable to expect the U.S. economy to grow more slowly in the years ahead. The 1990s were truly extraordinary, so much so that some came to believe the United States economy had conquered the traditional business cycle. It did not, and the decade ended with the bursting of the bubble in technology spending and stock values. U.S. firms, like their Japanese counterparts a decade earlier, had overinvested in boom times. The United States may not be destined to face a decade of Japanese-style stagnation and deflation, but its economy will require time to work through the excesses of the 1990s and deficits of the first half of the 2000s. Not surprisingly, the U.S. economy experienced recession in 2001–2002. What was surprising was how mild the recession turned out to be, in large part due to significant monetary and fiscal stimuli. But no government can stimulate indefinitely. The combination of interest rate cuts and tax cuts—along with large increases in defense spending prompted by wars in Afghanistan and Iraq—has led the United States to record fiscal and external deficits. The likely result of the eventual effort to bring these deficits under control will be slower growth.[31]

Slower growth complicates U.S. international economic strategy. It makes it more difficult politically for the United States to serve as the open market of last resort. A considerable segment of the U.S. public was skeptical of free trade even during the boom years of the 1990s. The Clinton administration was denied the trade promotion authority needed to advance free-trade agreements. Political pressure against liberalization is likely to intensify if U.S. growth slows, and likely will be directed at U.S. trade partners in East Asia that have run up large bilateral deficits with the United States. China, for both geopolitical and economic reasons, is the obvious target. The more U.S. officials succumb to the political pressure to confront China on the economic side, the more difficult it will be to manage a cooperative partnership with China on the security side.

A related consequence of slower growth is a decline in the attractiveness of dollar-denominated investment assets. By 2003, the dollar had begun a sharp decline against major currencies. A depreciating dollar means foreigners will be less likely to continue to finance U.S. current account and budget deficits, and their governments may become less inclined to hold the dollar as a reserve asset. Declining foreign investment could force the U.S. officials to raise interest rates more rapidly than anticipated, thereby slowing growth further. The more extreme and hopefully less plausible scenario—given that many currencies are tied to the dollar—is a cycle of competitive currency depreciation contributing to global deflation.

The economic rise of China will continue to compensate for slower growth in the United States. If, as expected, China shifts gradually from an overreliance on export-led growth to a greater reliance on domestic demand, it will begin to serve as a regional and perhaps even global engine of growth, alongside the United States. This will be good for the world economy in that two engines of growth are better than one. But it will also further complicate U.S. security strategy. China's economic influence will also translate into greater political influence, particularly in the East Asian region. A more economically powerful China will be a politically more assertive China, and unless U.S. and Chinese regional interests turn out to be remarkably consistent, a more assertive China will mean greater potential for conflict with a United States determined to play the dominant role in the East Asian region while it simultaneously undertakes the global war on terrorism.[32]

Conclusion

Some fifteen years after the end of the Cold War, the striking feature of contemporary world politics continues to be the disproportionate power position of the United States. U.S. officials consider stability in East Asia to be of vital importance, and they have adopted a hegemonic strategy in an attempt to maintain order and serve U.S. economic and security interests. The hegemonic strategy is likely to persist, but U.S. officials are likely to find the management and completion of hegemony more problematic in the years ahead. U.S. power, particularly military power, will remain unchallenged. But changes in U.S. foreign policy after September 11, developments in the world economy, and developments in East Asia suggest that the exercise of

U.S. power and U.S. relations with states in this all-important region of the world will become increasingly complicated and will demand more creative diplomatic efforts.

Notes

An earlier version of this chapter appeared under the same title in *International Relations of the Asia-Pacific* 5, no. 2 (Fall 2005): 177–96. It is reprinted with permission.

1. G. John Ikenberry, ed., *America Unrivaled: The Future of the Balance of Power* (Ithaca, N.Y.: Cornell University Press, 2002).

2. Michael Mastanduno, "Incomplete Hegemony and Security Order in the Asia-Pacific," in *America Unrivaled: The Future of the Balance of Power*, edited by G. J. Ikenberry (Ithaca, N.Y.: Cornell University Press, 2002), 181–210.

3. William C. Wohlforth, "The Stability of a Unipolar World," *International Security* 21 (1999): 1–36.

4. Robert G. Gilpin, *The Political Economy of International Relations* (Princeton, N.J.: Princeton University Press, 1987).

5. Bruce Cumings, "The United States: Hegemonic Still?" in *The Interregnum: Controversies in World Politics, 1989–1999*, ed. M. Cox, K. Booth, and T. Dunne (Cambridge: Cambridge University Press, 1999); G. John Ikenberry, *After Victory: Institutions, Strategic Restraint, and the Rebuilding of Order after Major War* (Princeton, N.J.: Princeton University Press, 2001).

6. Michael W. Doyle, *Empires* (Ithaca, N.Y.: Cornell University Press, 1986).

7. Christopher Layne, "The Unipolar Illusion: Why New Great Powers Will Rise," *International Security* 17 (1993): 5–51.

8. Ikenberry, *After Victory.*

9. Josef Joffe, "Bismarck or Britain? Toward an American Grand Strategy after Bipolarity," *International Security,* 19 (1995): 94–117.

10. Ralph A. Cossa, "U.S. Approaches to Multilateral Security and Economic Organizations in the Asia-Pacific," in *U.S. Hegemony and International Organizations*, ed. R. Foot, S. N. MacFarlane, and Michael Mastanduno (Oxford: Oxford University Press, 2003), 193–214 .

11. U.S. Department of Defense, *United States Security Strategy for the East Asia-Pacific Region*, Washington, D.C.: Government Printing Office, 1995; and Joseph Nye, "The 'Nye Report' Six Years Later," *International Relations of the Asia-Pacific*, Vol. 1 (2001): 95–104.

12. Thomas J. Christensen, "China, the U.S.-Japan Alliance, and the Security Dilemma in East Asia," *International Security* 23 (1999): 49–80.

13. Paul Midford, "China Views the Revised U.S.-Japan Defense Guidelines: Popping the Cork?" *International Relations of the Asia-Pacific* 4 (2004): 113–46.

14. Richard J. Ellings and Aaron L. Friedberg, *Strategic Asia: Power and Purpose, 2001–2002* (Seattle, Wash.: National Bureau of Asian Research, 2001).

15. John L. Gaddis, *Surprise, Security, and the American Experience* (Cambridge, Mass.: Harvard University Press, 2004).

16. United States National Security Council, *The National Security Strategy of the United States of America* (Washington, D.C.: Government Printing Office, 2002).

17. U.S. National Security Council, *National Security Strategy*, 1.

18. U.S. National Security Council, *National Security Strategy*, 30.

19. Joseph Nye, "The Case for Deep Engagement," *Foreign Affairs* 74 (July–August 1995): 90–102.

20. U.S. National Security Council, *National Security Strategy*, 28

21. Ralph A. Cossa, "Everything Is Going to Move Everywhere, But Not Just Yet," *Comparative Connections: An E-Journal on East Asian Bilateral Relations* 5 (April–July 2003).

22. Michael Mastanduno, "Preserving the Unipolar Moment: Realist Theories and U.S. Grand Strategy after the Cold War," *International Security* 21 (1997): 49–88.

23. Timothy Garton Ash, *Free World: America, Europe, and the Surprising Future of the West* (New York: Random House, 2004).

24. Anatol Lieven, *America Right or Wrong: An Anatomy of American Nationalism* (New York: Oxford University Press, 2004).

25. Zbigniew Brzezinski and John Mearsheimer, "Clash of the Titans," *Foreign Policy*, no. 146 (January–February 2005): 46–50.

26. David Kang, "Hierarchy and Stability in Asian International Relations," in *International Relations Theory and the Asia-Pacific*, ed. G. J. Ikenberry and M. Mastanduno (New York: Columbia University Press, 2003); David Shambaugh, "China Engages Asia: Reshaping the Regional Order," *International Security* 29, no. 3 (2004–2005): 64–99.

27. Michael Mastanduno, "Back to Normal? The Promise and Pitfalls of Japan's Economic Integration," in *Strategic Asia 2006–2007: Trade, Interdependence, and Security*, ed. Ashley Tellis and Michael Wills, 105–37 (Seattle, Wash.: National Bureau of Asian Research, 2006).

28. Jennifer M. Lind, "Pacifism or Passing the Buck? Testing Theories of Japanese Security Policy," *International Security* 29, no. 1 (2004): 92–121.

29. U.S. National Security Council, *National Security Strategy*, iv.

30. U.S. National Security Council, *National Security Strategy*, 18–27.

31. Stephan D. Cohen, "The Superpower as Super-Debtor: Implications of Economic Disequilibria for U.S.–Asian Relations," in Tellis and Wills, *Strategic Asia 2006–2007*, 29–63; Catherine L. Mann, "Perspectives on the U.S. Current Account Deficit and Sustainability," *Journal of Economic Perspectives* 16, no. 3 (2002): 131–52.

32. Evelyn Goh, *Meeting the China Challenge: The U.S. in Southeast Asian Regional Security Strategies*, East-West Center Policy Studies 16 (Washington, D.C.: East-West Center, 2005).

References

Brzezinski, Z. and Mearsheimer, J. "Clash of the titans," *Foreign Policy*, no. 146 (2005): 46–50.

Christensen, T. J. "China, the U.S.-Japan alliance, and the security dilemma in East Asia," *International Security* 23 (1999): 49–80.

Cossa, R. A. "U.S. approaches to multilateral security and economic organizations in the Asia-Pacific," in *U.S. Hegemony and International Organizations*, ed. R. Foot, S. N. MacFarlane, and M. Mastanduno, 193–214. Oxford: Oxford University Press, 2003.

———. "Everything is going to move everywhere, but not just yet," *Comparative Connections: An E-Journal on East Asian Bilateral Relations* (2003): 5.

Cumings, B. "The United States: hegemonic still?," in *The Interregnum: Controversies in World Politics, 1989–1999*, ed. M. Cox, K. Booth, and T. Dunne. Cambridge: Cambridge University Press, 1999.

Doyle, M. W. *Empires.* Ithaca, NY: Cornell University Press, 1986.

Ellings, R. J. and Friedberg, A. L. *Strategic Asia: Power and Purpose, 2001–2002.* Seattle, Wash.: National Bureau of Asian Research, 2001.

Gaddis, J. L. *Surprise, Security, and the American Experience.* Cambridge, Mass.: Harvard University Press, 2004.

Garton Ash, T. *Free World: America, Europe, and the Surprising Future of the West.* New York: Random House, 2004.

Gilpin, R. G. *The Political Economy of International Relations.* Princeton, N.J.: Princeton University Press, 1987.

Goh, E. *Meeting the China Challenge: The U.S. in Southeast Asian Regional Security Strategies.* Policy Studies 16. Washington, D.C.: East-West Center, 2005.

Ikenberry, G. J. *After Victory: Institutions, Strategic Restraint, and the Rebuilding of Order after Major Wars.* Princeton, N.J.: Princeton University Press, 2001.

Ikenberry, G. J., ed. *America Unrivaled: The Future of the Balance of Power.* Ithaca, N.Y.: Cornell University Press, 2002.

Joffe, J. "Bismarck or Britain? Toward an American grand strategy after bipolarity," *International Security* 19 (1995): 94–117.

Kang, D. "Hierarchy and stability in Asian international relations," in *International Relations Theory and the Asia-Pacific*, ed. G. J. Ikenberry and M. Mastanduno. New York: Columbia University Press, 2003.

Layne, C. "The unipolar illusion: Why new great powers will rise," *International Security* 17 (1993): 5–51.

Lieven, A. *America Right or Wrong: An Anatomy of American Nationalism.* New York: Oxford University Press, 2004.

Lind, J. M. "Pacifism or passing the buck? Testing theories of Japanese security policy," *International Security* 29, no. 1 (2005): 92–121.

Mann, C. L. "Perspectives on the U.S. current account deficit and sustainability," *Journal of Economic Perspectives* 16, no. 3 (2002): 131–52.

Mastanduno, M. "Preserving the unipolar moment: Realist theories and U.S. grand strategy after the Cold War," *International Security* 21 (1997): 49–88.

———. "Incomplete Hegemony and Security order in the Asia-Pacific," in *America Unrivaled: The Future of the Balance of Power*, ed. G. J. Ikenberry, 181–210. Ithaca, N.Y.: Cornell University Press, 2002.

Midford, P. "China views the revised U.S.-Japan defense guidelines: Popping the cork?" *International Relations of the Asia-Pacific* 4 (2004): 113–46.

Nye, J. "The case for deep engagement," *Foreign Affairs* 74 (1995): 90–102.

Nye, J. "The 'Nye Report' six years later," *International Relations of the Asia-Pacific* 1 (2001): 95–104.

Putnam, R. and Bayne, N. *Hanging Together: Cooperation and Conflict in the Seven Power Summits.* Cambridge, Mass.: Harvard University Press, 1988.

Shambaugh, D. "China engages Asia: Reshaping the regional order," *International Security* 29 (2004–2005): 64–99.

U.S. Department of Defense. *United States Security Strategy for the East Asia-Pacific region.* Washington, D.C.: Government Printing Office, 1995.

U.S. National Security Council. *The National Security Strategy of the United States of America.* Washington, D.C.: Government Printing Office, 2002.

Wohlforth, W. C. (1999) "The stability of a unipolar world," *International Security* 21 (1999): 1–36.

11

An Institutional Path
Community Building in Northeast Asia

Vinod K. Aggarwal and Min Gyo Koo

A T THE OUTSET OF THE COLD WAR, the so-called San Francisco system put Northeast Asian countries on a unique institutional path, characterized by a bilateral-multilateral institutional mix in both the trade and security issue areas.[1] Against the background of bitter memories of Japanese colonialism, unresolved sovereignty issues, and the ideological divide across the region, the San Francisco system offered America's Northeast Asian allies access to the U.S. market in return for a bilateral security alliance.[2] At the same time, U.S. allies were strongly encouraged to participate in broad-based, multilateral fora in areas of both security—the United Nations (UN), and trade—the General Agreement on Tariffs and Trade (GATT) and the World Trade Organization (WTO).

Aside from informal networks based on corporate and ethnic ties, the San Francisco system created few incentives for Northeast Asian countries to develop exclusive regional arrangements of their own. Hence the conventional wisdom argues that Northeast Asians are inherently unable to manage their own economic and security affairs in a collective manner without an external actor, namely the United States.[3]

In this chapter, we show how the traditional institutional equilibrium in Northeast Asia has come under heavy strain in the triple post period: namely post–Cold War, post–Asian financial crisis of 1997–1998, and post–September 11, 2001, attacks. Although Northeast Asian countries maintain their traditional commitment to bilateral alliance and multilateral globalism, the erosion of their confidence in the conventional approach is increasingly visible, as manifested by the proliferation of free-trade agreements (FTAs) and regional security dialogues, both official and unofficial, formal and informal, and bilateral and minilateral.

Much ink has been spilled over the uniqueness of Northeast Asian regionalism, but the existing literature fails to systematically assess the novel dynamics of rivalry and cooperation that is currently shaping a new institutional architecture in the region. Northeast Asia clearly remains sandy soil for cultivating regional institutions and a sense of community, leaving the future institutional trajectory wide open. Yet we believe that it is now timely to examine the origins and evolution of Northeast Asia's new institutional architecture in a more comprehensive and systematic manner, as this question is at the forefront of the minds of both academics and policymakers.

In the first section of this chapter, we explore Northeast Asia's traditional institutional equilibrium in trade and security. In the second section, we analyze the emerging institutional architecture, focusing on initial impetuses for change, the goods involved, individual bargaining situations, and institutional context. In the third section, we draw policy implications and conclusions with attention to possible linkages between trade and security issues.

Traditional Institutional Equilibrium in Northeast Asia

The growth of economic and security interdependence in Northeast Asia has been remarkable. Yet seen in comparative regional perspective, Northeast Asia's economic and security cooperation has lacked significant formal institutionalization at the regional level. Not surprisingly, many scholars have argued that Northeast Asia has the most pronounced formal "organization gap" of any area, as well as a growing inadequacy of long-standing informal alternatives. For them, the gap has stubbornly failed to close, thus bolstering the belief that Northeast Asian countries are incapable of overcoming the divides of history, virulent nationalisms, and the Cold War hostility.[4]

In economic issue areas, a number of proposals for a more exclusive Northeast Asian scheme largely failed during the Cold War period.[5] Most notably, Asia-Pacific Economic Cooperation (APEC)—a transregional agreement and Asia-Pacific's most ambitious institutional experiment, launched in 1989—includes the membership of all the Northeast Asian countries except for North Korea, but remains an essentially consultative forum. Fifteen years after its creation, most members continue to prefer loose family-type linkages to a formal institution.[6]

In contrast to the weakness of formal economic integration, the network of Japanese transnational corporations played a key role in forming a virtual economic community.[7] Alongside this Japan-centered economic system was the emergence of an informal business network, often referred to as "Greater China," in which Chinese communities in Hong Kong, Taiwan, and elsewhere in Asia promoted trade with, and investment in, China.[8] These informal networks based on corporate and ethnic ties delivered unprecedented rates of growth during the 1980s and the first half of the 1990s. The openness of the U.S. market, natural forces of proximity, and the vertical and horizontal integration of regional economies through Japanese investment and overseas Chinese capital seemed to have produced greater economic interdependence without substantial institutionalization at the regional level.[9]

On the security front, Northeast Asia has yet to host anything comparable to the highly developed North Atlantic Treaty Organization (NATO) and Organization for Security and Cooperation in Europe (OSCE), leaving regional security coordination underinstitutionalized. The ASEAN Regional Forum (ARF) is virtually the only permanent regional security forum in which Northeast Asian countries and the United States participate simultaneously.[10]

Given the heterogeneous policy preferences and strategies of the key players in Northeast Asia during the Cold War period, this may not be a surprising outcome. The United States remained principally concerned about how such a regional security dialogue might constrain its military forces and weaken bilateral alliances in the region. Sharing Washington's misgivings about the implications of security minilateralism in Northeast Asia, Japan shied away from pushing hard for more-substantive regional security dialogues. For fear of international intervention in and pressure on its domestic affairs, China obstructed any moves in this direction. From this perspective, the norm for regional security cooperation was the so-called concerted bilateralism—the structuring of a formal bilateral summit process in which major regional powers interact systematically with each other—rather than explicit multilateralism.[11]

In sum, the institutional architecture under the San Francisco system served Northeast Asia well for the Cold War period, while obviating the need for any significant regional arrangements. Most importantly, the United States served not only as the principal architect of the hub-and-spoke system in Northeast Asia but also as a power balancer between Japan and China, as well as between the two Koreas and the two Chinas, while gluing together its key allies through open access to its market.

The Evolution of New Institutional Architecture in Northeast Asia

In a dramatic turn of events, the traditional institutional equilibrium in Northeast Asia—a combination of bilateral and multilateral arrangements and an informal business network—has come under heavy strain in the triple post period.

On the one hand, the burgeoning interest in FTAs has generated positive expectations for the region's institutional future. Although Northeast Asian countries continue to pay lip service to their commitment to multilateral globalism, the erosion of their confidence is visible, particularly after the region-wide financial crisis and the collapse of the new WTO talks in the late 1990s.[12] On the other hand, there have been various official and unofficial, formal and informal, and bilateral and minilateral dialogues to resolve regional security issues in a post–Cold War era. Certainly, the strength and effectiveness of these fora remain unclear, falling short of filling the organization gap that has persisted in Northeast Asia. Nevertheless, the increasing number of channels for security dialogues and negotiations indicates positive and dynamic processes in exchanging information and opinions, which should be promising signs for regional peace and stability.[13]

To systematically analyze the evolution of a new institutional architecture in Northeast Asia, we focus on the interplay of four broadly defined causal elements, namely, external shocks, goods, individual bargaining situations, and the existing institutional context. The process of a shift from an initial institutional equilibrium to a new one generally comes about with some external shocks that create pressure for change. External shocks may stimulate or impede the supply of certain types of goods that pertain to either trade or security, or to both. The most significant elements that might affect national responses to external shocks and subsequent change in the provision of goods include countries' individual bargaining positions, consisting of their international positions, domestic power structures, and elite beliefs. Finally, if countries choose to create new regional institutions or modify existing ones, they must decide on the extent to which those institutions are to be influenced by the context of global multilateral institutions.[14]

The Triple Post Shocks

In Northeast Asia, the pressure for a shift from the traditional to a new institutional equilibrium has come about through three major external shocks—the end of the Cold War, the Asian financial crisis, and the September 11 attacks.

The Post–Cold War Shock

The San Francisco system began to undergo a gradual modification from the 1970s with the inclusion of China and other communist countries, but retained to a remarkable degree the Japan-centered and Washington-dominated form throughout the Cold War period.[15]

In the post–Cold War era, however, the fissure in the system became increasingly visible, as a result of the changing regional balance of power. In Northeast Asia, the Sino-Soviet-American strategic triangle has now been replaced by a new triangular relationship among the United States, Japan, and China. For all the power of the United States and Japan, the past two decades have been most notable for China's dramatic rise, and the resultant complexity of the regional power equation does not allow for a single pacesetter.[16]

The Cold War bipolarity in Northeast Asia acted as the source of regional reluctance to institutionalize economic and security relations, but its abrupt end has made it politically easier for Northeast Asian countries to consider institutionalizing their economic and security ties.[17] It can be reasonably argued that the end of the Cold War has reduced the significance of ideological divisions and broken down the problem of (in Gowa's term) the "security diseconomy" that had precluded tighter institutional integration between and within capitalist and communist blocs.[18]

The early 1990s produced an outpouring of proposals aimed at developing economic regionalism in Northeast Asia. In particular, various attempts focused on geographically contiguous parts of national economies located in the Russian Far East, northeast China, Japan's Hokkaido, North Korea, South Korea, and Mongolia.[19] In 1990, China presented one of the first proposals to develop the so-called golden delta of the Tumen River. In the following year, the United Nations Development Plan (UNDP) accepted the proposal as the Tumen River Area Development Program (TRADP), leading to the participation of China, Russia, South Korea, North Korea, and Mongolia (and later Japan as well). Although this collective development plan collapsed in the wake of the first North Korean nuclear crisis in 1993–1994 as well as the lack of coordination among local and national governments of the participating countries, it clearly marked an important departure from Cold War perceptions and divisions.[20]

In the security issue area, the United States exhibited a pronounced preference for bilateral security arrangements rather than minilateral ones within its spheres of influence in Cold War Northeast Asia.[21] For instance, the United States opposed an Asian equivalent of the Council on Security Cooperation in Europe (CSCE)—the predecessor of OSCE—primarily due to Soviet support for the idea. The United States feared that the Soviet Union would use a multilateral security forum to drive a wedge between the United States and its Asian allies. Japan followed the U.S. lead in opposing proposals for establishing regional multilateral security cooperation fora in East Asia.[22]

Yet by 1990 Japan began to fear that its fundamental security interests, including the U.S. alliance, would be seriously undermined if Japan did not participate in the emerging process of the post–Cold War institution building in the region. In July 1991, Japan proposed its own initiative for a multilateral security forum, thereby abruptly reversing its years of steadfast opposition to regional security multilateralism. This initiative, known as the Nakayama proposal, represented a bold departure from Japan's reactive policy toward regional security in the face of clear American opposition.[23]

The Nakayama proposal encouraged the formation of the ARF by promoting the idea of a multilateral security dialogue connected to ASEAN. To a large extent, the ARF came into being because the United States, with less strategically and more economically at stake in East Asia, ended its longstanding opposition to minilateral security dialogue in the region. Despite its operational feebleness as a security regime, the ARF began to bind Japan and China together into a regional institutional framework, allowing Japan to address its historical problem, China to address the fears of its neighbors, and both to avoid conspicuous balancing behavior toward each other. The ARF was also supplemented by numerous "Track Two" dialogues, involving government officials in their private capacities plus academics, journalists, and others. Prominent examples of Track Two dialogues include the North Pacific Cooperative Security Dialogue, the Northeast Asia Cooperation Dialogue, and the Council for Security Cooperation in the Asia-Pacific.[24]

For its part, China made an unprecedented attempt to integrate itself into the post–Cold War region. Many analysts note that China's broader strategic motive behind that regional economic arrangements was to integrate an increasingly powerful China into a regional economic and security regime parallel to China's integration into the global multilateral trading and security system through its bid for the WTO membership, on the one hand, and its proactive role in the UN Security Council, on the other. As the 1990s unfolded, China's relations with the region settled into a mix of unilateral bellicosity (over Taiwan and the South China Sea) and increasingly comfortable and skilled use of multilateral fora such as the ARF and ASEAN Plus Three (APT) to support those regional voices still concerned about excessive U.S. influence.[25]

The Post–Asian Financial Crisis Shock

The second turning point came in the wake of the Asian financial crisis of 1997–1998. The financial crisis revealed a number of institutional weaknesses that Northeast Asian economies shared.[26] With respect to informal market integration, the unprecedented economic shocks showed that the seemingly dense networks of Japanese and overseas Chinese business were quite vulnerable.[27] Asian economies could delay the ultimate bursting of their bubble as long as they were able to find export markets where they could sell the investment-fueled output that vastly exceeded the absorption capacity of domestic consumers. However, the structural problems finally exacted a heavy toll in the closing years of the 1990s.

Aside from the many structural problems underlying the Asian model of capitalism, such as its cronyism, unsound investments, and overcapacity, many in Asia found fault with the widespread practices of Western financial liberalism, which allegedly reinforced credit bubbles, empowered currency speculators, and created unstable collective irrationalities. This interpretation strengthened demands for a regional response to the globalization primarily led by the West.[28] Concurrently, Northeast Asian countries' commitment to a broad-based, multilateral trade regime eroded significantly, particularly since the debacle of the WTO ministerial meeting in Seattle in 1999. At the transregional level, APEC as a formal mechanism to facilitate economic integration came under fire for its inability to deal with the financial crisis across the region.[29]

Northeast Asian countries came to recognize that tighter institutionalization of intraregional commercial and financial ties might be a better commitment mechanism for providing economic security, and they started to weave a web of FTAs accordingly. In August 1998, the Japanese foreign minister first proposed the idea of a Northeast Asian Free Trade Agreement (NEAFTA), and feasibility studies have been conducted since then.[30] A tripartite cooperation among China, Japan, and South Korea also motivated the creation of the APT forum. Although APT is not based on any treaty or formal, binding agreement between the participating states and although it has no central secretariat, the web of relations between the members has grown quickly since the first meeting of the heads of government in December 1997. The first significant concrete product of APT was an agreement, reached at Chiang Mai in Thailand in May 2000, to establish a regional currency swap facility to enable the states to protect themselves better against any future financial crises.[31]

More specifically on trade and investment issues, the conclusion of Japan's first post–World War II FTA, the Japan-Singapore Economic Partnership Agreement (JSEPA), came at this critical juncture in 2001. China also signed a framework FTA with ASEAN countries in 2003 pledging free trade by 2010. In addition, other Asian countries have wasted no time in moving toward FTAs, departing from their traditional commitment to the WTO and, to a lesser extent, APEC. As of spring 2006, East Asia was engaged in 112 FTAs (in force, under negotiation, or under study), with more to come.[32]

On the security front, South Korean president Kim Dae-jung (1998–2003) proposed a six-nation Northeast Asian Security Dialogue (NEASD) involving the two Koreas, the United States, China, Japan, and Russia. The proposal was an extension of the four-party talks to resolve the first North Korean nuclear crisis in the early 1990s. While Japan and Russia (excluded from the four-party talks) have naturally supported the six-party NEASD forum, this and similar proposals for collective or cooperative security have fallen by the wayside because they have failed to gain the support of China and the United States.[33]

The Post–September 11 Shock

The latest turning point for the institutional order in Northeast Asia came with the September 11 terrorist attacks. The American global war on terrorism has called into question the fate of the Northeast Asian balance-of-power system. With its counterterrorism initiatives, the United States has accelerated its effort to reconfigure its traditional security policy in Northeast Asia for strategic and logistical reasons. It now solicits multilateral cooperation against terrorism through APEC, the ARF, and the Proliferation Security Initiative (PSI), while scaling down its forward deployment.[34] This represents a significant departure from its conventional emphasis on bilateral security ties.

In many ways, post–September 11 developments put unpredictable pressure on the strategic triangle among the United States, China, and Japan. On the one hand, the regional dynamic had been moving in the 1990s toward a mimesis of the Cold War cleavage, in the sense that while China and Russia moved ever closer, Sino-American rivalry became increasingly tense. The impact of America's neoconservative foreign policy since 2001 has accelerated this trend, while consolidating Washington's relations with Tokyo and Taipei in spite of Beijing's grievances. On the other hand, September 11 provided an escape hatch for China from this looming confrontation, as a result of Beijing's support for the grand antiterrorism coalition. Despite tensions, disagreements, and mutual misgivings, antiterrorism provides a convenient pretext for both the United States and China to restore the semblance of cordiality necessary to maintain regional stability.[35]

In a region with an already awkward balance between the United States, Japan, and China, the second North Korean nuclear standoff, which began in October 2002, has set everyone scrambling. Many analysts agree that North Korea has become the vortex of Northeast Asia's geopolitical and geoeconomic turbulence.[36] It may drive the United States, Japan, China, Russia, and South Korea together in a post–September 11 world. Yet one might also argue that such a crisis is likely to exacerbate incipient conflicts among these actors. The second North Korean nuclear crisis reflects the mixed results of previous multilateral efforts—such as the Nuclear Nonproliferation Treaty (NPT), the International Atomic Energy Agency (IAEA) safeguards agreement, and the Korean Peninsula Energy Development Organization (KEDO) based on the 1994 Agreed Framework between the United States and North Korea. In response, Washington's focus on North Korea shifted from preserving the international nuclear nonproliferation regime to preventing terrorist organizations and rogue states from acquiring nuclear weapons or fissile material.[37]

In the wake of rising tensions between the United States and North Korea, China began to host the six-party talks in Beijing in August 2003, extending an invitation to South Korea, Japan, and Russia to join the earlier ad hoc trilateral negotiations between the United States, China, and North Korea. China's new and remarkably proactive role sits in direct contrast to its hands-off approach during the first North Korean nuclear crisis in the early 1990s. Beijing has been particularly motivated this time by its desire not only to address Pyongyang's nuclear program but also to enmesh Washington in a regional minilateral process and prevent it from taking unilateral action as it did in Iraq.[38]

On September 19, 2005, North Korea pledged to abandon its entire nuclear program in return for security and energy guarantees from the other parties. The agreement, although vague, was the first real achievement of the six-party negotiating process and gave rise to the promise of a more permanent minilateral dialogue mechanism in Northeast Asia.[39] Unfortunately, this minilateral negotiating process has yet to produce concrete results. A core stumbling block in the talks remains the question of who takes the first step, with North Korea (as well as China and South Korea) emphasizing the Ukrainian example of the outside parties extending security and economic assurances first, while the United States (and Japan) contends that the onus is on North Korea to dismantle its nuclear weapons infrastructure, just as Libya did, before concessions can follow.[40]

The point was proven again immediately after the September 2005 agreement was announced. North Korea asserted that the provision of the light-water reactor to the North should be implemented up front. The U.S. government responded to this by stating that the issue of providing a light-water reactor to North Korea would be discussed only after North Korea returns to the NPT and abides by its promise to dismantle its nuclear program. To make matters worse, North Korea's involvement in counterfeiting U.S. dollars and its reaction to the U.S. government's sanction on a Macao bank, Banco Delta Asia, which had allegedly been linked to money laundering for North Korea, halted the fifth round of the six-party talks in summer 2006.[41] On October 9, 2006, North Korea defied international pressure and tested its first nuclear device, becoming the ninth nuclear power.[42] The sudden announcement sent shockwaves throughout the international community. The surprise nuclear test was an implicit but strong signal to the United States to free up North

Korean assets in Macao, thus opening a way for Pyongyang to return to the six-party talks without losing face.

Despite the lack of concrete progress, the current nuclear crisis on the Korean Peninsula and the formation of the six-party process to deal with the issue has given rise to the possibility that a more formal organizational framework for multilateral cooperation in Northeast Asia could be established, likely in the form of a Northeast Asian Security Dialogue (NEASD) or a Concert of Northeast Asia (CNEA).[43]

Goods: Trade Liberalization and International Security

The triple post shocks have significantly changed the provision of trade liberalization and international security as goods.[44] In many respects, Northeast Asia's new appetite for FTAs and regional security dialogues reflects a convergence of interests in securing inclusive "club goods" in the face of growing economic and security uncertainties. Put differently, the political initiatives and intrinsic interest in creating regional economic and security arrangements reflect the growing need for an insurance policy to realize free trade and collective security when traditional mechanisms under the San Francisco system have stalled or been dismantled steadily in the triple post period.

During the Cold War period, trade liberalization was provided for most Northeast Asian countries mainly through the GATT. To the extent that the GATT required membership, the provision of trade liberalization was a multilateral club good. But it contained a strong public-good characteristic, since Northeast Asian countries were allowed to pay less to get more out of the system. In the security issue area, the San Francisco system provided Northeast Asian countries with security as bilateral club goods, which were made available through their alliance with the United States or the Soviet Union. As with trade, the provision of security under the San Francisco system also contained a strong public-good characteristic, as the costs and benefits from the alliance relationships were asymmetric in favor of the superpower's Asian allies.

In the early post–Cold War years, the provision of trade liberalization through the GATT and national security through the alliance with superpowers remained as club goods, but their public-good characteristics declined. The main cause of this shift was the stalemated Uruguay Round of WTO talks and some early indications of U.S. disengagement.

In the aftermath of the Asian crisis, Northeast Asia's new appetite for FTAs reflected a convergence of interests in securing bilateral club goods. With traditional mechanisms within the WTO and APEC offering no salient solutions, one major option for the crisis-ridden countries was to secure preferential access to their export markets. With respect to security, it appears that the financial crisis had no direct impact on the provision of security as bilateral club goods, but the eroding U.S. defense commitment to the region further weakened the provision of security as virtual public goods.

Finally, in the post–September 11 era the multilateral mechanism for trade liberalization has yet to regain the full confidence of participating countries, while the pursuit of alternative trade mechanisms through bilateral and minilateral channels has proliferated. On the security front, the public-good characteristic of security as bilateral club goods for U.S. allies is in trouble, as the United States has begun to reconfigure its alliance politics in Northeast Asia. For instance, the U.S.-South Korea alliance has significantly weakened, whereas the U.S.-Japan alliance has been strengthened in spite of China's protest. Such new developments do not necessarily imply that the provision of public goods under the San Francisco system will be terminated any time soon. Nevertheless, it has prompted Northeast Asian countries to deal with new security challenges by collectively pursuing security cooperation as club goods.

Individual Bargaining Situations

While there are many factors that might affect state actors' individual preferences and strategies for choosing between different institutional alternatives, the most significant elements that determine national responses to external shocks and the changes in the provision of goods include (1) an actor's relative position within the international distribution of capabilities; (2) domestic power structures that reflect coalitions and political regime type; and (3) elite beliefs and ideas about issue linkages.

International positions

Two aspects of the international context have been the basis for exploring cooperation and conflict in trade and security. The first international factor concerns a country's relative position within the international continuum of economic development. For instance, a country with a large market—either actual or potential—is more likely to entice others to seek it out as a trading partner rather than the other way around. The approach that many East Asian countries have taken to obtaining China as an FTA partner illustrates the importance of a large market in enticing the negotiation of trading arrangements, which in turn provides China with a greater bargaining position.[45]

As to the second international factor, collective security concerns may also drive an interest in institutionalizing trade and security management. Countries may prefer trade with their (potential) allies, while avoiding trade with enemies, because the relative gains realized from free trade can cause changes in the relative distribution of power. Therefore, trade accords are more likely to overlap with alliance relationships. At the same time, allied relationships are more likely to be successful in institutionalizing their trade ties.[46] From this perspective, despite their troubled relations in the first half of the 2000s, the current quasi-alliance relationship between Japan and South Korea would likely evolve into a full-fledged alliance in the foreseeable future.[47] Thus, the question of an alliance in Northeast Asia and a prospective NEAFTA really comes down to whether China and Japan could form a substantial entente through a Franco-German type of rapprochement.[48]

This observation has both positive and negative implications for Northeast or East Asian regionalism. On the one hand, rising interdependence provides greater economic incentives for Northeast Asian countries to avoid costly conflict. On the other hand, Northeast Asia's rapidly increasing dependence on China means that the bargaining power of Japan and South Korea (as well as other East Asian countries) vis-à-vis China has declined significantly. As a result, China may now feel less constrained from challenging its neighbors than in previous decades, prompting greater relative gains concern in the rest of the region.[49]

Domestic Coalitions and Political Regime Type

In Northeast Asia, individual bargaining situations in terms of domestic coalitions and political regime type have changed significantly as a result of the end of the Cold War, on the one hand, and the financial crisis, on the other. Domestic political structures vary widely, ranging from highly democratic— the United States, Japan, and South Korea—to highly authoritarian—China and North Korea. Though to different degrees, the governments in the region have experienced challenges to their political legitimacy and actual political turnover, albeit peaceful, by opposition groups—the end of the ruling Liberal Democratic Party's electoral dominance in 1993 and the end of military rule in South Korea in the same year, for instance.

From one perspective, such developments have altered the economic and security payoffs confronting individual countries, as many, if not all, of them move toward liberalization, rendering cooperative outcomes at the regional level more likely and the requirements of institution-building less daunting.[50] Furthermore, the economic interests that the United States, Japan, and South Korea have in China might prevent them from standing up to China for fear of losing lucrative commercial opportunities. The democratic political systems of these countries are most likely to enable business communities to pressure their respective governments to adopt more conciliatory policies toward China. China would also be pressured by its domestic economic interests, though to a lesser degree, to maintain good relations with its rich neighbors.

By contrast, it can be argued that as Northeast Asian countries move from authoritarianism toward greater political pluralism, their political leeway to deal with complex economic and security interdependence may be constrained by domestic political pressures. Indeed the twin challenges of responding to nationalist sentiments and maintaining political legitimacy are major constraining factors that have grown more significant as liberalization has taken a greater hold in the region. Recent research suggests that countries with more veto players—including a legislature, an independent judiciary, an independent central bank, and the military—are less likely to cooperate. Where leaders confront an array of domestic groups with diverse preferences and the ability to block policy initiatives, it is difficult to forge international agreements.[51]

Furthermore, the advent of the Internet and information technology has not only made national political leaders less capable of censoring news that might provoke ultranationalist sentiments but also made it easier for otherwise small, poorly financed activist groups to mobilize support for their nationalist agenda. The brief but intense disputes between China and Japan, and between South Korea and Japan, in spring 2005 over Japanese history textbooks, and over the question of sovereignty over the offshore islands and the gas deposits in their vicinity, highlighted how domestic nationalist groups can hijack otherwise peaceful Northeast Asian relations.[52]

Elite Beliefs and Ideas

The third factor concerns elite beliefs and ideas about the causal connections among issues and the need to handle problems on a multilateral, minilateral, bilateral, or unilateral basis. In view of the rising pressure of assertive nationalism and fluid geopolitics in the triple post period, even the mere containment of economic and security tensions requires the skillful diplomacy and tireless efforts of national leaders. The Asian financial crisis has significantly undermined the traditional confidence in multilateral trade liberalization. At the same time, the erosion of America's commitment to Northeast Asia in the post–September 11 period led everyone to scramble in search of alternative security mechanisms. These changes have led to the construction of new ideational formulas that support regional alternatives for economic and security cooperation.[53]

Many in the region agree that the best strategy to hedge against potentially disruptive behaviors is to engage more with each other and to empower internationalist interests by institutionalizing economic and security interdependence. Indeed, many experts in the region now are part of an epistemic community and Track Two organizations, which share the view that regional arrangements can be trade- and security-creating rather than trade- and security-diverting in the face of a loosening San Francisco system.[54]

Demand for Institutional Fit

How can we best characterize the resulting institutional outcomes? We briefly summarize them in terms of the number of participants in, and the geographic coverage, nature, scope, and strength of agreements.

First, the latest enthusiasm for FTAs in Northeast Asia and, more broadly, in East Asia revolves around a bilateral FTA as a popular mode of participation, while there are also strong indications of minilateral participation, such as ASEAN Plus Three (1997), the China-ASEAN Framework FTA (2003), and the South Korea-ASEAN FTA (2006). In security issue areas, bilateralism and minilateralism are also popular modes of participation.

Second, Northeast Asia's new appetite for FTAs is geographically open with a focus on the emergent concept of an East Asian Community rather than on a NEAFTA.[55] In sharp contrast, the most recent bilateral and minilateral security dialogues in which Northeast Asia has engaged have tended to be geographically closed, although the United States has remained a key player.

Third, as countries attempt to meet their trade and security needs in a new environment, they often negotiate new arrangements or modify existing ones, while interacting strategically within the context of broader institutional arrangements such as the UN and the GATT or the WTO. In trade issue areas, many of the recent FTAs attempt to cover broader areas and elements beyond trade, indicating their WTO-plus nature or their institutional division of labor. At the same time, however, these arrangements are potentially incompatible with the WTO provisions since some sensitive sectors are deliberately excluded, thereby setting up the possibility of institutional conflict.[56] In the security issue area, the evolution of the ARF illustrates how a regional security arrangement can be nested within a broader one. If viewed as the opening stages of an attempt to build a regional security regime in an area notable for the absence of regional institutions, the creation of the ARF looks impressive. The cultivation of ideas such as "cooperative security" has been reinforced by the promotion of norms regarding peaceful settlement of disputes, regular multilateral dialogue at several levels, and adherence to some international arms control agreements such as those on nuclear nonproliferation. Although the process has largely been slow and often disappointing, such cultivation does lay the foundations for elements of an East Asian security regime.[57] In a similar vein, the invocation of the NPT and the IAEA system of safeguards in the September 19, 2005, agreement of the six-party talks indicates collective efforts at nesting the minilateral process in a broader security regime.

Conclusion

We began our analysis with the observation that the postwar trade and security order in Northeast Asia had remained multilayered under the San Francisco system, involving elements of bilateral alliance structures, global institutions for managing economic and security problems, and long-standing informal alternatives. In the wake of the three major external shocks for the past fifteen-plus years, however, the traditional institutional equilibrium in Northeast Asia came under heavy strain. As a result, countries are now pursuing greater institutionalization at the regional level, actively weaving a web of FTAs and security dialogues. Within two decades, Northeast Asia, and East Asia, have moved from lacking any significant regional organization to a point where new collaborative arrangements in both trade and security have mushroomed.

Explaining the emerging institutional architecture in Northeast Asia poses a challenge. In an effort to understand the shifting institutional dynamics, we examined external shocks, goods, countries' individual bargaining situations, and the fit with existing arrangements. We focused on the triple post shocks: the end of the Cold War, the Asian financial crisis, and the September 11 attacks. With respect to goods, we noted that the disturbances in the traditional mechanism for providing trade liberalization and international security have motivated countries to seek for club goods as a viable alternative. In looking at countries' individual bargaining situations, we focused on their international strategic and economic interests, domestic power dynamics, and elite beliefs about the value of pursuing regional alternatives. We also showed how the changing nature of broader institutions interacted with country characteristics to alter institutional payoffs in the region.

We argued that the pursuit of regional club goods replaced a more generalized commitment to global public goods in the triple post period, thereby undermining the myth that the combination of bilateral and multilateral arrangements under the San Francisco system and loose-structured production networks could be a viable alternative to tighter, formal institutionalization in Northeast Asia and more broadly in East Asia.

With respect to trade liberalization, the weakness of the WTO and APEC opens up institutional space for trilateral or bilateral FTAs in Northeast Asia by affecting the provision of public goods and thus the incentives for creating club goods. Yet much depends on the possibility of a Sino-Japanese entente. In the meantime, the establishment of a permanent security forum in Northeast Asia to address security issues may appear premature. Yet we argued that the current six-party talks as well as the ARF process have the potential to evolve into an NEASD or CNEA, albeit through the unforeseen and unplanned spontaneous development of consultations among the countries involved. In the post–September 11 environment, the prospect of establishing a framework for multilateral cooperation is enticing in a region where no such forum previously existed.

Northeast Asia faces the uncertainty of a host of multiple institutional alternatives for regional trade and security cooperation. In view of the tremendous political and economic uncertainties in the contemporary period, the paths to deeper and wider economic and security integration are likely to be complex. One can only hope that the burgeoning efforts to form FTAs and security dialogues may facilitate rather than impede this process.

Notes

1. The San Francisco system was codified through the 1951 San Francisco Peace Treaty between the Allies and Japan. For more details, see Kent E. Calder, "Securing Security through Prosperity: The San Francisco System in Comparative Perspective," *Pacific Review* 17, no. 1 (2004): 135–57; Kimie Hara, "50 Years from San Francisco: Re-examining the Peace Treaty and Japan's Territorial Problems," *Pacific Affairs* 74, no. 3 (2001): 361–82.

2. The U.S.-centered bilateral alliances include U.S.-Japan (1951); U.S.-South Korea (1953); U.S.-Taiwan (1979 Taiwan Act). In the communist camp, China and North Korea signed a friendship treaty in 1961; Russia and North Korea renewed a treaty on friendship in 2000; and China and Russia signed a new friendship treaty in 2001.

3. Barry Buzan, "Security Architecture in Asia: The Interplay of Regional and Global Levels," *Pacific Review* 16, no. 2 (2003): 143–73; Lowell Dittmer, "East Asia in the 'New Era' in World Politics," *World Politics* 5 (2005): 38–65; Paul Evans and Akiko Fukushima, "Northeast Asia's Future Security Framework: Beyond Bilateralism?" *NIRA Review* (Summer 1999), www.nira.go.jp/publ/review/99 summer/evans.html; Peter J. Katzenstein, "Introduction: Asian Regionalism in Comparative Perspective," in *Network Power: Japan and Asia*, ed. Peter J. Katzenstein and Takashi Shiraishi (Ithaca, N.Y.: Cornell University Press, 1997).

4. For more details on the concept of an organization gap, see Kent E. Calder and Min Ye, "Regionalism and Critical Junctures: Explaining the 'Organization Gap' in Northeast Asia," *Journal of East Asian Studies* 4, no. 2 (2004): 191–226.

5. Katzenstein and Shiraishi, *Network Power*, 12–22.

6. John Ravenhill, *APEC and the Construction of Pacific Rim Regionalism* (Cambridge: Cambridge University Press, 2002).

7. Under the rubric of the "flying geese" model, Japan exported many of its lower-tech industries to its neighbors, thereby creating concentric circles of investment, with South Korea and Taiwan in the inner circle, and Southeast Asia and China in the outer one by the early 1990s. See Mitchell Bernard and John Ravenhill, "Beyond Product Cycles and Flying Geese: Regionalization, Hierarchy, and the Industrialization of East Asia," *World Politics* 47, no. 2 (1995): 171–209; Walter Hatch and Kozo Yamamura, *Asia in Japan's Embrace: Building a Regional Production Alliance* (Cambridge: Cambridge University Press, 1996).

8. Dieter Ernst, "Partners for the China Circle? The Asian Production Networks of Japanese Electronics Firms," BRIE Working Paper 91 (Berkeley: University of California, 1997); Andrew MacIntyre, "Business, Government and Development: Northeast and Southeast Asian Comparisons," in *Business and Government in Industrializing Asia*, ed. Andrew MacIntyre (Ithaca, N.Y.: Cornell University Press, 1994).

9. Katzenstein and Shiraishi, *Network Power*, 40–41.

10. The ARF links together the Association of Southeast Asian Nations (ASEAN) member countries with their "dialogue partners," the United States, Japan, China, Russia, South Korea, Australia, New Zealand, Papua New Guinea, and the European Union. Initially, North Korea and Taiwan were not included, but after the inter-Korea summit in 2000, North Korea was invited to participate. See Buzan, "Security Architecture in Asia," 155.

11. Evans and Fukushima, "Security Framework"; Mike M. Mochizuki, "Security and Economic Interdependence in Northeast Asia," Asia/Pacific Research Center Working Paper (Stanford, Calif.: Stanford University, 1998).

12. Vinod K. Aggarwal and Min Gyo Koo, "Beyond Network Power? The Dynamics of Formal Economic Integration in Northeast Asia," *Pacific Review* 18, no. 2 (2005), 189–216; Vinod K. Aggarwal and Shujiro Urata, eds., *Bilateral Trade Agreements in the Asia-Pacific: Origins, Evolution, and Implications* (New York: Routledge, 2006); T. J. Pempel, ed., *Remapping East Asia: The Construction of a Region* (Ithaca, N.Y.: Cornell University Press, 2005).

13. Buzan, "Security Architecture in Asia"; Evans and Fukushima, "Security Framework."

14. For a theoretical discussion of this approach, see Vinod K. Aggarwal, "Reconciling Multiple Institutions: Bargaining, Linkages, and Nesting," in *Institutional Designs for a Complex World: Bargaining, Linkages, and Nesting*, ed. Vinod K. Aggarwal (Ithaca, N.Y.: Cornell University Press, 1998).

15. Calder, "Securing Security through Prosperity," 136–37.

16. Buzan, "Security Architecture in Asia," 152–62; Dittmer, "East Asia in the 'New Era' in World Politics," 41–42; Aaron L. Friedberg, "The Future of U.S.–China Relations: Is Conflict Inevitable?" *International Security* 30, no. 2 (2005): 7–45.

17. Edward J. Lincoln, *East Asian Economic Regionalism* (Washington, D.C.: Brookings Institution Press, 2004), 3–4, 250–51.

18. Joanne Gowa, *Allies, Adversaries, and International Trade* (Princeton, N.J.: Princeton University Press, 1994). Certainly, the potential problem of a security diseconomy has yet to be resolved in Northeast Asia. There is a deepening concern that China's growing trade surplus with the United States and Japan has yielded

hard currency with which to buy weapons, foreign investment for the expansion of strategic infrastructure, and technology transfer that may improve Chinese military capabilities. The dissatisfied rising power (i.e., China) would most likely challenge the existing regional order if it continued to favor the United States and Japan alone. Also, China is allegedly a classic model of authoritarian modernization, unconstrained by democracy and vulnerable to nationalism and militarism. At the same time, however, the presence of a security diseconomy may motivate both China and Japan to promote an appropriate minilateral venue for directly or indirectly reassuring each other as well as their neighbors about their security and economic policies, while maximizing their respective national interests. See Buzan, "Security Architecture in Asia," 153–54.

19. Evans and Fukushima, "Security Framework."

20. Chung Mo Koo and Dick Beason, "Prospects and Challenges for Northeast Asian Free Trade Agreement," *Journal of the Korean Economy* 3, no. 1 (2002): 139.

21. John S. Duffield, "Asia-Pacific Security Institutions in Comparative Perspective," in *International Relations Theory and the Asia-Pacific,* ed. G. John Ikenberry and Michael Mastanduno (New York: Columbia University Press, 2003), 343–44.

22. Paul Midford, "Japan's Leadership Role in East Asian Security Multilateralism: The Nakayama Proposal and the Logic of Reassurance," *Pacific Review* 13, no. 3 (2000): 372.

23. Midford, "Japan's Leadership Role," 377–84.

24. Evans and Fukushima, "Security Framework"; Brian Job, "Track 2 Diplomacy: Ideational Contribution to the Evolving Asia Security Order," in *Asian Security Order: Instrumental and Normative Features,* ed. Muthiah Alagappa (Stanford, Calif.: Stanford University Press, 2003).

25. Buzan, "Security Architecture in Asia," 155; Dittmer, "East Asia in the 'New Era' in World Politics," 40–41; Samuel S. Kim, "Northeast Asia in the Local-Regional-Global Nexus: Multiple Challenges and Contending Explanations," in *The International Relations of Northeast Asia,* ed. Samuel S. Kim (New York: Rowman & Littlefield Publishers, 2004), 17; David Shambaugh, "China Engages Asia: Reshaping the Regional Order," *International Security* 29, no. 3 (2004): 64–67.

26. Aggarwal and Koo, "Beyond Network Power?" 202–3.

27. Some scholars go a step further and argue that the particular pattern of Japanese and overseas Chinese investment contributed to the damaging crisis. The rapid expansion of Japanese and overseas Chinese regional production networks in East Asia in the 1980s and early 1990s began to show a tendency to follow investment fads rather than market demand, creating overcapacity in similar manufacturing sectors such as electronics and automobiles. See Walter Hatch, "Grounding Asia's Flying Geese: The Costs of Depending Heavily on Japanese Capital and Technology," NBR Briefing (Seattle, Wash.: National Bureau of Asian Research, 1998).

28. Fred Bergsten, "East Asian Regionalism: Towards a Tripartite World," *Economist* (July 15, 2000), 23–26; Robert Wade, "Wheels within Wheels: Rethinking the Asian Crisis and the Asian Model," *Annual Review of Political Science* 3 (2000): 85–115.

29. Douglas Webber, "Two Funerals and a Wedding? The Ups and Downs of Regionalism in East Asia and Asia-Pacific after the Asian Crisis," *Pacific Review* 14, no. 3 (2001): 339–72.

30. Koo and Beason, "Northeast Asian Free Trade Agreement," 146.

31. Webber, "Two Funerals and a Wedding," 339–43.

32. Aggarwal and Urata, *Bilateral Trade Agreements*; Lincoln, *East Asian Economic Regionalism*; Mireya Solis and Saori Katada, "Understanding East Asian Cross-Regionalism: An Analytical Framework," *Pacific Affairs* 80, no. 1 (2007).

33. Kim, "Northeast Asia," 15.

34. Buzan, "Security Architecture in Asia"; Dittmer, "East Asia in the 'New Era' in World Politics."

35. Dittmer, "East Asia in the 'New Era' in World Politics," 64–65.

36. Kim, "Northeast Asia," 27.

37. John S. Park, "Inside Multilateralism: The Six-Party Talks," *Washington Quarterly* 28, no. 4 (2005): 77.

38. Park, "Inside Multilateralism," 76–84.

39. Edward Cody, "N. Korea Vows to Quit Arms Program: Nuclear Agreement Set at 6-Nation Talks," *Washington Post*, September 9, 2005, www.washingtonpost.com/wp-dyn/content/article/2005/09/18/AR2005091800403.html.

40. Park, "Inside Multilateralism," 85.

41. Young-kwan Yoon, "The North Korean Nuclear Problem and Multilateral Security Cooperation in Northeast Asia" (paper presented at a conference titled "Northeast Asia's Economic and Security Regionalism: Old Constraints and New Prospects," Center for International Studies, University of Southern California, March 3–4).

42. Anthony Faiola and Maureen Fan, "North Korea's Political, Economic Gamble," *Washington Post*, October 10, 2006, www.washingtonpost.com/wp-dyn/content/article/2006/10/08/AR2006100801169.html.

43. Todd Bullock, "U.S. Hopes Six-Party Talks Can Be Model for Northeast Asia: State's Hill Says Talks on North Korea's Weapons Programs Strengthen Ties," Washington File, U.S. Department of State, 2005; Jack Pritchard, "Beyond Six-Party Talks: An Opportunity to Establish a Framework for Multilateral Cooperation in the North Pacific" (paper presented at the Hokkaido Conference for North Pacific Issues, Hokkai Gakuen University, October 7, 2004); Yoon, "North Korean Nuclear Problem."

44. For the distinction between different types of goods, see Aggarwal, "Reconciling Multiple Institutions," 8–9.

45. Elaine S. Kwei, "Chinese Trade Bilateralism: Politics Still in Command," in *Bilateral Trade Agreements*, ed. by V. K. Aggarwal and S. Urata. New York: Routledge, 2006, 121.

46. See Joanne Gowa, *Allies, Adversaries, and International Trade* (Princeton, N.J.: Princeton University Press, 1994); Edward D. Mansfield, Helen V. Milner, and Rachael Bronson, "The Political Economy of Major-Power Trade Flows," in *The Political Economy of Regionalism*, ed. Edward D. Mansfield and Helen V. Milner (New York: Columbia University Press, 1997).

47. For some analysts, the erosion of the U.S. defense commitment and common security threat from North Korea would likely cement the ties between South Korea and Japan. In sharp contrast, others hold a pessimistic view on the likelihood of a full-fledged South Korea-Japan rapprochement. See Victor D. Cha, *Alignment Despite*

Antagonism: The United States-Korea-Japan Security Triangle (Stanford, Calif.: Stanford University Press, 1999).

48. Aggarwal and Koo, "Beyond Network Power?" 213. Many scholars argue that the open hostility of China and Japan has become the driving force that militates against East Asian regionalism. For instance, in December 2005, the two countries made dueling claims in Kuala Lumpur at the ninth APT summit followed by the first East Asian Summit (EAS). With support from Indonesia and Singapore, Japan succeeded in inviting India, Australia, and New Zealand to be members in the EAS, as part of its push for universal values and open regionalism. Then, China gained Malaysia's consent for giving the APT meeting—rather than the EAS—the primary responsibility for building the East Asian Community (EAC), thereby leaving a big question mark over the future of EAS as well as polarizing the region. The tug of war in Kuala Lumpur may indicate that NEA regionalism and, by extension, broader East Asian regionalism through either APT or the EAS is in trouble (see Rozman, "South Korean–Japanese Relations"). Yet not all is grim in Sino–Japanese relations. Despite the persistent diplomatic tensions, the so-called cold-politics-*but*-hot-economics is likely to remain a defining feature of Sino-Japanese relations. Indeed, China and Japan both would suffer significant economic setbacks if the flourishing trade, investment, and capital flows between them were cut off due to a massive political conflict. See Min Gyo Koo, "Scramble for the Rocks: The Disputes over the Dokdo/Takeshima, Senkaku/Diaoyu, and Paracel and Spratly Islands" (Ph.D. diss., University of California, 2005), 189–91.

49. Koo, *Scramble for the Rocks,* 189–91.

50. For more details about the positive role of internationalist coalitions in creating a regional zone of peace, see Ethel Solingen, *Regional Orders at Century's Dawn: Global and Domestic Influences on Grand Strategy* (Princeton, N.J.: Princeton University Press, 1998).

51. Edward D. Mansfield, Helen V. Milner, and Jon C. Pevehouse, "Vetoing Cooperation: The Impact of Veto Players on International Trade Agreements," www .princeton.edu/~pegrad/ papers/milner.pdf.

52. Koo, *Scramble for the Rocks,* 135–36, 184–87.

53. Koo, *Scramble for the Rocks,* 252–56.

54. Job, "Track 2 Diplomacy."

55. Webber, "Two Funerals and a Wedding?"

56. John Ravenhill, "The Political Economy of the New Asia-Pacific Bilateralism: Benign, Banal or Simply Bad?" in *Bilateral Trade Agreements,* ed. V. K. Aggarwal and S. Urata, 31–45 (New York: Routledge, 2006).

57. Buzan, "Security Architecture in Asia," 154–57.

References

Aggarwal, Vinod K. "Reconciling Multiple Institutions: Bargaining, Linkages, and Nesting." In *Institutional Designs for a Complex World: Bargaining, Linkages, and Nesting,* edited by Vinod K. Aggarwal. Ithaca, N.Y.: Cornell University Press, 1998.

Aggarwal, Vinod K., and Min Gyo Koo. "Beyond Network Power? The Dynamics of Formal Economic Integration in Northeast Asia." *Pacific Review* 18, no. 2 (2005): 189–216.

Aggarwal, Vinod K., and Shujiro Urata, eds. *Bilateral Trade Agreements in the Asia-Pacific: Origins, Evolution, and Implications.* New York: Routledge, 2006.

Bergsten, Fred. "East Asian Regionalism: Towards a Tripartite World," *Economist* (July 15, 2000), 23–26.

Bernard, Mitchell, and John Ravenhill. "Beyond Product Cycles and Flying Geese: Regionalization, Hierarchy, and the Industrialization of East Asia." *World Politics* 47, no. 2 (1995): 171–209.

Bullock, Todd. "U.S. Hopes Six-Party Talks Can Be Model for Northeast Asia: State's Hill Says Talks on North Korea's Weapons Programs Strengthen Ties." Washington File, U.S. Department of State, 2005.

Buzan, Barry. "Security Architecture in Asia: the Interplay of Regional and Global Levels." *Pacific Review* 16, no. 2 (2003): 143–73.

Calder, Kent E. "Securing Security through Prosperity: The San Francisco System in Comparative Perspective." *Pacific Review* 17, no. 1 (2004): 135–57.

Calder, Kent E., and Min Ye. "Regionalism and Critical Junctures: Explaining the 'Organization Gap' in Northeast Asia." *Journal of East Asian Studies* 4, no. 2 (2004): 191–226.

Cha, Victor D. *Alignment Despite Antagonism: The United States–Korea–Japan Security Triangle.* Stanford, Calif.: Stanford University Press, 1999.

Cody, Edward. "N. Korea Vows to Quit Arms Program: Nuclear Agreement Set at 6-Nation Talks." *Washington Post,* September 9, 2005. www.washingtonpost.com/wp-dyn/content/article/2005/09/18/AR2005091800403.html.

Dittmer, Lowell. "East Asia in the 'New Era' in World Politics." *World Politics* 5 (2002): 38–65.

Duffield, John S. "Asia-Pacific Security Institutions in Comparative Perspective." In *International Relations Theory and the Asia-Pacific,* edited by G. John Ikenberry and Michael Mastanduno. New York: Columbia University Press, 2003.

Ernst, Dieter. "Partners for the China Circle? The Asian Production Networks of Japanese Electronics Firms." BRIE Working Paper 91. Berkeley: University of California, 1997.

Evans, Paul, and Akiko Fukushima. "Northeast Asia's Future Security Framework: Beyond Bilateralism?" *NIRA Review* (Summer 1999). www.nira.go.jp/publ/review/99 summer/evans.html.

Faiola, Anthony, and Maureen Fan. "North Korea's Political, Economic Gamble." *Washington Post,* October 10, 2006. www.washingtonpost.com/wp-dyn/content/article/2006/10/08/AR2006100801169.html.

Friedberg, Aaron L. "The Future of U.S.–China Relations: Is Conflict Inevitable?" *International Security* 30, no. 2 (2005): 7–45.

Gowa, Joanne. *Allies, Adversaries, and International Trade.* Princeton, N.J.: Princeton University Press, 1994.

Hara, Kimie. "50 Years from San Francisco: Re-examining the Peace Treaty and Japan's Territorial Problems," *Pacific Affairs* 74, no. 3 (2001): 361–82.

Hatch, Walter. "Grounding Asia's Flying Geese: The Costs of Depending Heavily on Japanese Capital and Technology." NBR Briefing. Seattle, Wash.: National Bureau of Asian Research, 1998.

Hatch, Walter, and Kozo Yamamura. *Asia in Japan's Embrace: Building a Regional Production Alliance.* Cambridge: Cambridge University Press, 1996.

Job, Brian. "Track 2 Diplomacy: Ideational Contribution to the Evolving Asia Security Order." In *Asian Security Order: Instrumental and Normative Features,* edited by Muthiah Alagappa. Stanford, Calif.: Stanford University Press, 2003.

Katzenstein, Peter J. "Introduction: Asian Regionalism in Comparative Perspective." In *Network Power: Japan and Asia,* edited by Peter J. Katzenstein and Takashi Shiraishi. Ithaca, N.Y.: Cornell University Press, 1997.

Kim, Samuel S. "Northeast Asia in the Local-Regional-Global Nexus: Multiple Challenges and Contending Explanations." In *The International Relations of Northeast Asia,* edited by Samuel S. Kim. New York: Rowman & Littlefield Publishers, 2004.

Koo, Chung Mo, and Dick Beason. "Prospects and Challenges for Northeast Asia Free Trade Agreement." *Journal of the Korean Economy* 3, no. 1 (2002): 133–50.

Koo, Min Gyo. "Scramble for the Rocks: The Disputes over the Dokdo/Takeshima, Senkaku/Diaoyu, and Paracel and Spratly Islands." Ph.D. diss., University of California, Berkeley, 2005.

Kwei, Elaine S. "Chinese Trade Bilateralism: Politics Still in Command." In *Bilateral Trade Agreements in the Asia-Pacific,* edited by V. K. Aggarwal and S. Urata. New York: Routledge, 2006.

Lincoln, Edward J. *East Asian Economic Regionalism.* Washington, D.C.: Brookings Institution Press, 2004.

MacIntyre, Andrew. "Business, Government and Development: Northeast and Southeast Asian Comparisons." In *Business and Government in Industrializing Asia,* edited by Andrew MacIntyre. Ithaca, N.Y.: Cornell University Press, 1994.

Mansfield, Edward D., Helen V. Milner, and Rachael Bronson. "The Political Economy of Major-Power Trade Flows." In *The Political Economy of Regionalism,* edited by Edward D. Mansfield and Helen V. Milner. New York: Columbia University Press, 1997.

Mansfield, Edward D., Helen V. Milner, and Jon C. Pevehouse. "Vetoing Cooperation: The Impact of Veto Players on International Trade Agreements." www.princeton.edu/~pegrad/ papers/milner.pdf (2004).

Midford, Paul. "Japan's Leadership Role in East Asian Security Multilateralism: The Nakayama Proposal and the Logic of Reassurance." *Pacific Review* 13, no. 3 (2000): 367–97.

Mochizuki, Mike M. "Security and Economic Interdependence in Northeast Asia." Asia/Pacific Research Center Working Paper. Stanford, Calif.: Stanford University, 1998.

Park, John S. "Inside Multilateralism: The Six-Party Talks." *Washington Quarterly* 28, no. 4 (2005): 75–91.

Pempel, T. J., ed. *Remapping East Asia: The Construction of a Region.* Ithaca, N.Y.: Cornell University Press, 2005.

Pempel, T. J., and Shujiro Urata. "Japan: A New Move toward Bilateral Free Trade Agreements." In *Bilateral Trade Agreements in the Asia-Pacific,* edited by V. K. Aggarwal and S. Urata. New York: Routledge, 2006.

Pritchard, Jack. "Beyond Six-Party Talks: An Opportunity to Establish a Framework for Multilateral Cooperation in the North Pacific." Presentation given at the Hokkaido Conference for North Pacific Issues, Hokkai Gakuen University, October 7, 2004.

Ravenhill, John. *APEC and the Construction of Pacific Rim Regionalism*. Cambridge: Cambridge University Press, 2002.

———."The Political Economy of the New Asia-Pacific Bilateralism: Benign, Banal or Simply Bad?" In *Bilateral Trade Agreements in the Asia-Pacific*, edited by V. K. Aggarwal and S. Urata. New York: Routledge, 2006

Rozman, Gilbert. "South Korean–Japanese Relations as a Factor in Stunted Regionalism." Paper presented at the conference "Northeast Asia's Economic and Security Regionalism: Old Constraints and New Prospects," Center for International Studies, University of Southern California, March 3–4, 2006.

Shambaugh, David. "China Engages Asia: Reshaping the Regional Order." *International Security* 29, no. 3 (2004): 64–99.

Solingen, Ethel. *Regional Orders at Century's Dawn: Global and Domestic Influences on Grand Strategy*. Princeton, N.J.: Princeton University Press, 1998.

Solis, Mireya, and Saori Katada. "Understanding East Asian Cross-Regionalism: An Analytical Framework." *Pacific Affairs* 80, no. 1 (2007).

Wade, Robert. "Wheels within Wheels: Rethinking the Asian Crisis and the Asian Model," *Annual Review of Political Science* 3 (2000): 85–115.

Webber, Douglas. "Two Funerals and a Wedding? The Ups and Downs of Regionalism in East Asia and Asia-Pacific after the Asian Crisis." *Pacific Review* 14, no. 3 (2001): 339–72.

Yoon, Young-kwan. "The North Korean Nuclear Problem and Multilateral Security Cooperation in Northeast Asia." Paper presented at the conference "Northeast Asia's Economic and Security Regionalism: Old Constraints and New Prospects," Center for International Studies, University of Southern California, March 3–4, 2006.

12

The United States and the East Asian Regional Order
Historical Recasting and Forecasting

Ki-Jung Kim and Myongsob Kim

T HE EAST ASIAN REGIONAL ORDER has experienced drastic changes since it first encountered Western expansion in the mid-nineteenth century. These changes were marked by many unprecedented historical incidents, beginning with the collapse of the traditional Sinocentric order and the enforced mechanism of unequal treaties, followed by the ensuing rise and fall of Japan as a modern militant nation, and ending with hostile confrontations taking place under the enduring shadow of the Cold War. The United States has undoubtedly played a key role in changing and shaping the East Asian regional order throughout the modern history of East Asia. However, in the post–Cold War era, East Asia is again faced with uncertainties. More careful attention should be paid to the role that the United States will play in the process of shaping a future order in East Asia.

Several questions can be raised regarding the topic of this chapter. Do certain patterns in the East Asian regional order that are distinct from those in other regions emerge? What has been the overall role of the United States in shaping the East Asian regional order? Can useful historical precedents be found for explaining today's political situation and foreseeing the next stage of regional order? What role can we expect the United States to play in mapping out the future of East Asia? This chapter aims to answer these questions by reviewing the historical experiences of the East Asian regional order.

Conceptualizing the East Asian Regional Order

Much ink has been spilled over the concept of order in post–Cold War academia.[1] This academic interest certainly reflects the fact that post–Cold War international relations (IR) is faced with new challenges in mapping out a new world order on one hand, and attempting to overcome the structuralism of IR studies on the other hand. Amid these fluctuating notions of order, James Rosenau, who sees the mechanism of sustaining and changing order on three levels, namely, ideation, behaviors, and institutions, seems particularly relevant.[2] The concept of power structure should be added to these three ingredients of order. A certain interrelated pattern of order tends to emerge among ideational and behavioral characteristics, compatible institutional settings, and power structure on a regional level. A change of regional order signifies a simultaneous or sequential change in these four interacting ingredients. In most cases, the ideational elements and power structure of a particular regional order in a given time reflect the leading actor's policy intentions and behaviors.

For analyzing the East Asian regional order, closer attention should be paid to the geographic position of actors and their dynamic and turbulent interactions: namely, the internal and external powers of the region. Since its integration into the world-system and through the subsequent intervention of external powers, East Asia could not be left alone per se as a closed system. The behaviors, interests, and intentions of external powers have determined the path of historical development in East Asia. Major intervention by external powers was occasionally equipped with coercive measures, not only against other external powers, but also against internal powers. Contrarily, the leading external power's stance often appeared as a cooperative engagement, by which the external power is likely to pursue its policy mostly on the basis of collaboration and consent from internal powers, due to a variety of factors, including an isolationist stance, beliefs in cooperation, or even abandonment.[3]

Another element that has shaped the East Asian order is the policy stance of a leading internal power against an external power's behavior. Entanglement in the expansion and intrusion of Western imperial powers since the early nineteenth century was an inevitable phenomenon of the East Asian experience of modernity. In terms of intentions, the policy stance of a regional power can be categorized into two different types: resistance and compliance. The former means a type of policy stance in which internal powers show a belligerent pattern of behavior against external powers. An internal power might challenge the external power's position and its order, showing a desire to create a new order. In the latter, internal powers show a somewhat benevolent attitude toward external powers. The interaction between external power and internal power has been a major source of both confrontation and cooperation in East

Asia, contributing to the emergence of a new regional order. This interaction has also determined the stability and instability of regional order.

In terms of recasting and forecasting the relationship between East Asia and the United States as an external power, the four ideal types of regional order can be conceptualized as follows.[4]

Confrontational order can be formed as a result of coercive engagement on the part of an external power coupled with a strong confrontational stance of an internal power. As the confrontational structure between the two leading powers prevails in the arena of regional security, the principles of balance of power mostly determine the contents of the security arrangement. This type of order appeared during the Cold War period, particularly during the 1950s and 1960s. The global feature of the bipolar confrontation between the capitalist bloc led by the United States and the socialist bloc led by the Soviet Union significantly affected the shaping of the East Asian regional order. During this period, the East Asian order was formed and maintained on the grounds of the regional bipolar structure and confrontational ethos between the Southern Trilateral (U.S.–Japan–South Korea) and the Northern Trilateral relationship (USSR–China–North Korea).[5]

The reactionary order of a region can emerge when a leading internal power, equipped with a strong resistant stance, strives for regional hegemony and meets surmountable resistance and challenge from external power(s). A leading external power's cooperative engagement comes from its calculation of the lack of national capabilities to surmount the resistant stance of internal power or from its choice to accept the internal power's revision as a way to secure its regional stakes. In this environment, a new working mechanism of regional order is suggested by a newly emerging regional power, which has a position as a challenger in terms of power structure. In this sense, this type of regional order is reactionary in nature.

TABLE 12.1.
The Four Ideal Types of Regional Order

		Leading External Power's Stance	
		Coercive Engagement	Cooperative Engagement
Leading Internal Power's Stance	Resistance	Confrontational order	Reactionary order
	Compliance	Imperial order	Multilateral order

The actual form of an East Asian reactionary order did not appear in the region's international history. But a relevant case that is similar to this ideal type was the new regional order sought by Japanese leaders under the banner of the Greater East Asian Co-Prosperity Sphere (*Daitowa kyoegeng*). The late 1930s and early 1940s marked the most intensive crisis in this case, which eventually led to a major war between the United States and Japan. The regional crisis was provoked and intensified by Japan's reactionary attempt to challenge the existing Washington Conference order (Washington Peace System) led by the United States as well as to eventually attain regional hegemony. Viewed from the perspective of order, this case could be considered as a reactionary attempt toward establishing a new regional order, which Japan tried to provide and enforce mostly through military means.

The imperial order can appear as a result of the combination of a coercive engagement by the leading external power and a compliant stance of the leading internal power. In this type, the prime principles for managing regional order are provided by the leading external power. The external power, possibly a global superpower, tends to set and enforce a workable framework of regional order and a security arrangement. Meanwhile, the internal power's willingness and capability to resist the dominant order might be limited in this type of order. A similar case can be found in East Asia during its integration into the modern world-system in the late nineteenth century. The regional system during that period was often identified as "the unequal treaty system," the leading power of which was Great Britain. A historian depicted the system as lying between European-style international relations and outright colonial arrangements.[6]

A multilateral order can emerge when the leading external power's cooperative engagement coincides with compliant intentions of the leading internal power. Hypothetically, this sort of environment could work as the testing ground for a new type of regional order in East Asia. A lack of motives for regional dominance from a leading internal power plus a posture of cooperative engagement from a leading external power can become good preconditions for establishing a new multilateral order. To consider a real case of this ideal type of regional order through multilateral arrangements, it is well worth reappraising the Washington Conference order (Washington Peace system).

Western Impact and the Emergence of Modern Regional Order in East Asia

When the West first encountered East Asia, the region was initially called the "Far East" (*Extrême-Orient*).[7] Nonetheless, until the end of the Second World War, this conception of the Far East was accepted as a popular geographical term designating the regional entity including "all Asia east of Iran and south of the Soviet Union, and the major offshore islands."[8] New principles and rules of international relations were introduced and enforced in East Asia, as this region was integrated into the modern capitalist world-system. The history of Western engagement was closely intertwined with the emergence of East Asia as a new geographic concept. While the Western powers' stakes and influences determined the types of internal power response and the patterns of survival, the internal powers' struggle against external power engagement surely became another foundation for the birth of East Asia as a region.

Prior to the encounter with the West, the Chinese Empire dominated this part of the world. Whereas the European regional order was based on relationships among countries of similar sizes and influences, East Asia as a modern regional order basically emerged from reaction both to the West and to the old Sinocentric system. The long-entrenched system of the *Deungkuo* (中國), which can be translated as "the central state" or "the core state," seemed to be an obstacle in the path to the realization of modern inter-state relations for the *Bianpang* (邊方; fringe states). Under the Sinocentric system and in the ethos of *Deungwha* (中華; splendid China), China led East Asian civilization through a coherent regional system called *T'ienhisa* (天下; all-under-heaven). According to the Sinocentric geopolitical concept, this regional system was presided over by *T'ien-tzu* (天子; the son of heaven), who possessed a "mandate of heaven" to rule the entire world.[9] Unlike in the competitive Mediterranean world in Europe, there was one paramount hegemon in this region, China. With a view of themselves as omnipotent, the Chinese felt little necessity to travel and trade. As Fernand Braudel has explained, China was already a sort of world-system.[10] The outsiders of this geopolitical system who wanted to deal with China were assigned to kowtow to the *T'ien-tzu*, which worked as a symbol of the Chinese world order.[11] In the Chinese conception, trade with other countries was regarded as a tribute, a mere recognition of the Sinocentric geopolitical system.[12]

This absolute Sinocentric system, which drew a line between the Chinese-dominated center and its periphery, could not coexist with a modern international system. Moreover, it could not expect any voluntary coherence when Asia was faced with challenges from other regional systems. The destiny of East Asian dynasties had become too dependent upon the ebb and flow of power in mainland China. The Western powers, more often multilaterally than unilaterally, expanded to enter into the Sinocentric geopolitical system. With the mechanism of "unequal treaties," this geopolitical system was entangled in the web of the world capitalist system. Thus the traditional Sinocentric system was faced with various threats from the West such as exploitation, unequal trade, concessions, protectorates, and colonization. The new regional order, much resembling the "imperial order" among the regional types suggested earlier, was suppressive by nature. The policies of the Western powers were mostly coercive, a good example of which was the gunboat diplomacy of the West toward East Asia beginning in the mid-nineteenth century. Great Britain, as a leading external power, was in the driver's seat when the Western imperial order was shaping the region. Ineffective resistance from regional powers could not alter the path of Western expansion based not just on a simple sense of superiority but on a messianic ethos for the *mission civilisatrice*. One example of those ideational aspects appeared in the form of racism based on Social Darwinism in the late nineteenth century.[13]

During the nineteenth century under the unequal treaty system, the United States acted as a quiet follower of British maneuvers with its so-called jackal diplomacy in East Asian politics. The historical legacy of the imperial order and colonialist ethos throughout the second half of the nineteenth century became a significant source of U.S. foreign policy toward East Asia in the early twentieth century.

Japan's Rise to Power and the U.S.-Japanese Confrontation

Japan as a Rising Sun

Competing with the Western expansion into East Asia was the emergence of Japan as a new center of modernizing East Asia, particularly with the eclipse of Chinese power. Although Japan had been a part of the Sinocentric system, the Japanese developed a new, different geopolitical concept beginning with its encounter with the West in the sixteenth century through the mission of Francis Xavier.[14] After the Meiji Restoration of 1867, as represented by Fukuzawa Yukichi's thesis of *Datsu-a* (脱亞; quit Asia), the Japanese developed a sense of superiority toward "Asian backwardness," an approach that later led to incredibly severe and cruel behavior toward "unrefined" Asian people and one that demanded more equal treatment from Western powers.[15]

But the Japanese could not tolerate being economically and psychologically isolated from Asia. This anxiety became the root of the fluctuating image of Japanese foreign policy during the first half of the twentieth century, namely, between Pan-Asianism and international collaboration. After its two unexpected victories over China and Russia, Japan's East Asia project was accelerated when Japan began to depart from Shidehara Kijuro's "international collaboration diplomacy" of the 1920s. International circumstances also provided temptations for Japan to expand because Western powers could not give their undivided attention to the Asia-Pacific agenda due to the impact of the Great Depression in the late 1920s. Japan's new idea of regional order was suggested as the "New Asian Order" (1938), and later refined as the "Greater East Asian Co-Prosperity Sphere" (1940) based upon a solidarity among Japan, Korea, China, and Manchukuo on the one hand, and upon a harsh and strong anti-Western (or anti-external) ethos, on the other.[16]

In the early 1940s, soon after the formation of the second Konoe cabinet, Japan made a concrete governmental commitment to the East Asia project. "The Principles of Basic National Policy" and "The Principles of Policy for Coping with the Situation in accordance with World Developments," which were approved soon after the Cabinet was organized, marked a turning point of epochal significance.[17] A close look at "The Principles of Basic National Policy" reveals the prominence given to the phrase "new order in East Asia." However, the term "a new order in East Asia" soon changed to "a new order in Greater East Asia" and it was not much later that government officials publicly aired the policy slogan of the new era, the "Greater East Asian Co-Prosperity Sphere."[18] In the process of defining the extent of Greater East Asia, three concentric belts were designed—Japan, Manchukuo, Mongolia, and China in the first belt; the outer *nan'yo* or South Pacific Mandate (Micronesian islands added to Japanese territory for the first time by the Treaty of Versailles) in the second area; Burma, India, Australia, and New Zealand in the third.[19]

Japan saw itself as the only country that had successfully resisted Western expansion against the incessant penetration by European powers, particularly the British, who had successively made victims of the Near East, Middle East, India, Burma, and China. East Asians became attuned to the marching cadence of Japanese boots, and while they might have been skeptical about Japan's plans for a "Greater East Asian Co-Prosperity Sphere," they liked the propaganda slogan that went with it: "Asia for the Asiatics [sic]." In developing the Greater East Asian Co-Prosperity Sphere, the Japanese relied successfully on pitting the "Asian spirit" against "Western imperialists." The aim was pronounced as a "revival of Oriental morality," and the "unity of Asians."[20]

Yet within the Greater East Asian Co-Prosperity Sphere, all partners were less than equal, and the Japanese sought to impose a unilateral Japanese version of Asian regionalism.[21] Japan could not incorporate the occupied region as successfully as the British had done during the Victorian expansion. With the military defeat of Japan, the Japanese project of regional community building rapidly lost its intellectual attractiveness.

The United States as an External Power

The Japanese Greater East Asian scheme marked an intensive movement toward a kind of regional order that eventually led to a major clash between the United States and Japan. Before vigorously confronting Japan, the United States was a passive actor in this region. For the United States, the mid-1890s marked a new threshold of its foreign policy beyond the Pacific.[22] As an emerging power, the United States began to be involved more actively in East Asian regional politics with two symbolic incidents: the acquisition of the Philippines in 1898 and the declaration of the Open Door policy in 1899. By that time, East Asian regional politics were becoming more complex in terms of power structure, as the power arrangement of the world-system was entering into a new phase after the decline of British hegemony. In particular, rivalry between Japan and Russia over Manchuria and Korea drastically intensified into a crisis.

Regarding the U.S. East Asian policy, the Open Door policy of 1899 was a turning point. Indeed, the Open Door policy aimed to propose a new principle for dealing with the Chinese market. It assumed collaborative suppression through noncolonial competition among the major powers for commercial opportunities in China. The Open Door policy aimed at securing commercial access to the market without administrative burdens, such as protectorates and colonization.[23] It meant that the United States would not commit itself militarily in the tangled competition. The United States, motivated by growing economic capabilities, tried to keep the huge China market open and not partitioned in order to avoid military conflicts with other powers. The principle, however, revealed something of a contradiction in America's overall foreign policy. Maintaining the Open Door principle with regard to China, the United States implemented exclusive imperial policies toward other countries such as the Philippines.

In the early twentieth century, the initial U.S. response to the emergence of Japan as a regional power was an appeasement policy. As Japan decided to stand firm against Russia in 1902, the United States virtually joined the power bloc made by the Anglo-Japanese alliance and supported Japan as a proxy ally against Russia in East Asia. The course of strengthening ties with the Anglo-Japanese alliance was determined by Washington's concern for maintaining the Open Door policy in East Asia. Japan was considered to be "playing America's game" against Russia on the front line.

The situation in East Asia after the Russo-Japanese War, however, did not develop as the U.S. policymakers had expected within the framework of Japanese-American cooperation; in fact, Japanese policy in Manchuria evolved to exclude foreign powers, somewhat similar to Russia's actions before the war. American commercial access to the Chinese market, expressed later as "Dollar Diplomacy," was blocked as Japan attempted to monopolize the region, resulting in the decline of American trade after 1906.[24] Moreover, Japan actually divided Manchuria into two spheres of interest through a secret agreement with Russia in 1907. The principle of the Open Door policy was never realized in China and remained only a "myth."[25] Instead, the policy remained a burdensome cornerstone for U.S. East Asian policy throughout the first half of the twentieth century.[26] It also worked as a source of conflict with Japan, which eventually led to the Asia-Pacific War during the Second World War.

The Washington Conference marked a turning point for the United States in terms of its intention to lead East Asian regional politics in initiating a new vision. Nevertheless, the United States remained powerless and quiet when Japan began to ignore the core principles of the Washington Conference during the 1930s, due largely to America's retreat into its old "isolationist" stance after the end of the First World War. The situation of the early 1930s provided maneuvering room for Japanese ambition toward regional hegemony. The regional crisis was provoked and intensified by Japan's reactionary attempt at challenging the existing Washington Conference order initiated by the United States. Japan's bold action was indeed a reactionary attempt to establish a new regional order, which Japan tried to provide and enforce mostly with military means. Even though it was a transitional, unstable order with its militant nature, the East Asian order of the 1930s came as a by-product of the Washington Conference order, which failed to maintain a sound framework of long-term stability and order in the region.

It was in the late 1930s when the United States finally decided to counter, with military means, Japan's strong resistance to the West and quest for regional domination. Consequently, the two powers resorted to military force, and the new reactionary order was eventually aborted. American stakes in the region were still so big that it did not give away its traditional engagement in East Asia. Moreover, Japan's concept of a Greater East Asia did not provide and was not even based on a productive consensus among its members. The so-called new order was a unilateral declaration made by Japan and was only a clumsy emulation of the imperialist behaviors that Japan had learned from the West.

The U.S. Remaking of East Asia during the Cold War

After the Second World War, U.S. foreign officials pursued a similar regional integration policy as a part of the American global strategy of containment. The U.S. regional integration policy in Western Europe and in East Asia had the common characteristic of "a market-widening arrangement."[27] The British strategy of *divide et impera* was replaced by the American strategy of *integre et impera*. The American containment policy applied at the global level seems to be a crucial factor that helped generate the differences of regional order between Western Europe and East Asia.[28]

Since the end of the Second World War, there has been an undeniable stagnancy in the shaping of the East Asian regional order. For a long time, scholars have focused on the internal factors of a region in order to explain the differences between East Asia and Europe. In fact, unlike the Mediterranean or European worlds where rival political units constantly vied for advantage, Asia had one coercive power that demanded subordination rather than coordination. Even the significant internal movement for the shaping of the East Asian order that grew up along with anti-Sinocentrism in the 1920s swayed toward the Japanese Greater East Asia Co-Prosperity Sphere.

While the U.S. "Unite 'em" policy in Europe during the Cold War was a great success, the U.S. role in East Asia showed flaws contributing to "the revival without rival" slogan of the crippled Japanese geopolitical project, which would remain as a stumbling block to the sound development of regional order in the post–Cold War era. The Japanese Greater East Asian Co-Prosperity Sphere was revived in the U.S. orbit without any checking power. As an ultimate shaper of regional order in East Asia, the United States failed to show adequate sensitivity and respect for deep-rooted ideational structures in the region.

Geir Lundestadt once coined the phrase "empire by invitation" to emphasize the role of the European initiative, rather than the imperialist interest of the United States, in the evolution of the European regional community.[29] However, the role of the United States as an external parameter of regional integration in the bipolar system of the Cold War was more of a determining factor not only of the successful Western European integration but also of the seemingly stagnant regional community building in East Asia. Even though the United States wanted a regional community against the putative Soviet "Power Complex," Americans were not free from the obsessive fear of the possible revival of Pan-Asianism, against which they had had to fight during the war. Instead of encouraging regional integration as it did in Western Europe, Washington seemed to have a deep-seated fear vis-à-vis the possible misuse of Asian regionalism for the purposes of Japanese expansion under the guise of Pan-Asianism.

The U.S. support of Japan's revival coincided with growing tensions with the Soviet bloc in Europe and the victory of Chinese Communists in mainland China. The course Washington adopted was the "reverse course" in Japan, which resulted in an "American-Japanese Consortium."[30] The American reinvention of East Asia was fully supported by Japanese leaders. Regarding America's pressure to subordinate Japanese interests to America's Cold War policies, Japanese prime minister Yoshida Shigeru predicted as follows: "Just as the United States was once a colony of Great Britain but is now the stronger of the two, if Japan becomes a colony of the United States it will also eventually become the stronger."[31] But the United States reinvention of a Japanese Greater East Asia was followed by the strong reservations of Japan's Asian neighbors, who had been included in Japan's former Greater East Asia project.

The U.S. regional integration policy in East Asia, which was essentially the renewal of Japan's regional economic bloc, gave birth to the East Asian economic convergence in the 1960s with a "flying geese model." This model was marked by a "vertical" chain of capital flow, technological transfer, and supply of manufacturing parts, thus bringing about a high level of intraregional integration based on market exchange.[32] This East Asian economic integration was supported by a chain of "patron-client" relationships and a chain of bilateral security arrangements instead of regional community building.

East Asia's confrontational regional order was sealed by the Korean War. During the war, Japan eventually reentered the international community with its signature on the San Francisco Peace Treaty. It was the direct result of the war that the structure of bipolar confrontation in East Asia emerged between the capitalist bloc led by the United States and the socialist bloc led by the Soviet Union. The confrontational regional order was strengthened by the antagonism between the Southern Trilateral (U.S.–Japan–Korea) and the Northern Trilateral relationship (USSR–China–North Korea). While the United States aimed to project its power in order to maintain its predominant position in the Southern Trilateral setting, China clearly showed its resistant posture against the United States' bid for regional dominance. The United States' will to intervene in the region was well demonstrated by its intervention in the Korean War and strong military ties with Japan, South Korea, and Taiwan.[33] Meanwhile, China had also maintained a strong resistant stance against the United States after Mao's declaration of "leaning to one side" in 1949 and the subsequent Sino-Soviet alliance. This regional bipolar-type confrontation later underwent a significant transformation due to the U.S.-China detente in the early 1970s. The transformation from that type of order into the four-power equilibrium and loose confrontational order was made possible by America's new China policy, which induced China into a diplomatic relationship with the United States.[34]

Some of the features of the East Asian regional order during the Cold War can be summarized as the following. At the ideational level, the key ingredients included a strong realist belief in international affairs. Relying on military means in order to secure national interests reflected this realist notion. The realist notion also worked as a source of the balance-of-power type of international order. In terms of the ideational source of the confrontational order, the two sides seemed to be strongly preoccupied with their own self-fulfilling ideologies, such as the belief in free-market capitalism, democracy, and anticommunism on the one hand, and strong beliefs in a revolutionary spirit and socialist ideas on the other. Likewise, various behaviors of the participating actors can be identified along this type of confrontational order.

At the behavioral level, states tend to show various kinds of balancing and confrontational behaviors toward other actors. These behaviors naturally develop into a chain of hostile interactions and provocative behaviors. Presumably, as long as there is no one-sided game and a minimal possibility of overwhelming domination by a single power under this type of order, major powers' behaviors can appear extremely cautious.[35] At the institutional level, sets of military alliances can be regarded as a main characteristic of the confrontational order. Those military alliances are supposed to work toward cementing the cohesion of each bloc, through which a regional security system is established. Indeed, East Asia under this type of order showed several sets of bilateral security alliances, namely, the Sino-Soviet alliance, the U.S.-Japanese alliance, and the ROK-U.S. alliance.[36] There is no doubt that the United States has played the key role in every level of regional order since the San Francisco Peace Treaty was signed in 1951.

East Asia and the United States after the Cold War

The United States has undoubtedly become a single dominant military superpower without historical precedent.[37] It is a global empire that defines in large measure the global standard. With regard to the way of managing regional order in East Asia, the primary institutional setting that the United States has designed in the San Francisco Peace System is the American-Japanese alliance. Another bilateral arrangement, the ROK-U.S. alliance, is attached to this backbone alliance of former enemies in the San Francisco Peace System. And many principles that the United States has proposed for the sake of maintaining regional order seem to be accepted by other regional and external powers: the necessity of regional peace and stability, the principle of nuclear nonproliferation, free trade, and denouncing terrorism. It is also true that the United States has been maintaining a quite active, if not coercive, engagement posture in East Asia, along with the public announcement of "engagement and enlargement" as a national strategy.[38] As long as no foremost challenging power emerges to reverse the regional mechanism at work, the United States, equipped with a strong intention of engagement, plays a central role in shaping and maintaining the regional order. Nevertheless, in reality, today's order is not a mere product of America's one-sided enforcement. The United States needs to secure various kinds of cooperation from other participants in order to maintain the current regional order, mainly because the United States cannot afford to provide the public goods to manage the order by itself.[39]

At the same time, China does not seem to be fully complying with the United States and is strongly resistant. As our recasting has shown, Sinocentrism, which seems to be replacing communism as the dominant ideology in China after the end of the Cold War, has deep historical roots. Current East Asian fears of a dominant China are reminiscent of the long-abiding antipathy toward the traditional Sinocentric geopolitical system. For a modern regional order, all members have to be vigilant that these fears should not develop into a Sinophobia. The web of multilateral and regional cooperative ties within East Asia also has to play an alternative role between deep-rooted Sinocentrism and Sinophobia.

As long as China possesses neither intentions nor capabilities sufficient to reverse the course of the current order, it is fair to say that China is partially adopting a kind of bandwagoning strategy to the United States. As an internal power, China is not only a quiet follower but also a potential challenger to the United States. In this light, it is noteworthy that China often shows its ambition by checkmating the United States' arbitrary behaviors in some issues, not only in the East Asian arena, but also in the global theater. Post–Cold War Sino-American relations still have many sources of conflict: the human rights issue, the Taiwan controversy, the Tibet problem, and the missile defense (MD) system issue.[40] In the sense of power relationship and intention, China's amicable moves toward Russia should be carefully noted. The two countries agreed to maintain a strategic partnership that might aim to curb the Bush administration's one-sided behaviors in the security agenda, including MD issues. Potentially, this rapprochement would be reminiscent in scale and scope to the challenge posed by the Sino-Soviet bloc to the United States, though this time China is likely to be the leader and Russia the follower.[41]

Moreover, many observers foresee that China could emerge as an economically strong state, could continue to keep up a high economic growth rate, and could possibly surpass the United States in gross domestic product in the mid-twenty-first century. Changes in China's capabilities will surely place a significant impact on regional order, because they will inevitably trigger changes in the existing power relationship. Keeping these possibilities in mind, it is necessary to monitor closely the current bilateral relations between China and the United States, as far as changes in the direction of regional order in the mid-twenty-first century are concerned.

Recasting and Forecasting

In East Asia today, unlike in Europe, many uncertainties prevail in terms of regional order. First, there is "sustained insecurity" in the region. Military buildup continues on the regional level. The Korean Peninsula still remains divided, and it does not seem easy to find ways of transforming the armistice system into a peace system. The Taiwan issue is an additional element that might ignite an already unstable situation. Second, "the historical legacies of confrontation and distrust" still dominate in the ideational realm.[42] The scars of many regional wars are deep and lingering. These include the Sino-Japanese War (1894–1895), the Russo-Japanese War (1904–1905), the Manchurian Incident of 1931, the Sino-Japanese War (1937–1945), the Pacific War (1941–11945), the Korean War (1950–1953), the Vietnam War (1964–1975), and the Sino-Vietnamese War (1978). The aborted militant attempt of Japan's search for regional hegemony in the 1930s also added another chapter to a tragic historical memory. In short, the dark shadow of East Asian modernity, which began with resistance to Western expansion and was propelled under the banner of "Rich nation, Strong army' (富國強兵), still remains in the present regional politics. In other words, as Alexander Wendt explains, rather than a Kantian concept, a Hobbesian concept of anarchy prevails in the ideation of regional international politics.[43] Third, the lack of an institutional setting that is capable of dealing with regional security affairs presents another problem. Unlike in Europe, no regional security arrangement has developed in East Asia. A multilateral security institution has yet to be formed, while many initial attempts have only reached the Track Two (or Track 1.5 at most) level. The ASEAN Regional Forum (ARF) is regarded as too ineffective to work as a regional security institution in managing regional security issues. Instead, only exclusive bilateral alliance systems are functioning as security devices, with the United States as the hub of the bilateral security alliances.

Based on the above analysis, it might be fair to say that the current East Asian order resembles something between the confrontational order and the imperial order, where the United States holds the driver's seat in managing regional affairs, with China perceived as a potential challenger. The more noteworthy point is that it is highly possible that a new order, if it emerges, would be likely to resemble a confrontational order if major powers, both internal and external, continue to be preoccupied with strong realist, conflict-oriented ideation. This speculation posits that East Asia is most likely to head toward a new Cold War, where China is regarded as a "threat" to the current (stable) order. A pessimistic conclusion on the future of East Asian security can be drawn from this speculation.[44]

According to the framework mentioned earlier, an ideal type of multilateral order can be viewed as a new type of regional order in East Asia. A multilateral order can emerge when the leading external powers' cooperative engagement coincides with the compliant intention of the leading internal power. A restraint of the leading internal power's desire for regional dominance and a posture of cooperative engagement by the leading external power are the sine qua non for establishing this sort of multilateral order.

It is also possible that a liberal notion, rather than a power-preoccupied realist orientation, can function as an ideational basis of this order. Likewise, insofar as no intention of regional domination prevails and coercive measures for strong engagement do not command, states' behaviors can appear in the form of a cooperative and nonmilitary diplomacy. In this regard, regional security can be identified as collective, not as an individual country's exclusive responsibility. The institutional settings are intended to work for the collective responsibility of regional security. The institutions are designed to perform the multilateral management of regional security and peace, which, for example, includes the establishment of security governance, multilateral security cooperation, and a concert-of-power type of institution.

Historically, many lessons can be drawn from the Washington Conference system for the multilateral arrangement of East Asia. It was indeed an unprecedented attempt to shape a new regional order where "institutional bargaining" was at work.[45] The 1920s were a time of the "policy experiment of liberal ideas" after the devastations of the First World War, as was noticeable in many of the events that took place, such as the birth of the League of Nations and the Kellogg-Briand Pact. The East Asian theatre was not an exception to the new waves of the epoch, as was evident in the newly emerging order of the Asia-Pacific. This was the product of the imperatives of the Washington Conference. Most Asia-Pacific states were focusing on a nonmilitary approach to international affairs and a regional security system equipped with a multilateral institutional setting. It was the United States that played a leading role in shaping the new multilateral order.

The key ideas of the Washington Conference, with regard to regional order, loomed in the Four-Power Treaty and the Five-Power Treaty. The Four-Power Treaty replaced the Anglo-Japanese alliance, which had been considered the cornerstone of the East Asian regional order in the eyes of British and Japanese diplomatic officials. While the Anglo-Japanese alliance was a bilateral alliance, the new Four-Power Treaty was a multilateral one among the United States, Great Britain, France, and Japan. The Five-Power Treaty was also a multilateral one regarding a naval limitation pact. It set a ten-year moratorium on the construction of capital vessels and also established a tonnage ratio for capital ships of 5:5:3:1.75:1.75 (United States: Great Britain: Japan:

France: Italy). This arms control treaty reflected the strong desire for a non-military solution to international problems. But the new pattern of regional order failed to provide a stable environment in this region because of several shortcomings, including a lack of enforcement provision in those treaties.[46] However, it is worth reappraising the significance of the Washington Conference system for deliberating on a new regional order in East Asia. Despite its eventual failure, or, to be more precise, because of its failure, the Washington Conference system has significant implications for the future regional order in East Asia. The design and actual attempt to achieve a multilateral setting to manage regional affairs is still noteworthy.

One of the often-raised questions on the future order in East Asia is whether a multilateral format will be feasible and workable in this region. Many scholars point out that any multilateral arrangement, including a concert-of-power or multilateral security cooperation, could not be easily accomplished in East Asia due to many reasons: cultural heterogeneity, the lack of leadership, historical legacies left by the Asia-Pacific War, and ideological cleavages among countries lingering in the region even after the worldwide Cold War.[47] Liberal ideational beliefs argue that the intention of an actor is often more significant than the actor's capability and systemic distribution of capabilities and that a collaborative multilateral security arrangement is not unachievable for the sake of order.[48] The sharing of liberal ideation can be a good starting point for creating an alternative type of order in East Asia. As the world's leading power, the United States should reprise a leading role, one that is more liberal evolutionary than conservative revolutionary, in shaping the future order of East Asia.

The past is a prelude to the future. What does this historical recasting portend for the future? This look back at historical cases shows that there are three essential questions to be considered in the shaping of the East Asian order. First, how can China constructively engage itself with East Asia as a partner of and contributor to shaping a new regional order without too strong a nostalgia for its long-abiding predominance in premodern East Asia? Second, how can Japan find a new role, attaining a status commensurate with its economic achievements without dreaming of a revival of the Japanese Greater East Asian scheme? Third, how can the United States maintain a properly engaged role, encouraging the web of multilateral and regional cooperative ties within East Asia, and readjust its place in this more complex and perhaps more flexible framework beyond the limit of the San Francisco Peace System?

The increasing influence of China, coupled with its far-reaching territorial claims and growing military strength, still provokes some concerns in East Asia.[49] China has been suspected of wanting to increase its political hegemony in the region and being unwilling to cede regional leadership to Japan.[50] In this regard, coleadership by China and Japan might be necessary in East Asia (like France and Germany in Europe), but it is still premature to project a picture of these two as coleaders. There still remain tensions and conflicts between the two countries, and the difference in economic and political systems between the two further complicates the problem. Under these conditions, it is possible to argue that "South Korea may be in a better position to make proposals and facilitate future regional cooperation."[51] But South Korea cannot assume this role alone. Cooperation with other countries is a sine qua non. The South Korean initiative for this cooperation might link Southeast Asian countries and Pacific countries as well, creating a ribbon-type geopolitical coalition for peace and prosperity. Southeast Asian countries, which have been variously colonized, invaded, or pushed around by China or Japan in the past, could take a more active role, serving as a geopolitical bridge across cultural boundaries.

With the end of the Cold War, the postwar U.S. "containment" policy that supported the San Francisco Peace system has been eclipsed. The time has come to reconsider the meaning of another regional scheme that has faded into historical oblivion. Even today, there is nothing comparable in East Asia to the web of multilateral and regional cooperative ties that binds Europe together. Our rereading of East Asian history leads us to think that the role of U.S. foreign policy is still a determining factor regarding the unresolved issue of regional governance in East Asia. The role of the United States in the East Asian regional project was well perceived by Winston Lord, assistant secretary of state for East Asian and Pacific affairs. According to his 1993 confirmation testimony before the Senate, a main goal that the United States should pursue in the Asia Pacific is "developing multilateral forums for security consultations while maintaining the solid foundations of alliances."[52]

Although the United States has given a nod to multilateralism and cooperation among the countries in the region, there has been a great deficiency in real efforts by the United States to incubate a stable regional order in East Asia. This deficiency has been growing since the awful tragedy of 9/11 and the United States' proclaimed "war on terrorism." Meanwhile, the United States has become a subject of "strategic otherness" in a series of discourses on East Asian identity. The blowback of "Americanization via globalization" has become one of the key phrases for explaining and understanding East Asia's increasing efforts to reinvent a regional identity. Some opinion leaders in this region are even trying to recapture the past Sinocentric order or Japanese Greater East Asia project as a means of escaping from the predominance of the U.S.-centered unilateral globalization. A more international than imperial effort to construct a new East Asian regional order, one that moves away from the legacies of the Cold War confrontation that was maintained on the basis of the San Francisco Peace System, is now more urgent than ever.

The United States has, no doubt, the most important responsibility in reinventing the San Francisco Peace System. The United States should find ways to define and secure its own national interests in East Asia with a policy stance of cooperative engagement rather than coercive engagement. Viewed from an institutional function standpoint at least, it is possible that a policy stance based on the exclusive, confrontational nature of the bilateral military alliances might be harmful to enhancing a cooperative order in the future. China and Japan, too, should be aware that the revival of their traditional rivalry will be inevitable if they believe it to be so, since not only power structure but also ideation and perception are critical elements of regional order. These two regional (internal) powers must seriously consider the possibility of a coleadership scheme based on cooperative ideation. At this critical juncture in history, the North Korean nuclear issue seems to be a litmus test for all the participants for shaping the future order in this region. The Korean Peninsula, even though the two Koreas have been relatively minor actors in regional politics, has determined the regional weather, mainly because of its geopolitical condition. If the clash of civilizations along a civilizational fault line moves like two enormous cogwheels in East Asia, then Korea is a small cogwheel turning between them. In most cases the small cogwheel is moved by the larger ones. But sometimes the smaller one can influence to a certain extent the larger ones. It is necessary to view the history of the two Koreas in general as the process of creating and developing two modern states by one nation, which were supported by different civilizations. Either a rapid or slow absorption by relying unilaterally on a particular civilization is not an appropriate course of action toward Korean reunification. Korean reunification is not to be a simple geographical expansion of *a* civilization in East Asia. The impossibility of this has already been proved through the history of wars in East Asia (1592, 1895, 1905, and 1950). A neutral federation of two different modern states is to be discussed rather than simply focusing on reunification based on the standard of *a* civilization.[53]

Notes

1. For a more comprehensive discussion of the subject of "order" in international relations studies, see N. J. Rengger, *International Relations, Political Theory and the Problem of Order: Beyond International Relations Theory?* (London: Routledge, 2000).

2. James N. Rosenau, "Governance, Order, and Change in World Politics," in *Governance without Government: Order and Change in World Politics*, ed. James N. Rosenau and Ernst-Otto Czempiel (Cambridge: Cambridge University Press, 1992), 14. Concerning the importance of ideational elements, Barry Buzan has also suggested a concept of amity and enmity among states, adding that a regional security subsystem can be seen in terms of patterns of amity and enmity that are substantially confined

within some geographical area. See Barry Buzan, *People, States, and Fear: An Agenda for International Security Studies in the Post-Cold War Era,* 2nd ed. (Boulder, Colo.: Lynne Rienner, 1991), 189–90; see also Barry Buzan, Ole Waever, and Jaap de Wilde, *Security: A New Framework for Analysis* (Boulder, Colo: Lynne Rienner, 1998).

3. A similar concept was introduced in Michael J. Hogan's work, which was concerned with U.S. policy toward Europe during the early period of the Cold War. See his *The Marshall Plan: America, Britain and the Reconstruction of Western Europe, 1947–1952* (New York: Cambridge University Press, 1987), 53.

4. The earlier version of this argument was introduced in Ki-Jung Kim, "Establishing Peace on the Korean Peninsula," *Korea Observer* 36, no. 3 (Autumn 2005): 497.

5. Thomas McCormick, *America's Half-Century: United States Foreign Policy in the Cold War and After,* 2nd ed. (Baltimore: The Johns Hopkins University Press, 1995), 72–124.

6. Akira Iriye, *The Origins of the Cold War* (Englewood Cliffs, N.J.: Prentice Hall, 1973), 9–10.

7. The Eurocentric absurdity of this term has already been pointed out by many scholars. For example, see John K. Fairbank, Edwin O. Reischauer, and Albert M. Craig, *East Asia: Tradition and Transformation* (Boston: Houghton Mifflin Company; Tokyo: Charles E. Tuttle Company, 1976), 1.

8. CIA, "ORE 69–49 Relative U.S. Security Interest in the European-Mediterranean Area and the Far East," September 12, 1949, PSF: Intelligence File, HSTP, box 257, HSTL.

9. The earlier version of this argument was introduced in Myongsob Kim and Horace Jeffrey Hodges, "Korea as a Clashpoint of Civilizations," *Korea Observer* 37, no. 3 (Autumn 2006): 521. About the concept of *T'ienhsia,* see John K. Fairbank, "A Preliminary Framework," in *The Chinese World Order: Traditional China's Foreign Relations,* ed. John King Fairbank, 1–2 (Cambridge, Mass.: Harvard University Press, 1968); and Gerrit W. Gong, "China's Entry into International Society," in *The Expansion of International Society,* ed. Hedley Bull and Adam Watson, 171–83 (Oxford: Clarendon Press, 1984).

10. Fernand Braudel, *The Perspective of the World,* cited in Gerald Segal, *Rethinking the Pacific* (Oxford: Clarendon Press, 1990), 23, 28.

11. Gong, "China's Entry Into International Society," 171–83; Segal, *Rethinking the Pacific,* 29.

12. Segal, *Rethinking the Pacific,* 370.

13. During the nineteenth and early twentieth centuries, for instance, the notion of "civilization" worked as a critical psychological factor in the making of American foreign policies to non-Western countries. For the explanation of Theodore Roosevelt's case, see Frank Ninkovich, "Theodore Roosevelt: Civilization as Ideology," *Diplomatic History* 10 (Summer 1986). Many current political remarks as well as academic notions of civilization seem to bear the historical legacy of the past, which include American political leaders' perception of civilization when they deal with the Middle East. See Ki-Jung Kim, "Civilization and International Relations: Clash, Co-existence, and Dialogue" [in Korean], *Emerge, Sae Chonnyon* [Emerge, A New Millennium] (August 2000): 107–17.

14. Kim and Hodges, "Korea as a Clashpoint of Civilizations," 522.

15. About Fukuzawa Yukichi's influence in Meiji Japan, see Albert Craig, "Afterword: Fukuzawa Yukichi: The Philosophical Foundations of Meiji Nationalism," in *The Autobiography of Fukuzawa Yukichi*, rev. trans. Eiichi Kiyooka (New York: Madison Books, 1992), 373–429. A wide range of works of literature exist regarding Japanese cruelty toward other Asian countries. This cruelty was directed against all other Asian nations, including Korea, but the active participation of some Koreans in the Greater East Asia scheme has drawn too little attention. Concerning *Datsu-a-ron*, see Masahide Shibusawa, Zakaria Hai Ahmad, and Brian Bridges, *Pacific Asia in the 1990s*, Royal Institute of International Affairs (London and New York: Routledge, 1992), 137–38.

16. Walter LaFeber, *The Clash: U.S.–Japanese Relations throughout History* (New York: W. W. Norton & Co., 1997), 189–97.

17. Yano, *Greater East Asia*, 10.

18. Yano, *Greater East Asia*, 11. According to Charles Nelson Spinks, one of the main architects of Japan's new order was Naoki Hoshino, the then chief secretary of the cabinet. See Charles Nelson Spinks, "The Man Behind in Japan," *Asia and Americas* 43 (April 1943): 218–21.

19. Navy Ministry, Kaigunsho Chosaka, *Kokubô kokka no honshitsu to Kôzô*, 228–29, cited in Henry P. Frei, *Japan's Southward Advance and Australia: From the Sixteenth Century to World War II* (Honolulu: University of Hawaii Press, 1991), 208.

20. The effect of Japanese policies on Asian independence movements has generally been well established. Testimony and exhibits of the International Military Tribunal for the Far East (IMTFE) reveal with unusual candor Japanese policy and conduct of control in Southeast Asia. A highly accelerated awareness of "Asian-ness" among conquered peoples was clearly one of the results. See the following studies based largely on IMTFE records: F. C. Jones, *Japan's New Order in East Asia* (London: Oxford University Press, 1954); Willard H. Elsbree, *Japan's Role in Southeast Asian Nationalist Movements* (Cambridge, Mass.: Harvard University Press, 1953); M. A. Aziz, *Japan's Colonialism and Indonesia* (The Hague: Martinus Nijhoff, 1955); Ralph Braibanti, "The Southeast Asia Collective Defense Treaty," *Pacific Affairs* 30 (December 1957): 322–23.

21. W. G. Beasley, *Japanese Imperialism, 1894–1945* (New York: Oxford University Press, 1987).

22. Robert L. Beisner, *From the Old Diplomacy to the New, 1865–1900*, 2nd ed. (Arlington Heights, Ill.: Harlan Davidson, 1986).

23. Thomas J. McCormick, *China Market: America's Quest for Informal Empire, 1893–1901* (Chicago: Quadrangle Books, 1967).

24. Michael Hunt, *Frontier Defense and the Open Door: Manchuria in Chinese–American Relaitons, 1895–1911* (New Haven, Conn.: Yale University Press, 1973), 108–9; Eugene Trani, *The Treaty of Portsmouth: An Adventure in American Diplomacy* (Lexington: University of Kentucky Press, 1969), 158–59.

25. Paul Varg, *The Making of a Myth: The United States and China, 1897–1912* (East Lansing: Michigan State University Press, 1968).

26. The Open Door principle, particularly the principle of "preservation of Chinese territorial and administrative entity," continued to appear repeatedly in U.S. East Asian policies: e.g., the Root-Takahira Agreement (1908), The Ishi-Lan-

sing Agreement (1917), the Nine-Power Treaty (1922), and the Stimson Doctrine (1932).

27. A Report to the President by the Council of Economic Advisers, January 12, 1953, Annual Economic Review, Leon H. Keyserling Papers, box 5, HSTL.

28. Myongsob Kim, "Intégrer pour régner: La strategie globale de l'administration Truman et l'origine de la regionalisation tripolaire" (These de Doctorat, Universite de Paris I-Pantheon Sorbonne, 1996), 138–40; John Lewis Gaddis, *The Long Peace: Inquiries into the History of the Cold War* (New York: Oxford University Press, 1987), 57; Thomas Alan Schwartz, *America's Germany: John J. McCloy and the Federal Republic of Germany* (Cambridge, Mass.: Harvard University Press, 1991), 301.

29. Geir Lundestad, *The American "Empire"* (Oslo: Norwegian University Press; Oxford: Oxford University Press, 1990).

30. The term "American-Japanese Consortium" is quoted from Immanuel Wallerstein, *Geopolitics and Geoculture: Essays on the Changing World System* (Cambridge: Cambridge University Press, 1991), 242.

31. On Yoshida Shigeru's remark, see Michael Schaller, *The American Occupation of Japan: The Origins of the Cold War in Asia* (New York: Oxford University Press, 1985), viii.

32. Zhang Yunling, "East Asian Regionalism and China," *Issues and Studies* (June 2002): 214.

33. Thomas McCormick, *America's Half-Century: United States Foreign Policy in the Cold War and After,* 2nd ed. (Baltimore, Md.: Johns Hopkins University Press, 1995), 72–124.

34. Dong Sung Kim, *China's Foreign Policy* [in Korean] (Seoul: Bopmunsa, 1988), 153–89.

35. Kenneth Waltz explains why bipolarity is relatively more stable than multipolarity in this light. See his *Theory of International Politics* (Reading, Mass.: Addison-Wesley, 1979).

36. The United States has maintained several separate bilateral security alliances. The security system was conceptualized as "the spoked-wheel" concept. The United States still seems to rely on the effectiveness of this "bilateral" security arrangement in the post–Cold War era.

37. G. John Ikenberry, "American power and the empire of capitalist democracy," *Review of International Studies* 27 (2001): 191.

38. The White House, *A National Security Strategy of Engagement and Enlargement* (Washington, D.C.: USGPO, 1994).

39. In this sense, the current global as well as regional system is defined as a "Pax-Consortis" system instead of a (revived) "Pax-Americana" or "American Hegemonic" system. In East Asia, a good example of this notion was the formation of the Korea Energy Development Organization for keeping up the nonproliferation principle in the region, which the United States played a critical role in initiating, though it must acquire cooperation from relevant states, including financial support. About the concept of "Pax-Consortis," see Kumi Ushida, "Posuto Reisenjidaini okeru Beikokuno Taigaisenryaku" [U.S. Foreign Policy in the Post–Cold War Era], *Shinboeironshu* 21, no. 1 (June 1993).

40. James Shinn, ed., *Weaving the Net: Conditional Engagement of China* (New York: Council of Foreign Relations, 1996); Richard Bernstein and Ross Munro, "China I: The Coming Conflict with America," *Foreign Affairs* 76, no. 2 (March–April 1997): 18–32.

41. Zbigniew Brzezinski, *The Grand Chessboard: American Primacy and Its Geostrategic Imperatives* (New York: Basic Books, 1997), 55.

42. Ki-Jung Kim, "Establishing Peace on the Korean Peninsula," 490–91.

43. See Alexander Wendt, *The Social Theory of International Politics* (Cambridge: Cambridge University Press, 1999), 246–312.

44. For instance, see Aaron Friedberg, "Ripe for Rivalry: Prospects for Peace in a Multipolar Asia," *International Security* 18, no. 3 (Winter 1993–1994): 5–33.

45. For the concept of "institutional bargaining," see G. John Ikenberry, *After Victory: Institutions, Strategic Restraint, and the Rebuilding of Order after Major Wars* (Princeton, N.J.: Princeton University Press, 2000).

46. J. Garry Clifford, Thomas Paterson, and Kenneth Hagan, *American Foreign Policy: A History since 1900* (Toronto: D. C. Heath, 1988), 340–42.

47. Susan Shirk, "Asia-Pacific Regional Security: Balance of Power or Concert of Power," in Lake and Morgan, *Regional Orders*, 267–68.

48. For a comparative summary of neorealist and neoliberal assumptions, see David Baldwin, ed. *Neo-Realism vs. Neo-Liberalism* (New York: Columbia Univ. Press, 1993). One of the critical distinctions between the two theories is, according to Baldwin, the intention of policymakers on a state's behavior vis-à-vis a state's capability.

49. Leni Stenseth, "The Imagined China Threat in the South China Sea," in Knut Snildal, comp., *Perspectives on the Conflict in the South China Sea*, SUM Workshop Proceedings (August 1999), 37.

50. Pierre G. Goad, "Asian Monetary Fund Reborn," *Far Eastern Economic Review* (May 18, 2000).

51. Jae-Seung Lee, "Building an East Asian Economic Community," *Les Etudes du CERI*, no. 87 (May 2002), 28.

52. Winston Lord, "Ten Goals for the Future," *Asia-Pacific Defense Reporter*, June–July 1993, 15; See also David Winterford, "Chinese Naval Planning and Maritime Interests in the South China Sea: Implications for U.S. and Regional Security Policies," *Journal of American–East Asian Relations* 2, no. 3 (Winter 1993): 370.

53. About the earlier version of this argument regarding Korea, see Myongsob Kim and Horace Jeffrey Hodges, "Korea as a Clashpoint of Civilizations," *Korea Observer* 37, no. 3 (Autumn 2006): 538–39.

References

Buzan, Barry. *People, States, and Fear: An Agenda for International Security Studies in the Post–Cold War Era*, 2nd ed. Boulder, Colo.: Lynne Rienner, 1991.

Buzan, Barry, Ole Waever, and Jaap de Wilde. *Security: A New Framework for Analysis*. Boulder, Colo.: Lynne Rienner, 1998.

Fairbank, John K., Edwin O. Reischauer, and Albert M. Craig. *East Asia: Tradition and Transformation* (Boston: Houghton Mifflin Company; Tokyo: Charles E. Tuttle Company, 1976)

Hogan, Michael J. *The Marshall Plan: America, Britain and the Reconstruction of Western Europe, 1947–1952.* New York: Cambridge University Press, 1987.

Iriye, Akira. *The Origins of the Cold War.* Englewood Cliffs, N.J.: Prentice Hall, 1973.

Kim, Ki-Jung. "Establishing Peace on the Korean Peninsula." *Korea Observer* 36, no. 3 (Autumn 2005): 489–510.

McCormick, Thomas. *America's Half-Century: United States Foreign Policy in the Cold War and After,* 2nd ed. Baltimore, Md.: Johns Hopkins University Press, 1995.

Morris, Dick. *Power Plays: Win or Lose, How History's Great Political Leaders Play the Game.* New York: Regan Books, 2002.

Mueller, John E. *Retreat from Doomsday: The Obsolescence of Major War.* New York: Basic Books, 1989.

Nau, Henry et al. *At Home Abroad: Identity and Power in American Foreign Policy.* Ithaca, N.Y.: Cornell University Press, 2002.

Noble, Gregory W., and John Ravenhill, eds. *Asian Financial Crisis and the Architecture of Global Finance.* Cambridge: Cambridge University Press, 2000.

Nye, Joseph. *The Paradox of American Power: Why the World's Only Superpower Can't Go It Alone.* Oxford: Oxford University Press, 2002.

Packard, George. *Protest in Tokyo: The Security Treaty Crisis of 1960.* Princeton, N.J.: Princeton University Press, 1966.

Pempel, T. J., ed. *The Politics of the Asian Financial Crisis.* Ithaca, N.Y.: Cornell University Press, 1999.

Rengger, N. J. *International Relations, Political Theory and the Problem of Order: Beyond International Relations Theory?* London: Routledge, 2000.

Rosenau, James N. "Governance, Order, and Change in World Politics." In *Governance without Government: Order and Change in World Politics,* edited by James N. Rosenau and Ernst-Otto Czempiel. Cambridge: Cambridge University Press, 1992.

Schwartz, Hans-Peter. *Die Gezähmten Deutschen: Von der Machtbesessenheit zur Machtvergessenheit.* Stuttgart: DVA, 1985.

Vogel, Steven, ed. *U.S.-Japan Relations in a Changing World.* Washington, D.C.: Brookings Institution, 2002.

Index

About the Contributors

Vinod K. Aggarwal is professor in the department of political science, affiliated professor of business and public policy in the Haas School of Business, and director of the Berkeley Asia Pacific Economic Cooperation Study Center (BASC) at the University of California, Berkeley. He is also the editor in chief of the journal *Business and Politics*. Professor Aggarwal received his BA from the University of Michigan and his MA and PhD from Stanford University. Aggarwal is the author or editor of fifteen books and he has published over seventy articles and book chapters on the politics of trade and finance. His most recent book is *Asia's New Institutional Architecture* (2007).

Paul Bacon is associate professor of international politics in the School of International Liberal Studies, Waseda University, Japan. He is assistant editor of *International Relations of the Asia-Pacific: A Journal of the Japan Association of International Relations*. He received his PhD from the University of Kent in the UK, and he has published numerous articles and book chapters on issues such as humanitarian intervention, democratic transition, and the international relations of Japan. Dr. Bacon is a former Foreign Research Fellow at the Institute of Oriental Culture, Tokyo University, and has also taught at Aoyama Gakuin University and Chiba University in Japan.

Avery Goldstein, professor of political science at the University of Pennsylvania, received his PhD at the University of California, Berkeley, specializing in international relations, security studies, and Chinese politics. He is the author of *Rising to the Challenge: China's Grand Strategy and International Security;*

Deterrence and Security in the 21st Century: China, Britain, France and the Enduring Legacy of the Nuclear Revolution; and *From Bandwagon to Balance of Power Politics: Structural Constraints and Politics in China, 1949–1978.* His other publications include articles in *International Security, International Organization,* the *Journal of Strategic Studies, Security Studies, Orbis, China Quarterly, Asian Survey, Comparative Politics,* and *Polity.* He is associate director of the Christopher Browne Center for International Politics and senior fellow at the Foreign Policy Research Institute.

G. John Ikenberry is the Albert G. Milbank Professor of Politics and International Affairs at Princeton University in the department of politics and the Woodrow Wilson School of Public and International Affairs. Professor Ikenberry is the author of *After Victory: Institutions, Strategic Restraint, and the Rebuilding of Order after Major Wars* (2001), which won the 2002 Schroeder-Jervis Award presented by the American Political Science Association (APSA) for the best book in international history and politics. The book has been translated into Japanese, Italian, and Chinese. A collection of his essays, titled *Liberal Order and Imperial Ambition: American Power and International Order,* was published in 2006.

Takashi Inoguchi, professor of political science at Chuo University, Tokyo, specializes in Japan and international affairs and has published some sixty books and numerous articles in English and in Japanese. Those in English include *Japanese Politics: An Introduction* (2005), *Values and Life Styles in Urban Asia* (2005), *Reinventing the Alliance* (2003), *American Democracy Promotion* (2000). He is emeritus professor at Tokyo University, former assistant secretary general of the United Nations, and president of the Asian Consortium for Political Research. In 2006 he was a visiting professor at Seoul National University.

Ki-Jung Kim is professor of political science and vice president for student affairs and services at Yonsei University, Seoul, Korea. He is a member of the editorial board of *International Studies Perspective.* Formerly, he was associate dean of the Graduate School of Public Administration at Yonsei University and also taught at Ewha Women's University, Sookmyung Women's University, and the University of California, San Diego.

Myongsob Kim is associate professor of politics and diplomacy at Yonsei University. Before joining the faculty of Yonsei University in 2003, he taught at Hanshin University as associate professor. He received his PhD from the Université de Paris I-Penthéon Sorbonne. He is author or coauthor of numerous books, such as *War and Peace in East Asia* (in Korean), and *Asia-Pacific and a New International Order: Responses and Options,* and has also had many articles published in various journals, such as *The Korean Journal of Defense Analysis, Korea Journal, Korea Observer, Issues and Studies,* and *International Political Science Review,* among others.

Woosang Kim is professor of political science at Yonsei University and director of the Institute of East and West Studies at Yonsei University. Formerly, he was professor at Sookmyung University, associate professor with tenure at Texas A&M University, and research associate at the Hoover Institution, Stanford University. He has published many articles in scholarly journals such as *World Politics, Journal of Conflict Resolution, International Studies Quarterly,* and the *American Journal of Political Science.*

Yongho Kim is associate professor of political science at Yonsei University and associate director of the Institute for Korean Unification Studies at Yonsei University. Formerly, he was research fellow at the Korean Institute of National Unification and journalist at *Joongang Daily Newspaper.* He has published several articles in scholarly journals such as *Asian Survey, Korean Journal of Defense Analysis, and Issues and Studies.*

Min Gyo Koo is assistant professor in the department of public administration at Yonsei University. He has published his research on East Asian political economy and Asia-Pacific security affairs in a wide range of journals and book chapters. He has also coedited (with Vinod K. Aggarwal) *Asia's New Institutional Architecture: Evolving Structures for Managing Trade, Financial, and Security Relations* (2007). Professor Koo received his BA and MA from Seoul National University and also holds an MA from the Johns Hopkins University School of Advanced International Studies. He obtained his PhD from the University of California, Berkeley.

Michael Mastanduno is Nelson Rockefeller Professor and associate dean of social science at Dartmouth College. A former special assistant in the Office of the U.S. Trade Representative and a member of the Council of Foreign Relations, Mastanduno directed Dartmouth's John Sloan Dickey Center for International Understanding for six years. He has received fellowships from the Brookings Institution, the Council of Foreign Relations, the East-West Center, and the Salzburg Seminar. In addition, Mastanduno is author or editor of *Economic Containment, Unipolar Politics, International Relations Theory and the Asia Pacific* and *U.S. Hegemony and International Organizations,* among other volumes.

Chung-in Moon is a professor of political science at Yonsei University and ambassador for international security affairs at the Ministry of Foreign Affairs and Trade, Republic of Korea. He served as dean of Yonsei's Graduate School of International Studies and as chairman of the Presidential Committee on Northeast Asian Cooperation Initiative, a cabinet-level post. He is currently an adjunct professor at the Asia-Pacific Studies Institute, Duke University. He has published over forty books and 230 articles in edited volumes and scholarly journals such as *World Politics, International Studies Quarterly,* and *World Development.* His recent publications include *Handbook of Korean Unification, Arms Control on the Korean Peninsula,* and *Ending the Cold War in Korea.* He served as vice president of the International Studies Association of North America, and is currently president of the Korea Peace Research Association, a member of the Pacific Council on International Policy (Los Angeles) and the Institute of International Strategic Studies (London), and a fellow of the Club of Madrid. He is a board member of the Korea Foundation, the Sejong Foundation, the East Asia Foundation, and the International Peace Foundation. He is also editor in chief of a forthcoming Hong Kong–based magazine, *Global Asia.*

Katharine H. S. Moon, associate professor and chairperson of the department of political science at Wellesley College, is also a nonresident scholar at the Sigur Center for Asian Studies, George Washington University. She is the author of *Sex among Allies: Military Prostitution in U.S.–Korea Relations* (1997; Korean edition, 2002) and other works on women and international relations, migrant workers, and social movements in East Asia. Currently, she is writing a book on "anti-Americanism" in Korea–U.S. relations from the perspective of Korea's democratization and the politics of social movements. Moon received a Fulbright Senior Research Fellowship in 2002 to conduct research in Korea and was a visiting scholar at the Woodrow Wilson Center and the George Washington University in 2002–2003. Katharine Moon has served in the Office of the Senior Coordinator for Women's Issues in the U.S. Department of State and as a trustee of Smith College. She serves on the editorial board of several journals of international relations and consults for NGOs in the United States and Korea. She also serves on policy task forces designed to examine current U.S.–Korea relations.

Seung-Won Suh is professor in the faculty of law, Kanto-Gakuin University, Japan. Recent publications include *Japan's Economic Diplomacy and China* (2004; received 2005 Ohira memorial award) and *Korea at the Center* (coauthored with Chung-in Moon, 2006).

William C. Wohlforth is professor of government at Dartmouth. Previously, he held positions at Georgetown, Yale, and Princeton. Wohlforth is author of *Elusive Balance: Power and Perceptions during the Cold War,* and editor of *Witnesses to the End of the Cold War* and *Cold War Endgame.* He has published numerous articles on international and strategic affairs and Russian foreign policy. Recent articles include "American Primacy in Perspective," *Foreign Affairs* (July–August 2002), "Responses to U.S. Primacy: Soft Balancing or Unipolar Politics as Usual?" *International Security* (Summer 2005) and "International Relations Theory and the Case against Unilateralism," *Perspectives on Politics* (Summer 2005), all with Stephen G. Brooks, and "Revisiting Balance of Power Theory in Central Eurasia." His most recent book, also a collaboration with Stephen G. Brooks, is *World Out of Balance: International Relations and the Challenge of American Primacy* (2008). Dr. Wohlforth received his BA from Beloit College and his MA (international relations) and PhD (political science) from Yale University. He has held fellowships at the Institute of Strategic Studies at Yale, the Center for International Security and Cooperation at Stanford, and the Hoover Institution.